B3

SHOPS AND SHOPP

INTERIOR OF BURLINGTON ARCADE, LONDON.

The Burlington Arcade is a sublimate of superfluities . . .
paintings and lithographs for gilded boudoirs, collars for
puppy dogs, and silver-mounted whips for spaniels, pocket
handkerchiefs in which an islet of cambric is surrounded
by an ocean of lace, embroidered garters and braces,
filagree flounces, firework-looking bonnets, scent bottles,
sword-knots, brocaded sashes, worked dressing-gowns,
inlaid snuff-boxes, and falbalas of all descriptions; these
form the stock-in-trade of the merchants who have here
their tiny boutiques.

GEORGE AUGUSTUS SALA, 1859

SHOPS

AND

SHOPPING

1800–1914

Where, and in What Manner
The Well-dressed Englishwoman
Bought her Clothes

ALISON ADBURGHAM

London
GEORGE ALLEN AND UNWIN
Boston   Sydney

First published in 1964
Second impression 1967
Second edition 1981

GEORGE ALLEN & UNWIN LTD
40 Museum Street, London WC1A 1LU

© Alison Adburgham, 1964, 1981

British Library Cataloguing in Publication Data

Adburgham, Alison
    Shops and shopping 1800–1914. – 2nd ed.
    1. Clothing trade – Great Britain – History
    2. Retail trade – Great Britain – History
    I. Title
    380.145′687′120942   HD9940.G8   80–41477

ISBN 0–04–942168–9

Printed in Great Britain
by Unwin Brothers Limited,
The Gresham Press, Old Woking, Surrey

TO
VICTOR STIEBEL

———————

'If I were to pass the remainder of my life in London, I think the shops would always continue to amuse me. Something extraordinary or beautiful is for ever to be seen in them. . . . There is a perpetual exhibition of whatever is curious in nature or art, exquisite in workmanship, or singular in costume; and the display is perpetually varying as the ingenuity of trade and the absurdity of fashion are ever producing something new.'

ROBERT SOUTHEY, 1807

'Shopping is very demonstrative.'

LORD MELBOURNE TO QUEEN VICTORIA

PREFACE TO THE SECOND EDITION

M UCH has changed on the shopping scene since this history first appeared. Gorringe's in Buckingham Palace Road, whose customers' letters I quoted in my introduction, is now no more. Woolland's of Knightsbridge, whose building pictured in Plate XI was then so familiar, has disappeared. Jolly's of Bath, which was then directed by a great-great-great grandson of the founder Jolly, is now one of the House of Fraser's many mansions. And Harrods' dignified banking hall has been transformed into a vast, glittering cosmetic department. The deep-seated green leather chairs in which gentlemen used to snooze the hours away behind *The Times* have been relegated to the fourth floor. It was rumoured that when one of the chairs was sent up in the lift, it was found to contain a somnolent gentleman *in situ*.

The octogenarian and nonagenarian residents of the Linen & Woollen Drapers' Cottage Homes with whom I talked some twenty years ago are unlikely to be available for interview now. Indeed, there can be few people living who remember the shops of Edwardian times, fewer still who can recall shopping when Victoria was on the throne. Yet when this book was published in 1964 there were many who wrote to tell me of the memories it aroused. For example, Miss Stubbs wrote from a nursing home in Droitwich: 'I have my Apprenticeship Deed which was compiled by Cavendish House Co. Ltd., Cheltenham, in 1895 and it is really most amusing to read now, when young people are paid so highly *to learn*. My dear Mother was left a widow with very little income and her most kind Aunt educated us. When the local shop owners told her they paid their Head Milliner £100 a year, she decided something of that kind would be best for me. So Cavendish House it was, and greatly I enjoyed every day of it.' Miss Stubbs's wages would probably have been one shilling a week for the first year, rising to five shillings at the end of her five-year apprenticeship. That was the going rate in 1900 at Hannington's of Brighton, a similar high-class establishment to Cavendish House.

Dorrien Brooks wrote from Richmond: 'My mother, born in 1887, was apprenticed to the drapery trade as a girl of fourteen, and my father came of a family of London horse-cab drivers, whose livelihood centred very much around the "carriage trade" to the famous West-End stores. Your book has crystallised for me the hours of fascinating reminiscences I have heard from my parents. You quote a shop rule—"any assistant allowing a customer to go away unserved without first appealing to the Buyer will be subject to instant dismissal". This was certainly the case, and not only in the classy shops, but very strictly adhered to in the Walworth Road where my mother began her career.'

Customers' memories were nostalgic. Mrs Bond wrote from East Horsley: 'I can remember the West End shops from the first decade of this century—the treat of being taken into Marshall's ribbon department, and the wonderful taste of the ice-cream delicacies at Selfridges, and the impact of their window-dressing on other establishments.' And Mrs Beecham, writing from Dartmouth, wondered if the Mrs Mason whom I mentioned as having made some of Princess May's trousseau 'could possibly have been the "Alice Mason" who made things for my grandmother and my mother and aunts, and who had a charming corner shop in Grosvenor Gardens. Why I specially remember it, is because both my mother and aunt kept their favourite hats, which Mrs Mason had made for them when they were in their teens, as they were so lovely, both exactly the same, round cream straw, with trimmings of small scarlet wax strawberries and blue satin ribbon. I adored them!' Why is it always hats that people remember so lovingly? And what a period note that letter gives—sisters in their teens wearing the same. Some sisters dressed alike even when quite grown-up.

From Wales, Mr Mytton Davis wrote: 'My father was Governor of Pentonville Prison, and my mother did a lot of shopping in the big West End stores, and took me with her in our carriage (I remember the coachman, Stephens, who wore a top hat with a black cockade in it). My nanny's uniforms were bought at Garroulds at the bottom of Edgware Road near Marble Arch. When we lived at Governor's House, mother did her household shopping in Islington at T. R. Roberts, an enormous department store next to the equally large Rackstraw's. She gave her orders each week in the grocery department, which was under the management of a tall, grey-haired man named Pound who always wore a frock coat. He greeted my mother obsequiously, just as you have described, and supervised her orders himself. And I remember the Haymarket Stores almost next door to Fribourg and Treyer, the Regency-windowed tobacconists in the Haymarket. It had a big square foyer with rails and hooks for tying up dogs, which were not allowed inside. It had a famous writing room which was always the rendezvous that my grandmother, great-aunt, uncle and mother used for meeting their friends in London.' The Haymarket Stores has long since gone; but Fribourg & Treyer are still there, still selling snuff as well as tobacco.

Another letter came from a lady who said she grew up in Tynemouth —'so I was particularly interested in your remarks about Bainbridge's and Fenwick's. My mother could remember Fenwick's marvellous new shop windows and when they sold bonnets, not hats; and I can remember the separate shops of Bainbridge's and Dunn's, though Dunn's gave up some years ago. I can also remember my mother scanning a dance programme of my eldest sister's, and saying she would not be allowed to any Newcastle dances if she continued to have Jack Bainbridge amongst her partners! Those were certainly the days!! pre 1914–18 war.'

Yes, those pre-1914 days belong to a far away era of clear-cut social divisions; and this history ends at that nineteen-fourteen turning point. Two world wars and a social revolution since then . . . no wonder the methods of retailing, the whole pattern of shopping, the attitudes on both sides of the counter, are altered. The loyalty of families to their favourite shops over long years, even over generations, tends to be a thing of the past, as does the affectionate loyalty of staff to their firms. All the retired members of the retail trade with whom I talked twenty years ago spoke of their old firms with great affection. None of them seemed to have any bitterness about the strict apprenticeships, long hours, short holidays, low wages, of their early days. Old hearts, of course, edit the past. The happy memories are selected, seasoned by a few odd quirks on the part of dictatorial employers—quirks which no doubt at the time caused deep resentment, but when looked back upon become the spice of reminiscence.

Additional pre-1914 information that has come my way since 1964 has been incorporated in this new edition, and I have updated to 1980 all references to current ownerships and premises. Although so much of the English shopping scene has altered, in one respect I have found remarkable continuity. Very many shops, and not only the small specialised ones, are still owned and directed by their founders' direct descendants; and despite the changing face of our cities, most of the famous pre-1914 department stores—not only in London, but also in the provinces—can still be found on their original sites. One must accept that many of the familiar names conceal new ownerships; but the very fact that the names are retained attests to the value still placed by this island nation upon long-established roots, upon tradition and upon a certain reassuring continuity.

ALISON ADBURGHAM, 1981

INTRODUCTION

A FAMOUS London store sent out a letter to customers who had not been using their accounts for a long time. Were they dissatisfied with the store's service in any way? Replies came back like voices from a vanished generation . . .

'I have no fault whatever to find, but I am nearly eighty-three and very lame and rather blind. I will try to shop sometimes and would like to continue to have your catalogues.' 'I have dealt with your store for fifty years, and every transaction has been a pleasure. The last regular business we had was about fifteen years ago when you supplied the school clothes for my grandchildren. I am now over eighty and crippled with arthritis so my needs are extremely few.' 'I am one of those trying to live on a small fixed income, and have to curtail my spending to bare necessities; you still have my custom, but it is over the counter, paid for by cash.' 'I am the third generation of my family to have an account with you.' 'Your store is to me an institution and I shall continue to shop there as long as I or it endure.'

This intense loyalty was built up through personalised service: 'I have always found yours a most delightful store. The assistants are invariably helpful and charming.' 'I recently bought some materials amounting to several pounds and was served by a most efficient and charming gentleman of the old school. It gave me much pleasure to ask his advice.' Things bought were recalled with affection: 'One of my earliest memories is of being taken to your store to buy a dressing-gown, a fat pink quilted one. It is the first garment I can remember consciously appreciating.' 'Without your warm full-length petticoats, I could not have stood the icy winds on the coast. I often recommend them.' 'A year last Christmas (I think) I bought some of the 19/11 a yard velvet for curtains. My niece wants some curtains, so when it is available will you please let her know.' But some nieces, even middle-aged nieces, were beginning to break away. . . . 'The reason I have not visited your store recently is that my son has left school and I no longer buy his clothes. The aunts I used to lunch with have died.'

Yes, the aunts have died, faithful unto death to their favourite store. Aunts, as a species, have a new look now, and a new outlook. But there are still many people who remember shopping before 1914, and some who remember it before 1900, not only as customers but as staff . . . 'I remember Mr Edwin Jones taking the scissors from my hand and showing me how to cut the material on the cross for my customer.' 'We had to dust everything before stock-taking, even the eyes of the needles.' 'It was all black stockings I sold then, except white stockings for corpses. My grandmother had hers ready in a drawer.' 'The model gown buyers behaved like queens.' 'There was a cellar full of bustles.' In conversation, such inconsequential recollections give intimations of time past.

Few shops have preserved comprehensive records of their history. The founder retires and takes his memories and mementoes with him; congested premises are cleared out for extensive alterations; old family firms are bought by larger companies, new brooms sweep clean, old selling methods are superseded. Through the hazards of wars, new buildings, and changing ownership, not much remains to show how the little shops grew bigger as their towns grew big, how their development into department stores is part of the social history of their neighbourhood. Such things as have survived take on significance through the very fact of their survival . . . a scrap book of press-cuttings and advertisements, an obituary notice, some old ledgers of department sales, a customer's letter, a centenary supplement, an architect's plan, a book of rules for the staff: 'Any Assistant allowing a Customer to go away unserved without first appealing to the Buyer will be subject to instant dismissal.'

It has been said that Sir Walter Scott's greatest contribution to historical understanding was when he observed that our ancestors were once 'as really alive as we are now'. And it is the little detailed things which make us apprehend that essential fact. To come upon a dress-maker's bill for £207 upon which a lady of great wealth has paid £10 on account, is to come upon someone we feel we know. Reading a letter from Sara Hutchinson to her cousin John Monkhouse, we share the anxieties of buying a hat in 1800: 'I will thank you to purchase for me at your friend the Chip Hat house a Chip Hat or Bonnet of the very *newest* fashion—I would have it coloured *pea-green*, else lilac I would prefer—a useful size, that is one to shade the face but not too large as you know that would be out of proportion, I have a small head. You can order it to be sent to the Idles who will pack it carefully up—mind no flowers or kickshaws about it, let it be very modest—not hemmed with Ribband or anything but simply the Hat itself. Don't be angry at the trouble we give you.' Then weeks of waiting . . . 'I will therefore trouble you once more to enquire what coach it was sent by, to what Inn at York and the Innkeeper's name' . . . and the petulant postscript, 'but as it is too late in the season it is of little consequence—you need not trouble yourself'. We know exactly how Sara felt.

The facts which have been fitted together to make this narrative of shops and shopping have been gathered from widely differing sources— a little information here, some confirmatory evidence there. It is a story bound up with the trade of our country and the vagaries of feminine fashion, with the emancipation of women, the changing social climate, and the continuity of the English character. History is from day to day, and nothing in our national life has been more daily than keeping shop and going shopping.

ALISON ADBURGHAM, 1964

ACKNOWLEDGEMENTS

I am indebted to all those who have given me access to material of interest in the history of their firms, and in particular to those who have so kindly lent their property for reproduction as illustrations. They are too many to name individually. I am also very grateful to Mr Donald Cave, former Secretary of the Linen and Woollen Drapers' Cottage Homes at Mill Hill, for his introductions to retired members of the trade; and I have greatly appreciated the help and interest of Mrs Madeleine Ginsburg of the Department of Textiles, Victoria & Albert Museum, and of Dr Ann Saunders when she was archivist of the St Marylebone Public Library. Mr J. G. Links has been most generous in lending rare books from his own library, which have been very valuable both for information and illustration.

A.A.
1964

CONTENTS

ILLUSTRATIONS

IN THE TEXT

Illustrations

Shops and Shopping

CHAPTER I

SHOPPING DURING THE
NAPOLEONIC WARS

*Travelling Tradesmen; Village Shops. London Drapers and
Shopping Streets. Wholesale and Retail in the City. Trade
Buyers from the Provinces. Effects of the Berlin Decree and
the Industrial Revolution.*

ᵥᵥᵥᵥᵥᵥᵥᵥᵥᵥᵥᵥᵥᵥᵥᵥᵥᵥᵥᵥᵥᵥᵥᵥᵥᵥᵥᵥᵥᵥᵥᵥᵥᵥᵥᵥᵥᵥᵥ

IT is January 8, 1801, and Jane Austen is writing from the Rectory
at Steventon to her sister Cassandra: 'Martha and I dined yesterday
at Deane to meet the Powletts and Tom Chute, which we did not
fail to do. Mrs Powlett was at once expensively and nakedly dress'd;
we have had the satisfaction of estimating her Lace and Muslin; and
she said too little to afford us much other amusement'.

And Miss Austen wrote too little in that particular letter to afford
us much information about Mrs Powlett's shopping habits; but it is
possible to hazard a reconstruction of them from other sources. The
paradox of her being at once expensively and nakedly dressed is
resolved by it being in the period of the 'naked fashions', stemming
from post-revolutionary Paris, where the simple unornamented dress
of the Greek city states was adopted as part of the endeavour to
establish a parallel culture. Officially approved by the Consulate, it
became a mode which, at its most modish, raised simplicity to a fine
degree of artificiality. It dispensed with corsets, reduced underclothes
to a negligible shift, raised the waist to draw attention to the bosom
and lowered the neckline to expose the breasts, throwing modesty to
the winds. It is difficult to explain how such exiguous clothing, devoid
of trimmings, could be expensive, except by observing that any mode,
at its most modish, is always expensive, however exiguous.

The English never went to such nude extremes as the Parisians; but
to be dressed nakedly in white muslin for a country-house dinner party

1

in January nevertheless suggests a devotion to fashion bordering upon the phrenetic. And many fashionable women, not always young, walked abroad at all seasons in deeply decolletée gowns, the transparency of the muslin revealing a minimum of pink underclothing, a slit at the side revealing pink-stockinged legs. Long gloves reaching almost to the short sleeves, little tippets and muffs, lace pelisses or cobweb shawls, were the only concessions to cosiness. James P. Malcolm, reviewing the state of Society in 1807, gave a contemporary gentleman's appreciation of current fashions:

> The ladies have at length, much to their honour, thrown aside those hateful attempts to supply Nature's deficiencies or omissions, the false breasts, pads, and bottoms; and now appear in that native grace and proportion which distinguishes an English-woman: the Hair, cleansed from all extraneous matter, shines in beautiful lustre carelessly turned round the head in the manner adopted by the most eminent Grecian sculptors; and the Form appears through their snow-white draperies in that fascinating manner which excludes the least thought of impropriety.

Later he had second thoughts about impropriety:

> But in the midst of this praise I must be permitted to make one observation; and that is, some thoughtless females indulge in the licence of freedom rather too far, and shew their persons in a manner offensive to modesty.

Had Mr Malcolm met Mrs Powlett, he might have included her among his thoughtless females. Although she lived in rural Hampshire and was but the wife of an undistinguished Colonel, it is likely she was an import from the fashionable world. Certainly she had run the gauntlet of provincial prejudice two years earlier when introduced to Steventon as a bride . . . 'Charles Powlett's wife is discovered to be everything that the Neighbourhood could wish her, silly, and cross, as well as extravagant'. Probably her gowns were made in London instead of, as those of most people, by the village dressmaker or a visiting sewing woman. The styles would be copied from the latest fashion plates. *Heideloff's Gallery of Fashion,* consisting of hand-coloured aquatints, was appearing monthly from 1794–1803; and *The Fashions of London and Paris* contained 'correct drawings of from ten to twenty of the fashionable dresses worn in those cities . . . a work of the highest utility to milliners, dressmakers, and private families in the country and in all parts of Europe'. Further valuable information about the *beau monde* could be found in *The Lady's Magazine* and *The Monthly Museum.*

Some of Mrs Powlett's lace may have been bought from the travelling laceman, who went round from village to village; and no doubt she, like any other lady living in the country, would make necessary purchases from the itinerant draper. In some parts of the country he was called the scotch draper or scotchman, in other parts the talleyman; and it seems likely the derivation of both terms comes from his being illiterate and making up his customers' accounts by a talley of notches, or scotches, on a stick, often giving them credit from one visit to the next. We know that Miss Austen bought from the Overton scotchman on November 25, 1789, some Irish to make six shifts and four pairs of stockings. We know, also, that some scotchmen were women, since on April 10, 1801, Parson Woodforde wrote in his diary, 'Nancy bought a New Gown of Mrs Batchelor of Reepham who travels about with a Cart'. The new gown would have been a length of material to make a gown. Even after ready-made clothes began to be sold in shops, dress materials were offered or advertised at so much 'the gown' or 'the dress', and people spoke of buying a gown or a dress when what they had purchased was the material for making it.

In any town of any size there were market stalls selling drapery and haberdashery; and in every village larger than a hamlet, there was a shoemaker and a village shop. In Miss Mitford's village the shoemaker was a man of substance: 'He employs three journeymen, two lame, and one a dwarf, so that his shop looks like a hospital'—a journeyman being an employee who had completed his apprenticeship. Miss Mitford's village shop was 'like other village shops, multi-farious as a bazaar; a repository for bread, shoes, tea, cheese, tape, ribands, and bacon; for everything, in short, except the one particular thing which you happen to want at the moment and will be sure not to find'. And Jane Austen's village shop had the same frustrating characteristic:

I went to Mrs Ryder's and bought what I intended to buy, but not to much perfection. There were no narrow braces for children and scarcely any netting silk; but Miss Wood, as usual, is going to town very soon, and will lay in a fresh stock. I gave 2/3 a yd. for my Flannel, and I fancy it is not very good, but it is so disgraceful and contemptible an article in itself that its being comparatively good or bad is of little importance. I bought some Japan Ink likewise, and next week shall begin operations on my hat, on which you know my principal hopes of happiness depend.

Poor Mrs Ryder no doubt found her customers difficult to please. She died during the January of that dinner party at Deane, and soon Miss Austen was writing:

The neighbourhood have quite recovered the death of Mrs Ryder—so much so, that I think they are rather rejoiced at it now; her things were so very dear!—and Mrs Rogers is to be all that is desirable. Not even Death itself can fix the friendship of the World.

Jane Austen was fortunate in often having the opportunity of shopping in London when visiting her brother Henry. Her fortune is our fortune, since her letters to Cassandra are unique in contemporary writing in their many references to shopping. For fashionable muslins she favoured Grafton House, and sometimes bought 'gowns' for her mother and sister as well. She never mentions the address, but it was possibly 164 New Bond Street on the corner of Grafton Street, at that time owned by drapers Wilding & Kent and later by the Grafton Fur Co. Another of her favourite shops was Bedford House, conveniently near her brother's house in Henrietta Street. She sometimes refers to it as Layton & Shear's, so it must have been the same shop advertised in *The Times* of 1821 as S. Shears & Co., Bedford House. Jane Austen also mentions Newton's which was in Leicester Square, where Stagg & Mantle's was established in 1812 and very much later became Stagg & Russell. She can hardly have failed to visit Swan & Edgar, established at No. 10 Piccadilly in 1812, nor Flint & Clark (established 1778 at 44 Wigmore Street, later Clark & Debenham) nor Harding Howell's grand Schomberg House, Pall Mall, with furnishings as well as fashions.

Another well-known establishment founded well before the nineteenth century was Nicholay's Fur and Feather Manufactory of 82 Oxford Street, a firm which was acquired by Debenham & Freebody in 1896. During the time when huge 'Gypsy Hats' bedecked with ribbons and feathers contrasted with the naked fashion of the dress, there were many plumassiers, such as W. H. Botibol of the Ostrich Feather Warehouse, 120 Oxford Street and Rust & Roberts (ostrich and fancy feathers, artificial flowers) of St Paul's Churchyard. But the prosperity of the plumassier was dangerously vulnerable to the vagaries of fashion. Nicholay did wisely to consolidate his feathers with the less ephemeral frivolity of furs.

1. Trade card of Cavendish House, Wigmore Street, in 1813, when Flint & Clark became Clark & Debenham.

The heart of the drapery trade was the City of London, the wholesale side being centred on St Paul's Churchyard. To the City of London came many ambitious young men from all over the country, some of whose names are still well-known in the drapery trade. William Cook, founder of Cook & Son wholesale outfitters, came as a very young man in 1806 to seek his fortune as a draper. Within two years he was established in Clerkenwell; fourteen years later he had his warehouse in Cheapside and was elected to the Worshipful Company of Drapers. Olney Amsden, the great wholesale haberdashers, were first established in Borough High Street in 1809, later moving to Falcon Street in the City. They still have an Amsden on the Board. Another famous wholesale haberdashery firm, Pawson & Leaf, was very early in St Paul's Churchyard.

In the early years of the century, the City was still a place where people lived as well as worked. The more prosperous merchants were beginning to move out from their place of business to the fine squares and terraces in the newly developing Bedford estate in Bloomsbury, or even as far north as Islington; but generally speaking, the shopkeeper still lived at his place of business. The principal shopping streets of London at this time are given in *The Picture of London*, a guide book for visitors, edition of 1803:

There are two sets of streets, running nearly parallel, almost from the Eastern extremity of the town to the Western, forming (with the exception of a very few houses), a line of shops. One, lying to the South, nearer the river, extends from Mile End to Parliament Street, including Whitechapel, Leadenhall Street, Cornhill, Cheapside, St Paul's Churchyard, Ludgate Street, Fleet Street, the Strand, and Charing Cross. The other, to the North, reaches from Shoreditch Church almost to the end of Oxford Street, including Shoreditch, Bishopsgate Street, Threadneedle Street, Cheapside, Newgate Street, Snow-hill, Holborn, Broad Street, St Giles, and Oxford Street.

The Southern line, which is the most splendid, is more than three miles in length; the other is about four miles. There are several large streets also occupied by retail trade, that run parallel to parts of the two grand lines, or intersect them, among the most remarkable of which are Fenchurch Street and Gracechurch Street in the City of London; and Cockspur Street, Pall Mall, St James's Street, Piccadilly, Kings Street Covent Garden, and New Bond Street, at the West end of the town.

In all these streets, in most of the shops, the proprietor-shopkeeper lived with his family above or behind his business premises and was more than a man who handled merchandise: he was a specialist in the goods he sold. Very often he was the craftsman who made them: shoemaker, tailor, staymaker, hatter, fan-maker, umbrella and parasol maker.

Hanging shop-signs over the pavement were gone by the end of the eighteenth century: their removal was enforced from 1762, because of their danger to passers-by when the supports became delapidated. Sir Ambrose Heal in *London Tradesmen's Cards of the Eighteenth Century* gives the last streets to keep their signs hanging over the pavements as Wood Street and Whitecross Street, where they remained until 1773. But there were exceptions allowed, such as the barber's pole and the pawnbroker's three balls. Mayhew mentions, as late as 1856, an umbrella shop having 'a bright crimson umbrella with a yellow fringe hung over the doorway'. With the removal of the signs (which were then often fixed flat over the doorways of the shops), the streets began to be numbered; previously shopkeepers gave on their trade cards, which usually carried an engraving of the shop-sign, detailed instructions about its locality as, for instance: S. Huntley, Linnen Draper at ye Single Crown; very Broad Fronted Shop Sashed in, almost over against ye East India House in Leadenhall Street.

Many shopkeepers had little or no window space for displaying goods, and drapers' shops were especially dark through the custom of draping the doorways with their wares. Nevertheless, James Malcolm wrote a very flattering account of London shops in 1807:

> The shop-keeper prides himself on the neatness of his shop-front; his little portico, and the pilasters and cornices, are imitations of Lydian, Serpentine, Porphyry, and Verde Antique Marbles; and those who have the good fortune to serve any branch of the Royal Family immediately place large sculptures of their several arms and supporters over their doors, and their own names and business in golden characters. The great windows of large panes exhibit the richest manufactures, and the doors of the Linen Drapers are closed by draperies of new muslins and calicoes. Some wags pretend indeed that the tradesman has a double motive in this proceeding—the darkening of his premises to prevent keen eyes from discovering coarse threads, and embellishing his shop.

Robert Southey wrote in the same year of plate glass as 'a refinement of very late date; indeed glass windows were seldom used in shops before the present reign, and they who deal in woollen cloth have not yet universally come into the fashion'. But English drapers seem to have been in advance of those in other countries in the use of their windows. Sophie von la Roche, a German lady who visited London in 1786, wrote home that she was struck by 'a cunning device for showing women's materials whether they are silks, chintzes, or muslins, they hang down in folds behind the fine high windows so that the effect of this or that material, as it would be in the ordinary folds of a woman's dress, can be studied'.

Such enterprising shopkeepers attracted carriage trade from beyond the immediate neighbourhood. Even customers who did not have their own carriages could come by public transport. *The Picture of London* lists these methods of transport available in 1803: hackney coaches, watermen (oars 7d, sculls 3d), chairmen, stage coaches (a coach every hour from the Mansion House to Kensington). For private hire: glass coaches, post chaises, one-horse chaises, and saddle horses.

There were no stated shopping hours. The proprietor who lived on his premises took down his shutters before breakfast and did not put them up again until he went to bed. Gas-lighting, although invented in 1792, was not general at the beginning of the century. The first British Gas Company, which was also the first in the world, obtained its Act of Parliament in 1810, and Westminster Bridge was lit by gas in 1813. The last oil lamps were removed from Grosvenor Square in 1846. Parish lamps, as street lamps were called before gas-lighting, burned inferior oil, and were recalled as 'despicable' by the Rev. J. Richardson in *Recollections of the Last Half-century*: 'A set of greasy fellows were employed to trim and light these lamps, which they accomplished by the apparatus of a formidable pair of scissors, a flaming flambeau of pitched rope, and a ricketty ladder, to the annoyance and danger of all passers-by'. But the more prosperous London shopkeepers had outside lights trained on their windows and were, according to Malcolm, 'of infinite service to the rest of the inhabitants by their liberal use of the Patent Lamp, to shew their commodities during the long evenings of winter. The parish lamps glimmer above them, and are hardly distinguishable before ten o'clock'. This seems to imply that the shopkeepers put out their lights at that hour.

No lady, of course, shopped after dark: nor did she shop in daylight except accompanied by her maid, her footman, or a page. Even those streets which were not regarded as actually dangerous or unsavoury were, for a gentlewoman, unseemly; and it was considered indiscreet for a lady to be in Bond Street in the afternoon. Bond Street for the first half of the century was very much a man's street, with hotels and apartments for gentlemen, hatters, tailors, hairdressers and perfumers, jewellers, and other expensive tradesmen catering for the exquisite tastes of gentlemen of fashion.

2. Outside reflecting lamp, japanned Maroon and Gold; opal glass lettered to suit all trades.

3. Looking West along Piccadilly from Coventry Street.

A great many London retailers were also wholesalers, supplying the trade; and trade customers came to London from all over England. In the early 1780's, when three coaches travelled once a week from Chester to London, taking six days on the journey each way, Elizabeth Towsey, who kept a little millinery and haberdashery shop in Chester with her sister Susannah, travelled to London regularly to select the latest merchandise. Later a Miss Legge, the forewoman, made the journey on her employer's behalf. When her purchases were delivered, an announcement in the local newspapers invited the public to inspect the new London fashions. Susannah Towsey married a druggist, Mr Brown, and their son eventually carried on the business . . . that was how the sisters' little shop became the famous Brown's of Chester. A notebook of Miss Towsey's still exists containing receipts from London firms and entries which show she was familiar with the City. A history of the shop, *Browns and Chester*, quotes the instructions she gave to her forewoman for the first day of a visit to London. This will surely give the modern stores buyer, accustomed to flying to foreign cities in a few hours, an idea of how hard her counterpart of over a hundred and fifty years ago had to work, following a six day journey by stage coach:

In the first place call at Steward Spavold and Smiths, where settle our accounts and look at modes of all sorts, at the white silk, the blue and green. Do not buy any. Ask if they have any black . . . coat, as had last at 62s. Then go to Harris and Penny, pay their bill, and just look at what kind of fancy gloves they have to sell. Tell them that the gloves they called maid were most of them small girls, that they were too dear, that as their account was a small one it had indeed been almost forgot, that I had advised Weatherall people we should draw them in favour of Harris and Co., but in hurry of business we had quite forgot it. Next place you may call at Moores, or not, as you will have a good deal to do and the morning will be pretty far advanced. You may then go to Bread Street. Just call in at Adams, and if they have any pretty fancy ribbons, pick out a few. Get the bill made out and take it with you to Drury's which is just by there. Perhaps they may not have sent out the goods last ordered. Get to look at the order whether they have or not, and you will be able to judge what is wanted of those kind of things. And be sure to get some white souflee for tippets as we have some bespoke for next week. If they have none done, as I do not suppose they have, they may perhaps let you have a yard or two of some that may be done for other customers, which we shall be obliged if they will let us have. A small quantity must be had at any rate to send on Wednesday.

You may call at Tibets and see if there is anything particularly pretty in the ribbon way there. As Barton and Simpson live in the same street call and balance their account, then go to Price and Cook who live in the same street, balance their account, look over their gloves, ask the prices of different sorts. If there is anything particularly nice you may look them out and order them to Drury's as the parcel from there will not be a large one.

More directions follow. A list of twelve addresses in Cheapside, Moorgate and nearby is given. The instructions end:

Go either to Tooly Street or Will Weaver, which is most convenient, where I fancy you will be glad to rest.

Glad to rest!—her feet must have been killing her after all that walking on the City cobbles.

It is surprising that a Chester milliner should send an employee on the six-day journey to London for her merchandise when Manchester was within easy reach; but the prestige of London fashions evidently made it worth the expenditure of time and money. In *Cranford*, Mrs Gaskell makes the principal shopkeeper, 'who ranged trades from grocer to cheesemonger to man-milliner', claim that he went straight to London for the fashions which he exhibited at the beginning of each season at his rooms in High Street. Miss Betty Barker, on the other hand, who set up a milliner's shop with her sister when they had both saved money enough from their situations as ladies' maids, and piqued themselves upon their aristocratic connection, were content to accept the pattern of an old cap of Lady Arley's, which they immediately copied and circulated among the élite of Cranford.

In London itself, merchandise from Paris was the thing; but there was no travelling abroad for this during the Napoleonic wars. It was a difficult period for trade in many ways, with foreign markets fluctuating, and imports of raw materials uncertain. But the ill winds of war blew favourably for the promotion of British fashions. Just as two centuries earlier Huguenot refugees had brought their skills to our weaving trades, so now the *émigrés* from the Terror, although mainly aristocrats, included a sprinkling of embroideresses, dressmakers, and other trained workers from the city of fashion. Moreover, the very presence of elegant French aristocrats was a stimulus to London Society. Amongst the *émigrés* in London, was Rose Bertin, Marie Antoinette's dressmaker, hairdresser, and cosmetician. This world-famous lady continued to dispatch from London her fashion dolls (or milliners' mannequins as they were called) to the courts of Europe; so for a time at any rate, London gained reflected fashion prestige.

Some British fashion trades prospered during the wars through being able to sell in foreign markets which were previously supplied from France. The ribbon trade was one of these. It also enjoyed an additional boom between 1812–15 through a fashion for purl-edged ribbons: that is, ribbons in which the shoot extends beyond the edge of the ribbon. This boom, known in Coventry as the Great Purl Time, illustrates the sensitivity of the ribbon trade to fashion. Only two years earlier, in 1810, the death of Princess Amelia, favourite daughter of George III, for whom twelve weeks general mourning was ruled, so depressed the fancy ribbon trade that several manufacturers went bankrupt. One, however, turned the disaster to good account by starting a mill weaving black ribbons only.

Napoleon's Berlin Decree of 1806 proclaimed his intention of going to war with any European country that traded with England. This cut off supplies of raw silk from the continent, making things difficult for English silk weavers; but it was the cause of an important new industry coming into being. Previously all sewing thread had been silk; and silk was used for the heddle eyes of cotton weaving looms, since that part needed to be particularly fine and smooth to permit the warp threads to be inserted. When silk imports from the continent ceased, the brothers Clark of Paisley, who provided equipment for looms, evolved a smooth cotton yarn for the heddle; and this soon became used as thread for hand-sewing. At first it was sold in hanks or skeins, and women had to wind it into little balls for use, like knitting wool. To help his customers, the first Mr Clark would often wind the skein on to a spool and charge them an extra halfpenny, which he refunded when the empty spool was returned. Presently, when thread was made in many thicknesses, reels were ticketed accordingly and included in the cost of the cotton.

In Paisley at this time, many mills were idle because the warm domestic-looking Paisley shawl was the very antithesis of a naked fashion. James Coats came of several generations of Paisley weavers, and was concerned with Canton crepe shawls, for which a peculiar twisting of yarn was required. This aroused his interest in thread making, and in 1826 he started a small mill at Paisley to produce his own thread. Soon, thanks originally to Napoleon, both Clark's and Coat's sewing threads were on every haberdashery counter in the British Isles, and thread was becoming an important British export.

❧   ❧   ❧

Although the Industrial Revolution began in the second half of the eighteenth century with Hargreaves' Spinning Jenny and Crane's warp knitting machine, it affected the fashion trade very little until after the Napoleonic wars, when Cartwright's power-weaving loom began to be felt as a new production force. The jacquard loom, introduced on the continent in 1801, did not come to England until the early 1830's. Heathcote invented his net-making machine in 1808, and this was really the beginning of machine-made lace; but it did not make any appreciable difference to the lace trade until Heathcote's patent expired in 1823 and many net-making firms were started. The first embroidery machine, introduced in 1829, gave further impetus to the production of lace and other trimmings. Hosiery continued to be a cottage industry longer than any other outworkers' trade except gloves; the power knitting frame for stockings, introduced in 1838, was not put into use until 1844.

Thus the new era of fabric production did not start before 1815; and it is also from 1815 that new methods of retail distribution began. At the beginning of the nineteenth century, the pattern of shopping was much as it had been for the whole of the previous century. The goods were sold by individual shopkeepers, who were proprietors of their own shops and lived on the premises, and who were often craftsmen making the goods they sold. Their customers came to them through word of mouth recommendation, and for the most part lived in the locality. There was no clear demarcation between retailers and whole-salers. After 1815, a change began.

CHAPTER II

AFTER WATERLOO

Nash's Regent Street. Tottenham Court Road. Oxford Street.
Swan meets Edgar in the Market. The Bazaar in Manchester,
London Bazaars, Pantechnicons.

Iꜰ Napoleon sneered at England as a nation of shopkeepers, Nash's Regent Street was the retort magnificent. When General von Blücher visited London after the Battle of Waterloo and was shown this fine new shopping street, he is said to have exclaimed: 'What a place to loot!'

Instigated by the Prince Regent, the Act for building Regent Street was passed in 1813. The site was a long unimportant street called Swallow Street, part of which still remains, cutting through from the south side of the Quadrant to Piccadilly. Regent Street started from the Prince Regent's residence at Carlton House, led up to the newly planned Portland Place and swept on to Regent's Park, which had been laid out in the old Marylebone Park. The whole length was finished in 1820. Seventeen years later, Tallis's Street View described it:

> The buildings of this noble street chiefly consist of palace-like shops, in whose broad shewy windows are displayed articles of the most splendid description, such as the neighbouring world of wealth and fashion are daily in want of. The upper part of these elegant structures are mostly let as apartments to temporary visitors of the metropolis.
>
> The Circus unites Regent-street with Oxford-street. It is a continuous style of architecture, with the houses above it, its form is one of the best which could be devised for the purpose; it gives an air of grandeur and space to the streets, and a free circulation of air to the houses. It affords facilities to carriages and horsemen in turning from one street to the other, and is as elegant in form as useful in application.

Nash himself said of his design for Regent Circus, as it was then called,

12

that it 'avoided the sensation of crossing Oxford Street'. Oxford Street was something which, like the poor, you avoided observing as you passed over from your dignified shopping in Regent Street to your fine new residence in Portland Place or Cavendish Square. Nevertheless, although not patronised by the exclusives of the *beau monde*, the straight mile originally called the Oxford Road, stretching due west from Tottenham Court Road to Tyburn toll gate, was a very busy, prosperous shopping street with a decided bias towards fashion merchandise. Tottenham Court Road itself was regarded as a high-class shopping street, serving the rich merchants' families who had moved out from the City to the dignified streets and squares built on the Bedford Estate and the Foundling Hospital property. On its western side, there was a reservoir of good customers in the newly developed Portland and Portman Estates, which had been made fashionable through being the favourite district of prosperous Academicians of the late eighteenth century.

To Tottenham Court Road in 1817 came James Shoolbred, whose drapery business had been established three years earlier as Shoolbred, Cook & Co., the Cook of the partnership being a brother of the founder of Cook & Sons, wholesale outfitters, of St Paul's Churchyard. Shoolbred's was to become one of the first department stores, branching out from its beginnings as outfitters and drapers into carpets and soft

4. The Quadrant, Regent Street; Swan & Edgar at left.

furnishings, and later into groceries and toys. It kept its high-class family connection even after the fashionable drift to the West caused Bloomsbury to decline in the social scale. The furnishing house of Maples was established in the adjoining block in 1842; and John Harris Heal, whose father had founded a mattress-making business in Rathbone Place in 1810, moved to Tottenham Court Road in 1840 because it was becoming known for furniture shops.

In Oxford Street, at this period, there were already two drapery shops with names which still belong to famous stores. Dickins & Smith opened in 1790 at the sign of The Golden Lion, 54 Oxford Street. In 1835 they obeyed the compulsion to move to the more fashionable Regent Street, and later became Dickins & Jones. In 1833 Peter Robinson, son of a Yorkshire haberdasher, opened a linen draper's shop at 103 Oxford Street, which still remains part of the present Peter Robinson site. Apart from these well-known names, the number and variety of Oxford Street shops which catered for the necessary and unnecessary items of women's clothing and adornment at the end of the Napoleonic wars, 'the whim-whams and fribble-frabble of fashion'', can be seen in *Johnstone's London Commercial Guide* of 1817:

33	Linen drapers	2	Silk and satin dressers and dyers
10	Straw hat manufactories	2	Drapers and tailors
6	Bonnet warehouses	1	India muslin warehouse
5	Woollen drapers	3	Fancy trimmings and fringes
5	Lace warehouses		manufactory
3	Plumassiers	1	Button manufactory
24	Boot and shoe makers	2	Calender and dyers
17	Hosiers and glovers	5	Perfumers
4	Silk mercers	1	Patent thread manufactory
1	Silk weaver	1	Tailor
4	Furriers	3	Stay and corset warehouses
12	Haberdashers and hosiers	1	Stocking warehouse
1	Ribbon warehouse	1	Ready made linen warehouse
1	Muslin and shawl warehouse	4	Umbrella manufactories

The terms 'manufactory' and 'warehouse' were not what we understand them to mean today. A manufactory was simply an establishment where the goods which were sold were made by hand in workrooms on the premises, as was so often the case. There were straw hat manufactories, flower and feather manufactories, and so on. A warehouse was any retail or wholesale establishment housing wares, which were not necessarily made on the premises, the term being used when the proprietor considered the size of his business merited a more impressive description than that of shop. The wares themselves could be much more frivolous and delicate than the term suggests to modern ears—there were flower, glove, and ribbon warehouses. Grafton House and Bedford House, Jane Austen's favourite shops, would have been described as warehouses; as would Swan & Edgar's shop at No. 10 Piccadilly.

No. 10 Piccadilly was the premises of the Western Mail Coach Office, the 'Bull & Mouth', and when Swan & Edgar acquired the property, they bought the Inn licence with it, which has never been allowed to lapse. William Edgar was the son of a Cumberland farmer, who came to London and started business with a stall selling men's cravats, socks, and haberdashery. It is not known where he had his stall, but it could have been in the rough and rowdy St James's Market, which was swept away by the construction of Regent Street. The Rev. J. Richardson wrote in his recollections:

> The site on which formerly stood St James's Market, and the filthy passage called 'Market-lane', though within a stone's throw of the palace of the heir apparent to the throne, were very properly avoided by all persons who respected their characters or their garments, and were consequently only known to a 'select few', whose avocations obliged or whose peculiar tastes induced them to penetrate the labyrinth of burrows which extended to Jermyn Street and westward towards St James's Square, and the formerly dirty district now occupied by more stately and appropriate edifices.

Stalls in open markets did a large part of the total men's outfitting trade at that time, and also of the drapery trade in provincial cities and country towns. William Edgar used to sleep under his stall at night, and George Swan, according to one legend, had a nearby stall. But all that is known for certain about Swan is that he died without issue, aged 44 years, on his premises at No. 10 Piccadilly in 1821. What strange perversity of fame! So brief an entry, so swift an exit, for this man Swan whose name, familiar as any famous name in England, has been written in large letters above Piccadilly Circus for over 150 years. Edgar, on the other hand, flourished not only financially but also socially: one of his three daughters married a baronet, Sir Henry William Peek. One of his three sons followed him into the business and begat eleven children. Only one of these eleven grandchildren went into the firm, which suggests that the others rose socially to a point at which they felt obliged to shake off their connections with retail trade. In 1886 the firm of Halling, Pearce & Strong of Waterloo House, Pall Mall East and Cockspur Street, was amalgamated, and a public company floated under the title of Waterloo House and Swan & Edgar Ltd.—'All business now to be carried on at Swan & Edgar of Regent Street and Piccadilly'.

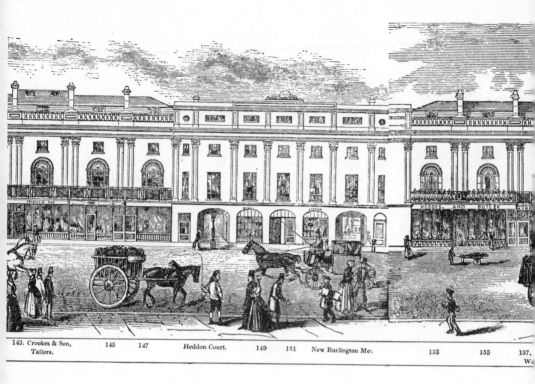

143. Crookes & Son, Tailors.   145   147   Heddon Court.   149   151   New Burlington M⸱⸱   153   155   157.
W⸱

VIGO STREET.   415   117   119. James Locke, Scotch Tartan Warehouse.   121   123   1⸱

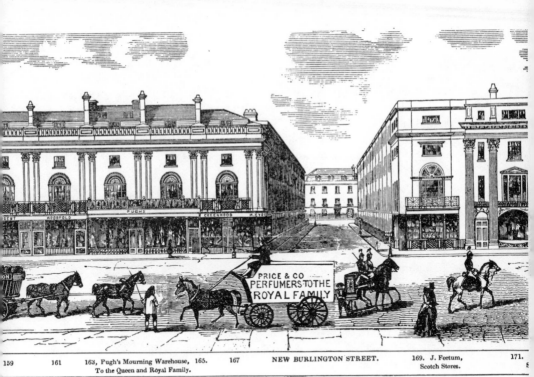

PRICE & CO PERFUMERS TO THE ROYAL FAMILY

159   161   163, Pugh's Mourning Warehouse, 165.   167   NEW BURLINGTON STREET.   169. J. Feetum,   171.
To the Queen and Royal Family.   Scotch Stores.

27. James Locke,   129   131. H. D. & J. Falcke,   LEICESTER STREET.   133   135   137   159
ch Tweed Warehouse.   Importers of Decorative Furniture, Paintings, &c.

A rather less humble start than a market stall was to hire a counter in a bazaar. A bazaar was usually a building of more than one storey under the management of one proprietor; it often had picture galleries and various kinds of exhibitions as well as the shopping stalls which were rented out to retailers in different trades. Exeter Change, built in the reign of Charles II on the north side of the Strand, was used as a menagerie as well from about 1773. Robert Southey described it in his *Letters from England* in 1807:

> Exeter Change is precisely a Bazaar, a sort of street under cover, or large long room, with a row of shops on either hand, and a thoroughfare between them; the shops being furnished with such articles as might tempt an idler, or remind a passenger of his wants. At the further end was a man in splendid costume who proved to belong to a menagerie above stairs. A maccaw was swinging on a perch above him . . .

Considerably smarter was the Royal London Bazaar in Liverpool Street where, according to an announcement in the *World of Fashion* of 1830:

> You may purchase any of the thousand and one varieties of fancy and useful articles, or you may lounge and spend an agreeable hour either in the promenades or in the exhibitions that are wholly without parallel to the known world. Carriages may either wait in the arena for orders, or at the Royal Entrance, Liverpool Street; or at the Gray's Inn Road entrance.

It was claimed that the Grand Saloon and promenades were crowded every day with beauty and fashion 'because it is the nearest emporium or mart where the many thousand of highly respectable inhabitants in an immense surrounding vicinity can immediately obtain all the variation of Fancy, Elegant, and Useful articles'.

※　　　　※　　　　※

The many thousands of highly respectable inhabitants of Manchester had the opportunity, not so very long after the wars with France were over, of shopping at a bazaar which in its conception had a great deal of similarity with the modern department store, and which did in fact develop into the famous store of Kendal Milne. It was a two-story building in which counters were hired by the proprietors to outside tradesmen and tradeswomen. This method was not dissimilar to that of 'the shop within a shop' which is such a feature of department store trading today, when cosmetic counters are hired and staffed by different cosmetic houses, and space in store fashion departments

18

rented to individual manufacturers of branded ready-to-wear clothes. The idea of the bazaar has come full circle.

The Manchester 'Bazaar' was established by John Watts, a farmer of Didsbury. He and his wife Betty had six sons, to all of whom they taught hand-spinning and weaving. Then the farmer, instead of sending out his sons to seek their fortunes, himself gave up farming and opened in 1796 a small office and draper's shop on the Salford side of Deansgate, where he could sell the hand-woven ginghams which were a speciality of his family. Soon he was able to take new premises on the opposite side of the road, and the first edition of the *Manchester Guardian* in 1821, then a weekly paper priced 7d, carried an advertisement for The Bazaar, General Drapers and Warehousemen. The younger brothers Samuel and James joined their father, and ten years later The Bazaar, by then a flourishing business, was rebuilt. The original prospectus of the rebuilt Bazaar, dated March 22, 1831, still exists. It sets out exactly how such an establishment was run:

THE BAZAAR

and the

EXHIBITION OF WORKS OF ART,

INCLUDING DIORAMA, PHYSIORAMA, ETC.

Deansgate & Police-Street, King-Street.

The Proprietor of this Establishment announces to Manufacturers, Artists, and Tradesmen generally, that having constructed the above Premises upon an extensive and splendid Scale, they will be open for business about the middle of March.

The great object in the general arrangement of this Bazaar is to promote the reciprocal Interests of Purchaser and Vendors, to give employment to industrious Females, and at the same time to secure to the Public the choicest and most fashionable Articles in every branch of Art and Manufacture, at a reasonable rate.

A portion of the Establishment will be appropriated for various interesting and amusing Exhibitions and Works of Genius.

GENERAL REGULATIONS.

For the well-being of this Establishment, it is essential that it should be conducted on liberal principles; and to render it mutually advantageous to the Public, and to those who may occupy Counters in it, careful attention to judicious regulations is imperatively necessary. The following Rules are therefore laid down for its government.

19

That all persons desirous of having Counters, shall give references to two respectable Housekeepers, who vouch for their general good character, and for their ability to introduce the best qualities of the Articles in which they propose to deal on the most reasonable terms.

That on their being accepted as Tenants, they shall respectively sign the Rules contained in this Paper, and pledge themselves to a strict observance of them in every particular, and shall contribute to the utmost of their power to uphold the character and respectability of the Bazaar.

That every principal shall name a substitute, not under 14 years of age, who, upon being approved of by the Manager, shall always be at command, so that in case of the illness, or any other unavoidable cause of absence of any parties, their Counters may be properly attended to.

That the Counters shall be let weekly, monthly, or quarterly, to suit the occupiers, who are to give notice to be equal to the time for which they may have engaged them.

That the Bazaar shall be open to the Public from half past nine o'clock in the morning, until eight in the evening, except on Saturdays, when it shall remain open until nine.

The Counters on the first floor will be let to males, and those on the second to females.

That whatever be the description of Goods, with a view to the sale of which any persons are admitted, they are to adhere to the precise Trade to which the Articles they purpose to deal in specially belong, and not enter any other class of Articles whatever, until they have received the decided sanction of the Manager in writing.

That the Prices shall be marked on all the Goods, from which no abatement shall be made; and all the Art shall be of good quality, and offered at very moderate prices.

That the strictest regard shall be paid to propriety of demeanour and of dress; each person must appear perfectly attired for business, clean, and becoming his or her station, and females will not be allowed to have their hair in papers, or to wear bonnets.

That any Article accidentally left by a Visitor, shall immediately be brought to the Manager, who shall see to its being restored to the owner with the least possible delay.

The private door in Hatter's Lane shall be opened every morning at half past eight o'Clock, and each Occupier of a Counter, or his or her Substitute, shall, under penalty of One Shilling, have it furnished and properly set by half past nine.

Every Person who may be admitted into this Establishment shall avoid all unbecoming liberty, and shall adopt obliging and pleasing address, in order to secure the entire satisfaction of the Visitors. There shall be no gossiping on any pretence whatever, nor any eating or drinking behind the Counters, a Room being appropriated for the purposes of Dinner and Tea.

The Proprietor of the Premises engages to pay all Taxes, to heat the Rooms with warm air, to have them cleaned out before eight o'Clock every morning, to provide a Porter for each entrance who shall prevent the intrusion of improper persons, and also to have the Premises watched, at his own expense. Yet he does not insure the Stallholders or Tenants, or take any responsibility upon himself, for risks, losses, or damages of any description, or from any cause whatever.

If any of the above Regulations are violated, it shall be at the option of the Manager to give the Parties two days' notice to quit, and quiet and peaceable possession shall be given of the Counters; and if it be not, he shall be at liberty to take the Goods and deposit them in a Room in the Bazaar, at the risk of the Owners, and to re-let the Counters.

As it is impossible to lay down Rules to meet all contingencies, it must be clearly understood, that the Manager and Inspectress, shall have full power to decide upon what is proper and what is not, and that his or her Orders, both as to propriety of Dress and Conduct, must be willingly and implicitly attended to.

Applications for Counters to be made to MR HAYES, the Manager, on the Premises.

❧ ❧ ❧

Three young men joined the Bazaar as employees when it was rebuilt: Thomas Kendal from Westmorland and James Milne from Scotland were both breaking their family traditions of farming; Adam Faulkner from nearer Manchester was probably already in commerce. These three became friendly with their employers, the Watts brothers, who in 1836 sold them the Bazaar and then founded the wholesale business of S. & J. Watts & Sons. In 1862, on the death of Adam Faulkner, Kendal, Milne and Faulkner became Kendal, Milne & Co.; but customers went on calling it affectionately The Bazaar until in 1872 the old building was demolished to make way for 'a stately four-storey store building with elegantly appointed windows where ladies of fashion alight from their carriages'.

Returning to the 1830's in London, the Pantheon, which was built by James Wyatt in 1772 and dedicated to 'the nocturnal adventures of the British Aristocracy' for balls and masquerades, had become a bazaar and picture gallery. This was in 1834; and in the interval since the original nocturnal gaiety, it had been an opera house, had been destroyed by fire, twice rebuilt, and in 1810 had been taken by a National Institute to Improve the Manufactures of the United Kingdom—a kind of nineteenth century Design Centre. Its subsequent history is that it became a wine store in 1870 and in 1937 was bought by Marks & Spencer, who dismantled and presented the original façade to the Georgian Society when they rebuilt it as their premier store. A clause in the deeds of the Pantheon, throughout its long history, has always been that the name of the building be retained, so that The Pantheon is now written upon a black granite marble frontage. In its days as a bazaar it dealt not so much in drapery and outfitting as in what we should now call accessories, and in children's clothes and books, sheet music, and all those things which come under the heading of 'fancy goods'. In the gallery, pictures were sold on commission, and an upper gallery was a toy bazaar. There was an aviary where cage birds were sold, and a conservatory for the sale of plants. Augustus Sala described it in *Twice Round the Clock:*

We alighted beneath the portico of the Pantheon. The affable beadle (whose whiskers, gold-laced hat-band, livery buttons, and general deportment are as superior to those the property of the beadle of the Burlington Arcade as General Washington to General Walker) receives the ladies with a bow. So into the Pantheon, turning and turning about in that Hampton-Court-like maze of stalls, laden with pretty gimcracks, toys, and papier mâché trifles for the table, dolls and childrens' dresses, wax flowers and Berlin and crochet work, prints, and polkas, and women's wares of all sorts. The young ladies who serve behind the counters behave to their lady customers with great affability. The gentlemen, I am pleased, though mortified to say, they treat with condescension mingled with a reserved dignity that awes the boldest spirit.

It is time that we quit this labyrinth of avenues between triple-laden stalls. I pass the refreshment counter where they sell arrowroot cakes, which I never saw anywhere else, and enter the conservatory . . . and as we entered by Oxford Street, with its embeadled colonnade, it becomes a bounden duty to quit the building by means of the portal which I assumed to have been in days gone-by the stage-door of the pig-tail opera-house, and which gives egress into Great Marlborough Street. Leaving my aunt and my cousin genteely bargaining, I slip through the conservatory's crystal precincts, inhale a farewell gust of flower-breeze, pass through a waiting-room where some tired ladies are resting till their carriages draw up, and am genteelly bowed out by affable beadle No. 2.

6. Regent Street looking South from the Circus, previous to taking down Carlton House in 1828.

It seems from Sala's genteelly bargaining relatives that the Pantheon did not, like the Bazaar at Manchester, rule that 'Prices shall be marked on all the Goods, from which no abatement shall be made'; but the Soho Bazaar opened in 1816, which occupied several houses on the north-west corner of Soho Square with counters on two floors, seems to have been run on exactly the same lines as the Manchester Bazaar. Knight's *London*, published in 1851, says that the Soho Bazaar 'was founded many years ago and stands at the head of its class. . . .

The stalls are rented by females who pay, we believe, something between two and three shillings per day for each. The articles sold are almost exclusively pertaining to the dress and personal decoration of ladies and children; such as millinery, lace, gloves, jewellery, etc.; and, in the height of 'the season', the long array of carriages drawn up near the building testifies to the extent of the visits paid by the high-born and the wealthy to this place.

Some of the rules of the establishment are very stringent. A plain and modest style of dress, on the part of the young females who serve at the stalls, is invariably insisted on, a matron being at hand to superintend the whole; every stall must have its wares displayed by a particular hour in the morning, under penalty of a fine from the renter; the rent is paid day by day, and if the renter be ill, she has to pay for the services of a substitute, the substitute being such an one as is approved by the principals of the establishment. Nothing can be plainer or more simple than the exterior of this bazaar, but it has all the features of a well-ordered institution.

The Baker Street Bazaar was opened as a horse bazaar; but after horses ceased 'to be exposed here for sale', the chief commodities became carriages, harness, horse-furniture and accoutrements, furniture, stoves, and furnishing ironmongery. The North London Repository was started in the early 1850's as a 'labour-exchange', at which the system of barter, exchanging articles according to the amount of labour the artificer who made it spent, was attempted. The scheme was a complete failure, and the building was turned into a kind of bazaar for furniture and carriages.

A relevant discovery is that the modern use of the word pantechnicon must have come from the Pantechnicon Bazaar in Motcombe Street, Belgravia. The O.E.D. gives the derivation of the word pantechnicon as 'a bazaar of all kinds of artistic work', date of origin 1830—which is the date when the Pantechnicon was built. Some time before the 1860's, the Pantechnicon was turned into a bazaar selling carriages of all types (each carriage with its selling price marked on a ticket), and furniture, also clearly ticketed. There was a wine department, and a small toy department. Soon it concentrated almost entirely on furniture, and the vans used by the Pantechnicon were having their name given to any furniture van. Other furniture depositories also began to adopt the same name. By the 1880's there was the Kensington Pantechnicon (proprietor E. L. Jackson) at 8 King Street, High Street, Kensington; and in 1887 a list of the premises occupied by Cavendish House, Cheltenham, included storage and strong rooms in the Pantechnicon, Regent Street, Cheltenham. The original building of the Pantechnicon in Motcombe Street, with certain interior alterations, is now Sotheby Belgravia—a branch of the famous Bond Street auctioneers.

7. A woman shopkeeper comes onto the pavement to serve the grand lady. *Punch*, 1844.

CHAPTER III

WOMEN SHOPKEEPERS

Mrs Caley of Windsor. Milliners and Corset Makers. Husband and Wife teams. Mrs Bell's Magazin de Modes. 'The World of Fashion' and other Journals. Maternity Corsets. The Footwear Trade.

MANY successful drapery businesses must have had their first origins, like Swan & Edgar, in the market stall. And although Kendal Milne is almost certainly unique in having started as a bazaar on the same site which it still occupies now just a hundred and sixty years later, the founders of many other big concerns may have started by renting a bazaar counter. Far and away the most usual beginning, however, was in the little family shop run by husband and wife and inherited by sons and grandsons. Often two brothers would establish a business together; and sometimes it was sisters, as in the case of Susannah and Elizabeth Towsey, the founders of Brown's of Chester.

It was another pair of sisters who began the long history of Caley's of Windsor, now a store in the John Lewis Partnership. The earliest record of the shop is an advertisement which appeared two years before the battle of Waterloo in the newly founded *Windsor and Eton Express* of October 1813:

M. Caley, Milliner, Dress-Maker & Haberdasher, late of Thames Street Windsor, begs leave to inform the Ladies of Windsor, Eton, and their Environs, that the above business will in future be carried on in Castle-street, in conjunction with her Sister, Mrs Noke. M.C. takes this Opportunity of returning the most grateful Thanks for the numerous and distinguished Favours hitherto so liberally conferred: and (jointly with her Sister) most respectfully solicits a Continuance of the same

Maria Caley, spinster, but maybe called Madame Caley in the millinery manner, was the first of the local dressmakers to make use of the fact that women were beginning to read newspapers, and her advertising campaign in the classified columns continued after the move to Castle Street. Rival shops were stimulated into advertising also, but M. Caley's announcements had a dignity and restraint that set her apart from less exclusive establishments such as that of Miss Hudson, whose Millinery, Dress and Corset Room opposite the 'Star and Garter' offered 'elegant morning dresses at 16s to £1 for ready money'. This did not, of course, mean made-up dresses, but dress-lengths of material.

By 1820 Miss Caley had achieved the tradesman's accolade of a Royal Warrant, and become 'Milliner to her Majesty and T.R.H. the Princesses and the Duchess of Gloucester'. Her sister Mrs Nokes had left the business, but she was joined by her brother John and they set up shop together at 19 High Street as John William Caley, Haberdasher, Silk Mercer and Laceman. John had two sons and by 1853 he and his sister Maria had retired and the sons were trading as Caley Brothers. Windsor was a very prosperous town by then. The railway had come in the late 1840's, the royal household grew larger and larger, and the Caleys added more and more departments until, in 1866, they described themselves as Silk Mercers, Linen Drapers, Lacemen, Furriers, Florists, etc. TO THE QUEEN, the Prince and Princess of Wales. A string of lesser royals trailed off into etc., etc., etc. Family mourning and undertaking was a profitable branch of their business, and there was a large dress-making workroom to execute the orders of their distinguished customers, to whom accounts were rendered twice yearly, five per cent interest being charged on anything outstanding after six months. In 1903 'Madame Caley' set up a Court Dressmaking establishment at 18 Albemarle Street, formerly a private hotel.

The early history of Caley's is interesting as an example of a family business built up by a woman in a locality exceptionally favourable for high-class trading. In London, it so happens that none of the big stores still trading under the founder's name today was founded by a woman. On the other hand, there were plenty of extremely vigorous business women in the retail trade during the first half of the nineteenth century. By the mid-century, successful women were tending to sell out to men, more from social than financial reasons: as they prospered, they aspired to be included in the genteel classes whose womenfolk did not work—or so it seems from Margaretta Gregg's diary of 1853:

Men in want of employment have pressed their way into nearly all the shopping and retail businesses that in my early years were managed in whole, or in part, by women. The conventional barrier that pronounces it ungenteel to be behind a counter, or serving the public in any mercantile capacity, is greatly extended.

However, two lines of business in Victorian times were always regarded as women's province: that of milliner and of corset-maker. Doubtless many of these ladies had husbands behind them; but behind them was definitely their place where millinery and corsetry were concerned. Where two sisters ran a business, they were often spinsters: Martha Wheatland and Sister at Queen Charlotte's Head, Milliners & Haberdashers, sound like two hard-working women on their own—unless, of course, the sister was called Mary. There is a suspicion of this since, besides the more usual merchandise of the trade, their shop stocked 'Necklaces and Earrings in the most Elegant Taste'.

Originally a milliner meant a vendor of fancy wares and articles of the kind for which Milan was famous: bonnets, straw hats, ribbons, gloves, trimmings of all kinds. But it is evident from the advertisements of the time that even before Victoria came to the throne millinery was beginning to mean more especially hats, bonnets and their trimmings. A hatter was always a man's hatter, although he would also make riding hats for ladies. There was a Heath, Hat-maker, at 393 Oxford Street listed in *Tallis's Street Views* of 1838. This was Henry Heath, est. 1822, who later moved to 105–109 Oxford Street, from where his fashionable beaver hats for ladies were much advertised in the 1880's. The firm became particularly famous for ladies' golfing hats in the early twentieth century.

Some women shopkeepers combined millinery, corsetry, and dress-making, as did Madame le Plastrier who moved into a new shop at 29 Ludgate Street in 1835:

Madame le Plastrier flatters herself that, from her long experience and extensive connection in the French metropolis, she will be enabled to offer such a succession of novelties of the most prevailing taste as cannot fail to ensure their patronage. Madame L. begs also to recommend her highly approved ELASTIC PARISIAN CORSETS, made under the directions of some of the most eminent of the faculty.

In the wholesale millinery trade of the post Napoleonic War period there was Mrs Piggott of 2 Chatham Place, New Bridge Street. She went over to Paris early in the Spring of each year and on her return would announce to 'the Ladies in the Business' that she was provided with the greatest variety of every elegant, fashionable, and useful article, for first-rate connections, and flatters herself that by her selection of the most admired and novel Parisian millinery, dresses, etc., and the original productions of her own inventresses of English fashion,

8.

she will be enabled to supply her friends on the best terms. Mrs Piggot took apprentices and improvers for moderate premiums. In Regent Street, among the numerous retail milliners, all of them Mrs, Miss, Mesdames, or Madame, two gentlemen's hatters claimed to be 'Hatters to the Queen': Mr Jupp and Son at No. 222 had the Royal Warrant within the first year of Victoria coming to the throne; Johnson & Co. at No. 113, on the corner of Vigo Street had the royal coat of arms over his entrance in prints of 1860.

Mrs Huntley of 294 Regent Street had the honour of being Stay-maker and Corset Maker to Her Majesty Queen Adelaide. She had at her rooms patterns of Parisian and English corsets, 'including her much improved Parisian Corset and full-boned stay, so exceedingly easy that the most delicate constitution may wear them with great advantage, being a general support without particular pressure in any part'. Mrs Huntley emphasised that hers was a *private house*, and she was 'At Home' to her clients from 12–5 daily. Invalids were waited upon in their own homes by Mrs Huntley in person. Her newly invented washing elastic stay prevented pressure at the chest, so destructive to the health of growing children and the young lady whose figure was forming. . . . . 'particularly recommended by Mrs Peter George to

ladies practising the Grecian Exercises, for producing that ease and
elegance for which her pupils are so distinguished'.

This elastic corset material was made by the new process of manufacturing india-rubber in fibres, invented in 1830, which replaced the
spiral brass wires which up till then had been used for corsets and
shoulder straps. Another woman who claimed to be inventor of the
elastic corsets and belts was Mrs Mills of 231 Regent Street. She also,
in 1838, claimed to have invented the 'wove stay'. This was probably
her own version of the woven corsets made on a loom with shaped
gussets, for which Jean Werly took out a patent in 1828. They were
very lightly boned, and continued to be made for another sixty years.
Mrs Mills was one of the women with a man behind her: Mr Mills was
a milliner and dressmaker at the same address.

Another husband and wife team of which the wife was a very active,
aggressive partner, was that of Mr and Mrs Bell. Mrs Bell directed
The World of Fashion and Continental Feuilletons, a monthly magazine
founded in 1824 and 'dedicated expressly to High Life, Fashionables and
Fashions, Polite Literature, Fine Arts, The Opera, Theatres, etc. It
carried a widely read gossip column under the heading of 'On-Dits of
Fashion', and was published by her husband, as was the *Gentleman's
Magazine of Fashion*, 'edited by several Literary and Fashionable
Characters'.

Some of the fashionable characters may well have been Mrs Bell in
disguise, for she seems to have been a woman of prodigious parts and
pretensions. In 1820 she had invented the Chapeau Bras, an ingenious
type of Calash, or hooped hood, which would fold up to carry in one's
'ridicule', as Regency reticules were called. At that time her shop was at
26 Charlotte Street, having been previously at 22 Upper King Street.
On the up and up, she moved to St James's, from where she directed the
World of Fashion and opened her Magazin de Modes with 'a novel
and splendid display of Millinery, Dresses, and Head-dresses, just
prepared in Paris exclusively for Mrs Bell'. Mrs Bell employed the
most competent and highly talented French, German, and Spanish
Milliners and Dressmakers, and she did both Wedding Dresses and
Family Mourning . . . 'the strict regard she has paid in adapting the
dresses according to the degree of relationship has given the utmost
satisfaction for its characteristic propriety. Ladies own materials Mrs
Bell does not object to make up'.

She also made court dresses, ladies' habits, fancy ball dresses and
foreign costumes. She was a corset inventress, holding the appointment
of Corset Maker to Her Royal Highness the Duchess of Kent. We do
not know the date of this appointment, but it is very possible that Mrs

Bell had the responsible honour, or onus, of making the corsets which cradled, so to speak, the embryo Queen Victoria. Her Bandage Corset was invented for use by ladies in late pregnancy and after accouchement, and also for ladies inclined to corpulency—which seems to cover the Duchess of Kent both in and out of pregnancy. Moreover, Mrs Bell's regenerating and Sleeping Ceinture was indispensible to ladies before and after accouchement . . . 'prevents flatulency, reduces protuberance, supports the stomach and bowels, relieves dropsical symptoms'.

These invaluable items by no means exhausted the specialities of this notable corset inventress. The corsets Elyvatone were highly ingenious:

By means of a spring these elegant corsets may be loosened at pleasure, if too tight, without damaging the dress, or the viability of the lace knotting, or the delicate skin tortured by the tags harshly coming in contact with it. A second spring affords the facility of completely and instantaneously unlacing the corset, by which the body may be indulged by reclining in a recumbant position, without the smallest inconvenience. Swoonings, vapours, oppressions, and spasms, are relieved by this corset; and as a Bathing Corset it is equally invaluable, from the rapidity with which it can be taken off and put on.

No wonder the fame of these corsets was such that imposters used her name and Mrs Bell had to announce that she had 'no authorised nor competent person in the Country, travelling and assuming her name of business. *Her Corsets have always been made in London, and can only be made there*, under her own superintendance, as her Patterns of Corsets are her own excellent invention; therefore all orders should be directed to Mrs Bell. Ladies are respectfully cautioned against Pretenders'. Further to defend herself against copyists, Mrs Bell made it a rule at her London shop that her novelties would only be shown to ladies giving their real names and addresses. Anyone who smelt of being connected with trade would be shown the door.

Mrs Bell's dominating position was no doubt achieved, and held, through her *World of Fashion*, which was a very handsomely produced magazine. It had colour engravings of Paris fashions and its editorial columns covered 'High Life and Fashionable Chit Chat, Continental Notes, and On-dits'. A great deal of advertising for Mrs Bell's own shop was disguised as editorial. Her husband not only published it and *The Gentleman's Magazine of Fashion*, but also the famous *La Belle Assemblée* whose sub-title was *Bell's Court and Fashionable Magazine*. This was founded in 1806 and was a leading arbiter of fashion until

1832. From 1832 until 1848 it became *The Court Magazine and Belle Assemblée*. Bell's *World of Fashion and Continental Feiulletons* in 1852 became the *Ladies' Monthly Magazine.* The vicissitudes of women's magazine publishing were no less hazardous in those days than in these.

❦   ❦   ❦

Another married couple in retail trade at this time were Mr and Mrs Carter. But they kept their business activities most strictly separate: Mr Alfred Carter operated a wholesale and retail boot and shoe warehouse at 6 Great Surrey Street; Mrs Carter's Parisian corset warehouse was at 6½ Great Surrey Street.

In the case of the Carters, one rather suspects that it was Mr Carter who had the more virile business. In 1830 he was advertising Wellington Boots to measure at 1 gn. a pair, and Ladies' Lasting or Prunella Slippers at 3/– a pair; children's dancing pumps, 1/6. He supplied public charities regularly, and drapers and country dealers advantageously. This shows that by 1830 shoes and boots were being sold by shops other than those owned by the craftsmen who made them. But footwear remained a handicraft trade up to the mid-nineteenth

45   247. W. C. Jay, 249.   251   253. W. Marchant,   OXFORD STREET.
          Mourning Warehouse.   Wax Chandler, Oilman, &c.

century, the most usual figure in both production and distribution being the producer-retailer—the boot and shoe-maker, the cordwainer, the clog maker. Neither machine nor power was used, and the method of organisation beyond what the single shoemaker could undertake was that of outworking.

Footwear in excess of what the shoemaker could himself sell to retail customers was distributed through other retailers such as drapers, household goods dealers and leather merchants, and stallholders at town markets and fairs—but in all these outlets, it was cheap footwear for the working classes. Footwear for gentlefolk was always 'bespoke'. They did, however, owing to the flimsiness of fashionable footwear, resort to clogs and various types of overshoes. Advertising in *The World of Fashion* (only read, of course, by the fashionable and would-be fashionables), a Mr W. Jackman of 347 Oxford Street introduced himself as an 'Inventor and manufacturer exclusively of the Health Preserver or Promenade Clog—a kind of cork and leather sole worn over shoes or boots'. Mr Jackman's Promenade Clogs were also sold by Molière and Co., the fashionable boot and shoe manufacturers of 223 Regent Street. Specialist footwear retailers, that is the tradesmen who did not make footwear but who specialized in its sale to the exclusion of other goods, were practically non-existent until well into the second half of the century.

Between the mid-1850's and the 1870's, a series of inventions revolutionized the shoemaking trade and led to the replacement of handicraft methods by machine manufacture . . . Blake's sewing machine, Crick's riveting process, the Goodyear welding apparatus. Even then, this factory-made footwear was badly made in poor leather, and often did not distinguish between right and left foot. Bespoke shoemakers would naturally have nothing to do with it, and drapers and general clothing shops only handled it in small quantities, the demand for it being entirely working class.

Shoemaker Daniel Neal, who started business in 1837 in the Edgware Road, was one of the old tradition of craftsman producer-retailers, who carried on an exclusively handmade trade. He made and sold everything himself, specialising in shoes for children. He was one of the first shoemakers to recognize that these should not just be miniature versions of adult shoes and boots. Lilley & Skinner, founded in 1842, were amongst the first shoemakers to combine both wholesale and retail trades, selling their wares through other retailers, and became pioneers of machine production in the shoe trade after the mid-century.

...sher's shop on the ...ner of St Martin's ...ne in 1830. The ...play of materials in the ...orway was very ...tomary with linen ...pers. From a water-...our by George Scharf.

The Strand from near Villiers Street, *c.* 1830, showing Manchester House Irish Linen Warehouse. From a water-colour by George Scharf.

II

The original
Pantheon in Ox
Street, built by
James Wyatt in
1772. From
an engraving by
Thos. H. Sheph
c. 1828.

Interior of the r
Pantheon of 183
reopened as a
bazaar and pictu
gallery. From a
contemporary
engraving.

CHAPTER IV

QUEEN ADELAIDE'S
'BUY BRITISH' CAMPAIGN

*French Dressmakers and Hairdressers at the British Court.
Spitalfield Silks. Imported Gloves and Hosiery. Lace Warehouses. Haberdashery and trimmings. Paper Patterns.*

IMMEDIATELY after William IV had come to the throne in 1830,
Queen Adelaide announced her intention of banning French fashions
from the Court. The redoubtable Mrs Bell, being a London dressmaker, was a fearless fighter for English fashions and a virulent
denigrator of French dressmakers. Her *World of Fashion* struck out in
its 'On Dits of Fashion' column in support of Queen Adelaide's 'Buy
British' campaign:

For her first Drawing room, fixed for the 24th day of February 1831, all the
ladies who attend are expected to appear in dresses of British manufacture,
and *which should also be made up by English dress-makers;* (Mrs Bell's italics);
the foolish mania of employing French dress-makers has subsided—their
arrogance and impudence have discarded them from the presence of English
ladies; the talents of the English dress-maker and milliner cannot be surpassed
by any foreigner.

We have before had occasion to speak of the patriotic partiality of our
beloved Sovereign and his royal consort for the arts and manufactures of the
nations over which they preside, and we are enabled to increase our plaudits
upon the present occasion, when we find that *English people* have also been
employed, to the exclusion of the arrogant and conceited foreigner. The most
honourable and honoured portion of the *beau monde* have awakened to a just
sense of the impropriety of employing the *vain* and *wanton* people of foreign
lands and, in confining their patronage to the natives of their own country,
have thrown the former into the shade and obscurity which they have long
merited, and which for the prosperity and welfare of Great Britain ought
to have been done long ago.

These were fine fighting words; and Mrs Bell, in the first flood of unleashed patriotism and self-interest, followed them up in the March issue of the *World of Fashion*, with an announcement that her new Magazin de Modes, lately removed to Cleveland Place (a strategic position for a Court Dressmaker, since it was just opposite St James's Palace) 'is opened with the view and intention of rivalling and surpassing every French Millinery, Dress, and Corset establishment in the Kingdom, that the Nobility and Gentry may patronise English talent, in preference to foreign, and upon such moderate terms as must secure patronage and approbation'. So far so fine, but the announcement continues:

> Agents in every foreign country provide Mrs Bell exclusively twice each week, with every foreign novelty. Her intercourse with the Continent has been established at considerable expense, and with the view of improving the manufactures of England, as well as increasing her fame as Milliner, Dress & Corset Inventress. The Millinery consists of Caps, Turbans, Tocques, Bonnets, etc., indeed every species of Head-dress, made under Mrs Bell's directions, by English and French assistants of the first eminence.

Clearly Mrs Bell was too shrewd a business woman not to make sure her bread was buttered on both sides. She intended to get her money back on the agencies she had secured in foreign countries; and she had too keen a fashion sense not to know that 'Buy British' would never be a profitable exhortation as far as the elegancies are concerned. In the same number of the *World of Fashion*, a reader's letter to the editor signed by 'An Englishwoman', reveals that even Queen Adelaide herself failed to practise what she preached. The letter began by praising the *World of Fashion's* campaign to persuade people to expend their money upon *'the productions of our own soil and in the employment of our own tradespeople'*, and continued:

> A considerable number of Her Majesty's Appointments have been conferred upon *foreigners*. . . . the dresses which decorate *(or are meant to decorate)* the *Queenly form*, are the work of the people of one *Madame* ——— (I dare say she is a *volume* of vanity if one knew all) and that the *perruquier* of the palace, and the Pavilion, figures and fidgets away in the fantastical person of Monsieur ———.

Famous hairdressers, it seems, had the same characteristics then as now; and this splendidly spiteful bit of writing makes one almost suspect that Mrs Bell wrote the letter herself. Can she, perhaps, have been disappointed in not receiving an appointment to the Queen? At this time she was Staymaker to the Duchess of Kent who was important as the mother of the heir to the throne, but some more elegant appointment in the dressmaking or millinery line to the Queen herself must surely have been the ambition of one who had done such great services to British fashions.

In April of that year Queen Adelaide appeared in 'a very handsome white and silver brocaded dress of Spitalfields produce'; thus attesting by evidence not to be contravened, that she really believed what she so patriotically expressed in her answer to the mechanics of Spitalfields upon their presentation of six fabrics of Spitalfields silks: 'As far as I can judge, or learn from others, best competent to give an opinion, *the English silks are very superior to the foreign'.*

In the circumstances, considering the handsome gift of Spitalfields silks, it was the very least she could say; and she does not seem to have influenced ladies of her court, (who did not get presents from Spitalfields), because the report continues:

Still, notwithstanding, we have yet to regret the unfeeling passion which still actuates many to lavish their patronage upon those whose foreign influence acts as a blight upon our industry; poisoning and withering the otherwise wholesome plants and produce of our native soil. Do such people imagine that with all their exotic finery, upon which has been executed all the *un-English* skill of some dress-decorator with an *outlandish name*, they can rival the graceful elegance and noble carriage of a Duchess of Northumberland, a Marchioness of Londonderry, who had the feeling and the good sense to attend the Drawing-room arrayed in robes the produce of British and Irish industry and skills?

✻   ✻   ✻

The 'Buy British' campaign was an attempt to counteract the delayed post-war slump in the British textile and fashion trades during the years 1826 to 1830. The hosiery trade, which was entirely supplied by outworkers in their own homes, was suffering from cheap imports from Saxony. The home industry itself, over-crowded and over-competitive, spoiled its own reputation by producing cheap goods: in particular there was the abuse of 'cut-up' hose—that is, stockings and socks not fashioned to the shape of the leg, but cut from a flat web and then stitched together. The glove trade, also an outworkers' industry, suffered an immense blow when the ban on foreign-made gloves was removed in 1825 and the market became flooded with cheap German imports and chic French kids.

The lace industry was also suffering badly from continental competitors whose merchandise was once more being imported—with all the prestige of being continental, all the desirability of having been unobtainable during the wars. A firm called Urling & Co., established

35

10. Part of the East Side of Regent Street, showing Urling's Lace Warehouse.

in 1817 as a British and foreign lace warehouse at 224 Regent Street on the corner of Argyll Place, announced that they had made arrangements in Paris to be supplied with the newest articles in French Blondes, Chantilly Veils, Valenciennes and Mechlin laces, 'at lower prices than can be furnished by agents to mere retail dealers— Urling & Co. keep none of the inferior articles manufactured for cheap shops'. But in the spring of 1831, when Queen Adelaide's 'Buy British' campaign was making news, Urling's came out with this intriguing headline:

FRENCH BLONDES ON THE DECLINE

The Queen, having patronized British manufacturers only in the appointment of tradesmen to the Royal Household, and required the observance of the same object at the ensuing Drawingrooms, a sudden change has been effected in the fashionable world, no less beneficial to this country than equitable towards France, *which entirely prohibits British lace from approaching its shores!*

G. F. Urling & Co., 224 Regent Street, have had the honour to supply Her Majesty with Dresses, Veils, etc., the work of BRITISH FEMALES, in *Imitation of French Blonde and Brussels Point* that challenge the criticism of the most fastidious. Urling & Co., not being interested in upholding the prejudice for foreign produce, can afford to offer their extensive stock of CHANTILLY VEILS, etc., selected by themselves in Paris, much under the usual prices.

Yet even this righteous firm had too much business sense to forgo the prestige attached to fashion goods from abroad, and there is a final line: *Regular arrivals of Continental lace of all kinds.*

Although Queen Adelaide gave her Royal Appointment to Urling's, they were not successful in gaining Queen Victoria's patronage. In Tallis's *London Street Views* of 1838, Dison & Co. Foreign and British Lacemen of 237 Regent Street, is *Principal Lace Man in Ordinary to Her Most Gracious Majesty* and the whole of the Royal family. Dison had a large establishment on the corner of Regent Street and Princes Street, and advertised that they sold every conceivable kind of lace 'from a quilling net at one half-penny per yard to a Brussels Point Veil at One Hundred Guineas'.

The decline of the British lace industry is illustrated by the fact that at the time of Queen Victoria's marriage in 1840, there were so few skilled workers left in Devonshire that it was difficult to find enough to make her wedding gown. It was composed of Honiton sprigs, and the pattern was immediately destroyed. The cost was £1,000; but a slight economy was made later by some pieces of the lace being used for the drapery of Princess Beatrice's wedding gown in 1885.

Lacemen were rarely women. The Misses Heywood, Dealers in British Lace at 211 Regent Street, were exceptions. Even when shops began to extend into department stores, the lace department was almost always staffed by men; and it was always a male lace buyer who travelled on the continent placing orders for his stock. One of the best known specialist houses was Hayward's Lace Warehouse of 73 Oxford Street, established in 1770, which by the 1850's had moved to 81 Oxford Street and changed its name to D. Biddle, Laceman to the Royal Family. In 1870 it reverted again to being Hayward, and by the 1880's, while still specialising in lace and 'made-up lace' (fichus, scarfs, collars, Spanish mantillas, stomachers, etc.) had expanded into being a general fashion house.

❧   ❧   ❧

Trimmings, lingerie (in its original meaning of fine linen collars, cuffs, fichus, frills, etc.), and haberdashery of all kinds gained an immense aura of elegance if they came from France. An advertisement in 1830 of C. & G. Roberts (late Rust & Roberts) warehousemen of 17 St Paul's Churchyard shows how much of the merchandise in which they traded was French; and it calls up a charming impression of all those etceteras and accessories to fashion which were so invaluable to the dressmaker's art. This advertisement is reproduced overleaf.

ARTIFICIAL FLOWERS, OSTRICH & FANCY FEATHERS

French Ribbons
French Blondes
Grecian Laces
British Blondes
French & English Tulles
French and English Worked
   Collars, Caps, Flouncings
Foundation Net & Linen
Coloured, and Figured Gauzes
   and Lisses
Gold & Silver Tissues
Trimmings, Braids
Gold & Silver Flowers
French & English Beads
French Tulle Dresses
French Tulle Garnitures
Willow Squares and Chips
Tiffanies and Waddings
Fancy Handkerchiefs
Bouffants

Covered Whalebone
French Sleeves
Silk Fringes & Trimmings
Silk, Worsted, and Cotton Braid
Bugle Fringes & Trimmings
Gold & Silver Hooks and Eyes
Silk & Cotton Buttons
Silk & Cotton Worsted Cords
Gauze, Satin, and Crepe Flowers
Wire & Wire Ribbons
Rolled & Book Muslins
Ivory & Painted Fans
Blonde Quillings
Gauze & Barège Scarfs
French White Cotton Hats
Chip and Tuscan Hats
Whalebone Drawn Bonnets
Imitation Leghorn Hats
Worked Muslin Trimmings

A constant supply of the Newest and Most Fashionable
PARISIAN NOVELTIES
Feathers, shawls, etc., cleaned

Similar merchandise was also kept by Hitchcock and Rogers 'the large haberdashery establishment at the very top of Ludgate Hill' where 'a prodigious quantity of novelties in Ribbons, Shawls, Silks and Lace are always on view'. But although there were still plenty of retail shops in the City neighbourhood, the drift to the West End was very strong; and in 1832, the old established firm of Wilks moved from the Strand to 186 Regent Street, where they sold EVERYTHING FOR THE WORKTABLE:

Cottons, Worsteds, Lamb's-wools, Floss and other Silks for Embroidery, Rug-work; Sewing, Knitting, Netting and Mending Needles; Pins and fine Cutlery; Gilt and Steel Beads, Tassels, Slides, Snaps, etc. for Purses; every article in Steel, Ivory, Pearl and Tortoishell for the finishing of Workboxes and suited to every description of Plain and Ornamental Needlework.

The sale of 'everything for the work-table' would mean good business in those days of private dressmaking and of ladies with a great deal of time on their hands to fill with needlework, plain and ornamental, useful and useless. And even in this side branch of the drapery trade, Queen

Adelaide's 'Buy British' campaign was a bandwagon worthwhile climbing on: 'Her Most Excellent Majesty, with that earnest desire to promote and patronize all branches of British manufacture, has been graciously pleased to appoint the long established firm of Kirby, Beard & Kirby to be *Her Majesty's Pin & Needle Manufacturers*. Their new manufacture, excelling anything of the kind ever offered, are the Royal Diamond Patent Pins and Needles'.

But at 202 Regent Street, there was a sinister foreign cell called Gotto's Berlin Repository. This was run by a lady named A. Gotto, importer of foreign needle work, manufacturer of fringe and fancy trimmings, braids, tassels, and cords; haberdasher and dealer in all kinds of lambswools, worsteds, floss, netting and other silks . . . 'A. Gotto begs to announce to the Nobility and Gentry, that her stock is most extensive and unique, every attention being paid by her agents on the Continent in the selection of articles of the newest fashions and most approved designs'.

✢   ✢   ✢

An auxiliary trade to dress-making and embroidery was the production of paper patterns. Although it was not until the mid-century that magazines began to carry paper-patterns for their readers (the *World of Fashion* of August 1850 was the first), the idea of paper patterns was conceived very much earlier as a service to dressmakers. The originator of paper patterns as a commercial proposition is not known; but a paper pattern model warehouse with a considerable operation was established at 4 Pilgrim Street, Ludgate Hill, well before the 1830's at any rate, and was so successful that it soon moved to 71 St Paul's Churchyard, the very heart of the drapery trade. It was run by a Mrs Smith in partnership with Mme La Poulli of the Boulevard des Italiennes, Paris. They supplied full size paper patterns, £1 the set to milliners and dressmakers. In March 1831 they were announcing that the new season's selection of Millinery and Dress Models, and full size paper patterns was ready . . . 'on no former occasion have they been able to produce a greater variety of novelties, particularly in elegant Pelisses, Dresses, Bonnets, and Caps. Ladies in business are requested to make an early call, as Mrs Smith and Madame La Poulli have brought over several Premier Assistants from the most celebrated *Marchands des Modes* in Paris, viz; Mme Muire, Laurent, Minette, Payant, Michel, Victorine, Heaubeaux, etc., and make up materials in a few elegant articles for the Trade only'. To those interested in patterns for embroidery they announced:

The past and present state of the French capital have rendered other resources necessary, and from the source of genius and invention, BERLIN, they have received an immense variety of Elegancies, among which will be found superb Embroideries and Appliqués, composed of a new Material made of *Whalebone* and *Carp Scales*, much in request for all fancy trimmings and ornamental work, together with an elegant display of Taste and Fashion.

However, the state of the French capital (this was the year after the July revolution which brought Louis Phillipe to the throne) cannot really have been very incommoding to the fashion trade, because by April of the next year Mrs Smith and Madame La Poulli were informing their esteemed customers that arrangements had been made with the leading Houses in Paris for a regular supply of every novelty of taste and fashion the moment they are produced in Paris. *Just received:*

Some very new and elegant hats and bonnets, caps, turbans, etc., and a few superb morning, dinner and evening dresses, completely made up in paper, price only a pound the complete set; and, as the Spring advances, and the novelty becomes multiplied, they intend throwing open to the *Trade* generally, one of the most superb and elegant Collations of Taste and Fashion ever exhibited in this country. They have already received six first-hand Milliners from the following Houses: Madame More, Rue de la Paix; Madame Michel, Rue Neuve des Petits Champs; and the Magazin of the Belle Anglaise, Rue de Richelieu. They earnestly entreat Milliners and Dressmakers, both in Town and Country, to inspect their Collection of Taste and Fashion before they make extensive purchases for the season.

At 71 St Paul's Churchyard and No. 2 Boulevard des Italiennes, two or three young ladies may be admitted on Improvement. Premium moderate.

(In a later announcement, the 'moderate' premium is given as 10 gns.— a considerable sum in those days; nearly as much as the girls would earn in their first year after their apprenticeship.)

In the Spring of the following year, the Paper Pattern Model Warehouse was announcing that Madame La Poulli was in Paris, 'selecting from first sources every novelty that is either made or in preparation for the season':

She has already obtained a great variety of Morning, Dinner, Evening, Ball & Opera Dresses, Pelisses, Hats, Bonnets, Caps, Turbans, etc., which are *made in models and full-size Paper Patterns* with an assemblage of beautiful millinery and fancy goods, and rarely if ever met with so early in the season, including a new bonnet, composed of Tuscan Grass and prepared whalebone, having the appearance of beautiful transparent Pearl. This elegant article can be had in Bonnets of every shape, or Trimmings for making up.

As Madame La Poulli remains in Paris for some time, every novelty will be forwarded the moment they appear in the French Capital.

Although this operation was probably the most extensive at the time, these two enterprising ladies were not the only paper pattern merchants. There was Mrs Hobson of 64 Russell Street, Bloomsbury Square. In October 1836 she was advertising to country milliners and dressmakers:

> Mrs Hobson solicits an early inspection of her French Paper Models, comprising a very superior and extensive display of Real Fashions, selected from the newest designs for Cloaks, Bonnets, Caps, Dresses, new Sleeves, Capes, with every new Pattern as they appear, at 8/– set of four articles, and 15/– for two sets of eight articles, packed in a box charged 3/– and forwarded to any part of the kingdom.

Also near Bloomsbury Square, established at 12 Hart Street before 1830, there was Mr B. Read, whose beautiful colour prints of men's and women's fashions were sold, together with paper patterns and his patent measure, at 8s the set from all booksellers in the kingdom. Mr Read was an instructor in cutting, who offered to perfect the system of cutting of other teachers and sold his own patent measures to them. He also examined and corrected the drawings of those who published fashion plates. He became a tailor of international repute by 1830, and had a branch on Broadway, New York. It must have taken him many long weeks travelling each way to visit his American branch, and he must surely be considered one of England's very early retail pioneers of British fashions in the New World.

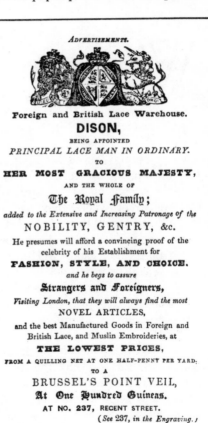

11. Advertisement in Tallis's *Street Views*, 1838, for Dison's Lace Warehouse.

CHAPTER V

THE ERA OF RETAIL ADVENTURERS

London shops begin to grow. Young men set out from the City to the Provinces. Shops in the fashionable spas. Scarborough, Harrogate, Cheltenham, Bath, Tenby, Brighton. Fashions at Victoria's accession. Dry-cleaners and Dyers.

ꚍꚍꚍ

WHEN the old king died and the young queen took his place, there was a spirit of expansion in the air. Ambitious and intelligent young men were beginning to establish shops which were very soon to grow into much larger concerns. It was the dawn of a great era of retail adventurers.

At 103 Oxford Street, between Oxford Circus and Great Portland Street, a young man named Peter Robinson, son of a Yorkshire haber-dasher, having served his apprenticeship in a small draper's shop in Paddington, set up on his own as a linen draper in 1833. And in 1835 Dickins & Smith, 'at the sign of the Golden Lion', moved from 54 Oxford Street where they had been established since 1790, to the magnificent new Regent Street that had become every ambitious shopkeeper's eldorado. They took Nos. 232 and 234, and grandly called their shop Hanover House. They took another partner into the business and became Dickins, Smith & Stevens. And they placed their Golden Lion above their new entrance, where it remained until the rebuilding of Regent Street in the nineteen-twenties. It was one of the last of the old shop signs to be seen in the West End.

But the West End had not yet drawn all retail fashion trade away from the City. One shopkeeper of King William Street, a Mr D. Nicholson, was in 1837 the founder of one of the earliest wholesale mantle manufactures; and in 1843 he joined with his brother in opening a retail and wholesale drapery establishment at 50–54 St Paul's Church-yard. They described themselves as 'Silk, Woollen, and Manchester Warehousemen'—Manchester goods being household and all kinds of

42

cottons. Nicholson's of St Paul's was to become the most important drapery and fashion store in the City; and within ten years they had also taken over the Argyll Rooms in Regent Street from 'The Fur Company' owned by Charles Cook, and established there the Argyll Mourning Warehouse . . . described in a contemporary guide book as 'the spacious and highly ornamental saloons of Messrs D. Nicholson & Co., the fittings of which are at once chastely elegant and appropriate'. Nicholson's was acquired by Debenham's after the Second World War, but remained in the City as Nicholson's of St Paul's until their building was demolished in 1963 to make way for the new Barbican. The business was moved to an entirely new store converted from a cinema in Bromley. Before the move, the Managing Director said: 'When we have left the City, there will be nowhere to buy a reel of sewing-cotton between Holborn and New Cross'. It was the end of retail drapery in the City of London.

Just before the Nicholson brothers opened their shop, an assistant employed by another draper in St Paul's Churchyard reversed the usual direction of ambitious young men and left the City of London to seek his fortune in Cambridge. This was Robert Sayle. In Cambridge he bought the well-established business of John Cooch in 1840, and announced in the local press the arrival of 'a new and well-selected stock of Linen, Drapery, Silk Mercery, Hosiery, Haberdashery, Straw Bonnets, etc., etc., etc.'. It is thought that he also stocked furs. But furs or no furs, and allowing for a certain amount of hyperbole in the etc., etc., of his announcement, it is clear that the young man from St Paul's Churchyard, with all the prestige of having come from the citadel of the drapery trade, very swiftly branched out into more various lines of merchandise than was usual at that date. His establishment was to become in 1934 a Selfridge Provincial Store, and came into the John Lewis Partnership in 1940. But it is still known as Robert Sayle's.

Another young man to take his London experience into the provinces was Emerson Muschamp Bainbridge, who was at Lewis & Allenby. This was an extremely high-class silk & shawl warehouse at 195 Regent Street which later was moved to a magnificent emporium at 63 Conduit Street. After his apprenticeship, Bainbridge returned to his home town of Newcastle, and in 1838 went into partnership with a draper called William Dunn. Bainbridge was a man of very advanced theories about retail selling, and three years later he decided to discontinue the partnership so that he could work out his progressive ideas with no cautious partner to hold him back. In point of fact, he visualized the idea of a department store. As early as 1849 he had twenty-three departments.

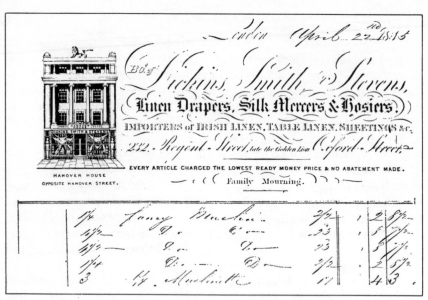

London April 22nd 1845

Bot of *Lickins, Smith & Stevens,*

(Linen Drapers, Silk Mercers & Hosiers,)

IMPORTERS of IRISH LINEN, TABLE LINEN, SHEETINGS &c.

252. Regent Street, late the Golden Lion Oxford Street

EVERY ARTICLE CHARGED THE LOWEST READY MONEY PRICE & NO ABATEMENT MADE.

Family Mourning.

HANOVER HOUSE
OPPOSITE HANOVER STREET.

12.

Bot of SWAN & EDGAR,

Silk Mercers, Linen Drapers, Haberdashers,

Furriers Hosiers Lacemen & Glovers,

9 & 10, PICCADILLY, & 47 & 49, REGENT QUADRANT.

Damask Table Linen Sheetings, Blankets Counterpanes, Flannels, &c &c.

13.

SILKS & FANCY DRESSES.

Bot of D. NICHOLSON & Co.

COSTUME,

MANTLE, SHAWL & JUVENILE WAREHOUSE,

GLOVES, LACE, HOSIERY, RIBBONS, Etc.

50 to 54, St PAUL'S CHURCH YARD,

& 66 PATERNOSTER ROW.

(CORNER OF CHEAPSIDE.)

SILK MERCERS TO THE QUEEN.

PARASOLS & FURS.

ESTABLISHED 1843.

TERMS,

NETT PROMPT CASH. Post Office Orders to be made payable at Chief Office, St Martins le Grand.

14.

Meanwhile in London, in the year of Queen Victoria's accession, James Marshall opened a shop at 11 Vere Street in partnership with a Mr Wilson. James Marshall was the youngest son of twelve children and had come from Yorkshire to work with Burrell, Son and Toby, a drapery shop at 10 Vere Street. The year after he left them to join Wilson was coronation year, and so an exceptionally good year for tradespeople. The business had a flying start, and was already prosperous when John Snelgrove obtained a post with Marshall & Wilson. Snelgrove had walked to London with half-a-crown in his pocket. He was the son of a paper manufacturer in Wells who made five pound notes—one of the first harsh Victorian fathers, one presumes, since he let his son set out without one five pound note. However, the Somerset boy made good, and became a partner in 1848.

It may have been because James Marshall came from Yorkshire that he conceived the idea of having a Scarborough branch . . . perhaps some of his numerous brothers and sisters were available to manage it. There is no record of the date of its opening, but it must have been very early in Marshall & Snelgrove's history, because the Scarborough shop is recorded as having moved from Huntriss Row to Harcourt Place in 1843. Later it was moved again to St Nicholas Street. The Scarborough branch was open only during the season, catering for the rich visitors to this very fashionable resort. Scarborough's era of fashion touched its highest point when the Franco-Prussian war made holidaying on the continent too hazardous; but even before that, all through the 'fifties and 'sixties, it was the most favoured resort in England, since it not only had the sea but was also a spa. Osbert Sitwell describes the Scarborough of this period in *Two Generations*:

The revels were led by the Lord and Lady Londesborough of the day, who possessed a summer residence in it, and the season flamed almost exotically through the town in July, August and September, and continued through October and November. In the summer, the terraces by the sea were heavy under the sun with patchouli and cigar-smoke, and the streets were full of elegant carriages, drawn by high-stepping, thin-ankled horses, the public houses crowded with footmen at noon. In the evenings, the stone decks of the Spa rustled with the swaying of crinolines, and echoed the blare of the German Band, while rockets traced their ascending lines into the sky and then blossomed into showers of stars, pink, green and yellow.

Small wonder that a shop with all the prestige of being a branch of the fashionable Marshall & Snelgrove's in London, did good business in this dazzling Scarborough. It was the married women who spent the money. Young girls had very small allowances, as was recalled by Mrs Campbell Swinton, one of the three daughters of Sir George Sitwell of that time. She was writing of the year 1837:

A girl thought herself rich with one silk dress and a few muslins, all untrimmed, and one summer and winter bonnet a year. Few had more; many, whatever their rank, had less, and wore no ornaments on neck or arms until they married. A fourth of the money now thought necessary (she was writing this in the 1880's) must then have been spent on clothes, and yet I am not sure that girls were not far more attractive than in these days of triumphant millinery.

Later on, Marshall & Snelgrove established another spa branch at Harrogate. This, like the Scarborough shop, was at first open only during the season.

Marshall & Snelgrove's near neighbour and rival in London, Clark & Debenham, seized even earlier the opportunities of the fashionable spas, acquiring a controlling interest in the Cheltenham drapery shop of Pooley & Smith, founded in 1818. The *Gloucester & Cheltenham Herald*, August 12, 1826, carried the announcement: New Establishment—Clark & Debenham of Cavendish House, Wigmore-street, London, at No. 3, Promenade, Cheltenham.

The history of Debenham's began when a little drapery shop called Flint & Clark opened at 44 Wigmore Street in 1778. William Debenham, the nineteen-year-old son of a Suffolk farmer, bought a partnership with Clark in 1813, after having served an apprenticeship with a Mr Swan of 10 Fore Street—one would like to think that this was George Swan of Swan & Edgar. Clark & Debenham's shop looked out to the north on a waste of dank pasturage called Harley Fields; but to the east was Cavendish Square where lived the rank and fashion, the nobility and gentry, to whom shopkeepers liked to address their announcements. So it was Cavendish House that they rather naturally called their little shop. When Clark retired in 1837, Pooley & Smith of Cheltenham bought his share of the partnership, Debenham acquiring a further interest in their Cheltenham shop. Then around 1851 Clement Freebody was made a partner, having married Debenham's sister. Freebody managed the Cheltenham Cavendish House, which had already expanded considerably, as this advertisement in the *Cheltenham Chronicle* (October 10, 1844) on the opposite page suggests. Also, this announcement shows that there was already a branch of Cavendish House at Harrogate, but we do not know whether Debenham's followed Marshall & Snelgrove's, or vice versa—either way it was a very close thing.

CAVENDISH HOUSE
Promenade, Cheltenham:
No. 44 WIGMORE STREET, LONDON,
and HARROGATE, YORKSHIRE.

DEBENHAM, POOLEY & SMITH

beg to announce their intention of OPENING their NEW and EXTENSIVE PREMISES on MONDAY NEXT, when they will offer for Sale a Stock unrivalled in extent, and selected with the greatest care from the British and Foreign Markets, consisting of every novelty in

SILKS, CACHMERES, SHAWLES, MANTELS, CLOAKS,
LACE and EMBROIDERY;
HOSIERY, FLANNELS and BLANKETS;
MOREEN, DAMASK, and CHINTZ FURNITURE;
SHEETINGS, DAMASK TABLECLOTHS,
and Linen Drapery of every description;
COBOURG AND ORLEANS CLOTHS;
A Large Lot of French Merinoes, Exceedingly Cheap;
READY-MADE LINEN, for Ladies and Gentlemen;
Baby Linen and Children's Dresses of every kind;

also

A CHOICE STOCK OF FURS
FAMILY MOURNING
FUNERALS conducted in the most careful manner, at moderate charges.

Debenham & Freebody's spa branches shared the same *Fashion Book* as the Wigmore Street Cavendish House. This was a book of steel engravings and fashion information which was sent out to customers from 1870 onwards, through which ladies could order by post clothes made to their own measure. The daughter shop seems to have been run on very similar lines to those of the old lady of Wigmore Street herself. But some time before 1870, the Cheltenham business became Debenham & Hewitt, and Mr Hewitt seems to have become the dominant force. When he retired in 1888, a public company was formed under the name of Cavendish House Ltd, and at some point, of which there is no record, Debenhams relinquished their interest altogether. But Cavendish House Ltd. has remained the name through all changes of ownership ever since. A famous name is an incalculable asset in the goodwill of a retail firm. A new owner drops it at his peril.

BATH EMPORIUM,

No. 12, MILSOM STREET.

JOLLY and SON have the honour to return their sincere thanks for the Patronage they have experienced at their Establishment in Old Bond Street, which has induced them to open

EXTENSIVE PREMISES at

No. 12, MILSOM STREET.

From the novel nature of their new Establishment, which will combine a SHOP and BAZAAR, they deem it requisite to point out *the peculiar advantages it will offer to Purchasers*. The distinguishing feature of the Emporium will be

ECONOMY, FASHION, and VARIETY.

The FIRST can only be obtained by an exclusive Ready Money System, *no Article being delivered unless upon prompt payment*. The advantages of this System are great. By it the Tradesman is enabled to purchase on the very best terms, and from the quickness of his return, and his not incurring any risk of loss from bad debts a very small profit will remunerate him; *the benefit thus arising to the Consumer can only be judged of by comparison*.

For FASHION and VARIETY, JOLLY and SON trust the EMPORIUM will be unrivalled, they having just completed most extensive Purchases in *London* and *Paris*, combining, with their former FOREIGN STOCK, a general Assortment of

LINEN DRAPERY, SILK MERCERY,

Hosiery, Haberdashery, Shawls, Merinos, Lace Nets, &c.

The BAZAAR Department will contain a Splendid Selection of

FOREIGN CHINA and BIJOUTERIE; OR MOLU and ALABASTER CLOCKS,

Italian ALABASTER URNS, VASES, and FIGURES;

British and Foreign Cabinet Goods; Jewellery; Perfumery;

STATIONARY; COMBS; BRUSHES; CUTLERY; a great variety of TOYS;

And almost all the multifarious Articles usually kept in Bazaars.

There will be no abatement made from the price asked, the profit on each article being too small to admit of any reduction.

The EMPORIUM will OPEN on THURSDAY, November the 3d, 1831.

Reproduced from "The Bath Chronicle," Saturday, October 29th, 1831.

15.

The great days of Bath ended with the eighteenth century. By the beginning of the nineteenth century seaside resorts were beginning to draw away the transient fashionables, and Bath became a place of residence rather than of revelry. The old glories had departed, but the city was still sufficiently favoured for James Jolly to move his business there in 1830. James Jolly was born in 1775, so was then over fifty. Originally he had owned a wholesale woollen merchants' business in the City of London under the name of Nice & Jolly, and later a retail business in Margate. Evidently he was not satisfied with the class of customer at that resort, which was never very elegant, and after a few years of trying out showrooms in Bath open during the season only, he transferred his whole business there, the opening being announced in the *Bath Herald* of May 22, 1830.

PARISIAN DEPOT.

MESSRS. JOLLY and SON have the honour of announcing to the Nobility and Gentry of Bath and its Vicinity, that *the Parisian Depôt will not be closed during the Summer, but will continue permanently open.* JOLLY and SON avails themselves of the present opportunity, to return their sincere thanks for the very great support and encouragement they have been favoured with; they also beg to solicit the attention of Ladies to their last new Importation of CACHEMERES, which is very extensive, and will be found worthy the notice of Ladies purchasing Shawls.——20, *OLD BOND-STREET.*

Only a year later they were announcing in the *Bath Chronicle* (October 29, 1831) that they had moved to No. 12 Milsom Street to be called The Bath Emporium, which would combine a shop and a bazaar. The illustration opposite shows the variety of stock they now carried, 'including all the multifarious articles usually kept in Bazaars', and they had the rule that there would be 'no abatement made from the price asked, the profit on each article being too small to admit of any reduction'.

Milsom Street was then the most fashionable residential street in the city. It was in Milsom Street that Jane Austen's General Tilney had lodgings; but even then trade was creeping in, it seems, since it was at a shop in Milsom Street that Isabella Thorpe saw 'the prettiest hat you can imagine'. Some of Jolly's property had already been converted from houses into shops before he took them over. A letter written to a member of the staff by a friend who lived in lodgings opposite shows that the new business certainly attracted 'carriage trade'; 'We watched your house on Thursday last. The number of sedan chairs and carriages was very great. You had two Lords' carriages at one time. Your shop was at times so crowded that ladies had to wait outside until others came out to give them room. Indeed, I thought that of all the ladies who passed on that side of the street eight out of ten went in.'

Jolly & Son featured in 'The Fusseltons in Bath' a series of poetical letters of 1836:

> And next down Milsom Street we went
> On various purchases intent;
> 'Twas just that fashionable minute,
> When the Bath world were walking in it,
> Smart belles were tripping side by side,
> With beaux in spurs—who never ride—
> Old dames, more rouged than is discreet,
> Led little dogs about the street,
> Whilst chairs, so long the pride of Bath,
> Did all but push me off the path.
> Papa met many former friends,
> Whom gout or vapour hither send
> And chose with them awhile to stop,
> While we went on to Jolly's shop.
> But oh! Louise, should I recite,
> The various things that greet one's sight,
> The dresses sold for next to nought,
> The work by skilful fingers wrought,
> The jewellery so much like gold,
> That scarce the difference is told.

It seems that Jolly's were not above trading in what we should now call 'costume jewellery'; but that would be in the Bazaar section. The main prestige of the firm was built up on its dealings with the silk trade. The partners and buyers went direct to the weavers in France, Italy and Switzerland, and were able to offer an exceptionally wide choice well in advance of the fashions shown by other shops.

A branch of Jolly's was opened at College Green, Bristol in 1858, and alterations and extensions were gradually made to the Milsom Street premises. The main entrance of the building today was built in 1879, adjoining houses were added, and by Edwardian times they were launching out as house and land agents, as builders and decorators, furnishers, and antique dealers. It was still a family firm in the 1960s, when a great-great-great-grandson of the founder was on the Board. Then it was acquired by the House of Fraser, the name of Jolly's being retained with its cachet of a famous 'carriage trade' connection.

Farther west than Bath, the watering-place of Tenby in Pembroke-shire was a favourite although unsophisticated resort in the nineteenth century. In particular it was favoured by retired officers of the army and navy. In large premises upon the sea front was the establishment of W. Bill Ltd, homespun merchants. William Thomas Bill started his business in Mold, Flintshire, in 1846. Originally his specialities were Welsh flannels and blankets; but at the Tenby shop his son, the second William Thomas Bill, began to offer tweeds, which were a great novelty after the broadcloths, serges, flannels, and smoothly woven cloths then generally used. In London, tweeds and shepherd's checks had become immensely fashionable since the opening of the Scotch Warehouses. Mr Bill was also in at the beginning of the fashion for hand-knitted Shetland underwear, and later outerwear. He even took up the vogue for oriental goods after Liberty in London had made them all the rage. Despite his remote location, the Bill enterprise became sufficiently well known to move to London in 1892, when Tenby had become less of a resort and more of a quiet family holiday place.

※ ※ ※

Brighton, as long as the Pavilion was a royal residence, had innumerable smart shops. Gentlemen were particularly well served, many of the shops being branches of London outfitters, hatters, tailors, and hosiers, all contributing their Bond Street and Jermyn Street atmosphere to 'London-super-Mare', as it was christened by Titmarsh. More exclusively for ladies, there was a branch of Sykes, Josephine & Co., at 56a Old Steyne. Sykes, Josephine were makers of anatomical corsets and belts, their main branch being at 280 Regent Street, near Oxford Circus. They also made expensive lingerie and layettes, and were still in Regent Street at the end of the century. In Market Place, Brighton, there was a Waterloo House, but this had no connection with the Waterloo House, Pall Mall East, which amalgamated with Swan & Edgar. Waterloo House, Brighton, was owned by Stephenson Pierpoint & Co., Linen Drapers and Thread Lace Manufacturers, importers of Irish Linens, French Cambrics, Sheetings, Damask, Table Linens, and specialists in Bombazeens and all articles for family mourning.

Brighton was a very smart place to die in, and fashionable funerals were undertaken by Robert Rogers, linen draper, silk mercer, lace manufacturer, hosier, and haberdasher of 16 North Street, Brighton, who besides 'furnishing' funerals, did brisk business in supplying the draperies of grief to the relicts and relatives. Also in North Street, at No. 22, was Lynden's Hat Manufactory, specializing in straws, chips,

and leghorns, whose main branch was in Oxford Street, opposite
Stratford Place. At this period, straws and chips were always hats of
English origin; Leghorns were foreign, but not always from Leghorn.
The favourite shop of Regency ladies was Hannington's, dating from
1808 when Smith Hannington bought 'a shop and room behind' in
North Street. A Royal Appointment was achieved in 1820, and the
firm remained in the founder's family until the death in 1966 of his
great-great-grand-daughter, Dorothy Smith Hannington, who left her
interest in it to two hospitals. They sold it to Charles Hunnisett, a
well-known Hove philanthropist, under whose chairmanship Hannington's continues as an independant store.

Brighton was to lose some of its cachet when Queen Victoria decided
that the Pavilion was not suitable for a family residence and began to
look for a holiday house for her growing family on the Isle of Wight,
which she had visited twice as a girl. She first rented the Osborne
estate in 1845 and bought it the following year. The existing house
being too small, it was demolished and rebuilt to Prince Albert's
design. In 1850 the Royal Pavilion was sold to Brighton Town, and
from then on Brighton slipped gradually into the Margate, Ramsgate,
and Broadstairs class: popular family seaside resorts, much too popular
to be smart, much too easily accessible by day excursions by train.

Margate and Ramsgate were also served by steam packet from
London. Families would stay in lodgings most of the summer, husbands
and brothers coming down by the packet boat on Saturdays or Sundays.
During the season, Brown & Hood of 28 Jermyn Street, London, had a
branch of their 'Ladies' Cheap Shoe Manufactory' on the Parade at
Margate. Their business must have been considerable, as it was
advertised as 'wholesale, retail, and for exportation'; but the word
manufactory is misleading. It did not mean a factory in the modern
sense of the word. It meant a place where articles were literally made
by hand—a shop which had workrooms and made its own stock. Even
cheap shoes, at this time, were not factory made.

✲ ✲ ✲

Fashion itself, when Victoria's reign began, was in an entirely different
mood from that of the first twenty years of the century. At the end of
the Napoleonic wars, the uncorseted classical style, flowing softly
from a high waist, was still in vogue; but the skirt was shorter than
during the Empire—well above the ankle. It was also narrower; and
since the hem was ornamented and stiffened with four or five rows of
braid, pleats, tucks, or dog-tooth trimming called 'dents,' it caused a

more sedate walk. Soon the waist began to drop and skirts to become fuller; and as they became fuller, they were supported at the back and the sides by pads or small bustles, usually called tournures. Necklines were low and square cut; shoulders were emphasized by enormous sleeves. In July 1833, Sophy Horsley writing to her Aunt Lucy said, 'I wonder if you will return from Paris with an immense monkey behind and stiff sleeves?'

It was not only dressmakers who constructed these great sleeves— even the tailors were infected by the fashion. When Sara Hutchinson, writing to Edward Quillinan from Brinsop Court asking him to instruct her London tailor, Mr Stultz, about making a new habit for her, she added an anxious P.S.: 'Pray desire Stultz will not make the sleeves outrageously large—remember I am an old and *little* Body and do not like extremes—Dora's was very neat—but some which I have seen are frightful'. She was fifty-four at the time. The letter itself shows how a lady living in the country got a habit made by a London tailor:

April 20th, 1829

My dear Friend,

I send you this parcel for Mr Stultz—and will venture to give you a com-mission—viz. to order me a riding habit, chuse the cloth, *good, stout*, and *dark* blue, pay for it and send me the amount of the *damage* and I will return the money by post—He used to charge 10gs. for a *full-sized* habit (2 yds. long) deducting 10/6 for each ¼ yd. shorter than this—So that as I shall not require a full-sized one, I tell you this lest they should charge you the full price—If you will be so kind as call & order Stultz to send for the parcel to your house he will in it find the measure and directions—so that you will have no trouble but chusing the cloth—and ordering him to send it by the Mail to Hereford 'to be left at the Greyhound for Mr H., Brinsop Court— and desire to be sent as soon as possible—I wish to pay for it immediately that I may have discount.

Ten guineas was a lot for a habit at that time, but Stultz was the most celebrated tailor. His name keeps cropping up in memoirs and novels of the period. Thackeray made him Major Pendennis's tailor; and Bulwer Lytton made him the tailor of his dandy hero Pelham, who set the fashion for black evening clothes and insisted that Stultz made his suits without padding.

By 1830, skirts had spread into wide bells. And the bustle, Sophie Horsley's 'immense monkey behind', was becoming universally worn, not just by fashionable women. In November 1834, Mrs Carlyle wrote 'The diameter of the fashionable ladies at the moment is about three yards; their *bustles* (false bottoms) are the size of an ordinary sheep's fleece. The very servant-girls wear bustles. Eliza Miles told me a maid of theirs' went out on Sunday with *three* kitchen dusters pinned on as a substitute.'

Underneath the ever-widening skirts, unobserved, the underclothes were thickening up. Gone were the pink stockings and drawers intended to be observed under the transparent muslins of the empire; gone were the 'patent elastic India cotton invisible petticoat, drawers, and waistcoats all in one', which had been advertised as adding much less to size than cambric muslin—elastic meaning then a knitted fabric, as opposed to a woven one. Calico, more bulky even than cambric, was becoming usual for underwear; and even woollen underwear and stockings were beginning to have their advocates. The era of flannel petticoats and linsey woolsey was fast approaching, and the tight-laced stay had already returned to torment its fair victims. Few people in England had, in fact, ever discarded their stays altogether—only the ultra-fashionable and flighty.

The exuberant hats with feathers and flowers had been replaced, some years before Victoria came to the throne, by prim oval bonnets usually called 'coal-scuttles'. This type of bonnet was introduced by Baroness Oldenburg on her visit to London in 1818. There are two stories about this lady, who was sister to the Czar of Russia. One version says she was so beautiful that everybody wanted to copy her bonnets; the other that she was so hideous that the bonnets were designed to obscure her face.

Bare shoulders and bosoms were now covered by pelerines or by that cosy but unglamorous piece of feminine equipment, the shawl. The shawl, of course, like the stays, had never been entirely discarded, especially by older women; but during the period of 'naked fashions' it had a very thin time. It is true that Thomas Lloyd had his muslin and shawl warehouse at 132 Oxford Street, thus selling the diaphanous material of fashion and at the same time the shawls to counteract its chilliness; but for the most part they would have been shawls of lace, gauze, crepe, or other fine materials, designed in the long shape of scarfs or stoles. The shawl industry at Paisley and at Norwich had been having a distressing period, during which most of the mills closed down.

Sometime between 1820 and 1830, Jn. & J. Holmes opened their Shawl Emporium at 171 Regent Street, selling shawls and nothing but shawls. The *World of Fashion* commented that 'from confining themselves to this elegant and indispensable article of dress, the extent of their sales enables them to effect their purchases with a facility which gives them a decided advantage over other houses'. Certainly they gained the Royal Appointment to the Queen within a year of her

Mess.rs Grant & Gask (late Williams & Co.)

59, 60, 61 & 62. Oxford Street, & 3, 4 & 5. Wells St.

16. Engraving of about 1860—it was still Williams & Co. in 1857.
Bourne & Hollingsworth moved here from Westbourne Grove in 1902.

accession. By that time, there were two other specialist shawl ware-houses in Regent Street, quite apart from other establishments which sold shawls amongst other merchandise.

Thus the full-skirted, tight-corseted, close-bonneted, shawl-shouldered figure which is generally thought of as Victorian had already arrived before King William was laid to rest. The paradox is that Victoria was not responsible for the Victorian look. She herself only began to be 'Victorian' after she had married her handsome but priggish young prince—'uncomfortably handsome' according to one contemporary, but also uncomfortably high-minded for those at Court who were accustomed to the ways of the Hanoverian kings. Before she was married, Victoria loved pretty clothes and dancing, and while under the spell of the worldly Lord Melbourne was enchanted with the elegancies of the cultured Whig Society of which he was so engaging an example.

No, the sober fashions which coincided with the beginning of Victoria's reign must not be attributed to Victoria herself. After the years of extravagance following the end of the Napoleonic wars, there was a general depression in trade, particularly fashion trades. In France,

industrial unrest and distress amongst the workers led to the July
Revolution of 1830 which brought Louis-Phillipe, the 'Bourgeois
King', to the throne. The excesses of the *Incroyables* and the Romantics
were finally checked. In England, an unaesthetic blight was spreading
from the industrial cities, where the manufacturers of the industrial
revolution, narrowly religious, bigoted, and totally without taste,
were beginning to influence public life. They expressed their new
wealth in conspicuous costliness, in sumptious and sound possessions,
amongst which they numbered their wives and daughters. Wives and
daughters must wear as many clothes as possible to show that their
husbands and fathers were 'well-lined'. There was no difference really
between the heavily upholstered furniture of their homes and the
heavily upholstered figures of their womenfolk. And the colours and
fabrics for each were thick and dark—no doubt partly as a reaction
against the white muslins and pale colours of the Regency and following
years, but also partly because the smoke of the cities, belching from the
new factory chimneys, made everything grimy. The miracle of 'dry-
cleaning' was yet to come.

❦   ❦   ❦

Dry cleaning came from France—and came through an accident, as
have so many inventions. It was 1849 when a Paris tailor called Jolly-
Bellin upset an unlit lamp over the table cloth while his wife was out
marketing. Impatiently he pulled the cloth off the table, flung it into
the corner, and continued his tailoring. Retribution, however, was soon
heard approaching with familiar footsteps. He hurriedly replaced the
cloth on the table, thinking to cover the stain with his work until he
had braved himself to face Madame and the music. But when he spread
it out he found that the parts soaked in turpentine were not only
unstained, but were cleaner than the rest. Eureka! Immediately,
Jolly-Bellin saw the possibilities of cleaning by spirits. No doubt there
was a *mauvais quart d'heure* before Madame could be won round to
seeing that there was money in the wasted oil and crumpled, patchy-
looking cloth. But soon he was inviting his customers to bring in their
coats and breeches, their wives' mantles and shawls, for *nettoyage à sec*.

Jolly-Bellin's method was to take each garment to pieces and clean
the sections separately in a pan of turpentine oil mixture he called
'camphene'. The pieces were brushed, dipped again, and dried in a

room to get rid of the smell. Finally the garments were sewn together again. A laborious process; but *nettoyage à sec* was soon practised all over France. It was not until 1866 that Pullars of Perth, who had been in business as dyers for about forty years, began a postal dry-cleaning service in the British isles. They soon improved upon Jolly-Bellin's 'camphene', using a mixture of petroleum, benzine, and benzol; and they discarded the whole process of unpicking and remaking. In 1870, when the Prussians were advancing on Paris, a young French dyer and his wife fled to London where they set up the Achille Serre dyeing and dry-cleaning business. Lush & Cook, established as dyers in 1842, were also among the earliest dry-cleaners.

There were many dyers who had been established from the beginning of the century, and their services were very important in domestic life. *Tallis's Street Views* of 1838 lists Boura of Paris, *Aux Mille Couleurs*, at 31 Rathbone Place. They are described as 'Dyers & Cleaners, etc.', but since this is ten years before Jolly-Bellin's discovery, Boura's cleaning may have been a laundry method. Dyeing would, in any case, have been the firm's main business. Clothes were handed down in big families, and dyed to freshen them and give them a different look. Often garments were unpicked at home, the material sent to the dyers, and then entirely remade to give the impression of a new garment altogether. But above all, there was good, steady business in dyeing black for mourning clothes. All firms gave priority to mourning orders; they were rush jobs, since their customers had to beat the hearse to the cemetery. Lush & Cook announced 'We dye blacks every day, and special mourning orders can be executed in twenty-four hours when necessary. Please note: only superior feathers look well after being dyed black.'

Ostrich feather fan, superior feathers. Debenham and Freebody.

CHAPTER VI

THE APPAREL AND
APPARATUS OF GRIEF

Court, National, and Family Mourning. Widow's Outfits.
Henry Mayhew at Jay's General Mourning Warehouse.
Other Mourning Warehouses. Funeral Monument Shops,
Undertakers and Funerals.

ᕙ᠇ᕤ᠇ᕙ᠇ᕤ᠇ᕙ᠇ᕤ᠇ᕙ᠇ᕤ᠇ᕙ᠇ᕤ᠇ᕙ᠇ᕤ᠇ᕙ᠇ᕤ᠇ᕙ᠇ᕤ᠇ᕙ᠇ᕤ᠇ᕙ᠇ᕤ᠇ᕙ

SERVICES to the bereaved and the deceased were the great stand-by of most Victorian drapers. 'Funerals conducted in a most careful manner' was a typical announcement implying criticism of the slapdash undertakings of rivals in the trade.

The custom of wearing black as a symbol of grief had obtained since the time of the Restoration, and 'family mourning and funeral furnishing' appeared on trade cards of the eighteenth century. There was, for instance, Gabriel Douce of Ye Black Spread Eagle, Shandoies Street, who moved to New Round Court in the Strand and set up as 'Ye Lamb & Black Spread Eagle next door to the Golden Goate'. This address indicates that it was before or not many years after 1762, when the numbering of streets was started. Gabriel Douce sold 'all sorts of silk stuffs, Norwich crapes, camletts, and all sorts of black silks for hoods and scarves at reasonable prices'. His shop was, in fact, a mourning house at least sixty years before Jay's General Mourning House was established in Regent Street in 1841, although to Jay's is always given the credit of being the first.

In 1786 a notice in *The Gazette* was the result of remonstrances from the City of London about the loss of trade in many industries owing to the unreasonable duration of Court Mourning:

His Majesty, in compassion to such manufacturers and people in trade as by the length of Court Mournings are, in this time of general scarcity and dearness of provisions, deprived in a great measure of the means of getting bread, hath been pleased to give directions for shortening all such mournings

58

for the future: and the Lord Chamberlain's orders for Court Mournings will be issued hereafter conformably thereto.

It was still not reduced enough, however, to prevent hardships. When Princess Amelia, the favourite daughter of George III died in 1810, national mourning was decreed for six weeks, and then extended for another six. One of the disastrous results of this was its effect upon the ribbon trade, as was related in Chapter I. And possibly it was the outcry from Coventry that was responsible for reducing national mourning on the death of Queen Charlotte in 1819 to not more than one month. During this period fashionable evening dresses were of black crape over white satin slips. For walking, black cloth pelisses were lined with white sarcenet and trimmed with white silk cord. Bonnets were of black Leghorn, and black bombazine dresses were the most general, although it was January . . . but, as a Victorian historian of English dress, Georgiana Hill, observed, 'To people who had been used to wearing white muslin in mid-winter, the incongruity was not apparent'.

On August 15, 1821, *The Times* carried the Lord Chamberlain's Court Mourning Orders for her late Majesty Queen Caroline-Amelia-Elizabeth, viz.

> The ladies to wear black bombazines, plain muslin, or long lawn linen, crape hoods, chamois shoes and gloves, and crape fans.
> UNDRESS: dark Norwich crape.
>   The gentlemen to wear black cloth, without buttons on the sleeves and pockets, plain muslin or long lawn cravats and weepers, chamois shoes and gloves, crape hatbands, and black swords and buckles.
> UNDRESS: dark grey frocks.

Tradesmen expected a big demand for black, since the country as a whole had sympathized with the unhappy Queen Caroline, considering her most cruelly treated by the king; and the same issue of *The Times* carried a number of advertisements, all assuring customers that no commercial gain would be made out of the national grief. Millard's East India Warehouses of 16 Cheapside announced:

> DEMISE OF HER MAJESTY. J. Millard most respectfully informs his friends and the Nobility he has to offer to their notice an excellent assortment of Family Mourning, at the most advantageous prices: his black bombazines at 1/– yard and every other article equally cheap, and in consequence of the demise of Her Majesty he has determined to sell off the whole of his present very valuable stock of white and coloured dresses, with a variety of other articles.

17. Flat Paper Patterns of Mourning Costumes, 2/6 from Madame A.
Letellier, 40 Tavistock Street, Covent Garden. *Sylvia's Home Journal*, 1879.

The Apparel and Apparatus of Grief

S. Shears & Co. of Bedford House, Henrietta Street (Jane Austen's favourite shop), pledged themselves to sell without one farthing advance every article suitable for mourning, viz.—bombazines, crapes, Italian nets, silk gauzes, rich satins, gros de Naples, Queen Silks, silk stockings and gloves, pelisses and habit cloth. Radford & Co., 188 Fleet Street, announced: NO ADVANCE ON BLACK. All these virtuous protestations suggest that an advance on black was the usual practice at times of national mourning. But then, look what they lost on colours—'Sacrificial Reductions' had to be made.

The general mourning ordered for His Late Lamented Majesty George IV, issued from the Lord Chamberlain's Office on June 26, 1830, was the same as that ordered for Queen Caroline. Mrs Bell, of the Magazin de Modes, interpreted this for her fashionable customers, and for the readers of the *World of Fashion*, as follows:

The Mourning will be made up strictly according to the Monthly fashions—the only difference will be in the materials used in the making of dresses, etc.

THE DRESSES will be made of black and white crapes, black bombazines, black gros de Naples, plain black gauzes, black Aerophanes, black printed muslins, with white figured stripes.

FOR BONNETS—black and white crapes and black gros de Naples—crape flowers.

FOR CAPS AND BERRETS, etc. etc.—Black and white crapes, and black and white crape lisses.

SHOES AND BRODEQUINS of black gros de Naples.

STOCKINGS—black silk.

THE ORNAMENTS WILL BE JET.

The use of the word berret is interesting. Mrs Bell uses it later with the modern spelling, beret, and it was most generally an evening head-dress rather than the sporting head-gear of the following century: 'Many berets of crape or gauze have no ornament whatever, others have a single ostrich feather placed near the top of the crown and turning round in a spiral direction.' Rather too gay, one would have thought, for mourning attire.

The duration of Court and national mourning varied according to the nearness of the deceased to the Sovereign, both in the geographical sense and in the sense of relationship. When the Queen of Hanover, aunt of Queen Victoria, died in 1841, mourning was only 21 days, and after the first two weeks was considerably relaxed: ladies could have coloured ribbons, fans and tippets with their black silks or velvets; or they could wear white and gold, or white and silver stuffs with black ribbons.

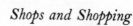

Quite apart from times of national mourning when business in black was particularly brisk, there was a reliable all-the-year-round trade. The annual mortality was very high. In 1831, in London, it was 31 in the thousand; in 1866 it was thirty-four in the thousand—as compared with approximately twelve in the thousand in 1964. There were times when it was astronomical such as during the cholera epidemic of 1849. Child deaths were accepted as a routine part of family life—and not only in poor badly-housed families. Even in Harrod's catalogue of 1900, children's funerals were quoted at 'From £2.10.0 according to age and appointments'. At that time cremation was described as 'this new method'. The first cremation in England was in 1882.

⚘   ⚘   ⚘

Family mourning was always more prolonged than Court or national mourning and widows had the worst of it. Two years of black crape was considered seemly. In *Middlemarch* (published in 1871, but set in the 1830's) Dorothea, still in her twenties, was in mourning two years for her disagreeable old husband. Her maid, Tantrupp, says to her after the first year,

> And most thankful I shall be to see you with a couple o' pounds' worth less of crape. There's a reason in mourning as I've always said; and three folds at the bottom of your skirt and a plain quilling in your bonnet is what's consistent for a second year. At least, that's *my* thinking; and if anybody was to marry me flattering himself I should wear those hideous weepers two years for him, he'd be deceived by his own vanity, that's all.

Etiquette demanded that upon a death in the family the whole household must go into mourning, including children and servants. Every kind of relative was mourned according to the relationship, distant cousins according to the distance. A married woman had to mourn her husband's relatives as well as her own. Who to mourn, how deeply and how long, seemed to be a perpetual worry to the ladies of Alderley. In 1844 Lady Stanley of Alderley wrote to her daughter-in-law who was staying in London, 'I suppose the Court mourning still continues or if not I hope you will put it on for Sir Gregory Way; he is my first cousin and there are several of the family in town who might observe and be hurt if you did not'. Two years later, she was writing about another cousin, 'I *ought* to be in mourning, for George Way, but I think I shall only mourne in *black wax*, which you shall see *next* time so as not to *alarm* you now'.

Black-edged writing paper went into black-edged envelopes sealed with black wax. Simply to seal ordinary envelopes with black wax was a compromise. Again to her daughter-in-law, Lady Stanley wrote: 'Mrs Whitby was my first cousin, Aunt to Albert—but she has lived so long out of the world that I never thought of your mourning for her, or doing so myself tho' I did seal with black to Emmy'. Emmy was evidently a stickler for etiquette. Some relatives were very inconsiderate in their date of decease, particularly those who passed on, or over, in the Spring when one was looking forward to getting into light summer dresses: 'We have just heard of the death of Mrs Gibson (Lord Stanley's sister)—I thought she would die soon when I got a coloured poplin from Ireland the other day'.

The demand for black was insatiable. Even little children had to wear mourning. *Answer to a correspondent in Sylvia's Home Journal,* 1879: 'The usual time for children to remain in deep mourning for their father is 7 months crape, 6 months black, 3 months slight. For relatives outside the immediate family they were given black-edged handkerchiefs. When King Edward VII died, Sonia Keppel was a child of ten, but 'black clothes appeared for me with black ribbons threaded through my underclothes'.

Non-blood relatives and even non-blood connections had to be mourned: Caroline Meysey-Wigley wrote to the Rev. Archer Clive in 1840 asking him to bring her back a gown from London 'pretty enough for the bazaar but very quiet—I shall be in mourning for a month for poor Carry Stevens'. Carry Stevens was one of her brother-in-law's sisters. Five years later when the married Clives were holidaying at Rome, they heard that a third cousin was dead. So they refused various attractive invitations and stayed in for four nights out of etiquette. Much later on, the finer points of mourning etiquette caused matrimonial disputes between Lady Jebb and her husband, as she retailed in a letter to her sister:

> Black is very tiresome and unbecoming, and when for a change I put on my grey cloth of last year, Dick could not express sufficient delight at the change. But I entirely refused to accept an invitation to a fancy ball, 'How can we go to a ball in fancy dress', I asked him, 'when we are using the deepest of black-edged paper and cards?' I refused to accept unless he bought narrower edges, convincing even him that to answer a ball invitation on that paper savoured of the ridiculous. He wanted very much to go to the ball, about which I don't care a farthing, so I gained my point as to the paper.

Magazine editors were constantly consulted upon points of mourning etiquette; and in 1881, *Sylvia's Home Journal* had two articles which dealt exhaustively with the subject, the first with particular reference to the widow, and the second with other degrees of relationship. This included complimentary mourning to be worn by slight connections: 'Mothers for the mother-in-law or father-in-law of their married children should wear black for six weeks or so without crape. Second wives for the parents of the first wife, should wear complimentary mourning for about three weeks'. . . . That really does seem to be straining the compliment beyond the demands of reasonable courtesy. *Sylvia* gives the following list as being ample for a widow's outfit:

One best dress of Paramatta covered entirely with crape.

One dress, either a costume of Cyprus crape, or an old black dress covered with Rainproof crape.

One Paramatta mantle lined with silk, and deeply trimmed with crape.

One warmer jacket of cloth lined and trimmed with crape.

One bonnet of best silk crape, with long veil.

One bonnet of Rainproof crape, with crape veil.

Twelve collars and cuffs of muslin or lawn, with deep hems, several sets must be provided, say six of each kind.

One black stuff petticoat.

Four pairs of black hose, either silk, cashmere, or spun silk.

Twelve handkerchiefs with black borders, for ordinary use, cambric.

Twelve of finer cambric for better occasions.

Caps either of lisse, tulle, or tarlatan, shape depending much upon age; young widows wear chiefly the Marie Stuart shape, but all widows' caps have long streamers. A good plan to buy extra streamers and bows.

Summer parasol of silk, deeply trimmed with crape, almost covered with it, but no lace or fringe for the first year. Afterwards mourning fringe might be put on.

Muff of Paramatta, and trimmed with crape.

No ornaments except jet, for the first year.

Furs are not admissible in widow's first mourning, though very dark sealskin and astrachan can be worn when the dress is changed.

The first mourning is worn for twelve months. Second mourning twelve months also; the cap in second mourning is left off, and the crape no longer covers the dresses, but is put on in tucks. Elderly widows frequently remain in mourning for long periods, if not for the remainder of their lives, retaining the widow's cap, collar and cuffs, but leaving off the deep crape the second year, and afterwards entirely discarding crape, but wearing mourning materials such as Victoria Cords, Janus Cords, Cashmere, and so on.

Business in mourning was business worth getting. Glovers did particularly well through the custom of presenting a pair of black kid gloves to all guests attending the funeral. It was a sensible idea to simplify shopping for the bereaved by concentrating all the necessary items for complete mourning under one roof, and conducting from the same address the business of funeral furnishing and undertaking. Mr Gabriel Douce's Black Spread Eagle warehouse may well have been

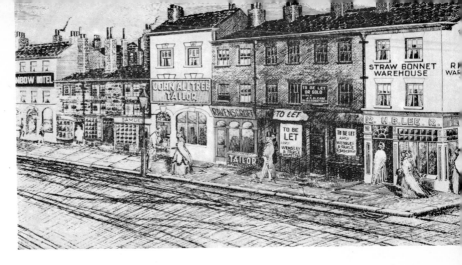

III

Mr Lee's Straw Bonnet Warehouse in 1853, at the corner of Basnett Street and Leigh Street, Liverpool, from a contemporary drawing. George Henry Lee gradually extended along the whole of this block.

Big and beautiful colour prints were sold in the 1830's by B. Read, Tailor, of Bloomsbury Square, London, and Broadway, New York, with paper patterns, 8s. the set.

VIEW IN THE REGENT'S PARK, LONDON.

FASHIONS for 1838 & 39. by B. READ & C? 12, Hart St. Bloomsbury Square, LONDON, and Broad Way, New York, AMERICA.

IV

Trade card of Scott Adie's Roy
Scotch Warehouse, established
1854 (actual size). The origina
is in full colour.

For French visitors to London: the Royal
Scotch Warehouse card is 4½ in. × 6 in.
and has a list of specialities in French
on the reverse.

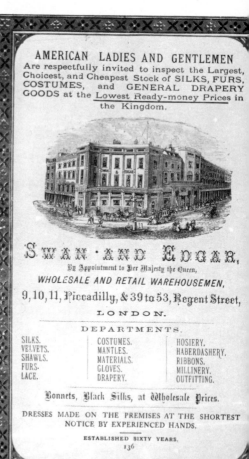

Swan & Edgar set out to attract
American visitors in 1872. Card
8¼ in. × 5 in., gold, blue, and red
border.

18.

only one of many at the beginning of the century. But undoubtedly Mr W. C. Jay's warehouse operated from its opening in 1841 on a much larger scale, and attracted unprecedented publicity in the editorial columns. His magnificent establishment occupying the whole of three houses in Regent Street, Nos. 247, 248, and 249, was, according to one contemporary, 'An inexhaustible theme for the speculative pen-dashers of the diurnal press'. One of these pen-dashers was Henry Mayhew, who in *The Shops and Companies of London* (1865) describes a visit to Jay's which he paid with his Aunt when he was a small boy:

We recollect passing down a long vestibule and up a long flight of steps, and at last emerging in a large, lofty room. This room had tall gothic windows; it was softly carpeted, so that you scarcely heard your own footsteps as you trod along. We had plenty of time to look about us, for our good aunt was a lady slow of choice, and once involved in the mysteries of crape and paramatta, we were sure of a good half-hour's quiet observation. We noted the quietness, the harmonious so to speak hush of the whole place, and were impressed with the total 'unshoppy' character of the establishment.

Mayhew goes on to describe Jay's as it was at the time of writing:

After gazing for some time at the tastefully arranged window, and inspecting the variety of mourning garb there exhibited, let us walk inside. Here we are once more struck with the total 'unshoppiness' of the place . . . On either side of the doorway are massive mahogany tables, by the side of which we can take our seat, and call for any possible kind of mourning we may require.

Let us walk upstairs into the spacious show-rooms. Here we can lounge about on the most comfortable of sofas and easy chairs; we can look at ourselves in the most dazzling of mirrors; and . . . we have a bevy of bright eyed fair damsels, clad in black silk, who will lay before us every description of mourning we may require to purchase for our wife, who may have just lost an uncle.

Mantles all a-bristle with bugles and beads, and trimmed with every variety of gimp ornamentation—marvels of design and workmanship. White silk Zouave jackets, whose sheen is dazzling, and whose braiding is a mathematical puzzle.

Putting aside those massive curtains which drape the doorway, we wander into another department, and here we see a wonderful assemblage of caps, which seem to range in density from the frosted spider-web to the petrified 'trifle'. We observed one widow's cap which was a marvel: this wonder was under a glass-case; for it was as light in texture as thistle-down, with long streamers like fairies' wings.

Bonnets of the most subtle design and most ornate specimens of sable floriculture nod at us from every table; and should you wish to purchase a cloak, one of the aforesaid young ladies will immediately put it on to show you the fit thereof. Boxes taken from their shelves reveal collars of white crape, of black crape, of tulle and of muslin, collars dotted with black and edged with black; also the clearest muslin Garibaldis, which, with a ruche of the faintest mauve-coloured ribbon, will constitute slight mourning.

Wander into the silk department, look tenderly on the massive black silks and satins—glance carefully at the delicate shades of slate-colour, grey, mauve, and purple, and go not hence till you have seen a certain delicate robe of the palest violet tint fairly frosted with crystal spots.

Mayhew is then taken upstairs to see the workrooms, and introduced to 'the lady who superintends the producing of these wonders, and who is frequently in Paris in search of novelties'. He is led into another room where 'two artistes are putting the finishing touches to one of those marvellous bonnets'. He concludes that 'in the present day our ashes must be properly selected, our garments must be rent to pattern,

19.   ARGYLL
GENERAL
MOURNING
AND MANTLE
WAREHOUSE
The Argyll
Rooms, 246–248
Regent Street, in
1853.

our sackcloth must be of the finest quality, and that our grief goes for nothing if not fashionable'.

Jay's General Mourning Warehouse did not long remain alone in Regent Street in its glooming glory. Pugh's Mourning Warehouse opened at 173 Regent Street in 1849; and Peter Robinson opened a Court and General Mourning House at 256, 258, 260, and 262 Regent Street, which soon became affectionately known as Black Peter Robinson's. The Nicholson Brothers of St Paul's Churchyard took over the Argyll Rooms from Charles Cook, the furrier. These, on the corner of Little Argyll Street, had until 1830 been assembly rooms for extravagant balls and soirées. Here Nicholson's opened the Argyll General Mourning & Mantle Warehouse, and advertised in the death column of the *Morning Post* in 1854, 'respectfully begging to intimate to ladies whose bereavements demand the immediate adoption of mourning attire, that every requisite for a complete outfit of mourning can be supplied at a moment's notice, and that many unpleasant occurrences arising from delay on melancholy occasions are thereby obviated'. They issued a book called *Mourning Etiquette* gratis in order that 'all trouble may be avoided in deciding the degree of mourning proper to be worn under various losses'.

That made four mourning warehouses in one street!—and there were others elsewhere, such as the West General Mourning Warehouse run by Howitt & Co. at Albion House, 226–230 High Holborn, and Cater's Mourning Warehouse, 1–4 Finsbury Place, and 88–91 Chiswell Street, E.C.

Henry Mayhew was not the first to turn a satirical eye upon the fashionable aspects of mourning. In the first number of *Hood's Magazine and Comic Miscellany* (1844) there was a farce which must have drawn its inspiration from Jay's. It was called The House of Mourning, and these are a few extracts:

Lady: I wish, sir, to look at some mourning.

Shopman: Certainly; by all means. A relict, I presume?

Lady: Yes; a widow, sir. A poor friend of mine who has lost her husband.

Shopman: Exactly so; for a deceased. How deep would you choose to go, Ma'am? Do you wish to be very poignant?

Lady: Why, I suppose, crape and bombazine, unless they're gone out of fashion. You had better show me some different sorts.

Shopman: We have the very latest novelties from the Continent. Here is one, Ma'am, just imported—a widow's silk—watered, you perceive, to match the sentiment. It is called 'Inconsolable', and is very much in vogue in Paris for matrimonial bereavements. And we have several new fabrics introduced this season to meet the demand for fashionable tribulation.

Lady: And all in the French style?

Shopman: Certainly—of course, Ma'am. They excel in the funèbre. Here, for instance, is an article for the deeply afflicted. A black crape—makes up very sombre and interesting. Would you allow me, Ma'am, to cut off a dress? Or if you would prefer a velvet, Ma'am—

Lady: Is it proper, sir, to mourn in velvet?

Shopman: O quite!—certainly. Just coming in. Now here is a very rich one— real Genoa—and a splendid black. We call it 'The Luxury of Woe'.

Lady: Very expensive, of course?

Shopman: Only 18/- a yard, and a superb quality—in short, fit for the handsomest style of domestic calamity.

Lady: And as to the change of dress, sir; I suppose you have a great variety of half-mourning?

Shopman: Oh! Infinite—the largest stock in town. Full, and half, and quarter, and half-quarter, shaded off, if I may say so, like an India-ink drawing, from a grief *prononcé* to the slightest *nuance* of regret.

As well as the specialized mourning warehouses, nearly all drapers of any size had mourning departments, and very often carried out undertaking as well. Even to this day, when the drapery side of death has altogether died out, the undertaker in many small towns is still a draper. In 1862, the *Windsor, Eton & Slough Express* carried an advertisement by Caley Bros.: 'Mourning orders expeditiously and tastefully executed. Funerals entirely furnished. Servants' mourning.' Another of their advertisements in the same month extolled the advantages of a new kind of coffin:

> WOOD COFFINS ENTIRELY SUPERSEDED AND LEAD ONES REN-DERED UNNECESSARY BY THE USE OF THE PATENT AIR-TIGHT METALLIC COFFIN, which contains all the advantages of a wood shell, lead and oak coffin. In addition to the economy of these coffins, their great advantage is that no matter what the cause of death, however infectious the disease, there can be no possibility of danger to the relatives or inmates of the house from the escape of any noxious effluvia. In a sanitary point, therefore, these coffins offer decided advantages over ordinary Wood or Lead.

Choosing your coffin was not by any means the ultimate purchase: you were not home and dry until you had settled on suitable grave furnishings. The most fashionable shop for these, right up to Edwardian times, was in Regent Street at the corner of Air Street. It was described by Augustus Sala in *Twice Round the Clock* (1859):

> Then there was the funeral monument shop, with the mural tablets, the obelisks, the broken columns, the extinguished torches, and the draped urns in the window, and some with the inscriptions into the bargain, all ready engraved in black and white, puzzling us as to whether the tender husbands, devoted wives, and affectionate sons, to whom they referred, were buried in that grisly shop— it had a pleasant, fascinating terror about it, like an undertaker's, too.

And A. R. Bennett describes the undertaker's share in the final pageant in *London & Londoners in the* 1850*'s and* 1860*'s:*

> The undertaker was of course in black, and equally of course wore a pot-hat turbaned with a wealth of weeping crape. Two of his men bearing draped wands invariably stood motionless on each side of the door of the house of mourning. These were the mutes. If the deceased had rejoiced in a coat-of-arms his escutcheon was displayed in front of the dwelling. This was the hatchment. The hearse was a long black box on wheels, closed on all sides, without glass, and bearing sockets in which plumes could be placed. The black horses bore tall black plumes nodding on their heads, acquiring therefrom a touch of the majestic. The coffins were covered with black cloth tacked on with innumerable brass-headed nails. A very familiar street sound of those days was the tack, tack, tack of the undertaker's hammer. He did it with a kind of rhythm which rendered the process unmistakable.

CHAPTER VII

THE TARTAN EPIDEMIC AND HIGHLAND FEVER

George IV's visit to Edinburgh. Sir Walter Scott and the Romance of the Highlands. Effect of Industrial Revolution on Scottish textiles. Tartan at Balmoral. Tweeds & Shepherd's Check Plaids. Scottish Warehouses in London.

THE unaesthetic vogue for tartan, and the establishment of so many shops in London dealing exclusively in Scottish merchandise, is often attributed to Queen Victoria's devotion to her highland estate at Balmoral. But this epidemic, variously called 'Highland Fever', or 'Tartanitis', broke out in England long before the Queen first rented Balmoral. Indeed, it had begun before she and Prince Albert had ever been in Scotland at all—their first visit took place in 1842, when they went no farther north than Perthshire.

Twenty years earlier, in August 1822, George IV had made a state visit to Edinburgh. Thinking to pay Scotland a pretty compliment he dressed as a Stuart in tartan trews, but only succeeded in making himself a laughing stock. An ex-Lord Mayor of London, Sir William Curtis, was one of the English contingent on this expedition, and he was also splendidly but inappropriately clad in the Stuart kilt, to which he had no claim by birth. The king was welcomed to the city by Sir Walter Scott, whose smiles of greeting may have camouflaged amusement at the caperings of these prominent Sassenachs; but the fact of the matter is that Sir Walter himself had a good deal to do with the fashionable infatuation for tartan, because his Waverley novels, of which a new one was published nearly every year from 1814 to 1831, had disseminated romantic ideas about Scotland.

There was that; and there was also the profit motive. The canny Scots business men were only too happy to cash in on the romance of the Highlands, and they had been given the power to do so by the Industrial Revolution. At the beginning of the century, the Scottish textile industry had begun to receive impetus from mechanization, and had been busily adding new designs to the traditional native 'weaves' for the delectation and temptation of non-Scottish customers far beyond the Highlands. After the fall of Napoleon, there was a great vogue for tartans in Paris, which can most plausibly be explained by the excitement, once the long wars were over, of being able once more to import foreign goods . . . tartans spoke their country of origin more loudly than any other import. Moreover, there had for a long time been sentimental ties between Scotland and France created by the sojourns in France of Mary Queen of Scots, and later of Prince Charles, two of history's most romantic figures.

Those Scottish mills which had adapted new techniques of mechanized spinning and weaving were capable of large outputs. They were able to meet the sudden demands of the export trade after the wars were over, and also to develop a growing domestic market which was being created by the new prosperity brought to parts of Scotland by the Industrial Revolution. This new domestic market was no more fussy than the French about the origins of the weaves; and so the mill owners happily invented new tartans, and retailers encouraged people whose names were far from Gaelic to discover that they belonged to a 'Sept' or division of a clan, which qualified them to wear a kilt or plaid. On a trade card of the 1840's, Kendal, Milne & Faulkner of Manchester included amongst their lines, 'Clan Tartan' and 'Saxony and Gala Plaids'. All this was before Queen Victoria lost her heart to the Highlands.

Nevertheless, although the Queen did not start the craze for tartans, she fanned it to fever heat by the naïve and boundless enthusiasm with which she entered into Highland life when she was at Balmoral. Ivor Brown writes of her arrival after the rebuilding of Balmoral:

Having arrived in a tartan-decked barouche on her first entrance to the Paradise, the Queen continued to spread herself in the invention of new 'weaves' and in the use of her inventions as well as the traditional designs. The upholstery, the curtains, the chintzes, the covers of sofas and chairs were either tartan or had a thistle pattern. To carry lamps, there were beautifully designed Highlanders. Lady Augusta Stanley summed up the *décor* by calling it 'all highly characteristic, but not all equally *flatteuse* to the eye'. . . . The Prince designed the Balmoral Tartan of black, red, and lavender on a grey background, which is still kept in use. The Duke of Edinburgh wore handsomely a kilt of this colour scheme at the Braemar Games in 1952. The Queen arranged her own Victoria tartan, mainly employed in furnishings,

71

and saw that the new Balmoral was be-tartaned from linoleum to the roofs of the rooms. The Royal Stuart (red and green) was also favoured: there were carpets both of this and of Hunting Stuart.

In London, her Majesty's loyal subjects could decorate their houses and themselves in similar fashion, if they so desired, by patronizing the many tartan warehouses, some of which were well-established before Queen Victoria ever went to Scotland. Probably the earliest of these was James Locke's Scotch Tartan Warehouse at 119 Regent Street. And it was a clerk in James Locke's office who, through a mis-spelling, was responsible for giving the name 'tweed' to the characteristic cloth woven in the Border country. This woollen merchant's clerk wrote tweed in mistake for tweel: tweel being the Scottish word for twill. Mr Locke (evidently an enlightened employer with a flair for publicity) did not reprimand the clerk for carelessness but congratulated him upon the inspired nature of his error. He saw at once that, with the current enthusiasm for the novels of Sir Walter Scott, and with Sir Walter living on the banks of the River Tweed near Galashiels, centre of the weaving industry, the word tweed would be excellent for promoting Scottish tweel.

Galashiels was at that time just pulling itself out of a recession. In 1829, twenty firms in the town had failed. Their cheap coarse cloths in greys, drabs, and blues, made from Cheviot wool which was often very tarry, had been outclassed in quality and undercut in price by Yorkshire cloths made from finer wools. What really saved Galashiels was the sudden fashion for black-and-white check shepherds' cloaks to be used as gentlemen's wraps, followed by a fashion for having trousers made of shepherds' check. Once more, Sir Walter Scott comes into the story, for he is credited with having first worn these trousers. That is the legend; but the first authentic record is that of an Edinburgh woollen merchant called Archibald Craig. In 1830, Craig had an inquiry from London for 'a coarse woollen black and white checked stuff made in Scotland and expected to be wanted for trouserings'. He sent a cutting from the seam of a shepherd's cloak, and it turned out to be what was wanted.

The first mixed-coloured twills, tweels, or tweeds, also originated, like the name tweed, in a happy blunder. About 1832, a quantity of shepherd's check had been made in which the white was so dirty from being mixed with grey wool that the cloth was unsaleable. Someone with an economical turn of mind dipped it in brown dye. This hid the fault and produced a black and brown check, which was sent to London as 'a new style'. It sold so well that it was followed up with blue and black checks, and then by green and black. Success again! Throwing all Scot's caution to the winds, they sent cloth in a whole range of shades, and introduced novelties by combining different coloured threads and by mixing wools of many colours before carding, to produce the granited and heather mixture yarns which became almost the most popular of all. Before the end of the 1840's, there was such a demand in England for these new tweeds that James Locke was able to open a retail establishment called the Scotch Tweed Warehouse at 127 Regent Street, in addition to their existing Scotch Tartan Warehouse at 119 Regent Street. By 1866 they had extended into No. 117 as well.

Meanwhile, two brothers called Gardiner, who were tailors in Glasgow, had come South in 1839 and opened a shop in Aldgate for Scottish tweeds and tartans. They called their business The Scotch House, and moved to the West End in 1900, choosing a prominent site on the triangular peninsular between Brompton Road and Knightsbridge—where the Scotch House remains today, with its library of 320 tartans, its kilted staff and its Pipe Major commissionaire in Highland dress. There are five other Scotch House branches in London now, and one in Edinburgh; but the owners are Great Universal Stores.

At 264 Regent Street, a gentleman called Joseph M. Crouch set up as The Royal Scotch Jeweller: 'the only house in London with a large selection of Scotch stones set in silver and gold.' His speciality was 'a combination of Scotch gems with diamonds and gold and silver worked into national signs and emblems'. Thistles, no doubt, would predominate. Somehow the diamonds sound rather out of place.

The London Scotch Warehouse upon which Queen Victoria bestowed her Royal Appointment was that of Scott Adie, who had a handsome building at 115 Regent Street, on the corner of Vigo Street. Scott Adie were established there in 1854; and although they have no records of an earlier shop in London or elsewhere, it seems almost certain that they must have been an already established concern, since they opened in Regent Street in such a grand building, and were given the coveted Royal Appointment at least by 1860. They still have ledgers going back to 1860 in which, under the heading of Queen, Her Majesty the (account to Miss Weiss), is recorded Her Majesty's purchases. There are also entries for seven of her children; headed by Prussia, H.R.H. The Crown Princess, and continuing Alice, H.R.H. The Princess, down through Helena, Louisa, Arthur, and Leopold, to Beatrice. There are other entries for foreign royalty, and the royalty of riches is represented by Rothschild, Baroness Adolphe, Naples. The aristocracy of birth is represented by names from many of the most famous families of England. It would surely not have been possible to have built up such a scintillating list of customers by 1860 if they had only started in business in 1854. And in the *Morning Post* an advertisement of July 7, 1854, gives an idea of the large range of merchandise it carried at that date:

SCOTT ADIE'S ROYAL CLAN TARTAN & SCOTCH SHAWL WAREHOUSE

Ladies VENTILATING WATERPROOF Travelling Cloaks, highly recommended for invalids and summer wear, made of Shetland home-spun Tweed expressly for Scott Adie. SCOTCH SPUN SILKS, in all the clans and new fancy patterns.

ABERDEEN LINSEY WOOLSEYS in granite, heather, and natural wools, an extra width and quality.

SHETLAND SHAWLS and VEILS in great variety.

Gentlemen's and Boys' WRAPPING MAUDS, SHETLAND KNITTED VESTS, and TROUSERING FOR RIDING.

Patterns sent to the country.

It is confirmation of the enthusiasm in France for all things Scottish that one of Scott Adie's early price-lists, which carries an engraving of a shooting scene in the Highlands, is written in French. Most of their catalogues have an introduction in French as well as in English, with the motto *Toujours mieux faire coûte que coûte*. An illustrated shopping guide called *A Visit to Regent Street* (*circa* 1860), which may have been a sponsored publication by some of the principal retailers in the street, included an entry for Scott Adie which speaks of extensive alterations having recently been made, and the illustration shows the Royal coat of arms already proudly set above the principal doorway:

This establishment is essentially a Scotch Emporium, to which the very latest productions and novelties of the hand-looms of the North are conveyed. Amongst the last *recherché* fabrics is *Vicuna*, an exquisite material made from the Down of the South American antelope, and freed from the hair by the prisoners at Elgin. It is woven in its natural colour, and is admirably adapted for Ladies' Cloaks and Gentlemen's Costumes. The Heather, Granite, and other Highland Mixtures for Ladies have all been carefully selected, and fully justify the high patronage extended to them, while their close imitation of the colour of the natural objects surrounding the *Sportsman* have rendered them an absolute necessity for the pursuits of the rod or gun. The new Tartan Spun and Glacé Silks are likewise on view. Ladies' Waterproof Cloaks and Jackets in great choice and suited to all seasons and climates. Ladies' Shetland Shawls and Veils, Scotch Hosiery. Perth Lawns and Linens plain and striped, for Dresses and Petticoats, adapted for the country, continental travelling, yachting. LINSEY WOOLSEY MANUFACTURER TO HER MAJESTY AND ALL THE FOREIGN COURTS.

20. HER MAJESTY'S
ROYAL TARTAN
WAREHOUSE
SCOTT ADIE

115 Regent Street, on
the corner of Vigo Street
circa 1860.

It was later on that Scott Adie erected their famous giant thistle over the doorway—a fantastic gas bracket which burst into a blaze of lights as dusk fell, a gas jet on every spine of the thistle. This conspicuous landmark remained in position until the rebuilding of Regent Street in the 1920's, when the firm moved to 38 Conduit Street, by which time their appointments were to Her Majesty Queen Mary and Her Late Majesty Queen Alexandra. Bombed out from Conduit Street during the Second World War, they moved first to 29 Cork Street, and then to their present address at 14a Clifford Street—where they still treasure the last few yards of a bale of cloth from which one of Queen Victoria's cloaks was cut.

Macdougall & Co. of 42 Sackville Street, Piccadilly, was a Scotch Warehouse which seems to have gone in for more feminine fallahs than the others. The *Englishwoman's Domestic Magazine* of April 1867, wrote in its 'Spinnings in Town' column of their splendid store of plaid ribbons for those 'whose heart warms to the tartan'. It was suggested these ribbons be bought to plait around the chignon: 'About three yards and a-half of tartan ribbon compose this pretty coiffure.' Macdougall's also had a special jupon which was 'not one, but a dozen

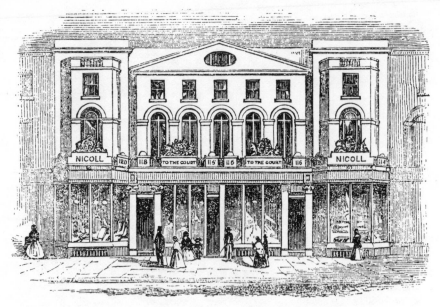

21. H. J. & D. Nicoll, 114–120 Regent Street, *circa* 1860.

22. Ground floor showroom of H. J. & D. Nicoll.

petticoats. The substratum is of black rep; on this is a plain tartan edging, attached by an ingenious device, which extends nearly half a yard upon the jupon higher than any dress would be raised. Petticoat edges can be had of scarlet, blue, brown, buff, plain trimmed or fluted, to wear over and with this elegant jupon. A lower skirt, of American leather cloth, can be worn with this petticoat, protecting it from splashes and mud. The idea is most ingenious, and the jupon elegant and ladylike in the extreme. It is called the *Isabella* jupon, and is already in favour with the élite'.

Twenty years earlier, the Duchess of Montrose, decidedly of the élite, used tartan for even more intriguing garments. Edward Stanley wrote to his wife from a shooting party at Black Mount on September 28, 1847: 'The Duchess wears plaid trousers and short petticoat about halfway down below her knees. She seems good humoured and un-affected but it may cause that worthy man the Duke some uneasiness as she is quite at home amongst the horned beasts of the Forest.' His description of the Duchess's outfit, short petticoat over trousers, sounds very similar to Mrs Bloomer's costume. Mrs Bloomer did not come to this country until 1851, but she had been campaigning for some years in America before that, so, it is just possible that the Duchess of Montrose was, in fact, an *avant-garde* Bloomer. On the other hand, she may never have heard of that essentially middle-class lady. In which case she should be regarded as one of the first Englishwomen to adopt a special costume for sport. This was some forty years ahead of Lady Harberton and her rational dress campaign.

Mr Macdougall of the tartan trimmed petticoats was to make his Scotch Warehouse famous for ladies' sporting clothes. In 1887, *The Lady's World* wrote:

Mr Macdougall, who designs stalking and hill costumes, as well as those for riding, yachting, boating, and Alpine climbing, finds no textures more serviceable than vicunas and homespun. He declares the former cloth to be so soft and light that it answers both for foundation skirt and drapery, while it runs little risk from sea and sun. He thinks braiding answers better on this substance than the introduction of another material, and the rich designs he shows in the same colour as the cloth are usually brightened by having a thread of untarnishable gold or silver interwoven with the worsted.

Vicuna, braided with gold and silver, shows Mr Macdougall to have been a creative designer rather than a traditional tailor; His glittering thread woven into the worsted, and his use of very soft, light woollen materials for tailored outdoor clothes, anticipates the fashions of our own day.

Another tailoring house creating original designs in the manner of a couture house was that of H. J. & D. Nicoll. In *A Visit to Regent Street* (c. 1860), Nicoll's dress designing is paralleled with the contemporary movement for applying art to industry:

> Gaudy or extravagant changes of dress will never again be tolerated in this country, or perhaps any other; but there is no valid reason why an artistic sense of the beautiful in design should not be applied to the garments we wear upon our bodies as well as to the commonest and meanest utensils which surround us. . . . The stolid absence of invention which everywhere prevails, is after all the great difficulty to be encountered on this subject, and whenever any improvement is brought out at once containing the elements of originality and good taste, it cannot be too highly recommended. As regards this matter, and the progress of British design of late, in its connection with industrial art, it is impossible to avoid noticing this year the Establishment of the Messrs Nicoll of Regent Street.

The book goes on to describe some of H. J. & D. Nicoll's models. There was the new highland cloak for ladies, 'a singularly graceful garment suited either for morning or for being worn at night over evening dress. It has a charming little hood, *à la Capucine*, which is elastic; and it resembles in its flowing contour the old French Roquelaire, originally invented by the eccentric Duke of that name, who had the mixed reputation of being at once the wittiest and the ugliest man in France.' There was 'The Zouave Morning Jacket' . . . 'one of the most charming and coquettish garments that ever improved a pretty figure. It is made like the full-dress pelisse worn by the *vivandières* attached to French Hussar regiments. It is elaborately braided, but the colours are of course sober and subdued. This piquant garment fastens at the neck, and is altogether unique in its originality and good taste.'

H. J. & D. Nicoll were in advance of their time in being men's tailors with a very large ladies' department in which creative designing was done; most men's tailors made ladies' riding habits and cloaks, but nothing of more feminine design. Nicoll's were also in advance of their time in having two London shops, two Liverpool branches, and a Manchester branch. They could almost have been called the first multiple tailors, if they had not been so expensive and superior—they held Royal Appointments to the Queen and to a long list of British and foreign royalty. Undoubtedly they were pioneers in expanding their business by opening shops in different districts and different cities. They were still bespoke, craftsmen tailors; but they had broken away by the 1860's from the one man proprietor-craftsman-shopkeeper pattern which had obtained in the tailoring trade for so long.

CHAPTER VIII

COUNTRY CLOTHES, WATERPROOFS, AND UMBRELLAS

*Ladies increase their mobility. Country dress and Balmoral
Boots. Macintosh and Hancock; Mandleberg, Aquascutum.
Waterproof Tweeds. Thomas Burberry. Umbrella Shops and
Umbrellas for Hire.*

BEFORE Victoria's reign, none but the rich and aristocratic travelled
for pleasure or to reach the places of pleasure. But as the nineteenth century advanced, a new monied middle-class emerged.
Railway travel supplanted stage coaches and private carriages; more
people began to take holidays, to pay visits to friends and relations, to
venture on the continent. The first Cook's tour to Switzerland was in
the summer of 1863—the same year as the first underground railway
was opened between the City and Paddington.

Horse omnibuses in the cities had improved in service and comfort
since 1829 when George Shillibeer's pioneer omnibus ran between
Paddington and the Bank via the Angel. By 1850 it was quite respectable for a lady to go in an omnibus. They were too expensive for
the working-classes who still lived sufficiently near to their place of
work to walk there on foot . . . so gentlefolk need have no fear of being
contaminated by their proximity. The knife-board top omnibuses which
were introduced in 1849 had only a ladder to the roof. But even
when this hazardous method of ascent was superseded by a stair in
1864, it was not considered proper for a lady to travel on top. Proper
or improper, the tight, trained dresses of the late 'seventies would have
made the ascent impossible. Nevertheless, all this travelling about,
whether on business or pleasure, whether in cities, country, or abroad,
meant that women were at least beginning to feel the *need* for more
practical clothes.

At the beginning of the century, gentlewomen did not require waterproof clothing since they simply did not go out in bad weather. If they got caught in a storm, serious illness if not death was foreseen as a result, as we know from the novels of that time. Shoes were scarcely stronger than dancing slippers, since ladies did not walk but were conveyed. The real countrywoman had wooden clogs, which she wore as over-shoes—this applied to the lady of the house as well as the dairy-maid. Galoshes came from America about 1847.

However, once the Queen began to fling herself into Highland life, going for long expeditions over the hills, she set an example which had its influence upon outdoor clothes of all kinds. In *The Habits of Good Society: A Handbook of Etiquette for Ladies and Gentlemen*, published anonymously about 1860, we read:

> One point of dress has been much amended lately, owing to the good sense of our Queen. It was formerly thought ungenteel to wear anything but thin Morocco shoes, or very slight boots in walking. Clogs and galoshes were necessarily resorted to. 'The Genteel Disease' as Mackenzie calls it, has, however, yielded to the remedies of example. Victoria has assumed the Balmoral petticoat, than which, for health, comfort, warmth, and effect, no invention was ever better. She has courageously accompanied it with the Balmoral boot, and even with the mohair and coloured stocking. With these, and the warm cloak, the looped dresses, the shady hat and, to complete a country walking dress, soft gloves of the kind termed *gants de siècle*, the high-born lady may enjoy the privileges which her inferiors possess—she may take a good walk with pleasure and safety.

The Balmoral boot had brass eye-let holes, patent leather ornaments, and elaborate stitching. It was worn with Balbriggan stockings. These came originally from Balbriggan near Dublin. They were a very fine cotton stocking made on hand machines. The fashion for them quickly spread, and the name became generic to stockings of the finest Egyptian cotton wherever they were made. The Balmoral petticoat was a white or grey horsehair petticoat worn instead of a cage crinoline. Fast young ladies wore Balmoral boots with quite a heel, and preferred broderie-anglais petticoats.

Certainly Queen Victoria's Balmoral boots (and no doubt her petticoats) were sturdier than those of the fast young ladies who appear in *Punch* pictures of this period, lifting their looped skirts to reveal a frisk of underskirts and six inches of horizontally striped stockings. The Queen's were probably more like the alpine boot, which was a speciality of James S. Carter, one of the earliest shopkeepers to call himself a Tourist Outfitter. Carter was established at 369 Oxford Street from about 1806, and moved to 16 South Molton Street in 1886. This

FOR TOURISTS.

Throw the Maud over the left shoulder and let about half a
yard hang in front, pass the longer end *under* the right arm,
across the chest, and *over* the left arm, so as to let an equal
length to the other side come over the right arm ; both
shoulders will in this way be protected from the cold and the
breast kept warm.

FOR THE RAILWAY.

Open the Maud out full size, take it in the centre and bring
it over your head from behind, then gather up the two corners,
tie the fringes together and pass it over your head.

23.

Alpine boot, 'applicable alike to the mountain, field, and moor, with
durability, elasticity, and ease on long pedestrian journeys' was made
for ladies as well as for gentlemen. Let us hope that Dorothy Wordsworth had a pair for all those long tramps in the Lake District.

⚜   ⚜   ⚜

The mists of time have partially blurred the beginnings of waterproofing. But about 1817 James Syme, son of a Scottish landowner and
Writer to the Signet, began his medical curriculum at Edinburgh
University. Some laboratory experiments led him to discover a substance obtainable from coal-tar which had the property of dissolving
india-rubber so that it could be used to make textiles waterproof. His
formula was communicated to the Glasgow firm of Charles Macintosh
& Co., and in 1823 they patented it. James Syme later became a great
clinical teacher, one of the most celebrated surgeons of his time, and

81

an ardent advocate of medical reform; but to Charles Macintosh has been given the imperishable glory of the invention that has meant so much in our damp island story. It is his name (with an inexplicable spelling change) which has been immortalized in the English dictionary.

Even before James Syme's discovery, there had been commercial experiments in waterproofing. *The Picture of London*, 1803, gives one of the industries of London as a waterproof manufactory at Chelsea. But this would not have been a garment factory, and the material they turned out was probably a kind of tarpaulin, that is, canvas impregnated or coated with tar—not a material that could have been tailored into clothes for man or woman. However, *The Times* of August 15, 1821, carried an advertisement for Fox's Aquatic Gambroon Cloaks, 'the best of which are warranted never to get wet when properly made up—may be had of the principal tailors, or purchased of the patentee, stamped on the back G. Fox's Patent Gambroon—28 King-street, Covent Garden'. Gambroon is defined in the Oxford Dictionary as a twill material used for linings; and it seems that in this case at any rate there was mohair in it, because the advertisement says that these Gambroon cloaks 'are fallen 20% owing to the increased importation of mohair'. We do not know whether G. Fox was father of Samuel Fox of umbrella fame, but it is nice to imagine that father and son were waging war against the English weather with different weapons of defence.

When Charles Macintosh took out the patent of 1823, he had already won considerable notice for his method of making waterproof fabrics by cementing two thicknesses together with india-rubber dissolved in naptha. And the year after the patent he received a commission from the famous explorer Sir John Franklin for the supply of waterproof material for use on an arctic expedition. Works were started in Manchester for carrying out the invention, and Macintosh was elected a fellow of the Royal Society. Part of the capital for the factory was supplied by Messrs Birley.

Meanwhile, Thomas Hancock had been working quite separately to discover a reliable waterproofing method, and had been competing with Macintosh in the manufacture of many kinds of rubber things such as diving-dresses, boots, air-beds, air-cushions, and hot-water bags. Each firm held patents that were necessary to the other; and in 1830 they very sensibly came to a working agreement, Hancock becoming a partner in Macintosh's Manchester firm. But they were not at all successful in getting garment manufacturers to use their waterproof material. This was due, according to Hancock, to the tailors' indifference, ignorance, and unwillingness to follow Macintosh's advice on making up the cloth. They therefore decided that their own firm should produce ready-made garments instead of supplying the waterproofed cloth for others to make up. This went well until trade fell off with the end of travelling by stage coach and the introduction of closed railway carriages. In 1836, Macintosh won an action for the infringement of the patent by a firm of silk mercers, Everington and Graham of Ludgate Street. Several eminent scientists gave evidence, and the trial excited a good deal of useful publicity. After that, they were able to enlarge the Manchester factory and start making all kinds of india-rubber articles.

It was Hancock who discovered in 1844 the process of vulcanizing rubber. In the same week Charles Goodyear announced a similar discovery in America. Thus the mackintosh is father to the motor-tyre. Vulcanizing got over some of the worst disadvantages of the original mackintosh material—its stickiness in warm weather and hardness in cold—but there was still the smell. Protected as the sodden inhabitants of the British Isles were for the first time against their climate, they still found something to grumble about. These wonderful waterproof garments smelt. In muggy weather you could smell them across the street. In an extreme case, in a small market town, on a wet market day, the smell had stopped the church clock. Such, or some such, were the nose-witness accounts handed down from the early days of the mackintosh. It was Joseph Mandleberg of Lancashire who, when he started in a modest way to put a bit of style into the making of *Ladies', Gents' and Children's Waterproof Outer-garments*, decided to tackle the smell. Useless, he realized, to make garments in good style if they were in bad odour. After much patient trial and hideous error, his Company registered its first proud trade mark: F.F.O. Free From Odour. What a boon and a blessing! No longer did your best friend recoil when she met you in your waterproof.

Free from odour though it was, the Mandleberg waterproof was still too stiff and clumsy to tailor well, and had the disadvantage of being brittle in cold weather so that the fabric cracked. Also, being non-porous and airproof, it prevented evaporation of skin perspiration so that in warm weather the wearer became drenched with sweat. It was a tailoring firm called Bax and Company of 46 & 48 Regent Street, who invented a showerproof wool fabric which could be tailored with style and was comfortable to wear. This was in 1851, and Bax and Company exhibited their 'Aquascutum' cloth at the Crystal Palace, thus gaining immediate publicity not only in England but also abroad through overseas visitors and trade representatives at the exhibition. When the Crimean War started in 1854 army officers equipped themselves with Aquascutums against the rigours of the campaign.

The original chemical formula for Aquascutum (which made fabric

24.

water-repellent without either sealing the pores or stiffening the fabric) was lost when the Nazi blitz destroyed Aquascutum's archives and also the Patent Office records for those years. But the firm has a receipt dated April 17, 1852, which was after Bax & Co. had sold the business premises and invention to a firm of tailors called Emary & Co. The splendid billhead (above) shows the original shop on Piccadilly Circus. Aquascutum's shop is now at No. 100 Regent Street.

Edward Prince of Wales was soon an Aquascutum customer. *Vanity Fair*, the first weekly to have a regular column on fashions for men (by 'The Man in the Mall') recorded every variation of the Prince's attire; and comparison of their photographs with Aquascutum's early catalogues shows that his Aquascutum wardrobe included many items from the range offered for public sale: informal daytime and sporting clothes, dress coats worn on state occasions, and evening capes and coats. What was worn by that great trend setter the Prince of Wales was soon worn by everyone with any pretensions to fashion, including most of the monarchs of Europe. But not by the ladies. Only in the early years of the present century did Aquascutum open a ladies' department.

The needs of the ever more sporting ladies were not, however, ignored by other firms. Scott Adie's Royal Tartan Warehouse was advertising in the *Morning Post* of July 1, 1854, 'Ladies Ventilating Waterproof Travelling Cloaks'. These may have been merely rubberized cloaks with ventilation holes in various places, but it is possible they were made with some kind of showerproofed tweed, since much experimenting was going on at this time. A brochure sent out to the trade about 1860 by Sélincourt & Colman, wholesale mantle makers, is introduced as 'Our new book of Designs for Waterproof Cloaks'. The cloaks are only described as being in 'plain, tweed, or check', and it is possible they may have only been waterproof in the sense of being made in very closely woven fabrics and being voluminously designed to cover the wearer completely from head to foot: they are full-length and include a hood. (Fig. 44).

During 1866 there were advertisements in the *Illustrated London News* for 'The Celebrated Shrewsbury Waterproof Tweed: cloaks, jackets, and gentlemen's overcoats, patterns post free from I. E. & W. Phillips, 37 High Street, Shrewsbury. Also stocked by Jay's of Regent Street, London.' In the same issue, Peter Robinson advertised 'Waterproof Mantles for travelling. The Salzburg Sac in waterproof tweed and in black cloth bids fair to supersede entirely the Waterproof Cloaks which have been so long in use. The Seacoast Cape in Shrewsbury Waterproof Tweed is made with or without sleeves.

Also advertised in the 1860's, was Ford's Waterproof Cloak, with hood, warranted to resist many hours' rain, obtainable from H. Ford of 78 Edgware Road. The founder of Thomas Wallis, Charles Meeking, owner of the woollen warehouse, 111 Holborn Hill, had waterproof tweeds, serges, patent velveteen and other materials for ladies' jackets and mantles; and in 1868 the *Englishwoman's Domestic Magazine* carried advertisements by H. J. & D. Nicoll of 'Waterproof Tweed and Melton Travelling Costumes, ditto skirts, made without the least mixture of cotton, hence they are so durable and impermeable'. But it could have been that this use of the term waterproof simply meant they were good stout, closely woven tweeds, coverts and cords which would keep the wearer dry during quite a lot of rain—just as the sheep's own fleece keeps the sheep dry. Amongst provincial shops, Brown's of Chester advertised in 1871 'the New Waterproof Costumes and Cloaks and the Chester Guinea Waterproof'.

Meanwhile, Thomas Burberry, who had been born in the Surrey village of Brockham Green in 1835, where he had learned the rudiments of his trade with a country draper, started his own business in Basingstoke in 1856. This young man's name was, like that of Charles Macintosh, eventually to achieve immortality in the English dictionary. Burberry approached the problem of waterproofing from the agricul-

AQUASCUTUM LTD.
REGENT STREET
LONDON W.

Burberry-
Proofs

SLIP-ON

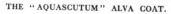

THE "AQUASCUTUM" ALVA COAT.

26.

Light Weight "Aquascutum"
From 3½ Gns.

Hand-Woven Tweeds
From 4 Gns.

Made in a variety of charming materials. The improved sleeves will meet the requirements of those who dislike the "Aquascutum" sleeve.

25.

tural point of view, because his customers were mostly farmers. Agricultural workers and shepherds wore linen smocks—useful garments, giving freedom of action, ventilation in summer, warmth in winter. They were easy to wash and kept the wearer moderately dry, but only moderately. Burberry realized that their ability to keep out wet depended on close weave and voluminous fashioning. He experimented in making sporting overcoats and suits of the same unproofed linen; but their loose cut made them objects of almost as much ridicule as Jonas Hanway's umbrella in 1756.

And so Burberry switched his experimenting to the fabric itself, trying to find some method of proofing which would yet leave the material porous. He co-operated with the owner of a cotton mill, and together they eventually produced a cloth of long staple Egyptian cotton, proofed in the yarn before weaving by a process using no rubber. The cloth was then closely woven and reproofed in the piece by the same process. The result was weatherproof and virtually untearable, but it did not obstruct air. It therefore kept the body in 'a wholesome and eupeptic condition in all temperatures and weathers'. In fact, it would not upset the digestion.

Burberry called this cloth 'gabardine', and took out a patent for it in 1879. He then began designing gabardine clothes for field sports, at which he himself was expert, incorporating many innovations for special uses into the classic lines of county tailoring. The fame of Thomas Burberry spread, and orders came from all over England. From 1899 he took a London hotel room once a week to give fittings; and two years later opened a small shop in the Haymarket as a branch of his Basingstoke business. Soon the metropolitan tail was wagging the provincial dog, and Basingstoke became the branch. A few more years and the address was: Burberry's of 30, 31, and 33 Haymarket, London, and at Basingstoke, Paris, Berlin, and New York. It is satisfactory to see Basingstoke loyally placed before Paris, Berlin, and New York.

❧   ❧   ❧

England was not the only country to be developing waterproofing processes, although she was the first. At the Health Exhibition of 1884, a process called 'Warnerizing', discovered by an American lady named Warner, was given prominence. It was claimed that Warnerizing enabled all kinds of material from tweeds to silk, velvet, and lace to to be made 'water repellent so that rain can hurt neither them nor their wearers, yet the material remains quite pervious to air'. After the Health Exhibition, a Warnerizing Company was formed and took offices in Queen Victoria Street, London. Mrs Ada Ballin, in *The Science of Dress* 1885, commented on the Warnerizing process: 'To think that ordinary outdoor garments can thus be made thoroughly waterproof seems almost too good to be true,' . . . which seems to indicate that the earlier 'waterproof tweeds' were not more than showerproof.

Whether it was the Warnerizing process at work or some other, Nicholson's of St Paul's were advertising in their *Jubilee Catalogue of* 1887:

NEW RUBBER DOLMAN, superior to anything of the kind hitherto made, in Black Alpacca 16/9, with hood 1 gn.; New Shot Silks, various colours 1 gn.

In very superior Bright Silk, novel colours, 1½ gns. to 3 gns. with hoods. A choice collection of Rubber Dolmans in Shot and Striped Silks and other Fabrics in the Sling Sleeve and Brighton shapes from 1 gn.

They also had 'Indiarubber Cloaks', in silk, at 1–3 gns., in a neat waterproof bag for an extra 1/–.

These wet day dazzlers do not seem to have been taken up to any great extent, for Georgiana Hill, in her *History of English Dress* published in 1893, bemoaned that:

Everything for daily use. must be quiet and unnoticeable, able to stand wear and tear, rain and dust, tumbling and creasing. The omnibus and tram-car have much to answer for in the toning down of our costume from gay to grave. In these democratic days everybody rides in public vehicles, and this custom not only tends to produce a sober uniformity in dress, but is a great bulwark against any huge extravagance of fashion.

It seems 'these democratic days' were with us even in the class-conscious 1890's.

Miss Hill concluded with a plea for more individuality in clothes and colours, quoting from an article in which the writer called for more colour in the streets, 'humorously suggesting that emerald green, scarlet, and orange should be used for mackintoshes and umbrellas'. On this Miss Hill commented, 'It is not impossible that this should

27.   THE ANTIPLUVIUM
          PERFECTUM
      designed by Abbot, Anderson,
      and Abbott, 15 Queen Street,
      London. *Lady's World*, Oct.
      1887.

come to pass'. Indeed it has in our day. In her day, although black was the usual colour for umbrellas, the trade catalogue of I. & R. Morley for the year 1879 lists ladies' silk umbrellas (not parasols or sunshades, which are on a different page), in brown, myrtle, navy blue and black. Cotton, regina, alpaca, and gingham umbrellas were all black.

Umbrellas had been made with ribs of whalebone up to the 1840's and then there were cane ribs. Ribs of tubular steel had been patented by Holland of Birmingham in 1840 and redesigned in 1850, but at that date metal frames were still more expensive than cane ones. It was in 1850 that Samuel Fox patented his Paragon Umbrella Frame with ribs of U-shaped steel, which gave maximum lightness and maximum strength. In the years 1855–66, Fox made a small fortune making cold-rolled strip for crinolines.

Undoubtedly Sangster's, a firm founded in 1777 at 94 Fleet Street, were *the* people for umbrellas and parasols. John Sangster wrote a history of the umbrella and was a recognized authority on all its foul and fair weather aspects. They opened a shop in Regent Street in 1839 and had other branches in Cheapside and Cornhill. Since they made their umbrellas as well as sold them, they must surely be counted as one of the first manufacturers owning a 'chain' of their own shops. John Sangster introduced and patented his alpaca umbrella about 1855, and by 1860 it was selling upwards of half a million annually—almost certainly through other retail channels as well as his own shops. The En-Tout-Cas sunshade and umbrella in one was launched towards the end of the 1850's. Both elegant and practical, it had considerable success; and it is described by Debenham & Freebody in their '*Fashion Book*' of 1877: 'For Country and Travelling, a tussore umbrella with short, stout handle, and lined with colour, 7/6.'

There were innumerable other umbrella makers, such as R. Williams who had a parasol and umbrella manufactory at 44 Ludgate Hill before 1830; Ben Cox, of 7 North Audley Street, 69 Chancery Lane, and 180 Aldersgate, who also sold walking-sticks and carved bamboo canes; James Smith whose business was founded in 1830 and moved to Hazelwood House, New Oxford Street in 1867, where it still is. It is, in fact, one of the very few mid-Victorian shops still to exist in London exactly as it has been for a hundred years, with the interior, shop front, and windows unchanged. It is still stuffed, not only with umbrellas, but cases of whips and walking-sticks. The brass stallboard underneath the windows has: James Smith & Sons, Umbrella Warehouse and Stick Factory.

James Smith was one of the first umbrella makers to use Fox Frames. At one time there was a Smith branch in a passage linking Savile Row with Mill Street, which had Mr Gladstone and other famous Victorians among its customers. Umbrellas were made on the premises in a space four feet wide, the complete stock being stored in the window. The second James Smith was a man of prolific interests, having six other businesses including a hatter's and a barber's shop. He also had a prolific family of eight sons and a daughter. The daughter's son, Mr R. H. Mesger, is the present Managing Director.

A hire service for umbrellas was an ingenious idea. The London Umbrella Company had stations all over Central London equipped with umbrellas for hire. The terms were set out on the hiring ticket, one of which is in the Museum of London in the City. These are the terms it gives:

> 4/- deposit and 4d. for 3 hours or less up to 9d. for from 12–24 hours. Each subsequent day 6d.
>
> Cheaper rate for nights, between 9 at night till 9 next morning.
>
> Deposit back when umbrella returned, with this ticket, at same or any station.

The ticket is unfortunately undated; but from the style of printing it is thought to be between 1840 and 1850. Certainly there is something deliciously Victorian about this London Umbrella Company operation. One imagines Thomas Carlyle constantly losing his hiring ticket and/or the umbrella, and Charles Dickens's wife finding umbrella tickets in his pocket that had been issued from compromising hiring stations.

28. William & John Sangster's Regent Street Umbrella Shop, *circa* 1860.

CHAPTER IX

SHOPS OF THE CRINOLINE ERA

Invention of the Crinoline and Commercial Interests. Crinoline and Stay Warehouses. Gaylor & Pope of Marylebone High Street. Gas Lighting and Window Display. Shawl and Cloak Emporiums.

'MR SMYTHE dined with us yesterday', wrote Caroline Clive in her diary on May 5, 1842. 'He is just come from London whence among other gossip he brought word that Lady Aylesbury wears forty-eight yards of material in each of her gowns, and instead of crinoline she wears a petticoat made of down or feathers which swells out this enormous expanse and floats like a vast cloud when she sits down or rises up.'

Crinoline, in that context, meant fabric stiffened with horsehair, from the French *crin*; it was a good ten years before the cage crinoline was invented. Lady Aylesbury may have bought her down petticoat from Mrs Addley Bourne of 37 Piccadilly, the great specialist in underwear, who advertised Arctic Down Petticoats for 17/6. Or possibly it may have come from W. H. Bateson & Co., who claimed (in the *Illustrated London News* of 1867) to be the original inventor of the genuine eiderdown petticoats. Lesser ladies than Lady Aylesbury were piling on the petticoats of flannel and of cotton stiffened with starch or horsehair, achieving a somewhat comparable circumference but with much less bouyancy. It was the dragging weight of all these garments which, becoming intolerable, led to the introduction of the cage crinoline.

Henry Mayhew, in his *Shops and Companies of London* (1865), describes the cage crinoline as 'consisting of slight steel hoops covered by bands of tape, which appeared in England shortly after the Great Exhibition of 1851'. Most fashion historians date the introduction between 1854 and 1856, but Mayhew was writing while the crinoline was still being worn, and was a very conscientious journalist; it is unlikely he would be far out in dating it. Indeed, one can well imagine some gadget-minded genius was inspired by that remarkable exhibition to experiment with a mechanical petticoat distender, for a great many of the exhibits in the 'Articles of Clothing Section' were more curious than chic. There was, for instance, buttonless, reversible, self-sustaining, self-opening, ventilating, one-piece, and even 'Mathematical' underwear; there were unpickable pockets, unsinkable yachting outfits, hats that eliminated all risk of concussion from railway travel, and corsets that opened instantly in case of sudden disorder. It was a time when outfitters were advertising such novelties as hats with patent air-valves; and when a Conduit Street tailor, B. Benjamin & Sons, designed a doctor's suit contrived so that, in the event of the owner being called up in the night, he could don coat, waistcoat, and trousers at once, and as if they were one garment. It sounds like an early version of Churchill's wartime siren suit.

Clearly, the inventive genius of the nation was at full stretch; and combined with the Englishman's boyish love of gadgets, it was almost inevitable that someone should arrive at a petticoat distender in the shape of a parrot's cage. Certainly, by July 1854, Mrs Potts & Son of 28 Pall Mall was advertising the Jupon Clochette in the *Morning Post*. This was not necessarily a steel crinoline. It could have been a petticoat with a band of horsehair or whalebone inserted in the hem, which was an early method of holding out the dress skirt. Other petticoats were made of piqué with as many as five rows of very thin and supple whalebone from hem to knee, giving the petticoat a bell-like, or cloche, shape. Without doubt, however, the cage crinoline with steel hoops was an established fashion in England by the summer of 1856, when Francis Wey visited England:

> From 5 o'clock to 6 o'clock is the smart time in Kensington Gardens. Taste has improved enormously of late. It is not unusual to meet women very well dressed despite the bold flights of fancy they indulge in where contrast of colours is concerned, and which is their stumbling block. They also have a habit of puffing out their skirts from waist to hem by means of whalebone or even wire hoops. These skirts swing about like bells and give their wearers a jerky gait which is not graceful.

What is chiefly interesting about this extract is that it reveals the crinoline to have been well launched in England before it was worn in France: Francis Wey was a Parisian of good position in Society, and yet clearly regarded the crinoline as an English folly, if not freak. It was evidently in full swing in Kensington Gardens before Charles Frederick Worth made it fashionable in Paris. His son, J.P.Worth, in *A Century of Fashion* does indeed say that an English inventor brought the crinoline to his father, who saw its possibilities and at once proceeded to launch it. Yet, such is the irony of fashion fame, that the credit (or blame) for the crinoline is usually attributed to Charles Frederick Worth and his most illustrious and conspicuous customer, the Empress Eugénie. Here again, Mayhew gives a clue by saying 'It is alleged that the Empress of the French first put on a large crinoline to conceal her interesting situation'. The Prince Imperial was born in March 1856, so this may well account for the customary dating of the crinoline.

In England, Messrs Thomson in the City, and Mr Philpott of 37 Piccadilly soon became leading manufacturers of the crinoline; and there was also Carter's Crinoline and Stay Warehouse at 4 Ludgate Hill, sometimes advertised as

CARTER'S CRINOLINE SALOONS

. . . open to the public with every new pattern in Real Horsehair Petticoats: Ladies objecting to steel crinoline skirts will find the largest stock in London of Tucked, Puffed, Flounced, and Fluted, real Horsehair Petticoats, Skeleton Skirts and Over Petticoats; together with the New Imperatrice Elastic stay and bodice, as worn by the Empress of the French. Also the New Patent Sylphide Elastic Stay, perfectly free from Indiarubber, and quite inodorous.

Carter's also had 'the new Balmoral White and Grey Horsehair Petticoat without steel'; and in this connection it should be noted that Queen Victoria never wore a crinoline, but was one of its most fervent opposers: on August 1, 1863, she addressed a letter *To The Ladies of England* expressing the pain with which she read 'the account of daily accidents arising from the wearing of the indelicate, expensive, dangerous, and hideous article called Crinoline'. Another severe critic was the lady who at that time was the most worshipped woman in England, Florence Nightingale. Yet the royal condemnation by the Queen, the divine disapproval of Miss Nightingale, the thunderings of the clergy, the warnings of the faculty, and the pronouncements by coroners on deaths by fire caused by crinolines, all failed to influence fashion.

Moreover, by this time trade interests were deeply involved. As early in the crinoline period as July 18, 1857, it was reported in *The Times* that 40,000 tons of Swedish iron had been imported for the manufacture of crinolines . . . 'One Sheffield firm alone has taken an order for forty tons of rolled steel for crinoline, and a foreign order has been given for one ton a week for several weeks'. Eight years later Henry Mayhew was writing:

That a great and important interest is involved in the sale and manufacture of crinoline is best proved by the fact that crinoline has become a special and distinct branch of trade. It is no longer a mere accessory of the milliner's or haberdasher's shop. There are great factories where nothing else is made but crinoline wires and hoops; there are warehouses where nothing else is stored, shops where no other commodity is sold. In fact, crinoline has become; at certain emporiums, *the* leading article.

Cheap non-steel crinolines were sold in all the little draper's shops: 'Huge, awkward, unwieldy hen-coops hung out of the doors of the cheap "selling-off" shops. Made of buckram and split sugar cane, they swing about and block the pavements.'

The Regent Street branch of Carter & Houston stocked 'Crinolines and Stiff Petticoats to suit all tastes'—but of course Regent Street taste would not approve of anything really cheap. Carter & Houston were corset makers established in 1812, who had a large factory in the Blackfriars Road, a branch at the Crystal Palace, and another in Stockwell Street, besides the Regent Street shop. They sent corsets 'daily by post to every part of England, Ireland, and Scotland'. The ordinary cage crinolines must have defeated the possibilities of the parcel post; but later on the 'Ondina' was invented which was 'so light and compressible that it might almost be rolled up and carried in the pocket'— the sort of claim made, in modern times, for lightweight girdles.

The great volume of ladies' dresses posed many problems—on the railways, in omnibuses, and mounting into carriages. It is no wonder grand ladies preferred, when shopping, to remain seated in their carriages and have the shop keeper come out onto the pavement to serve them. William Gayler, founder of Gayler & Pope, Marylebone High Street, recalled this custom to Mrs Baillie Saunders when,

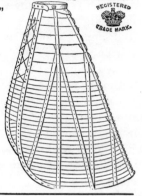

THOMSON'S "ZEPHYRINA" OR "WINGED JUPON,"

A NEW SAFETY CRINOLINE,

Registered Jan. 16th, 1868.

An entirely new form, which no written or pictorial description can possibly convey. Complete freedom of motion. No possibility of the feet becoming entangled. Made in two shapes, one the most perfect train ever effected in Crinoline; the other a round shape, specially adapted for walking costume dresses. Can be had in both shapes half-lined, if preferred.

W. S. THOMSON & CO.,

MANUFACTURERS OF THE "GLOVE-FITTING" CORSETS.

29. Leading manufacturer introduces the crinolette as an alternative to the round parrot-cage shape.

in 1907, she wrote a Jubilee book for his firm. He also recalled something more directly attributable to the crinoline: he had to have the counter of his little draper's shop set back ten inches and made hollow underneath like a davenport, to allow the crinolines of his customers to fit underneath.

That was in 1857, when William Gayler was twenty-three years' old and had served his apprenticeship at Harvey Nichol's. He bought a rat-ridden butcher's shop in Marylebone High Street and turned it into a little drapery establishment. At that time there were ten other small drapers in Marylebone, one of them being Peter Jones, who later moved to Chelsea. Another was the firm of Spencer, Turner, and Boldero, whose shop was in the then fashionable street of Lisson Grove. It was they who first employed the young John Barker when he came to London from Kent in 1858. Later, Barker left Spencer, Turner and Boldero to become an assistant to William Whiteley.

William Gayler and his young wife lived over their shop, and both worked hard all day and until late every evening. They never closed before eight o'clock, even in the winter evenings when the shop was lit by candles. Gas lighting was by this time general in the streets, and was installed in most of the big shops and public buildings, but not the smaller shops in quiet residential districts. Peter Robinson still had a great brass lamp hung over the door with a chain and swivel. Every evening at dusk it was ceremoniously lowered to be lit by his two apprentices and then hoisted back into position until, late in the evening, at this time nine o'clock, it was lowered again to be extinguished. Buckingham Palace was still lit by oil lamps and candles in the 1850's, and many private houses and even mansions followed its example: gas was so garish. Not having gas was probably a kind of snobbery, like not having television nowadays.

Mr Gayler recalled that when he started his shop bonnets were large round 'pokes' with a heavy curtain draped at the back of the hair. They were supposed to take exactly 4½ yards of ribbon to trim, and sarsenet ribbon was a particular favourite. Little lace and muslin cap-fronts were worn inside the bonnets to give a frame for the face. White cotton stockings were much in vogue. Mr Gayler, when he was at Harvey Nichol's, had sold them at 4/11½ per pair; but when he came to Marylebone, where the customers were often working class women wearing shawls over their heads, the popular price was 4½d a pair. When buying materials there was 'almost a kind of religion of rubbing everything between one's finger and thumb before making a choice. A good "thumber" who sturdily doubted the quality of the goods offered was considered a genius amongst shoppers.'

Although Gayler & Pope of Marylebone High Street, and many other little shops in the quieter neighbourhoods of London and other cities were still lit by candles, the general tendency, particularly in drapery shops, was towards a brilliant display of gas works. In Manchester, the very progressive emporium of Kendal, Milne & Faulkner installed Bude Lighting in 1842. London shop lighting was described by Charles Knight in 1851:

> To whatever part of London we direct our steps, we shall find that the drapers' shops—including in this term those which sell cotton, linen, silk, and worsted goods—are among the handsomest. In Whitechapel and other wide through-fares at the East End, the goods exposed in these windows are generally rather of a humble and cheap kind; but the windows are nevertheless glazed with plate-glass and lighted with a profusion of gas-jets, such as only the gin-palace can equal . . . When we arrive at St Paul's Churchyard we come to a very world of show. Here we find a shop whose front presents an un-interrupted mass of glass from the ceiling to the ground; no horizontal sash bars being seen, and the vertical ones made of brass. Here, too, we see on a winter's evening a mode of lighting recently introduced, by which the products of combustion are given off in the street, instead of being left to soil the goods in the window: the lamps are fixed outside the shop, with a reflector so placed as to throw down a strong light upon the commodities in the window.

This was the establishment of George Hitchcock & Sons, which occupied four houses on the corner site north west of the Cathedral, only a stone's throw from their great rivals, Nicholson's. Hitchcock's was much the older firm of the two, having been founded as silk mercers in 1760. They became linen drapers, haberdashers and carpet makers as well.

Hitchcock's method of lighting their display windows from outside, thus keeping the heat of the gas away from the goods, soon became general to all big shops, and remained the method up till the introduc-tion of electricity. Knight goes on to describe a shop in Ludgate Hill which was one of the first to give an illusion of brilliancy and vastness by 'clothing walls and ceiling with looking-glass, and causing these to reflect the light from rich cut-glass chandeliers. Farther on we see the first shop in London, as far as we are aware, in which the first floor was taken to form part of the shop itself, and one window carried up to the double height.' Protection at night could be secured by fitting the revolving iron shutters patented in 1837 by Bunnett & Co. and first used by Swan & Edgar.

The reason why drapers' shops were more numerous and brilliant than shops dealing in other merchandise is explained by Knight:

MODEL Nº 1.

DEBENHAM & FREEBODY, LONDON & CHELTENHAM.

V

Morning costume of brown *Satin-de-laine*, with wool fringe. Engraving from Debenham & Freebody's 'New Fashion Book', October 1870: a book of designs for ordering by post.

An Elias Howe sewing machine, decorated gold and mother-of-pearl inlay.

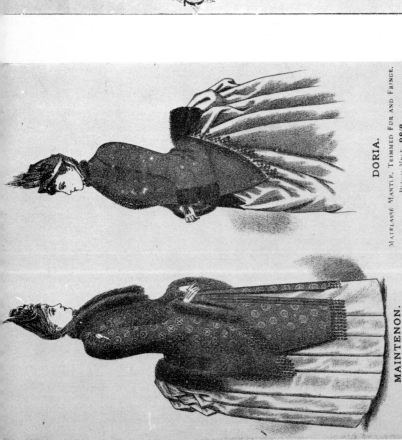

VI   Sheet from a folder of twelve designs for autumn 1887.

(Right) Cover of catalogue carrying fabric patterns attached to designs.

30. Handsome Globe lamp and bracket for showroom.

31. The Leo incandescent gas lamp.

The shops devoted to the sale of wearing apparel are the most remarkable in London. The principle of competition has been driven further in the drapery business than in most others, and hence the linen-drapers' shops exhibit the effect which this competition produces more strikingly perhaps than most others. The rise of the cotton manufacture in England has had much to do with this matter; for when woollen fabrics were the staple of English dress, the comparative costliness prevented any very eager competition, and the fabrics themselves were not of so showy a character. It is true the mercer had attractive silken goods to display in his window; but the immense consumption of cotton in female dress has been the chief moving power towards the production of the present remarkable display in the drapers' shops. The mills, the labour, the capital employed in this manufacture have led to so large a production that the manufacturer is anxious to 'do business' in any quarter, and this anxiety leads to a constant increase in the number of retail shops.

Eight years later, in 1859, George Augustus Sala published his *Twice Round the Clock* in which he describes, not the brilliant lights directed on to the plate-glass at eight o'clock in the evening, but what went on behind the plate-glass windows at eight o'clock in the morning:

In the magnificent linen-drapery establishments of Oxford and Regent Streets, the vast shop-fronts, museums of fashion in plate-glass cases, offer a series of animated *tableaux of poses plastiques* in the shape of young ladies in morning costume, and young gentlemen in whiskers and white neckclothes,

97

faultlessly complete as to costume, with the exception that they are yet in their shirt sleeves, who are accomplishing the difficult and mysterious feat known as 'dressing' the shop window. By their nimble and practised hands the rich piled velvet mantles are displayed, the moiré and glacé silks arranged in artful folds, the laces and gauzes, the innumerable whim-whams and fribble-frabble of fashion, elaborately shown, and to their best advantage.

✤   ✤   ✤

One of the magnificent establishments in Regent Street through whose windows Augustus Sala must have gazed, was the shawl emporium of J. & J. Holmes, occupying Nos. 171, 173, and 175 Regent Street, opposite Archbishop Tenison's chapel. Thirty years earlier, J. & J. Holmes were describing themselves in the *World of Fashion* as 'the most splendid establishment even in that vicinage, deserving the flattering enconiums bestowed on it by the fashionable who visit it'. They sold shawls from 1 gn. to 100 gns. and held the Royal Appointment to the Queen.

Shawls were an almost inevitable corollary to the crinoline; and their coming back into fashion can be seen to date from the increasing volume of skirts which gathered momentum from 1830 onwards—the more voluminous skirts became, the more difficult it was to wear mantles and capes over them: a very large, warm shawl was very often worn outdoors instead, even in the winter. In the summer, shawls were advertised 'for Flower Shows, Fetes, and Races'. Not all women took naturally to this cosy but incommoding article of dress, and the fashion magazines gave advice about how to wear them gracefully. One article in *Sylvia's Home Journal*, 1861, entitled 'How to Wear a Shawl' ends with an almost spiritual exhortation:

> We may add that all shawls should be as much as possible draped upon the woman who wears them, and sustained by the arms being pressed upon the bust; but we must also add that we have only displayed to our readers the material part of this difficult art. Unfortunately it is the only one we can analyse, for grace cannot be demonstrated, and taste is a natural gift which escapes every definition and all commentary. Wealth cannot replace it, nor can experience supply its want.

It is difficult to imagine a woman looking graceful, whatever her natural gifts, when she is sustaining her shawl by her arms being pressed upon her bust; and that stiff, prim, silhouette which the wearing of a shawl imposed is the typical silhouette we think of for the lady of the crinoline period—even the young ladies. One of the worst features of this ugly period was that the fashions made every woman look middle-aged or old.

ADVERTISEMENTS.

M ESSRS. J. & J. HOLMES,

SHAWL MANUFACTURERS,

BY APPOINTMENT,

TO

HER MAJESTY THE QUEEN;

HER ROYAL HIGHNESS THE

DUCHESS OF KENT;

Her Royal Highness the Princess Augusta;

AND

*Her Royal Highness the Duchess of
Cambridge.*

AN IMMENSE VARIETY OF

INDIA SHAWLS,

AND

ORIENTAL CURIOSITIES.

171, 173, 175, REGENT STREET
(*See* 171, 173, 175, *in the Engraving*)

32. Advertisement in Tallis's Street
Views, 1838.

Paisley and Norwich were flourishing again, making large square shawls woven or printed with Indian designs which became known as 'Paisley patterns'. The genuine Indian shawls of fine cashmere were imported, and also French cashmere shawls, but they were very, very expensive. Many other shops, besides that of J. & J. Holmes, were able to do well 'by confining themselves solely to this elegant and indispensable article of dress'. At least four of them were rivals of J. & J. Holmes in Regent Street: William C. Jay at 217; Simpson & Co. at Nos. 247 & 249; William's Cloak and Shawl Warehouse at Regent Circus; and at Nos. 211 & 213, T. Williams had his India and British shawl warehouse, specializing in Oriental and Sultan Long Shawls. This house not only sold shawls, but bought and exchanged them, and had a shawl cleaning service for customers. Not very far away, at 95 New Bond Street, was Owen's India Shawl Warehouse; while in Fleet Street, Howes & Hart's India Warehouse did its best to attract customers away from the more fashionable West End, advertising in the *Morning Herald* of October 30, 1835: 'Ladies with carriages are respectfully informed that the above establishment is situated only sixty doors from Temple-bar, and the approach from the west is remarkably good, since the great improvement made in the thoroughfare by the widening of the Strand.'

Somewhere between 1849 and 1854, the shawl warehouse of J. & J. Holmes was taken over by Farmer & Rogers, who renamed the premises The Great Shawl and Cloak Emporium, and advertised:

The largest and most magnificent collection in England, comprising the latest designs of India, Gold, Delhi, Benares, Decca and Lahore. Shawls and scarfs the most economical and the most costly.

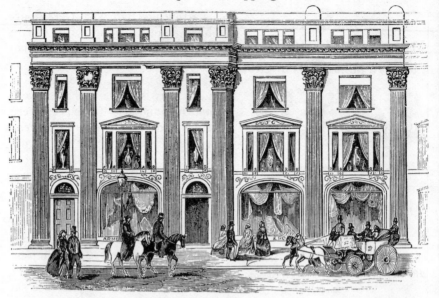

33. Farmer & Roger's Great Shawl and Cloak Emporium, 171–175 Regent
Street. *circa* 1860.

The great Indian empire had been opened up like Pandora's Box
and was spilling over with exquisite treasures, scattering its riches
more prodigally in Regent Street than in any other shopping street in
the world. By 1860, Farmer & Rogers were branching out into other
lines besides shawls, and were able to redecorate their emporium 'in
a most superb style' besides undergoing 'considerable alteration to
meet the exigencies of increased trade, and afford additional comfort to
the numerous visitors'. *A Visit to Regent Street* enthuses:

> This renowned emporium of fashion is the most celebrated of its kind in
> Europe. Although here may be found articles of the most costly description,
> the firm do not confine themselves exclusively to this branch, but endeavour
> to offer Shawls, Cloaks, and Dresses of first-class taste and quality, at very
> moderate prices. India, China, French, Paisley, Norwich, and French Shawls.
> Every description of Cloak and Jacket for the carriage, promenade, and
> opera. Plain and Fancy Silks, Irish and Norwich Poplins, etc.

To this renowned emporium of fashion came in 1862 young Arthur
Liberty, an eighteen-year-old apprentice. Twelve years later he was to
found his own business—Liberty's of Regent Street, which is one of
the very few world-famous stores remaining in London still under the
ownership and management of the founder's direct descendants.

CHAPTER X

TRAFFIC PROBLEMS AND
WEST END SHOPPING

Advertising vans in the Strand. Regent Street at 4 o'clock.
Lewis & Allenby's new building. Gorringe's of Buckingham
Palace Road. Bonnets and Flowers. The Burlington Arcade.
Perfumers and Glovers. Fans and Parasols.

TRAFFIC problems were acute in the West End in early Victorian times. Tradesmen themselves were partly responsible for some of the worst blocks, because their advertising vans moved as slowly as possible so that their slogans would be read. Pasted over with advertisements, they crawled about the streets at the busiest times of the day, the Strand being particularly favoured for their operations—as many as nine vehicles might congregate at one spot, completely stopping the traffic. Some were less vulgar than others: Knight's *London* illustrates a light two-wheeled gig shaped as a gigantic hat, emblazoned 'Perrings Light Hats'—a rather elegant turn-out.

When the Strand was widened in 1835, giving a better approach for carriages, drapers in the City of London, Fleet Street, and the Strand hoped to win back some custom from Regent Street, Oxford Street and Bond Street. But the prestige of West End shopping, which dated from the planning of Regent Street as the finest shopping street in the world, was too great; and all the time there was the social emigration to the west, all the time the City was being deserted by its most prosperous residents and their families.

Not only was fashionable shopping concentrated in the West End, but it was concentrated into one part of the day: from two o'clock to four o'clock was the elegant time in Regent Street. . . . 'To be seen to the best advantage' wrote Tallis in 1838, 'it should be visited on a summer's day in the afternoon, when the splendid carriages, and elegantly attired pedestrians, evince the opulence and taste of our magnificent metropolis.' Twenty years later, Augustus Sala wrote of the shops as being 'innately fashionable' . . .

REGENT-STREET IN THE SEASON—SEE NEXT PAGE.

34. Fashionable shopping hour in Regent Street, 4 p.m. *Illustrated London News*, 1866.

Indeed, Regent Street is an avenue of superfluities, a great trunk-road in Vanity Fair. Fancy watchmakers, haberdashers, and photographers; fancy stationers, fancy hosiers, and fancy staymakers; music shops, shawl shops, jewellers, French glove shops, perfumery, and point lace shops, confectioners and milliners; creamily, these are the merchants whose wares are exhibited in this Bezesteen of the world.

No wonder the fashionable world flocked to this Vanity Fair; contemporary drawings show the confusion of carriages and footmen, pedestrians, dogs and horse-riders, to have been a wild turbulence seething in all directions. The fact of the matter was that Society, and the apers and gapers of Society, looked upon Regent Street as a fashionable parade ground. One stopped to talk to one's acquaintances and to flirt with one's beaux, regardless of other carriages trying to proceed. The term 'through traffic' had not yet been invented: Regent Street was a shopping street, not a road, nor a route, nor a highway . . . . 'Only here', wrote Francis Wey, 'Only here could you find the fashionable world so perfectly at home in the middle of the street.'

The congestion was not only crowded into one time of day, but into one season of the year. 'With the West End no contrast can well be greater than that presented by fashion's haunt in and out of the season', wrote the *Illustrated London News* in 1866. 'In the former case, all is bustle and gaiety; in the latter, gloom and desolation. The brilliant ever-shifting scene presented daily in Regent Street during the season is dizzying in its confusion. On days of court ceremonial strings of carriages filled with beauty, rank, and fashion, creep at a snail's pace towards St James's or Buckingham Palace. At other times, the fireflies of fashion glance rapidly hither and thither, and the West End streets are thronged with a promiscuous jungle of carriages, horsemen and horsewomen, cabs, omnibuses, and wagons; the pavements being crowded with fashionable loungers. With what dignified ease the gorgeously bedizened footmen attend to their mistresses or lounge about in attitudes of studied grace.'

Nash's graceful colonnade was removed from the Quadrant in 1848. The villain of this piece of vandalism was, according to *Modern London*, 1887, Mr Frederick Crane, head of Sandland & Crane, hosier, glover, inventor and maker of the Patent Belt Drawers. Mr Crane was familiarly known as 'the father of Regent Street', being the oldest merchant in that thoroughfare. The writer of *Modern London* seems to have considered Mr Crane did a public service in this demolition: 'It was he who caused the unsightly colonnade to be removed from the street thirty years ago, and he was an active promoter of many other improvements which have made Regent Street the first thoroughfare in the world'.

There are, of course, Mr Cranes in every era, campaigning for unsightly 'improvements' aimed at the benefit of tradespeople. But in Augustus Sala's opinion, he not only ruined Regent Street, but did himself and his fellow tradespeople no good, no good at all:

> Whatever could have possessed our Commissioner of Woods and Forests to allow those unrivalled arcades to be demolished! The stupid tradesmen, whose purblind, shop-till avarice led them to petition for the removal of the columns, gained nothing by the change, for the Quadrant as a lounge in wet weather, was at once destroyed; it not only afforded a convenient shelter beneath, but it was a capital promenade for the dwellers in the first-floors above. The entresols certainly were slightly gloomy; and moustached foreigners, together with some gaily-dressed company still naughtier, could with difficulty be restrained from prowling backwards and forwards between Glasshouse Street and the County Fire Office. But, perambulating Regent Street at all hours of the day and night, as I do now frequently, I see no diminution in the number of moustached or rouged, or naughty faces, whose prototypes were familiar to me, years agone, in the brilliant Quadrant.

The traffic blocks in Bond Street were almost as bad as those in Regent Street. In 1866, Redmayne's of 192 New Bond Street and 35 Conduit Street advertised, 'Ready access will always be found in Conduit Street when Bond Street is blocked'. This advertisement tied up with an article in the same issue of the *Illustrated London News* (April 14, 1866) on London street improvements:

> Among the noticeable facts of the present day is that of the marvellous improvements in the street architecture of the metropolis. On all sides we now see springing up buildings for commercial purposes, such as a few years ago were not dreamed of, except for the palatial clubs of Pall-mall. Wherever the requirements of business or private enterprise demand reconstruction of premises, the improvement is most striking. At the West End, the spirit of progress is evident, and a remarkable example of the kind is the noble building that has been erected by the well-known firm of silk-mercers, Messrs Lewis and Allenby. The lower portion is devoted entirely to business purposes. The upper part contains a commodious library and sitting and sleeping rooms for their large staff of assistants. The front of the building is entirely of stone. The columns and the cornice of the lower portion are of polished Aberdeen granite. The architecture is of the purest Italian style, and is from the designs of Mr James Murray, the architect of the Palace Hotel and many of our new large buildings.

Lewis & Allenby's must have been one of the very earliest retail firms to construct a whole new building entirely for showrooms, workrooms, and staff. It is true that the shops in Regent Street were

35. New Conduit Street building of Lewis & Allenby, Silk Mercers. *Illustrated London News*, 1866.

all built as shops, but shopkeepers only rented the ground floor, the upper floors being let as apartments. . . . Sala says, 'the furnished apartments are let, either to music or operatic celebrities or to unostentatious old bachelors'.

It was to Lewis & Allenby that the great Charles Frederick Worth was apprenticed, according to his son, J. P. Worth, in *A Century of Fashion*. But his biographer Edith Saunders comes to the conclusion, through obituary notices and other convincing evidence, that Swan & Edgar are correct in claiming him as their apprentice. The explanation could perhaps be that on completing his seven years' apprenticeship there he took up an appointment for a short time at Lewis & Allenby, who were undoubtedly the most famous silk-mercers in London, before setting out on his Paris adventure. If that were so he would very likely have talked more to his son about Lewis & Allenby than about the less exclusive establishment of Swan & Edgar.

Happily the name of one of Lewis & Allenby's assistants in the 1830's is certain. This was Emerson Muschamp Bainbridge, who later founded Bainbridge's of Newcastle. And Bainbridge's, as will be shown in a later chapter, have a strong claim to be considered one of the first department stores. The name of Lewis & Allenby is no longer seen in the West End, as the firm was acquired by Dickins & Jones in Edwardian times. But the prestige of their speciality, silks, was transferred to Dickins & Jones, who then took over, in 1903, the stock and goodwill of George Hitchcock & Sons, City silk-mercers since 1760. Dickins & Jones also acquired a large silk warehouse in Manchester, and their silk department has always remained particularly strong.

The continuity of esteem for some particular branch of drapery is one of the most warming things in the history of retail distribution. A shop may change owners many times in the course of a century, its premises, its directors, buyers, and assistants, will change even more; yet its particular pride, its reputation for some one line of merchandise, is handed down from generation to generation.

❧   ❧   ❧

Far away from the brilliance of Regent Street and the high fashion of Bond Street, in quiet Buckingham Palace Road, Frederick Gorringe set up a little drapery shop in 1858, with two assistants. The neighbourhood was a very quiet one, almost it felt like the country, and his shop was so sited that it became known as the village shop for Buckingham Palace—the ladies of the royal household could slip out of the backdoor of the palace to get whatever they needed in the way of haberdashery or materials for their needlework.

It was not far to walk to Gorringe's from the fashionable Belgravia district, which had only recently been developed; and the little shop soon had many esteemed customers amongst the nobility and gentry, all of whose particularities and peculiarities were studied with a care and solicitude amounting to reverence by Mr Gorringe himself. When in 1928, the shop celebrated its seventieth anniversary, many customers wrote affectionately recalling the old days. One customer was a hundred and two years old when she wrote, and she recalled purchasing from Mr Gorringe 'a fancy Tuscan straw bonnet, trimmed with white ribbon, edged with steel, and having a deep silk curtain with bows and ends. This must be seventy years ago.'

In fact, it must have been the very year that Frederick Gorringe opened his shop. Strange alchemy of a hat, that it can remain in its wearer's memory, down to the white ribbon edged with steel, when seventy years have passed! Another customer wrote of the one-window shop of 1865 at which she used to buy pink geraniums for her

bonnet. At that time, she recalled, Grosvenor-gardens were merely
fields. Another wrote: 'I remember perfectly my mother taking me to
Mr Gorringe's shop in 1864 and ordering black straw bonnets and
bows of cherry-coloured velvet. In 1878 my bridesmaids' bonnets and
my going-away bonnet all came from you.' Mr Gorringe's little shop
in those early days was a general drapery business—and yet it was
nearly all bonnets that were remembered in these seventieth anniversary letters. What magic is there in millinery that makes it immortal?
Hats must possess some poetic quality that the romantic heart, which
saves what it can, remembers.

Flowers and ribbons, but above all flowers, were essential to the
atmosphere of a bonnet—and it was all bonnets, no hats, in this period
of crinoline and shawl. A milliner who advocated flowers at all costs,
was J. & E. Smith of 151 Regent Street—even at the cost of looking
too gay when etiquette required mourning:

FASHIONABLE PARISIAN MILLINERY,

in the best taste by first-rate artistes: Light bonnets, with flowers 10/6;
glacé bonnets, with flowers 16/6; mourning bonnets with flowers, 12/6.

Respectable grief, no doubt, dictated black flowers for full mourning,
purple for half-mourning, shading out to delicate parma violets for
complimentary.

Artificial flowers, their making and importing from France, was a
very considerable side-line of the fashion industry. Foster & Son of
60 Wigmore Street, Plumassier and Florist, specialized in dressing
and mounting ostrich plumes and in French flowers; and Hill & Wil-
liamson of the Flower & Glove Warehouse at 29 Regent Street was
another specialist. At Nos. 24 and 25 in the Burlington Arcade there was
Madame Marion, Artiste in Artificial Flowers, who created head-
dresses, caps, fichus, and won prizes for artificial flowers at the Crystal
Palace. Her business was taken over in 1867 by Mrs Harriet Rowley.
Next door, there was Madame Parsons, British to the core no doubt,
but Madame by courtesy and convention like most milliners and
corsetières.

Madame Parsons made trips to Paris, and each new season invited
her clients to a display on her return. Her Guinea Bonnets were famous;
and she must have prospered exceedingly because she had an establishment at 92 Regent Street as well as her main premises at Nos. 26, 27,
and 28 Burlington Arcade. Could hers, possibly, have been the 'friendly
bonnet|shop' which is mentioned in the *Survey of London?* The *Survey*
records that upper chambers over a friendly bonnet shop were used for
prostitution, and men of position who wished to 'avoid publicity in

their amours' dreaded being seen in the vicinity of the Arcade at certain hours. If Madame Parsons were the friendly milliner it would account for her prosperity—and be a further reason for her being 'Madame'. The furnished apartments over her Regent Street branch would make a convenient second house, which would lessen the hazards of 'men of position' meeting each other.

The Burlington Arcade was described by its architect, Samuel Ware, as 'a Piazza for all Hardware, Wearing Apparel and Articles not Offensive in appearance nor smell'. Only one of the original shops still trades under the name of its first owner—Nos. 66–70, the outfitting shop of D. H. Lord, who took possession when the Arcade was opened in 1819. By the time Augustus Sala came to write of it, in 1859, it had evidently got rid of the hardware and the goods with negative virtues, and specialized in luxury merchandise. Sala described it as 'a sublimate of superfluities, a booth transplanted bodily from Vanity Fair', and went on:

I don't think there is a shop in its *enceinte* where they sell anything that we could not do without. Boots and shoes are sold there, to be sure, but what boots and shoes? Varnished and embroidered and be-ribboned figments, fitter for a fancy ball or a lady's chamber, there to caper to the jingling melody of a lute, than for serious pedestrianism. Paintings and lithographs for gilded boudoirs, collars for puppy dogs, and silver-mounted whips for spaniels, pocket handkerchiefs, in which an islet of cambric is surrounded by an ocean of lace, embroidered garters and braces, filigree flounces, firework-looking bonnets, scent bottles, sword-knots, brocaded sashes, worked dressing-gowns, inlaid snuff-boxes, and falbalas of all descriptions. These form the stock-in-trade of the merchants who have here their tiny *boutiques*.

36. Gloves by Noble Jones, Burlington Arcade. *Lady's World,* 1887.

Sala does not mention gloves, but surely they would have been represented amongst all these scented luxuries, although the Burlington Glove and Fan Depot. at 22 and 23 Burlington Arcade, run by S. W. Greves, was not founded until 1862. Noble Jones, who ran the French Glove House at Newington Causeway, moved to the Burlington Arcade in 1881, where his shop is now owned and managed by the fourth generation of the Noble Jones family.

All the most elegant gloves were French; and certainly the 'Ladies Gloves beautifully and permanently perfumed' sold by Wheeler & Co. of 210 Regent Street (Est. 1817) would come from Paris. Indeed gloves were often sold by perfumers; and one of the most famous perfumeries was Rimmel's, No. 96 The Strand. Rimmel's gloves were all perfumed, as were their Artificial Bouquets which 'finely imitated natural blooms both in texture and scent'. They also sold roses and violets with collapsible stems which contained the scent of the flowers; and their perfumed fountains 'not only refresh the atmosphere but scent it at the same time'. One was placed in the boudoir of the Princess of Wales at Windsor Castle on the day of her marriage. Rimmel's perfumed crackers for balls and parties contained 'mottoes selected from the best poets and a small metallic tube, filled with the best rose-water which may be squirted by mischief-loving maids, even into the eyes of their partners without causing pain'.

Rimmel's shop was essentially a perfumery with accessory sidelines. L. T. Piver, Perfumer and Glover of 160 Regent Street and at 10 Boulevard de Strasbourg, Paris, also specialized in fans. Only at Piver's Parisian establishment in Regent Street could real Jouvin's gloves with the patent Fastenings be obtained . . . where also were stocked 'the finest and largest collection of Fans in London'. The scented elegancies of Piver's were described in *A Visit to Regent Street:*

> The mere title of the House of Piver is redolent with fragrance, and gives rise to all sorts of delightful thoughts, having joy and pleasure for their chiefest themes. Its *façade* is the purest example extant of the architecture of the most refined period of French history, and its interior evidences a taste and elegance which, while defying criticism, leaves nothing that the most fastidious can desire.

Later on, L. T. Piver was to be the only French perfumer to obtain the First Class Medals at the Great Exhibitions of 1851 and 1862; and after that success he paid a compliment to England by naming three of his new perfumes 'Guard's Club', 'Belgravia', and 'Forget-me-not'.

Piver's claim to stock the 'finest and largest collection of Fans in London' was almost certainly an exaggeration, for Jules Duvelleroy

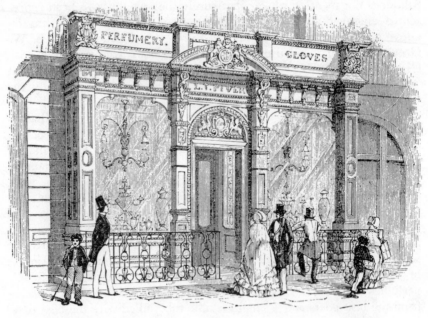

37.

(established in London in 1847) was undoubtedly the most important maker and dealer in fans, with a long list of royal appointments starting with the Queen and trailing off into 'members of all the Courts of Europe'. His shop at 167 Regent Street was a branch of his Parisian business; fans were his sole trade and he sold them from 6d to £300. His workrooms were above the showrooms; and he also had a department for repairing fans.

The making of fans is something that the English have never excelled at—indeed, it would be true to say that they have never really tried. Any fan-makers resident in England were almost invariably of French origin. Anne Buck in *Victorian Costume and Costume Accessories* says:

At the time of the Fan Exhibition at South Kensington in 1870, it was stated that fan-making as a trade was little represented in London where, out of seven or eight firms given in the directory, one only was English. the rest being French.

Primarily an instrument of flirtation rather than a practical means of keeping cool, fans are perhaps too frivolous a weapon to be created in our climate where we understand love and war, but not the finer shades of give and take. And yet, although the English do not take to it naturally, they can be taught. Those were the days when flirtation was a required study for all young ladies. Ballroom strategy hinged upon the skilful deployment of a fan, upon the Nelson touch in not seeing the signal of a chaperon's lorgnette.

⚘   ⚘   ⚘

Parasols could be equally useful weapons if properly handled; and these, unlike fans, were beautifully made in England. This could be explained by our having more aptitude for outdoor sports than indoor games. R. Williams of The Fashionable Parasol & Umbrella Manufactory at 4 Ludgate Hill was one of the principal suppliers to the trade as well as selling retail. Williams made parasols to match ladies' dresses, and carried 'a splendid assortment of *Highly Improved* and beautiful Parasols made of all the leading and most fashionable shades and colours'. Then there was the Parasol Warehouse of Savoker & Co., at 22 Rathbone Place. Savoker's were also general drapers and haberdashers and had been in Rathbone Place since at least the 1830's.

As the century advanced, retail shops selling only parasols seem to have disappeared, and parasols and sunshades were sold in umbrella shops and the larger drapers' shops dealing in different kinds of fashion goods. Usually, oddly enough, parasols were to be found in the fur department. The explanation of this could be that it gave the department a balanced turnover in both winter and summer—by the same token as an ice-cream manufacturer will also make sausages.

At the beginning of Victoria's reign, parasols were very small with slender sticks, usually jointed to fold. There was a special 'Victoria Parasol' for open carriages, which was so diminutive as to be used like a fan, just to shade the face. The folding sticks of these miniature elegances were most often of wrought ivory, and the parasols were silk, trimmed with fringes or embroidered borders. In 1844, Sangster's the umbrella·makers patented the 'Sylphide' parasol, which had a

PARIS

EVENTAILS ARTISTIQUES
ET DE MARIAGE

DUVELLEROY

BY APPOINTMENT

167, REGENT STREET. W.
FANS REPAIRED

LONDON

EVENTAILS ANTIQUES
DE TOUS STYLES

38.

spring at the end of the handle so that the parasol could be closed with the hand which was holding it.

Folding sticks and fringes went out in the 1860's, and parasols became larger and plainer. Before this, about the end of the 1850's, it occured to some sensible umbrella maker that there was no reason why a parasol should not also be an umbrella. Thus was launched the 'En-Tout-Cas' for sun or rain. Common sense, however, is rarely a marketable commodity in fashion merchandise. The heart responds to rhyme not reason, and clothes and their accessories are affairs of the heart. The shape of an umbrella and a parasol may be identical, the material they are made of similar, their handles not unlike; yet there is an entirely different atmosphere about them. The umbrella is tainted with utility; the parasol is a gay and decorative adjunct. Umbrellas are associated with rain and disappointments; parasols, like sundials, mark only the sunny hours.

39. Handles of new parasols at Dickins & Jones, 1887.

CHAPTER XI

HOME DRESSMAKING AND PRIVATE DRESSMAKERS

*The first Sewing Machines; Sewing Machine Shops. Fashion
Magazines with Paper Patterns. Buttericks come to Regent
Street. Madame Goubaud's Paper Models. The dominating
Dressmaker.*

✹✹

THE invention of the sewing machine could well have been not so
much a stroke of genius as of desperation, caused by the ever
increasing amount of sewing required to clothe a fashionable
woman. Up till the 1850's, every seam of every mantle, jacket, and
dress, every stitch of all those innumerable petticoats and voluminous
undergarments, whether made at home or by a dressmaker, or whether
bought in a shop, had been stitched by hand. The sewing machine
arrived in England in the nick of time for the era of maximum clothing;
but the invention was not a miracle worked by *force majeure*, but was a
development from much earlier beginnings.

A French tailor called Barthélemy Thimmonier made a chain-stitch
sewing machine as far back as 1829. When he introduced the machine
into his Parisian clothing factory where army uniforms were made, it
was wrecked by outraged, frightened tailors; but he persisted and
improved his invention, obtaining further patents in France, England,
and the U.S.A. The revolution of 1848 ruined him in France, but he
exhibited at the Great Exhibition of 1851. Strangely enough, no
interest was taken in his machine, and he died a disappointed man.

The next moves came from America. About 1832, William Hunt
invented a machine using a needle with an eye at the point and a
double thread, or lock-stitch; and in 1845, Elias Howe devised one
with a curved needle moving through the cloth at the end of a swinging
arm. The Howe patent was sold to an English corset manufacturer,
William Thomas of Cheapside, for £250. In America, Allen Benjamin

Wilson developed a number of improvements, which Isaac Merrit Singer incorporated in a machine which he patented in 1851. Singer lost no time in making his machine easily available to professional and amateur dressmakers through retail shops: the first in the British Isles was in Glasgow in 1856. Three years later, the Jones sewing machine, made under the Howe patent, was launched, and the Jones Company also opened retail shops in many large towns. But Singer's always kept ahead: by 1877, there were over a hundred and sixty Singer shops. Jones in 1880 pioneered hire purchase.

In his *Retail Trading in Britain*, J. B. Jefferys gives Singer's as the first manufacturers of any kind of goods to develop a chain of retail shops specializing in their product to the exclusion of any other. Singer's certainly developed this form of retail distribution fast and on a country-wide scale. Sangster's umbrella factory had four retail shops in different parts of London in the 1840's, when Carter's corset factory also had a retail shop and mail order service. Thirty years after Singer's, Fleming Reid's Scotch Wool Shops began their chain, selling mainly knitting wool at first. In actual clothing, during nearly the whole of the nineteenth century it was only manufacturers of cheap footwear who were multiple shop owners, and they did not start this method until the 'seventies.

During the 1860's, innumerable firms launched their own makes of sewing machines. Grover & Baker's Celebrated Prize-medal Elasti-stitch Sewing Machine, 'unrivalled for family use in dress and mantle-making, embroiders as well as sews' was advertised in the *Illustrated London News* in 1866. By the next year there were advertisements for three more machines: the Wheeler & Wilson, W. F. Thomas & Co.'s New Patent Sewing-machine, and the Dagmar Sewing Machine named after Princess Alexandra's sister Dagmar, who married the Czar of Russia.

The *Englishwoman's Domestic Magazine* of April 1868 carries the announcements of no less than six different makers, new names being Wright & Mann's Excelsior ('tucks, hems, frills, gathers, cords, quilts, braids, and embroiders'); Willcox & Gibbs; Weir's; Newton & Wilson's; and the Florence Sewing Machine. Machines poured into clothing factories and dressmaking workrooms, as well as into private houses for the use of sewing maids, visiting dressmakers, mothers, daughters and maiden aunts. They gave immense impetus to the clothing trade and to fashion for the middle and lower middle classes. At the same time women's magazines were beginning to provide much better fashion services for their readers.

It was in August 1850 that the *World of Fashion* began to include, in each month's issue, a collection of patterns 'in order that ladies of distinction and their dressmakers may possess the utmost facilities for constructing their costumes with the most approved Taste in the Highest and most Perfect Style of Fashion . . .

These IMPORTANT NOVELTIES will be supplementary, and in addition to the present attractive features of the *World of Fashion*, and without any additional charge, the Price of this Magazine, the Only Authority for Ladies Fashions, being still one shilling only

The *World of Fashion* was rather naughty in calling itself 'the Only Authority for Ladies Fashions', since in 1850 there were being published from London:

La Belle Assemblée
The Ladies Magazine by Jasper Goodwill
Townsend's Quarterly Selection of Parisian Costumes
Le Petit Courrier des Dames
Le Follet Courrier des Salons
The Lady's Gazette of Fashion
The Ladies' Cabinet of Fashion, Music, and Romance
Le Journal des Demoiselles
The Lady's and Gentleman's Diary

And during the 1850's came a new downpour of women's magazines:

The Ladies' Companion at Home and Abroad (1850)
The Englishwoman's Domestic Magazine (1852, published by Mr Beeton who founded the *Queen* in 1861)
The Ladies' Monthly Magazine (1852, previously the *World of Fashion*)
The Ladies' Treasury (1858)
The What-not, or Lady's Handbook (1859)

The inclusion of free paper patterns with the *World of Fashion* was a brilliant circulation-getting idea, and great variety was promised:

Dresses for Morning and Evening, for Balls and for the Sea-side, Sleeves, Bodices, Trimmings, Capes, Caps, Embroideries in great variety and, in fact, everything appertaining to a Lady's Toilette, immediately that it is introduced and accepted in High Society.

More than one pattern was engraved on the tissue paper folded into the magazine. The designs crossed one another, but . . . 'The models may be traced with ease by the peculiar style of line devoted to each. The first issue contained diagrams for a dress, a bonnet, and a capote on one large sheet of tissue. The next month there was a collection of embroidery patterns for 'Capes, Collars, Pantaloons, Veils, Handkerchiefs, Chemises, Spriggs, Medallians, etc. Wreath for bottom of Trowsers'.

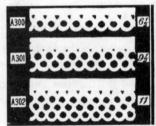

40. I. & R. Morley's
Everlasting Trimming.
White cotton edgings
in three widths,
obtainable in all
haberdashery depart-
ments. 1879.

41. Two examples of black
Chantilly lace and
(bottom) black silk
Maltese Guipure lace.
Debenham &
Freebody Catalogue,
1886.

The inclusion of pantaloons and trousers is unexpected—most fashion historians attribute the wearing of these long-legged under-garments to the cage crinoline, which was not invented when these patterns were issued. In repose, the cage crinoline appeared very modest and lady-like; but in a high wind, or when tilted to go through a narrow doorway, or when its wearer was climbing into a carriage or omnibus, it could be embarrassingly immodest. Its whole function was to allow women to dispense with the many layers of clinging petticoats which had been necessary to support the spreading dress skirts, and which had become a dragging weight. For this purpose, it was eminently successful. Mayhew quotes 'a lady's own testimony . . . In walking it permits a degree of comfort and freedom in movement to which before its use I had been an utter stranger.' And in *Period Piece*, Gwen Raverat recalled:

> Once I asked Aunt Etty what it had been like to wear a crinoline. 'Oh, it was delightful', she said. 'I've never been so comfortable since they went out. It kept your petticoats away from your legs, and made walking so light and easy.'

It was this keeping of your skirts away from your legs, of course, which made the swing and tilt of the crinoline so titillating to male observers. Some sort of decorous clothing to disguise the female anatomy was, in the moral climate of the time, an inevitable adjunct to the crinoline. But since the *World of Fashion* included embroideries for pantaloons and 'wreath for trowsers' in 1850, we must suppose that these were fairly familiar garments before the cage crinoline made them necessary ones. With the shorter crinolines worn in the country for walking, such excitements as red flannel and tartan knickerbockers were not unknown—nor unseen, when climbing over stiles.

⚘   ⚘   ⚘

In America, the 'invention' of paper patterns is claimed by the Butterick Company to have been the brain-wave of Ellen Butterick, wife of a New England tailor, in 1863. But there is evidence that there were paper patterns before that—which indeed seems more than likely since, as related in Chapter IV, paper patterns were in use in England from the beginning of the century. Butterick's may have put them on a more efficiently commercial basis; and certainly when they established an English branch in first floor offices in Regent Street in 1873 it was an immediate success. They claimed that their patterns were produced 'upon principles of the highest scientific accuracy, and by a process the secret of which rests with ourselves' . . . and maybe they were less complicated than the English ones, with their many designs on one sheet. At any rate, business for Butterick's was brisk, and they soon moved into three houses vacated at the closure of Farmer & Rogers, Nos. 171 to 175 Regent Street, and set up a large factory at Chalk Farm.

By the 1880's, Butterick's had a staff of thirty to forty assistants at Regent Street. The monthly output from the factory was between forty and sixty designs, priced from 3d to 2/–. They posted coloured fashion plates to tailors and costumiers in all parts of the world. In addition, they ran a publishing department, with large printing offices near the Old Bailey, equipped with machinery brought from America. Their publications were listed in *Modern London*, 1887:

The Delineator—monthly, ladies', misses', and children's fashions.
The Metropolitan Catalogue—a very fine publication, issued March and September each year, replete with handsome engravings and valuable letterpress.
The Ladies' Monthly Review
The Quarterly Report of Metropolitan Fashions
The Children's & Youths' Semi-annual
The Tailors' Review—monthly—a fund of valuable information and a selection of fine plates and engravings of gentlemen's and juvenile fashions.

Besides the main New York depot, Butterick's had 2,500 agencies in the U.S.A., and several hundreds in Canada. There were between three hundred and four hundred in the United Kingdom at this time, and agencies in all British dependencies and English-speaking countries.

The agents were almost certainly drapers; but unfortunately Butterick's have no record of when such agencies began to be arranged. A year after Butterick came to Regent Street, Madame Adolphe Goubaud opened in Rathbone Place 'a depot for the sale of Berlin wool and needlework patterns in connection with the Paper Model business now so successfully established'. This was the wife of Adolphe Goubaud of 92 rue Richelieu, Paris, with whom in 1860 Samuel and Isabella Beeton arranged a pattern service in their *Englishwomen's Domestic Magazine*. She may not necessarily have come over herself to operate in Rathbone Place, but simply have installed a French manageress. There was also a Madame A. Letellier in Tavistock Street whose models appeared regularly in *Sylvia's Home Journal*. Hers seems to have been a post order business. Bainbridge of Newcastle have a record of having opened a *separate* department for paper patterns in 1881, so one may presume that they sold them in the needlework department or haberdashery for some time before that. Between 1879 and 1895, four Weldon's magazines started publication, carrying their own dress patterns and embroidery transfers.

A pattern issued with *The Young Englishwoman* (another Beeton publication) of October 1867, in the author's possession, carries diagrams for an under-bodice (5 pieces) and a Lady's Chemise (3 pieces). There are engravings of the finished garments, and a price-list of Madame Goubaud's paper models which could be bought either flat or, for an extra charge, tacked together and trimmed. The list of patterns available gives a good indication of what a lady of 1869 wore:

Zouave jackets
Zerlina vest
Veste Russe, for wearing under
    Zouave jackets
Chemise Russe, a kind of tightly-
    fitting Garibaldi Shirt
Short loose jacket for the house
Princess breakfast dress
Senorita bodice and sleeve
Full bodice, for muslin dresses
Louis XIII bodice and sleeve
Low bodice for evening wear,
    including a pretty berthe
Lace pelerines
Fichu Antoinette, with ends to
    cross behind
Zerlina fichu, Gazelle ditto
Loreline capeline
Plain gored skirt
New gored skirt, without pleats
    in front
Lady's peplum
Cloaks for evening wear
Lady's sack dressing-gown

UNDER-LINEN
Chemise
Nightdress
Drawers
Ladies' knickerbockers, for
scarlet flannel
Petticoat body
Nightcap, with strings
Summer ditto, without strings
Train-gored crinoline
Frilled-gored petticoat
Habit-shirt and sleeve
Bathing dress, complete

New cloaks and mantles, tacked together and trimmed, 3s 6d each, including
a flat pattern to cut from.

The *Young Ladies' Journal* was another magazine which carried free paper patterns. They evidently had a tie-up with Nicholson's of St Paul's Churchyard because Nicholson's advertised in the magazine that they could supply all the goods represented by the illustrations, and would send a thousand patterns of their newest silks and dress materials post free. A thousand patterns seems rather overdoing it— an embarrassment of choice. The *Young Ladies' Journal* called their sheets of patterns a Gigantic Supplement, and not without reason

42. WALKING DRESSES FOR COUNTRY AND SEASIDE WEAR.

Flat Pattern, 3/1d. by post from Madame A. Letellier, 40 Tavistock Street, Covent Garden.

These styles may be obtained from James Spence & Co., 76-79 St Paul's Churchyard, E.C. Estimates Free. *Sylvia's Home Journal*, October 1879.

since, when the sheet is unfolded, it measures 49" × 33". One dated July 1885 has full-size patterns for a chemise with stomacher front and for a French chemise with embroidery. The embroidery designs are also given. There is a 'Notice to Subscribers':

The Proprietors of the *Young Ladies' Journal* beg to solicit special attention to their MADE-UP and FULL-TRIMMED Patterns, which they think will be found cheaper and better than any yet sold elsewhere. All the *Young Ladies' Journal* made-up patterns are tacked, not gummed, so that they can be taken to pieces to cut from, rendering flat patterns unnecessary in addition to the Made-up ones. Flat patterns ONLY may be had as given below. The patterns, unless otherwise ordered, are supplied a medium size and are so perfectly cut that they can be readily adapted to suit any figure.

In order to ensure earliest receipt, direct from Paris, of all Novelties in Ladies' and Children's Dress, we have made special arrangements with MADAME RUDOLPHINE to reside in Paris, for the purpose of paying daily visits to all the producing Fashion Houses, obtain Designs, and send us MODELS EVERY WEEK.

On the reverse side of the giant sheet, there are no less than seventy-three fashion engravings listed, with detailed descriptions, of which this is an example:

No. 47. *Visiting Costume.* The skirt is of fawn beige, ornamented with bows of ruby ribbon and steel buckles; the polonaise is of ruby beige, lined with fawn satin, looped with a bow of ruby ribbon; the polonaise shows a waistcoat of fawn satin pleated in folds at the waist, a velvet band catches it across the front, the collar and cuffs are also in velvet. Price of pattern of dress, trimmed 4/6. Polonaise, trimmed 3/6; flat 1/-.

With such extreme complications of dressmaking, and at such a price, it seems likely that many of the purchasers would be professional dressmakers who could make use of the patterns over and over again for many different clients.

⚜   ⚜   ⚜

The 'Court Dressmaker' (or couturière) whose premises consisted of salon, fitting rooms, and workrooms, and the 'Private Dressmaker' who received clients in her own house or fitted them at their homes, were still the most important factors in fashion . . . very human factors, whose livelihood depended on creating clothes, both for the fashionable and the frumpish, from the materials and trimmings which were the stock in trade of drapers' shops. The private dressmaker tended to be humble and anxious to please; the court dressmaker, if her business was successful, could become a despot. Mrs Ada Ballin, herself a very strong-minded woman who never pulled her punches, had this to say of dressmakers in *The Science of Dress:*

> It wants both knowledge and firmness to get a dress properly made; for the maker as a rule has a powerful store of arguments by which she defends her errors, and the genus dressmaker is too apt to keep the genus lady in a state of hopeless and miserable subjection. I think it is time that we should strike against this tyranny, and refuse to employ any couturière who will not allow us to have some voice in the construction of our own garments. Why not form an Anti-Dressmakers' Tyranny League, something in the same style as the Early Shopping Association? Surely we have our rights as well as the lower classes, although philanthropists too generally ignore them. All garments which can be made by a tailor should be so made. For tailors are not only more accurate in their fit than dressmakers but they are also more attentive to instructions, and less pig-headed, if I may be allowed to use that very suggestive expression.

She did not seem, in fact, to have much diffidence about using suggestive expressions, and it would be a brave dressmaker indeed who tried conclusions with Mrs Ada Ballin. But there were plenty more timid ladies who lived in spiritual subjection to the women they paid to attend to their bodily adornment. . . . and there were thousands of still more timid seamstresses who were paid very little to work long, long hours on the elaborate creations decreed by the dressmakers for their clients.

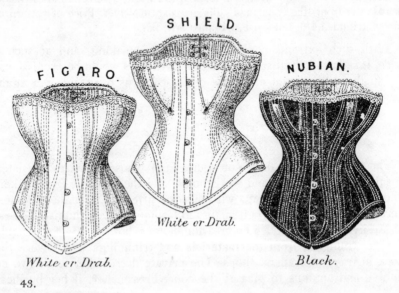

SHIELD.

FIGARO.

NUBIAN.

White or Drab.

White or Drab.

Black.

43.

CHAPTER XII

THE EARLY DAYS OF
READY-TO-WEAR

Ready-made Mantles. Part-made dresses; Made skirts with un-made bodices. Promenade costumes, Yachting Suits, and Bathing Dresses. Trousseaux and India Outfits. End of the Crinoline and of the Second Empire.

'I cannot determine what to do about my new gown; I wish such things were to be bought ready-made.' We are back with Jane Austen's letters, and the date is December 24, 1798. Miss Austen lived for another nineteen years, but she would never have been able to buy a ready-made gown. A mantle or cloak, perhaps, but not certainly. The earliest wholesale mantle manufactory in the City is said to have been founded by D. Nicholson of King William Street in 1837, and this would have been well established supplying shops before he joined his brother in 1843 to open the retail and wholesale drapery establishment of Nicholson's of St Paul's.

Lady Stanley of Alderley wrote to her daughter-in-law, Lady Eddisbury, in August 1849: 'When I was in Chester I went to Brown's to buy a gown and was tempted by "the next article", a love of a cloak, like Blanche's in some respects but black instead of brown and longer, and two such delightful pockets in front. I shall wonder how I ever did without it in the cold weather.' In writing of a gown, Lady Stanley will have meant a length of material to make a gown; but clearly the cloak, with its two delightful pockets, was a made-up garment. That does not mean that it was bought by Brown's from a wholesale mantle manufactory: it was much more likely, since Brown's was an 'exclusive' establishment, to have been designed and made in their own workrooms.

Although dresses were not sold ready-made, it was possible to buy them part-made, even before Victoria came to the throne. In 1830,

16, Cannon Street,

Gentⁿ

We have the pleasure of submitting our New Book of Designs for Waterproof Cloaks.

In some of the styles we think you will recognise a great improvement upon those of last year; the Brighton Coat, the Ramsgate, and Atlantic Wrap are all likely to be leading & popular shapes.

Our former price list, having led to a considerable increase of trade, the present quotations have been framed on the same tariff.

Soliciting your orders large or small,

We are, Gentⁿ
Your obedᵗ Servants,

Sélincourt & Colman.

OSBORNE.

(PLAIN IN TWEED ONLY)

BLUE TICKET QUALITY

| Nº 31 | length 52 inches | fullness 172 | 18/- |
| 32 | 56 | 188 | 19/6 |

ORANGE TICKET QUALITY.

| Nº 131 | length 52 inches | fullness 172 | 21/6 |
| 132 | 56 | 188 | 23/6 |

ATLANTIC.

(PLAIN, IN TWEED OR CHECK)

BLUE TICKET QUALITY.

| Nº 71 | length 52 inches | fullness 144 | 16/9 |
| 72 | 56 | 156 | 17/9 |

ORANGE TICKET QUALITY

| Nº 171 | length 52 inches | fullness 144 | 19/6 |
| 172 | 56 | 156 | 21/6 |

WATERPROOF CHECK

| Nº 271 | length 52 inches | fullness 144 | 19/6 |
| 272 | 56 | 156 | 21/6 |

44. Three pages from Sélincourt & Colman's catalogue to the trade, *circa* 1860. Other designs illustrated were named BRIGHTON, TORQUAY, EDINBORO', LONDON, WINDSOR, RAMSGATE. The last page gave a measurement diagram for shops placing special orders.

The Early Days of Ready-to-wear

T. Challinier of 109 New Bond Street advertised in the *World of Fashion:*

Muslin Bodices exceedingly useful to the country trade . . . the dresses can be completed for wearing in a few hours' notice.

This firm evidently sold wholesale to country drapers and dressmakers to whom it would be a great convenience to have the latest styles from London already cut out and partially put together, requiring only one fitting on their customers before completion. The bodices of the 1820's and 1830's, with their enormous sleeves, must have presented severe complications of cutting and construction. In any case, all dresses were made with separate bodices and skirts until the 'Princess Dress' began to come in during the 'sixties.

Some of the larger London and provincial shops sold clothes part-made, which their customers own dressmakers could finish to fit. And there was also the scheme by which skirts were sold completely finished, with material and trimmings to make the bodice of the dress. This method appears in shop catalogues and advertisements right up to the end of the century, and even later. Harrods' 'ever popular unmade robes' advertised in 1908 were probably partially made as well as cut out. Peter Robinson's 'un-made dresses' of that time 'only required joining up the back'.

It is possible that Bainbridge of Newcastle were one of the first, if not the first, to stock completely ready-made dresses, since in 1845 they were including in their list of goods stocked 'Sewed Muslin Dresses'; but again, we cannot tell if they were completely finished. Without doubt, however, Jay's had completely ready-made dresses in 1866, as they were advertising in the *Illustrated London News:*

JAY'S PATENT EUTHEMIA, a self-expanding bodice, recommended to ladies in cases of sudden bereavement or any less painful emergency, when a ready-made and stylish dress is required at a moment's notice.

They had devised an ingenious method of overcoming deviations from the female norm without having to stock dresses in many different measurements.

One of the earliest wholesale firms to make ready-to-wear clothes other than mantles was that of Sélincourt & Colman of 16 Cannon Street in the City. Charles de Sélincourt was of a Huguenot family, and his son Martin Wilfrid carried on the business after him. During the first year of their business, 1857, they numbered amongst their customers such important shops as Harvey Nichols' and Shoolbred's in London, Jolly's of Bath, Hannington's of Brighton, and the two Reading firms, Heelas & Son, and Wellsteed's—all shops that were still on the books of Sélincourt & Sons a hundred years later. Although they began with mantles, by 1869 their records show that they were also supplying waterproofs, costumes, shawls, and children's clothes. They issued illustrated brochures to the trade, one of the early 1860's is shown in Fig. 44. When the author met Miss Saunders, she was a nonagenarian living at the Linen & Woollen Drapers' Cottage Homes. She told how she was apprenticed to Sélincourt & Sons in 1886, and used to start work at 5 o'clock in the morning. She remembered particularly their long opera cloaks with Medici collars, made of black plush with jet embroidery. These they supplied to all the better class shops such as Dickins & Jones, Peter Robinson, Marshall & Snelgrove, and Gorringe's. The buyers used to come on Mondays and Tuesdays to pack up their orders and take them away.

✢   ✢   ✢

Julius Price in his *Dame Fashion*, published in 1909, says that the years 1854–60 saw the opening of 'large shops where ready-made costumes could be bought—the forerunners of the huge emporiums'; but it was not so much that new large shops were being opened but that the existing shops, such as those on Sélincourt's list of customers, were extending their premises and carrying more varied merchandise, including ready-made garments. In 1866, Redmayne & Co. of 19 & 20 New Bond Street and 35 Conduit Street were advertising 'Made-up skirts for walking'; and Horsley & Co. of 71 Oxford Street announced: LADIES' VELVETEEN SUITS—Velveteen short costumes, with petticoat complete. John Harvey & Son of 69 Ludgate Hill advertised 'Coloured serge costumes at 25/6 to 50/–'.

   Chas. Ammott of 61 and 62 St Paul's Churchyard was at this time offering a handsome catalogue which contained 'portraits' of thirty fashionable but anonymous ladies. These prototype gentlewomen were dressed in such up-to-date attire as Serge Suits (1 gn) and Rich Velvet Suits, which included jacket, skirt and petticoat, for 2 gns. This use of the word suit is interesting, as the more usual name for a two piece outdoor walking outfit was costume. The term costume obtained until after the First World War, when it was changed to 'coat and skirt'. It was not until the 1930's that they became suits again. In 1866, Chas. Ammott had a sale and offered 'Several hundred Made Dresses and Costumes at reduced prices in Yeddo Poplin, Russian Silk Linseys, Paris Silk Poplins, Aberdeen Wincey, Nanking cloths, etc.' This sounds rather as though it were a bankrupt's stock bought up cheaply to appeal to non-wealthy customers; but in 1866

45. Bathing Costumes from Marshall & Snelgrove, Oxford Street.

Bathing-dresses do not materially alter from year to year, and the fabrics are but limited. Swimmers show a preference for striped flannelette which is pretty to look at and light to wear; serge and ordinary flannel find more general favour, and a few who love the water use thick bunting. Sometimes the trousers are cut in one with the bodice, and sometimes are separate.

Lady's World, August 1887.

127

not many low income women read newspapers and magazines. An advertiser in the *Illustrated London News* would be out for carriage trade.

Peter Robinson, at this time, was evidently a great believer in the influence of this weekly, because his advertisements appear in the classified column each week, usually several announcements in each issue, of which this is an example:

> An endless variety of ready-made suits in Navy Blue Tweed, Serge, Diagonal Cloth, White serge Flannel, Velvet Pile, Llama, Grenadine, Alpaca, Lustre, Cashmere. Fancy Summer Cloth, and Beach Linseys. Yachting, Seaside, and Summer Jackets in endless variety. The Inverness with cape; the Seacoast with hood and sleeves. Circular Waterproof Mantles in Shrewsbury Waterproof Tweeds, A., B., & C. sizes.

This itemizing of three sizes indicates that the manufacture of ready-made garments was becoming more organized. Sélincourt & Colman had, even earlier, been supplying mantles in three different lengths and fullnesses; but suits and jackets required much more detailed sizing. The sewing machine was now well entrenched in clothing factories and workrooms, and was an essential factor in the ready-to-wear movement—indeed, the prime factor. It was about 1856 that John Barron's clothing factory in Leeds first used sewing machines; and three years later they were operating the band saw for cutting several thicknesses of cloth at one time.

Running parallel with the trend towards ready-made, was the idea of designing clothes especially for leisure occupations and activities. Clothes for the rain were the first ready-made women's garments designed to meet specific conditions. Croquet costumes, which occasionally figured in the fashion magazines of the 'sixties, might be said to be the first designed for a particular activity—although by no stretch of the imagination could those crinolined or prodigiously petticoated dresses be called sports clothes. Archery was very popular at country houses in the 1870's, but had no attire of its own—one simply wore garden-party dresses. Roller skating, or 'rinking', a sudden craze of the early 70's, lost favour very quickly mainly because the current fashions ordained tighter and ever tighter skirts. Eventually a fashionable dress made it impossible to walk upstairs, let alone skim round a rink, stoop to adjust a skate, or struggle up after a fall. The second great craze for roller skating came in Edwardian times. Skirts were then gored and flared, and the craze lasted longer.

Seaside holidays were indulged in by many more people as the century progressed, and gave inspiration for special fashions. As we have seen, Peter Robinson was advertising yachting and seaside jackets

I   Whiteley's in Westbourne Grove at the fashionable shopping hour of 4.30 p.m., *c.* 1900.

Customers leaving Bradley's Arctic Fur Store, Chepstow Place, after a parade of models in 1911.

VIII

Kensington High Street in 1860.

Kensington High Street *c.* 1910, John Barker's

in the mid-'sixties; and H. J. & D. Nicoll of Regent Street also announced serge, tweed, and cloth Promenade Costumes especially designed for the seaside holiday. These thick, heavy materials scarcely confirm that the summers were warmer then, although one must take into account that the seaside season went on until the beginning of November. Even Farmer & Rogers' Shawl Emporium rather surprisingly advertised, in 1867, an Atlantic Yachting Suit of Royal Naval serge . . . 'a very durable and pretty suit for Seaside Wear'. Unfortunately there is no picture or any detailed description; it would be interesting to know how these specialists in such soft and feminine things as shawls and oriental fabrics tackled tough naval serge.

Six years earlier, the *What-Not, or Ladies' Handbook* illustrated a seaside costume. Immensely crinolined, it was made of white piqué, with many seamed bodice, plaited stomacher, and elaborate sleeves. This may have been durable, but was hardly practical with its hem dragging along the sand. A round hat of Fribany straw, ornamented with a black velvet ribbon and two velvet cockades completed the costume. The round hat was the great seaside craze for several seasons from 1861.

Unlikely though it may seem, the young ladies who dressed themselves in these elaborate and beribboned garments for the beach— garments which covered tight-laced corsets and a multitude of under-clothes—did actually bathe. So, also, did their stout-hearted and stout-bosomed mothers. Undressing and dressing in the bathing hut must have been an interminable and tortuous exercise. Several London shops at this period were advertising ready-made bathing costumes of navy serge and flannel. The *What-Not* of 1861 preferred the former:

The chief draw-back to ladies swimming is the bathing-dress used in this country. The most commodious, and at the same time the most pleasant to the wearer, is a garment consisting of a dress and drawers in one, made of grey serge, and having a band to confine the waist. They are also far preferable, in all cases, to the common blue flannel, which, when saturated with water, becomes very heavy and inconvenient.

Grey serge, when saturated with water, would surely be equally dragging around the limbs, as Victorian legs were called. But generally speaking, the ladies did not swim: they bobbed about screaming in the shallow water. There were, however, some advocates of swimming for young ladies: 'We hope our fair readers will not be shocked if we say a few words on swimming. No one can experience the real pleasure of bathing unless they possess this, to some persons, unfeminine accomplishment.'

Most women made their own underclothes, and always by hand, even after the sewing machine got into the house. The mystique that under-clothes must never be sewn by machine obtained well into the twentieth century. There were, however, all through the Victorian period, specialists in lady's under-linen from whom ladies ordered their trousseaux, or actually bought ready-made. But, even when ready-made, they had been sewn by hand. In the 1830's there was Graham's Family Linen Warehouse at 207 Regent Street, specializing in Marriage and Outfitting Orders, and Ladies' and Gentlemen's ready-made linen. Outfitting was the euphemism employed for both men's and women's underclothes. Before the 1850's, there was the Maison Brie at 43 Conduit Street, *Spécialité de Lingerie*. Established in 1851 in Regent Street, there was the redoubtable Mrs Washington Moon, Ladies' and Children's Outfitter, who basked in the sunshine of the Royal Warrant. Mrs Washington Moon was evidently quite the lady herself, because her husband was a Fellow of the Royal Society of Literature and an author. Later she moved to a house at 16 New Burlington Street which was formerly the residence of Lord de L'Isle and Dudley and afterwards of Mr Dion Boucicault the dramatist. In fact, it was a high-class liaison of literature and lingerie.

The Princess of Wales, although coming from Denmark to be married, ordered her wedding trousseau with Christian & Rathbone of 11 Wigmore Street and later her layettes. At this time, wedding trousseaux and layettes were always listed together in advertisements and catalogues, the one requirement following the other in swift sequence. Maternity clothes are never mentioned, except in corsetry, and it seems probable that ladies adapted their own garments. From the 1830's until the end of the crinoline, the enormously full skirts conveniently hid a lady's 'interesting condition' until the last. But the dresses of the 'seventies and 'eighties, which swathed the body from bust to knee, must have forced pregnant fashionables to cancel their engagements much earlier than their mothers had done for them.

The trade in ladies' ready-made underwear increased after the mid-century. In the 1860's, George Roberts had a Ladies' Outfitting Warehouse at 183 Oxford Street, and a branch at 11 Lowndes Terrace, where he sold stays, underskirts, hosiery, and ready-made linen. And Chas. Ammott & Co. of 61 and 62 St Paul's Churchyard advertised, in 1867, a sale of underclothes upon such a scale that one would think it was wholesale stock for trade buyers, if it were not that the announcement appeared in the *Illustrated London News*: '700 very fine flannel petticoats in scarlet or white; 1,000 camisoles; tucked drawers; long-cloth chemises; Horrocks's long-cloth tucked petticoats, banded'.

The appearance of Horrocks in this advertisement is significant, for it was very early for a manufacturer's name to be given. Moreover, these Horrocks's underclothes would be some of the first machine-sewn undergarments. In the 1879 trade catalogue of I. & R. Morley, there are plenty of hand-made lines; also several pages of lock-stitched underclothing, '*Our Own Manufacture—warranted well made: Long-cloth night dresses, Long-cloth Chemises, Long-cloth Drawers, and Knickerbockers.* Machine-made underclothing, not lock-stitched, was listed as '*Our Own Manufacture—warranted well made: Calico Bodies, Camisoles, Long-cloth and Nainsook*'. Ladies' underclothing, sets of nightdress, chemise and drawers were offered '*neatly arranged and Boxed for Window or Show Room*'. The largest section in Morley's catalogue was of woven underwear: merino, merino finish, Segovia, lambswool, cotton, silk and spun silk, India gauze, and gauze merino.

In the 1860's the best known underclothes specialist was Mrs Addley Bourne, Family Draper, Jupon and Corset Manufacturer to the Court and Royal Family—37 Piccadilly, opposite St. James's Church. Mrs Addley Bourne circulated her customers with a Book of Illustrations which contained fashion information and all the New Designs in Underclothing—crinolines, corsets, camisoles, etc.—and included the 'Alice', 'Maude', 'Helena', 'Beatrice', and 'Dagmar' nightdresses. It was evidently not *lèse majesté* to name an article of underclothes after the princesses of the blood royal, as long as the garments themselves were not unmentionable. Petticoats and chemises were named after Royalty, but never drawers. Morley's dared an Alexandra corset.

In 1866 Mrs Bourne launched her Sansflectum Jupons, in which no steel was used. The Demi-Sansflectum, 2 yds round 10/6; the Full Sansflectum, 2½ yds round, 12/6. The *Morning Post* reported these to be 'a great refinement of the hoops or farthingale'; and *Le Follet* commended them as 'Elegant in form and moderate in proportion'. The *Queen* was more specific in describing them: 'The circles are like indiarubber.' They may have been a type of inflatable crinoline made with rubber tubes. These had a vogue for some time, exaggerated by *Punch* with jokes about punctures and suggestions for filling the tubes with water as a precaution against fire-danger.

Like all underclothes specialists, Mrs Addley Bourne made a feature of 'India Outfits'. She also listed outfits for Japan, China, and Australia, from £20 to £100. These were the days when young brides set sail on the long, long voyage for the unknown East with bridegrooms who were usually almost as unknown. Courtships had to be conclusively conducted during leave from the Indian Army, the Indian Civil Service, from a tea plantation, or some other far-flung post in the parts marked

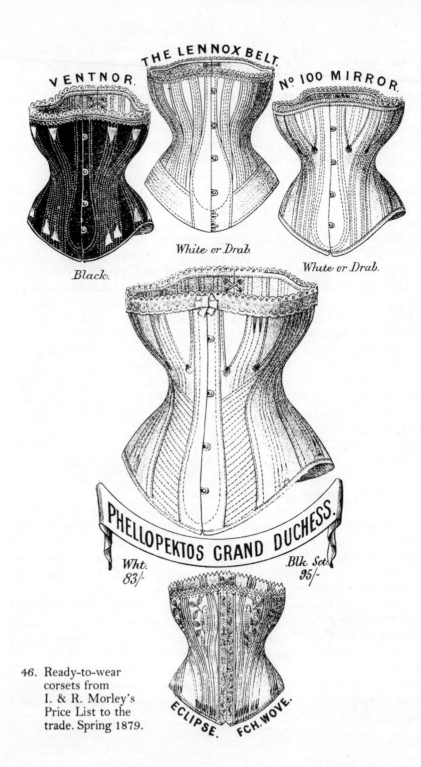

VENTNOR.

Black.

THE LENNOX BELT.

White or Drab.

Nº 100 MIRROR.

White or Drab.

PHELLOPEKTOS GRAND DUCHESS.

Wht.
83/-

Blk. Set.
95/-

ECLIPSE.   FCH. WOVE.

46. Ready-to-wear
corsets from
I. & R. Morley's
Price List to the
trade. Spring 1879.

pink on the map to denote British Empire. Sometimes a bride ordering an 'India Outfit' was sailing out to be married overseas, and must have been in equal trepidation about the country she knew nothing of, and the fiancé she had not seen for, perhaps, several years. Often unmarried daughters, not so young, were sent out to relatives on a last hope bid to find a husband in the lands where, in contrast to England, the number of marriageable men exceeded the number of eligible girls.

An 'India Outfit' was very similar to a trousseau, except that the garments were made in cooler materials. This was Mrs Addley Bourne's £20 trousseau of 1866:

6 Beatrice chemises	1 Printed cambric dressing-gown
3 Alexandra ditto	1 Coloured flannel ditto
4 Alice nightdresses	1 White hair cord dressing jacket
2 Maude ditto	12 Pairs white cotton hose
6 Pairs long-cloth drawers, tucked	6 Hem-stitched ditto
3 ditto, trimmed with work	12 Cambric pocket-handkerchiefs
2 Long-cloth petticoats, tucked	6 Hem-stitched ditto
1 ditto, trimmed with work	1 Pair French wove corsets
3 Camisoles, trimmed with work	1 Patent sansflectum crinoline
3 ditto, extra good	6 Fine huckaback towels
3 Merino vests	Haberdashery (an assortment)
3 Flannel petticoats	

Something of the size of Mrs Addley Bourne's business can be guessed at from the fact that in 1866 she was advertising in the *Illustrated London News:*

A THOUSAND CRINOLINES AT HALF-PRICE . . . commencing at 5/11, usually 10/6. Piccadilly Puffed Jupons 15/6; striped Linsey 8/3. Beautiful shapes but a little dusty—offered for a short time during stock-taking.

Crinolines must have been very difficult merchandise to store in a shop; and yet Mrs Bourne claimed a stock of over a thousand! And although she gives as her reason for selling them off at half price that they are a little dusty, one suspects that this shrewd business woman had realized the days of the crinoline were numbered . . . a Paris newspaper's description of the ball-dress worn by a well-known leader of fashion at the Tuileries in 1865 had ended with the significant words 'No Crinoline'.

Nearly three years later, in April 1868, that busy little fashion columnist 'Silkworm' of *The Englishwoman's Domestic Magazine* was in raptures over some pretty jupons that had arrived from 'dear, sweet, darling Paris' at Jay's. These petticoats were in 'a soft material, quite new, composed of silk and wool'. Soft materials of any kind were excitingly new for petticoats. 'Silkworm', however, disappointingly goes on to report, 'A very nice crinoline was also shown..It is gored, or rather shaped, so as to almost fit the figure at the top. It is made of real crinoline, and has a full fluting round the edge, supported at top and edge by a row of the finest steel.'

Messrs Jay's were no doubt catering with this crinoline for their more old-fashioned customers, the die-hards in the last ditches of the shires. For in 1866 *Punch* had pictures of maid servants apeing their betters by leaving off their crinolines; . . . and in the winter of 1867, crinolines had become so completely *vieux jeux* that Paterfamilias is depicted using his daughters' discards to cover delicate garden shrubs against frost. Georgiana Hill wrote in 1893 that by 1868, or there-abouts, the crinoline was practically gone:

> A council was held in Paris by the leaders of fashion anent the crinoline, and there was a good deal said in its favour. One argument was that the high heels of the shoes made women walk so badly they could not support the weight of their gowns without the crinoline. The conference ended in a compromise. The crinoline was modified into a petticoat, with some stiff bands round the bottom and up the back.

Nevertheless, the same issue of *The Englishwoman's Domestic Magazine* which carried 'Silkworm's' description of the crinoline at Jay's also advertised Thomson's Sephyrina or Winged Jupon (Fig. 29), which was definitely made of steel in the shape which later became known as the crinolette.

However, the news from Paris was soon changed from fashions to battles. In July 1870 came the Franco-Prussian War. In September, as the Prussians closed in upon Paris, the Empress Eugénie, crinoline's most glamorous promoter, escaped from the Tuileries by a back entrance. Escorted by her American dentist and one lady-in-waiting, she fled to England. The Tuileries, scene of so many extravagant balls, was burned down by the populace and the City of Fashion became a city under siege.

The year 1870 was a significant milestone in the story of British fashion and the evolution of ready-made clothes. The crinoline had at last ended its long sway, and fashion was no longer dictated from Paris: the English tailor-made costume began its era of supremacy. Debenham & Freebody still have a copy of their *New Fashion Book* of October 1870, in which they say: 'Having made arrangements for an early supply of Models from Paris, our Mantle, Costume, Millinery, and Lingerie Departments contain as much Novelty and Variety as in any previous season.' In other words, they had seen the Prussians coming, and made their Paris purchases in time to get delivery before Paris was surrounded.

This *New Fashion Book* was the second catalogue of its kind that they had sent out to customers in town and country. It contains very beautiful steel engravings of model gowns and costumes, and the text shows that there were four ways of buying them:

1. Made to measure in the Dressmaking Department.
2. Buying the skirt ready-made and having the jacket or bodice made up in the workrooms to one's own measurements. (This system was particularly recommended in the Mourning Room, which contained 'a ready assortment of made skirts suited to any degree of mourning').
3. Ready-made.
4. Post Order. Patterns and designs were forwarded free to all parts of Great Britain, India, and the Colonies. An outline figure indicated what measurements should be sent; alternately, ladies could send an old bodice to be used as a guide for size.

Naturally, all the beautiful models illustrated could not be obtained ready-made; but 'The increasing taste for Made-up Costumes, in every material, has compelled us to enlarge our Costume Room since last season. This alteration will provide increased convenience to Ladies, and enable us to keep a larger stock of these Goods than formerly'.

The charges in the Dressmaking Department are:

Making Plain Dress	10/6
Making Dress, with fancy trimmings from	12/6
Making Evening Dress, of light material, with low bodice from ..	10/6

EXTRAS

Silk body lining, 5/6; silk sleeve lining, 3/6; silk low body and sleeve lining, 5/6; lawn sleeve lining, 2/6; sundries, 1/6.

Charges for Making Bodices to Complete Costumes and Ball Dresses

Bodice Complete to Ball Dresses of Tulle and Tarlatan	12/6
Bodice Complete to Costumes or skirts of light summer materials	12/6
To ditto ditto in Winter materials from	12/6
To ditto ditto in Silk from	15/–

By this arrangement Ladies may select their Dresses and Costumes in the various Rooms, and have them completed at a small expense.

The *New Fashion Book* reveals that the term lingerie had come to mean underclothes, whereas previously it had meant collars, cuffs, jabots, frills, fichus, and all those delicate frothy things made of lace and fine linen at which the French excel. Here there is no doubt that it means underclothes:

LINGERIE DEPARTMENT. We would respectfully invite attention to this Department, which contains every requisite for Wedding Trousseaux,

Indian Outfits, etc. A new suite of private Show Rooms secures every con-
venience to Ladies selecting their goods. Competent persons wait upon
Ladies at home in any part of the country. Catalogues and Estimates for
Wedding Outfits, from £20 to any amount, forwarded by post.

Although the engravings in this Debenham catalogue are of very
dignified gowns and costumes, there was a confusion of styles after the
fall of Paris in 1870. There were 'classic' figures and 'Grecian Bends';
and a very popular panniered style, with looped up skirts and polonaise,
which was variously called the Pompadour, Louis XV, Watteau
Costume, or Toilette la à Shepherdess. In the same genre was the style
called 'Dolly Varden Costume'. This was designed in 1870 soon after
the death of Dickens and the sale of the painting he had commissioned
from W. P. Frith of the coquettish heroine of *Barnaby Rudge*. Dolly
Varden hats were worn everywhere; although the complete Dolly
Varden costume was not so ubiquitous. It comprised a soft flower-
sprigged dress with puffed polonaise and paniered skirt over a different
coloured underskirt, and was particularly popular at the seaside and as
a garden-party dress. One would say that it was only appropriate for
coquettish daughters; but a certain number of ill-advised middle-aged
women wore it as well. In *Victorian Best-seller* there is an account of
the visit of Miss Elizabeth Wordsworth, first Principal of Lady Margaret Hall, to the home of Charlotte M. Yonge, the novelist. It was
in 1872, when Miss Yonge was forty-nine years old—decidedly
middle-aged for a Victorian. She was in the drawing-room after dinner,
and Miss Wordsworth described her hostess as looking 'more like an
old French *Marquise* than ever, in a red and black Dolly Varden dress,
with pink skirt . . . and showing a very pretty pair of feet in white
open-work stockings'.

It seems that Miss Yonge, like many other literary ladies, had a
penchant for dressing rather spectacularly on important occasions; but
she also had the reputation of being normally extremely untidy in her
personal appearance. Certainly she seems to have had small confidence in
herself: coming out of church on the Sunday morning of this visit, she
whispered to Miss Wordsworth, 'Do tell me, *is* my hat on hind side
before? I have had such horrid misgivings about it'.

CHAPTER XIII

THE BEGINNING OF THE
DEPARTMENT STORES

Bon Marché, Paris; Kendal Milne, Manchester; Bainbridge,
Newcastle. Drapery Shops into Stores. The prosperous new
Middle Class. Growth of London and Travel Facilities.
Shopping in the 'seventies. The Paget Elopement.

S TRANGE irony of fame that the Bon Marché of Paris should have
the reputation of being the first department store in the world!
The French, who sneered at the English as 'a nation of shopkeepers', have been given the palm for pioneering modern methods of
retail trading. Yet the innovations which Monsieur and Madame
Bouçicaut introduced to Parisian shopkeeping in the 1850's would not
have been new in London. And there were provincial English shops
which developed into department stores long before the Bon Marché
first opened selling piece-goods only.

The explanation may be that American business men 'discovered'
the Bon Marché, wrote about it, and based their own great stores upon
its methods. Few travellers from the New World will have visited
Bainbridge's of Newcastle nor Kendal Milne & Faulkner of Manchester
before 1850. But these two shops can with justice be nominated as the
first department stores, with the proviso that there may possibly be
other provincial shops with equal claims whose early days have not
been studied for this history. The great London stores were a little
later in branching out into diverse lines of merchandise; but even so
many of them already operated some of the principles which Monsieur
and Madame Bouçicaut introduced to Paris. Let us take the Bon
Marché story first.

In 1852, the Bouçicauts opened a small retail shop on the unfashionable Left Bank, selling piece-goods only. Soon they added dresses and

137

ladies' coats, and by about 1860 had separate departments for under-wear, millinery, and shoes. From the beginning, they pioneered several important customer services hitherto unknown in Paris. The first was to offer only goods with marked prices, instead of allowing the current practice of individual bargaining. The second was that anybody could enter the shop and look around without the obligation to purchase which dominated the atmosphere of other Paris shops. The third was to give customers the right to exchange goods or get their money refunded. Competing retailers called these innovations *'du romantisme en boutique'* and prophesied disaster. But Bouçicaut went forward with courage. His next innovation was to announce periodical sales of goods at bargain prices. He then started daily deliveries to every part of Paris by van and by foot-porters, and gave quality guarantees on higher grade articles with cash refunds for goods which proved below standard. All these things brought the Bon Marché such brisk business that they were able to reduce profit margins. The current practice with piece-goods was to sell with a slow stock turn and a high mark-up; but the Bon Marché went for quantity sales with lower profits.

Now let us compare the story of Kendal Milne, or, as their shop was originally called 'The Bazaar'. From its establishment in 1831 there was the rule that *'Prices shall be marked on all the goods, from which no abatement shall be made'*; and one of the attractions of the Bazaar method of trading (which has been described in Chapter II), was that people could walk round and look at everything on the different counters without feeling any obligation to buy. In 1837, one year after Kendal Milne & Faulkner had acquired the business, they announced 'a sale of silk mercery, linens, shawls, Tuscan and straw bonnets and other items essential to the lady of fashion'. As soon as the shop next door became vacant, the partners acquired it, and added upholstery and carpets to their merchandise, and about the same time became also 'Funeral Undertakers and suppliers of complete mourning outfits'. Soon cabinet-making was added. All this was before the Bon Marché opened, selling piece-goods only. Kendal, Milne & Faulkner's trade card on the opposite page gives the full range of their trading, and shows the well-designed shop front of the Bazaar, with recessed doorways for maximum window display.

The story of Bainbridge's of Newcastle also begins in 1830, when Emerson Muschamp Bainbridge was apprenticed, at the age of thirteen, to a Newcastle draper called Robert Kidd, who had a wholesale and retail business in Side. After serving his time with Kidd, Bainbridge spent two years getting London experience with Lewis & Allenby of Regent Street. He then returned to his birthplace, and in 1838 was

47. Trade card of 1847 listing Kendal, Milne & Faulkner's specialities at The Bazaar.

taken into partnership by William Dunn, who had two small shops in Market Street which he called Albion House. By 1841, Bainbridge was advertising that he intended to run 12 Market Street on his own as Albion House. Dunn continued in No. 13, and seems later to have claimed the name of Albion House. Bainbridge countered with the equally loyal and much more contemporary name of Albert House.

So far, the story of Bainbridge is much the same as that of many ambitious young men apprenticed to the drapery trade who realized the value of gaining London experience before starting out in their own home towns. But Bainbridge was evidently exceptionally enterprising, and set about introducing a number of innovations in advance of his time—and very much in advance of the Bon Marché. By 1845, seven years before the Bon Marché opened, Bainbridge's stock included dress and furnishing fabrics, fashion accessories, furs, and family mourning, as well as 'sewed muslin dresses'—an early form of ready-to-wear clothes. The shop already had ten assistants, and by 1849 their stock books show they had expanded to twenty-three separate sets of takings. Moreover, from the time Bainbridge was on his own, that is from 1841, he abolished bargaining and labelled all his merchandise with fixed prices. He also encouraged shoppers to walk round without obligation to purchase. By these means his turnover was so quick that he could work on a lower mark-up than smaller, more specialist, shops. An advertisement of 1856 said that Bainbridge's 'had no hesitation in stating that they will sell all Goods in the Woollen Branch of their Business at Prices with which exclusively Woollen Houses cannot compete'.

In 1852, the year that the Bon Marché opened their little piece-goods shop, Bainbridge's acquired yet another shop in Market Street, to open ready-made clothing and men's mercery departments; and by that time there was also a flourishing wholesale section. In 1865, Bainbridge's bought a stretch of buildings over five hundred feet long running back from Market Street to Bigg Market, and later rebuilt this area on four storeys. In 1883, they entered the manufacturing business, with a factory in Leeds for men's and boy's clothing; four years later they added a boot and shoe factory to supply their own men's and ladies' shoe departments. Factories for women's clothes, knitted stockings and even mattresses came later.

J. B. Jefferys in his *Retail Trading in Britain* takes his definition of a department store as 'a large retail store with four or more separate departments under one roof, each selling different classes of goods of which one is women's and children's wear'. He also introduces a category of 'part department store' to suggest a large firm that had more than one retail department, but would not appear to have reached the status of a full department store as defined above. He then goes on to say that in the middle of the nineteenth century there would appear to have been no full department stores existing in Great Britain, but some part department stores were already trading. Yet Kendal Milne and Bainbridge's, also Shoolbred's in London, were full department stores under his definition by the mid-century.

Certainly many of the innovations attributed to the Bouçicauts were already current practice in England. It was routine, for instance, for shopkeepers to undertake delivery of their customers' purchases; and sales of goods at bargain prices were held from very early in the century, although the regular bi-annual stock-taking sales were not established until later. The sending of patterns of materials to country customers, which the Bon Marché started in France, was again a service that many London and provincial shops already offered. We know of at least one shop which, before 1840, had the rule that *'any garment bought and taken away, if not satisfactory, will be exchanged, if not worn or injured.'*

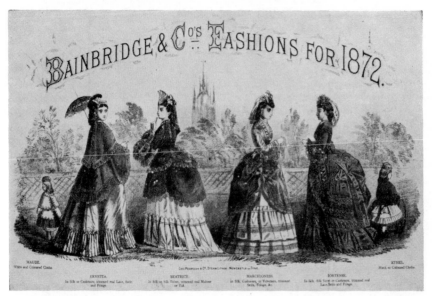

48. Lithograph fashion plate, with Newcastle Cathedral in the background.

This was Benjamin Hyam & Company of Liverpool, the tailors and outfitters which young David Lewis joined as an apprentice in 1839; and when he left to establish his own business in 1856, Lewis had this rule in his own shop, and also another that Hyam's had operated long before: '*All goods are marked in figures at the lowest selling price from which no abatement can be made.*'

Haggling over prices was never so prevalent in England as in France. As we have seen, Kendal Milne in 1830, and Bainbridge in 1831, were marking their goods with prices; and even the high-class shops of the West End of London did not disdain price tickets: Farmer & Rogers of the Great Shawl and Cloak Emporium in Regent Street, for example, mentioned in their advertisements 'All goods marked in plain figures'. Even the shops which marked their goods with hieroglyphs understandable only to themselves, did not expect customers to bargain when the price was named. The fact of the matter was that, once a shopkeeper employed several assistants, he could not rely on their bargaining skill as he might on his own, and it became necessary to fix prices. In France, shops remained smaller, with few if any assistants, and bargaining between owner and customer was part of the day's work.

In the small select shops of London in Bond Street, St James's, Jermyn Street and Piccadilly, the proprietor-shopkeepers were far too dignified to enter into any haggling. Writing in 1856, Francis Wey from Paris says this of them:

The detached attitude of shopkeepers in London is amazing . . . in London shopkeepers do not extol their wares, they seem quite indifferent as to whether you make or do not make a purchase . . . I had the greatest difficulty in getting the assistant to show me more than two fingers of each glove, as though displaying the entire article was beneath his dignity. The cashier took my money with the attitude of a man receiving a subscription for some charitable purpose, and my parcel was handed to me by the shopman with a benevolent expression as though he were making me a small gift. Sometimes even, they seem so averse to parting with their goods that you feel you are depriving them of cherished possessions.

It is not advisable to bargain in London shops as we do in Paris. The assistant thinks at first that you have misunderstood him, but when he realizes what you are driving at he stiffens visibly like a man of honour to whom one has made a shady proposal. He gives you to understand, politely but plainly, that his prices being equitable, cannot be reduced. His resolute bearing is so unmistakeable that only a fool would insist. Hawkers, dealers in booths or stalls, or small nondescript shops are the only tradespeople that you can drive a bargain with. In fact, the higher the commercial class the more conscientious is the price quoted.

From the mid-century onwards, the number of drapery shops which were expanding into considerable stores was so great that it is possible to mention only a few. In Holborn, the general drapery shop of Thomas Wallis, founded in 1826 by Mr Charles Meeking on what was then Holborn Hill, seems very early to have begun to sell both carpets and household drapery, as well as general drapery; and in St Paul's Churchyard, both Nicholson's and George Hitchcock were selling general drapery, corsets, fancy goods, and costumes. Shoolbred's, founded in 1817 in Tottenham Court Road, had a nearby rival as far as their furniture and furnishings went in Maple's, founded 1842. Lewis's of Liverpool bought additional premises in Bold Street in 1859, and started to deal in fashionable goods, announcing that their buyers visited both London and Paris. In 1854, John Heelas, who already had a drapery establishment at Wokingham, Berkshire, bought the business of Mr Hutchinson in Minster Street, Reading, for his two sons David and John. They added to the existing Linen, Woollen and Silk departments with Household Linen, Carpets and Family Mourning.

In the West End of London, Peter Robinson's great expansion began in 1854 with the acquisition of two more shops in Oxford Street, Nos. 105 and 106, adjoining his original premises at 103 Oxford Street. In 1856, he took over 107, in 1858, 108; and in 1860 the purchase of 104, gave him one solid block of six shops. He was already, in 1856, specializing in 'court millinery, mantles and dressmaking; widows' families' and children's mourning; flounced silk skirts, plain or trimmed with velvet'. All these were advertised with definite prices, so that one can presume they were also price-ticketed in the shop.

A young man called John Lewis, who came of a Somerset family of shopkeeping craftsmen, was Buyer of silks and woollens for Peter Robinson. In 1864, at twenty-eight, he set himself up in a small shop on the corner where Holles Street turns out of Oxford Street. He did not advertise like Peter Robinson, but he realized more clearly than most of his competitors the importance of offering a wide assortment of sizes and colours in the goods that he stocked. In Regent Street, Dickins & Jones of Hanover House were fast extending their business; and at Piccadilly Circus, Swan & Edgar made extensive alterations and additions in 1866, which included a new suite of showrooms for the display of fashions, and a mourning department.

Many different factors brought about the development of drapery shops into department stores. The industrial wealth of England, so proudly on view at the Great Exhibition of 1851, was creating a new spending population, a new middle class in which enormous importance was attached to the signs and symbols of prosperity: expensive clothes, handsome household furnishings, carriages, servants, a large establishment, and a prodigious number of children. The family, indeed, was all important. Tradesmen called themselves Family Drapers, Family Butchers, Family Furnishers, Family Mourning Warehouse. Families were 'waited upon' with everything they required in life and in death, from baby linen to funeral furnishings—almost, but not quite, from womb to tomb: they sold layettes but not maternity dresses. The only garments we know to have been especially designed for expectant mothers were corsets. But there may well have been specialists in maternity wear patronized by the *enceinte* élite, small establishments much too exclusive to advertise.

The members of the newly prosperous class looked for good value for their money. They saw that the shops which were expanding into department stores were buying advantageously in bulk, and so reducing their prices below those of the small retailers. Indeed up to the 'nineties, department stores were looked upon as essentially places for good value at low cost. Cash transactions were essential to their economy—they could never have operated upon the old yearly credit system, in which the richer the customer, the longer the expected credit.

Another factor in the development of the department stores was the

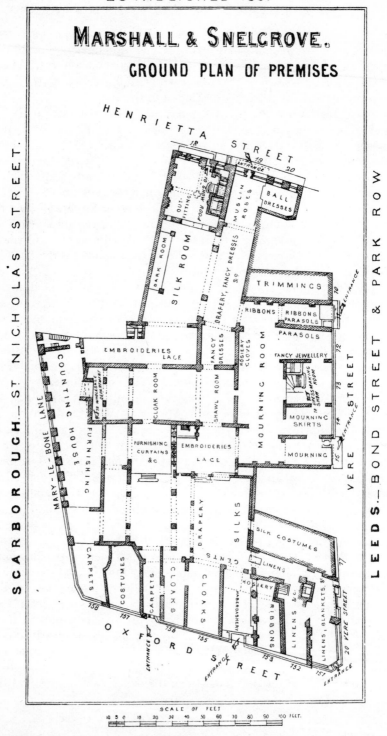

49. Ground plan of Marshall & Snelgrove at the erection of their present building in 1876.

improved railway services which brought shoppers into the large towns from suburban and country districts.

In the cities themselves, omnibuses now enabled people to move from shop to shop in streets quite far apart in search of exactly what they wanted at the price they were prepared to pay. In 1853, there were three thousand horse omnibuses in London, each carrying three hundred people daily; and in 1856, the small omnibus companies were absorbed by the French General Omnibus Company of London and more regular services assured. The habit of having a day's shopping in town began, and shopping now included 'window shopping'. The windows, stuffed from floor to roof, from back to front, with as much merchandise as they could possibly display, all clearly price-ticketed, were certainly not aesthetic. But they gave the shopper a very good idea of what she could find inside the shop.

Between 1821 and 1831 the boroughs of Paddington, St Marylebone, and St Pancras had doubled their population; and it was said at that time that 'Kennington, Camberwell, Hackney, Bethnal Green, Stoke Newington, Highbury, Chelsea, Knightsbridge, and even Kensington were 'hastening to join hands'. In 1851, there were twenty-five High Streets included in the metropolis; and London's population was growing so fast that out of every thousand, sixty-three were emigrants from other parts of England. Other cities, in particular the industrial cities of the Midlands and North, were growing almost equally fast. With this growth, the value of land and property in city centres increased. Rents and rates soared, and shopkeepers realized that it was no longer economic to expand horizontally by buying adjacent properties; expansion must be upwards. Thus the less highly-rated upper floors of property in Regent Street, Oxford Street, and other expensive shopping districts, which had previously been used mainly as staff rooms, workrooms, and offices (at this time nearly all the shop assistants lived-in), were brought into use for selling space. Staff hostels and workrooms were built or acquired in cheaper streets nearby. In the main buildings, the increased space allowed for larger and more clearly segregated departments. In 1870, the departments at Debenham & Freebody's numbered twenty-seven:

Coloured silks	Juvenile room
Black ditto	Hosiery
Mantles	Gloves
Shawls	Parasols
Furs	Household drapery
Costumes	Muslin curtains
Dresses	Embroidered muslins

Ball dresses	Ribbons
Printed muslins	Trimmings
Lace	Haberdashery
Embroideries	Family mourning
Fancy goods	Millinery
Ladies' outfitting (underwear)	Dressmaking
India Outfits	

*   *   *

Nevertheless, it would be a mistake to give the impression that either the shopping habits of 'the nobility and gentry' or the obsequious manners of the tradesmen who served them, had altered to any noticeable extent by the 1870's. The élite still patronized the little shops that their mothers and grandmothers had patronized; and if some of these little shops were becoming bigger shops, it would not alter the relations between the staff and their most valued customers. The lure of the 'inexpensive' was not for them, and not for one moment would they dream of paying cash. In an article entitled 'The Ethics of Shopping' in the *Fortnightly Review* of January 1895, Lady Jeune recalled shopping as it was twenty-five years earlier, when she was a girl:

There was little or no display in the windows. Each shop had its own speciality, and the more expensive and costly its goods, the more unremittingly conservative was the way of carrying on its business. Jones sold the best silks, Smith the best gloves, Brown the best bonnets, Madame X was far and away the only good milliner and dressmaker. . . . We bought our goods at these various shops, and dutifully followed in the steps of our forefathers, paying for the things at the end of the year, for no well-thought-of firm ever demanded or expected more than a yearly payment of debts. If residence in the country made a visit to London to choose what was wanted an impossibility, Jones, Brown or Smith knew the need of their particular customer, and the orders sent were expedited and despatched with unfailing accuracy.

With what interest and excitement the arrival of the case containing the garments was awaited, and the new mode canvassed! How quietly but certainly the appearance of the new garments at church heralded a reproduction of the same in the persons of the parson's wife and the smaller ladies of the community, who considered the big lady a faithful apostle of the gospel of dress! Even the dwellers in big cities carried on their shopping in a dignified and easy way, and the time devoted to shopping was laid aside as a concession which every woman felt bound to devote to the mysteries of her clothes. An afternoon's shopping was a solemn and dreary affair, when one was received at the door of the shop by a solemn gentleman in black, who in due time delivered one to another solemn gentleman, and perhaps again to a third, who found one a chair, and in a sepulchral tone of voice uttered some magic word such as 'Silk, Mr Smith' or 'Velvet, Mr A'. and then departed to seek another victim. One bought what was wanted and nothing more, and having secured the goods left the shop as seriously as one arrived. The whole performance left an impression of responsibility and sadness on one's mind and whether desiring wedding or funeral garments, the same solemnity characterized it, and with a great sense of relief the large doors closed behind one.

Poor Lady Jeune does not seem to have enjoyed shopping when she was a girl. Doubtless she was a dutiful and docile daughter, and always went shopping with Mamma in the shops which had rejoiced in Mamma's custom all her married life and her Grandmother's before that. But at least one girl of the 1860's shook off her Mamma and found romance in shopping. The elopement of Lady Florence Cecilia Paget is claimed by Swan & Edgar to have taken place by her leaving her carriage at their Piccadilly entrance and walking out through the Regent Street door to meet her lover. But in an old cuttings book at Marshall & Snelgrove's, there is an account of the elopement by Mrs T. P. O'Connor in her weekly 'Letter from London' to the *Washington Herald* (March 6, 1916). Mrs O'Connor's account names the shop as Marshall & Snelgrove; and since she was acquainted with the jilted man in his old age, I am inclined to accept her version of the story, which is this:

I suppose it is a rare thing for a woman with a taste for romance to enter M. & S.'s artistic shop without remembering a story connected with it. As long ago as 1864, a beautiful young girl, Lady Florence Cecilia Paget, third daughter of the Marquis of Anglesey, torn between love and duty, but with love in the ascendant, entered the shop with her fiancé, Henry Chaplin— who was then young, and, I hope, slim; now he is old and enormously fat— by the Oxford Street Entrance. She left him while she looked at the beautiful lingerie of her trousseau, and he never saw her again until he met her as the Marchioness of Hastings. She had stopped to look at the fairy-tale garments of linen and lace, but had left the shop by the Henrietta Street Entrance, been met by the Marquis of Hastings and got married that morning.

The Marquis does not seem to have appreciated his prize as he should for Mrs T. P. O'Connor's story continues:

It was said that the year after the marriage her husband's heart was broken by not winning the Derby. The horse, first favourite, stood to win, but a mysterious and never-discovered enemy had drugged him. At any rate, Lord Hastings died in 1869, four years after the famous runaway marriage, and his beautiful young widow married, later, Sir George Chetwynd, a well-known racing landed gentleman who for many years drove a splendid four-in-hand, was a great favourite of King Edward VII, and only died a few years ago living to a great age.

Was the mysterious enemy Henry Chaplin? Perhaps even Sir George Chetwynd? At any rate, a man who could have his heart broken by a horse only a year after a young girl had thrown her reputation over the windmill for him, was clearly a dislikable man, if not a cad, and deserved to have enemies. As to the trousseau, presumably Marshall & Snelgrove completed the order and delivered it to the headstrong young Marchioness of Hastings, and the bill to her parents—who no doubt paid up, as parents do.

In the one-time ducal residence of Schomberg House, Pall Mall, a firm called Harding & Howell had from 1796 conducted what was virtually a department store—selling furs, silks, lace, haberdashery, gloves, fans, millinery, perfumery, *objêts d'art*, and furnishing fabrics. A tea-room with a view over St. James's Park served wines, tea, coffee and sweetmeats, and was an elegant society rendezvous. In 1820, two of the Schomberg House partners, Howell and James, defected to start their own shop at No. 9 Regent Street, and the faithless *beau monde* followed them to buy their costly fabrics, furnishings, jewellery, ceramics and glass. There was a wine department, and an *haute couture* salon. Coachmen and footmen waiting for their ladies were served with free beer and bread and cheese in the basement. It was Howell & James who precipitated the collapse in 1849 of Lady Blessington's resplendent menage at Gore House by foreclosing on their bill for furnishing it thirteen years earlier. Long credit indeed! But suppliers always gave titled clients a lot of rope before the noose was tightened.

Oxford Circus in 1849 (then called Regent Circus) from *The Grand Architectural Panorama of London.*

CHAPTER XIV

WESTBOURNE GROVE—THE
BOND STREET OF THE WEST

Bayswater residential development. William Whiteley, the
Universal Provider. John Barker at Whiteleys. Bradley's
Arctic Fur Store. William Owen. Bourne and Hollingsworth.

᚛᚛᚛

ALL the time London was growing. All the time, a residential
migration westwards was in progress. From the mid-nineteenth
century, the trend to replace dwelling houses in central London
by shops and offices became much more pronounced. The residential
population of the City fell from 128,000 in 1851 to 75,000 in 1871.
Westminster, Holborn, Finsbury and St Marylebone started to lose
residents after 1860, although the sharp decline in the population of
these districts dates from the early 1870's.

The most fashionable new residential district was north of Hyde
Park, along the Bayswater Road. Fine solid family houses, pompous
and porticoed, had been built for prosperous city magnates, merchants,
and professional men—houses fit for Forsytes to live in. At first these
houses backed on open land to Paddington, but during the 1840's the
Westbourne Grove area filled up. To the south, the view over the trees
and greensward, where sheep and cows still grazed in summer, was
worth the price of expensive leaseholds; and the land behind the
Bayswater Road, hitherto rough, untidy, squalid waste land, was now
laid out in handsome terraces and squares with social cachet. The
children, escorted by nannies and nursemaids, benefited by their daily
walks in the Park.

Public transport was improving, and a second era of important
street improvements in central London was started. The Great Exhibition of 1851 had produced an omnibus boom; and many more vehicles

149

were put into service. Omnibuses still had only a ladder to the roof, where the seats were back to back in 'knifeboard' fashion; but in 1864 those running between Portland Place and Piccadilly were given a stair, and others soon followed. In 1863, the first Underground Railway was opened. This was the Metropolitan Railway, linking the City and West End. It ran from Farringdon Street to Bishop's Road, and served the Great Western Railway terminus at Paddington. Through its Gower Street Station, the Metropolitan Railway brought many new customers to Shoolbred's in Tottenham Court Road; and not far from its Bishop's Road Station, in Westbourne Grove, William Whiteley bought a small draper's shop a few weeks after the underground railway opened. With all the newly built squares, terraces, and residential roads nearby, Westbourne Grove was, in William Whiteley's eyes, a road with a future. Its past was not encouraging to a tradesman. In fact, it was known in the drapery world as Bankruptcy Row on account of the many businesses which had failed. But Whiteley foresaw not only good custom from the rich new residents of the district, but also that the new underground railway and the more comfortable and frequent omnibuses might persuade shoppers to come to Westbourne Grove from other districts, if they could be attracted by exceptional value and unusual customer services.

William Whiteley was not a man to rush in with his eyes shut. He was a North countryman of singular foresight, and knew exactly what he was doing and what he intended to do. The idea of him as a commercial buccaneer is completely misleading. For years he had been preparing himself for the time when he was ready to set up his own business, and was taking no risks of its being a failure through lack of experience. He had been apprenticed in 1848, when he was seventeen, to Harnew and Glover, the largest drapery shop in Wakefield. His first holiday was in 1851, and he used it to visit the Great Exhibition. This visit fired him with the ambition to make his future—and his fortune—in London. His indentures with Harnew and Glover expired in 1855; and the very next day he left Wakefield for London, and set himself to master, patiently and systematically, every detail of the London drapery trade. His plan was to begin among the old-established firms in the City and work his way through shop-keeping practice along traditional lines. His first position was with R. Willey & Co. of Ludgate Street. After fifteen months behind the counter, he moved to the Fore Street Warehouse—an important wholesale business, with a country-wide reputation, then trading as Morrison & Dillon. It was Mrs Morrison, a customer of Peter Robinson, who encouraged the young John Lewis, when he was Silk Buyer there, to set up on his own.

Whiteley next set to learn the ribbon trade by joining two ex-employ-ees of the wholesale haberdashers Leaf & Sons of Old Change (later Pawson & Leaf of St Paul's Churchyard), who were setting up their own business. All this time, Whiteley lived frugally, saving money from the pittance then paid to employees in the drapery trade. His last move before he had enough capital to start his own business was to another large wholesale drapers, Bradbury, Greatorex, and Beall of Aldermanbury in the City.

It seems that Whiteley hesitated in his choice of district between Upper Street, Islington, and Westbourne Grove. In Islington there would have been severe competition, because Upper Street was an extremely fashionable shopping street—a reputation it held until the end of the nineteenth century. In 1962 the author talked to a resident at the Linen & Woollen Drapers' Cottage Homes for retired members of the trade who remembered when it was all 'carriage trade' in Islington. Every afternoon, he recalled, carriages were drawn up on both sides of Upper Street. In 1881, *Sylvia's Home Journal* wrote, 'Girls with trousseaux on their minds had better haste to Islington's classic ground and do some shopping there'—it seems that Islington was particularly noted for underclothes. There was, for instance, E. Avis & Co. specialists in hand-made underclothing and 'Spatula Corsets'; and Mr R. Allin of 73 Upper Street and 464 Kingland Road who, while specialising in hand-made underclothing, stocked sufficient variety of goods to call himself The Universal Outfitter. One wonders whether Mr Allin called himself the Universal Outfitter before William Whiteley called himself the Universal Provider, or vice versa. Which-ever way it was in the beginning, it was the Universal Provider who became rich and famous, and the Universal Outfitter who found himself in a declining neighbourhood from which the carriage trade gradually drifted away as the residential migration from central London continued . . . westwards, always westwards.

Whiteley began by selling ribbons, lace, trimmings, and fancy goods—the haberdashery which he had learned so much about in his long years in the City. He started with two young lady assistants—one of whom he soon married, so assuring himself of her unpaid assistance twenty-four hours of the day instead of the twelve to fourteen hours a day which were the normal working hours in shops. Within a year of opening he had fifteen assistants, a cashier, and two errand boys—a staff far beyond the average for the neighbourhood. By 1867 he had added silks, linens, mantles, drapery, and dresses, millinery, haber-dashery, ladies' outfitting, gloves and hosiery, jewellery, furs, um-brellas, and artificial flowers. He had also acquired an assistant called

ALL THE DIFFERENCE!

Haberdasher (to Assistant who has had the "swoop"). "WHY HAS THAT LADY GONE WITHOUT BUYING?"

Assistant. "WE HAVEN'T GOT WHAT SHE WANTS."

Haberdasher. "I'LL SOON LET YOU KNOW, MISS, THAT I KEEP YOU TO SELL WHAT I'VE GOT, AND NOT WHAT PEOPLE WANT!"

50. *Punch.* June 16, 1877

John Barker, a young man of exceptional industry and enthusiasm.

John Barker had come to London the hard way, like Whiteley himself. Born in 1840 in Maidstone, he had been apprenticed to a Maidstone draper before he was thirteen. When his indentures were completed, he became a junior assistant with a Folkestone draper, and then a Dover one. At eighteen, he came to London and was employed by Spencer, Turner and Boldero in Lisson Grove. Lisson Grove was then a smart shopping street, in the fashionable borough of St Marylebone, an exclusive residential area before the decline of population started in the 1870's. Like Whiteley, John Barker had an instinct for the up and coming district, and he probably already sensed the future decline of Lisson Grove as a fashionable shopping street when he left it to join Whiteley.

Within a few years William Whiteley made Barker a department manager at a salary of £300 a year. The business was prospering so well that he soon demanded a further increase; and Mr Whiteley agreed to double his salary if he doubled the business in the next year. The business was doubled, and so was the manager's salary. As

Whiteley continued to expand his business, buying more properties on each side of his original shop and branching out into many different lines of merchandise, John Barker asked to be taken into partnership. Mr Whiteley refused, but offered to increase his salary to £1,000 a year. This was in 1870; and a thousand a year was an unheard of salary for a drapery employee. Nevertheless, it did not satisfy John Barker, who wanted more responsibility in the actual running of a business. He had many ideas of his own which he wanted to put into practice. So he left Whiteley's and Westbourne Grove to set up on his own in another swiftly developing district, Kensington High Street.

Although Barker's departure must have been a blow to Whiteley, his business was forging ahead with too great momentum to allow of any serious set-back. Before Barker left in 1867, Whiteley's had already seventeen separate takings, whose sales were as follows:

Silks	£5,700	Trimmings	£3,000
Dresses (including funerals)	£5,900	Gloves	£2,500
Linens	£3,000	Hosiery	£1,000
Drapery	£3,000	Ribbons	£3,000
Mantles	£2,000	Fancy goods	£1,000
Millinery	£2,000	Jewellery	£2,000
Ladies' outfitting	£3,000	Lace	£3,500
Haberdashery	£800	Umbrellas and furs	£1,500

It is interesting to note that, apart from silks, dress materials and funerals—always the mainstay of a drapery business before the era of ready-to-wear—the largest sales were in the lace department. A lace department, in those days, did not just stock lace by the yard, but also all those things which came under the category of 'made-up lace'; jabots, fichus, collars, cuffs, caps, handkerchiefs, dressing-jackets. It also included household lace: curtains, afternoon tea cloths, duchess sets, antimacassars, draperies, doyleys, and little mats of all descriptions. Big drapers such as Peter Robinson, who was particularly strong on lace, sent their own buyers on annual trips to Europe to place orders in all the famous lace-making districts of the Continent. And the extent of the lace business is shown by the stock of P. Steinmann & Co., Wholesale Lace Merchants, of 8 Piccadilly (1st floor), whose advertisements listed:

Point de Bruxelles, Point d'Alsace, Point de Vence, Milano, Genoa, and Greece; Medici lace; real Valencienne and imitation Ecru; real and imitation black Spanish and Chantilly laces; fichus, ties, wrappers, falls, mantillas, handkerchiefs; hand-made embroidered underlinen, trousseaux, layettes, trimmed baskets, cots, etc.

Although P. Steinmann were wholesalers supplying drapery shops and dressmakers, they became retailers as well. There is a bill of theirs amongst the Heather Firbank records at the Victoria & Albert Museum, which shows they were even more thriving in Edwardian times, since the address is then 185 and 186 Piccadilly (1st floor), almost opposite the Royal Academy. That was, indeed, the absolute peak period for lace, when it flowed and frothed on tea-gowns, blouses, and lingerie.

Another of Whiteley's departments in their list of 1867 is significant, not to the drapery trade in general, but to Whiteley's own particular line of development. This is the Jewellery Department, an indication that he was beginning to trade in lines which were not traditional drapery merchandise. And in 1870 he opened a Foreign Department for the sale of cheap Japanese and other imported fancy goods. These would have been popular interpretations of the oriental cult which young Arthur Liberty was helping to disseminate from the Oriental Warehouse of Farmer & Rogers in Regent Street. From now on, Whiteley was to extend into all those un-drapery departments and services to customers which enabled him to call himself 'The Universal Provider'.

Buying up adjoining properties in Westbourne Grove and Queen's Road, he added shop to shop to accommodate his new departments: in 1872 a House Agency and a Refreshment Room; in 1874 a cleaning and dyeing service; two years later a Hairdressing Department. Such activities were a source of great indignation to local shop-keepers, who did not consider it fair trading for a draper to start selling meat and books, ironmongery and houses, or to go into catering, dry-cleaning and hairdressing. The only service to the customer that it was traditional for a draper to offer was the ultimate service of undertaking.

It was probably the influence of local publicans which caused his application for a licence for his Refreshment Room to be refused. The Paddington magistrate did not, however, give this as his reason for refusal. Remarking that 'Mr Whiteley had got enough irons in the fire already, and would not require any more', he turned it down 'in the interests of morality'. . . . 'Many of Mr Whiteley's customers might be ladies, or females dressed to represent them, and the place might be made a place of assignation.' Swan & Edgar, with its situation on Piccadilly Circus, might well have been felt to be in more danger of its restaurant becoming 'a place of assignation'; but fortunately they never had to apply to the Westminster magistrates for a licence. Their site included that of the Western Mail Coach Office, the 'Bull & Mouth'. When the property was acquired by Swan & Edgar during the Regency, they took over the Inn's licence, and never afterwards let it lapse.

One way and another, even before the series of disastrous fires which five times broke out in Whiteley's buildings and were national news, the Universal Provider was always good for a headline. *The Bayswater Chronicle* can scarcly have had an issue without some reference to the goings on at his unique emporium. William Whiteley never took paid advertisement space, since he got sufficient publicity through his own newsworthy personality and activities. And he was probably one of the first tradesmen to contrive disguised advertising in editorial form. He and some of his fellow shop-keepers in Westbourne Grove arranged a series of 'letters' in the *Bayswater Chronicle* supposedly passing between two fashionable young ladies signing themselves 'Claribel' and 'Evelyn'. These letters mixed modish chit-chat and local gossip with references to the merchandise in the Westbourne Grove and Queen's Road shops. In this connection it is interesting that Spence, one of the big drapers of St Paul's Churchyard, commissioned the famous journalist George Augustus Sala in 1879 to write an article in their catalogue.

Unfortunately for posterity, one of Whiteley's most ambitious publicity ideas did not become realised. This was to have his emporium the subject of a painting by W. P. Frith. The enormous success of Frith's huge detailed canvases, for which vast sums were paid, had by the early 'seventies exhausted the Royal Academician's ideas for subjects. He let it be generally known that he would pay large rewards for suggestions. To one man who called to offer a subject he said, 'If you can propose to me a subject for a picture of the size and importance of 'Railway Station' or of 'Derby Day', I will give you two hundred pounds'. Frith recalls in his autobiography that one day he was brought a letter signed William Whiteley, asking for an interview on a matter of business . . . 'I was much puzzled as to what the "business" could be, as I owed Mr Whiteley nothing at the time; indeed, the principles on which he conducts his business are such as to prevent the possibility of anybody owing Mr Whiteley anything for an unreasonable time.' But his caller had come to propose a subject for a painting: 'Whiteley's at Four o'clock in the Afternoon'. . . .

I should leave it to your discretion, sir, to choose either the inside of the place or the outside. If you take the former, you would have the aristocracy making their purchases. You might introduce the young ladies who do me the honour to assist in my establishment, many of whom are very pretty. Then there are what are called shopmen, with fine heads, and every conceivable detail for your back and fore grounds. If, on the other hand, you select the outside of the shops, you could introduce the commissionaires who, as you may have observed, wear a picturesque livery created by me; you would have the nobility and gentry stepping into their carriages with—forgive my suggestions, they are subject to your criticism—street beggars, toy-sellers—think of the contrast between them and my customers—and all the variety of characters that Westbourne Grove always presents. There is but one stipulation that I venture to make, namely, that the whole length of the shops be shown, care being taken that the different windows should display the specialities of the establishment.

Frith's account of the interview continues: 'Then, as if reading my thoughts, Mr Whiteley said: "I never advertise; I never spent a shilling in that way in my life. My notions of the advantage of advertising take the form of good things at so small a profit as to make the purchasers recommend their friends to come to my shops; and I have found that method of advertising so satisfactory that I feel no inclination to spend the enormous sums that some of my brethren in trade find, or think they find, profitable".'

There could have been no more profitable advertisement for Whiteley's than a painting by Frith, then at the height of his fame. We do not know whether Whiteley also intended, besides getting this magnificent free advertisement, to exact payment for the 'idea', because unfortunately Frith turned it down—not forthwith, but after thinking the matter over. And it seems he rather regretted having done so: 'I have often thought since that, though I should fear to undertake it, much might have been done'. We also must regret the decision. Shopping, for all that it is a daily activity and a colourful part of social life, has seldom been depicted by painters, although draughtsmen and cartoonists have from time to time explored its rich seam.

By the time *Modern London* was published in 1887—that is, twenty-four years after Whiteley opened his haberdashery shop—the felicities of this fashionable new district were well-known to the world at large . . . 'Bayswater has become of late years one of the most pleasant and attractive of London suburbs, and Westbourne Grove has developed attractions which have resulted in it being termed *The Bond Street of the West*.' There follows an ecstatic eulogy of Whiteley's:

Depot, emporium, bazaar, warehouse—none of these seem to possess the slightest descriptive power. Whiteley's is an immense symposium of the arts and industries of the nation and of the world; a grand review of everything that goes to make life worth living passing in seemingly endless array before critical but bewildered humanity; an international exhibition of the resources and products of the earth and air, flood and field, established as one of the greatest 'lions' of the metropolis.

Mr Whiteley's system of delivery by his own vehicles is as well-nigh perfect in its operation as possible. The scheme has a radius of 25 miles from the Bayswater centre. For long journeys extra depots have been instituted at Hayes, Croydon, Epsom, and numerous other places, where relays of horses are to be had. A stud of 320 horses and a total of 145 vehicles are impressed into the service of this immense delivery system.

A FISH BAR is attached to the fishmongery department, where tempting little fish luncheons popularly denominated SNACKS may be had at all hours.

The Fish Bar with its snacks has a very modern ring about it. More out-of-date to our ears is the sound of Whiteley's laundry, which he started for his customers in 1892. It only became really successful when he hit upon the idea of having the family's laundry decontaminated from that of their servants by wrapping theirs separately and marking it with blue.

        ✧   ✧   ✧

The spectacular success of Whiteley had encouraged many other retailers to the district. In Chepstow Place which leads off Westbourne Grove in the direction of the Bayswater Road, a Mr Bradley opened in 1870 The Arctic Fur Store. The next year, S. Bradley & Co., Silk Mercers and Furriers, according to *Modern London*, opened an establishment called Ulster House at 129 and 131 Westbourne Grove, having been established elsewhere in 1858. There is nothing to tell us that these two were in any way connected, but it is very likely they were relatives, since furrier businesses run in families. The Arctic Fur Store was a business which not only made up furs, but also traded as direct importers of raw skins, and was one of the first firms to have a series of cold air chambers for storing furs. Much later, in the present century, Bradley's were to become an immensely high-class dressmaking and tailoring establishment as well as furriers—a model house for couture furs and clothes with workrooms and showrooms occupying an area of nearly six acres, with eighty-six private fitting rooms. It was run under the direct control of members of the Bradley family until 1953, when it was acquired by Debenham & Freebody.

Another extremely modish denizen of the district was Mr A. Abrahams, who was established as 'Fashionable Bootmaker' at 11 Westbourne Grove in 1851, twelve years before Whiteley came. Mr Abrahams had an unusual speciality in 'painted boots and shoes and embroidered shoes of every kind'. He designed and executed monograms on boots, shoes, and slippers, employing designers on the premises for these and other novelties.

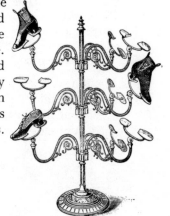

51. Handsome all brass branch Boot Stand, with patent ornamented bracket. Harris & Sheldon, 1888.

Measuring and fitting was done on 'correct anatomical principles' by 'a large staff of assistants'. Abrahams made riding, hunting, fishing, and shooting boots and in the 1880's claimed to have nearly ten thousand pairs of lasts registered on his books, making the spacious assertion that 'repeat orders are received from all parts of the universe'.

In 1873 Tom Ponting, one of four brothers from Gloucester, opened as a fancy draper in Westbourne Grove, while his brothers set themselves up in Kensington. Also in 1873, an enterprising Welshman named William Owen opened a shop at 12a and 14a Westbourne Grove, just opposite Whiteley's, and called it The Bayswater Trimming Shop. It was a modest start, although his trimmings were supplemented by gloves, ribbons, lace, haberdashery and fancy goods. It would be very similar to the kind of fancy goods shop to be found in any country town. Yet in the next thirteen years William Owen bought twelve shops in Hatherley Grove nearby, and by 1888 owned fifteen shops in Hatherley Grove, two in Westbourne Grove, and employed three hundred and fifty assistants. From the description of William Owen's emporium in *Modern London*, it sounds as though he aimed at a rather higher class fashion trade than William Whiteley:

On the First Floor, up a particularly handsome staircase in American walnut of the most artistic design, is the main showroom for gowns and millinery, probably unsurpassed in size and elegance of appointment by any similar exhibition saloon in London. The arts of the skilled *modiste* stand here exemplified in all their highest phases . . . velvets and velveteens, crapes and mourning goods, laces, hosiery, wools, art needlework, costume clothes, underclothing, corsets, baby-linen, straws, flowers, feathers, and dressing-gowns.

William Owen particularly prided himself upon his delivery service. This was not so far-flung as Whiteley's which penetrated twenty-five miles into the country and had depots or agencies in many country towns; but it was extremely smart, with the most elegant horses:

The delivery department gives employment to a very large number of horses and men—the stables being a model of modern convenience and arrangement. They are the only stable in London, with the exception of Tattersalls, that has patent mangers divided into apartments for the reception of hay and other sorts of provender. The horses are all of the best, and everything that can add to their comfort is done.

Although Whiteley and Owen were intense rivals in business, Owen showed considerable sympathy for Whiteley over the various mysterious and disastrous fires which occurred at his emporium. And he joined Whiteley in an enterprise to try and attract more customers to

Westbourne Grove from North London. Together they approached the London General Omnibus Company and asked for a bus service to be inaugurated from Camden Town to Bayswater. The Company refused on the grounds that it would be uneconomic, but said that if anyone else started a service they would start their own in competition. To a man of Whiteley's temperament this was a challenge which could not be ignored. He persuaded other Bayswater tradesmen to join in running a service from Camden Town, past the Zoo, through St John's Wood and Warwick Road, to Bayswater Road. There was a fleet of ten buses, eight of which Whiteley had specially built. Distinctive with chocolate body and yellow wheels, they carried the announcement TO WHITELEY's and TO OWEN's, which seems to indicate that only these two can have been financially involved. It was a brave, pirating gesture—and a costly one. The shopping bus service was not continued for very long, but it did have the effect of making the London General Omnibus Company improve its own services to the district. As a publicity campaign it was worthy of the showman in Whiteley. William Owen, with his more discreet establishment and high-class clientele, may well have had his regrets.

It was in 1894 that a Mr Bourne and his brother-in-law Mr Hollingsworth set up a small draper's shop in Westbourne Grove with £600 capital and another borrowed £600. Perhaps they found that the competition of Whiteley's and Owen's was too much for them; or perhaps they were possessed with the kind of instinct that warns when a district's fashionable years are numbered. Whiteley was guided by such an instinct when he decided against Islington at its most modishly prosperous in favour of Westbourne Grove when it was known as 'Bankruptcy Row'. Mr Bourne and Mr Hollingsworth may already have foreseen, in 1902, the future decline of Bayswater. At any rate, in that year they moved from Westbourne Grove to 116 and 118 Oxford Street.

That was just five years before the Universal Provider was shot dead in his own shop by a young man claiming to be his illegitimate son. William Whiteley thus departed from the scene of his successes in a final blaze of unbought publicity.

CHAPTER XV

KENSINGTON AND THE SUBURBS

*Residential development of Knightsbridge. The Kensington
Improvement Scheme. John Barker, Derry & Toms, the
Ponting Brothers, and Seamen, Little. Streatham, Holloway,
Brixton, Kingston. Tradesmen's Country Residences.*

K ENSINGTON retained the quiet character of a country town for a
remarkably long time. It was a very proud little borough. It had
its own royal residence, Kensington Palace; its own aristocratic
mansion, Gore House, where Lady Blessington had held sway with the
elegant Count d'Orsay; and its own country house where all the great
Whig families used to gather—Holland House, surrounded by its own
gardens, woodlands, and cricket field.

Kensington High Street was part of the coaching road from London
to Oxford and the West Country; but well into the 1860's it remained
narrow and picturesque, with small, austere Georgian houses and little
shops with wooden shutters. North of the High Street, there were
shady tree-lined roads with quiet houses secluded in charming mossy-
walled gardens. Nothing there had altered since the 1830's, when Fanny
Horsley lived near the Gravel Pits and used to run with her sister down
the hill to buy ribbons at Breeze's in the High Street—or, for more
important shopping expeditions, took Chancellor's omnibus to Bond
Street, sometimes getting off at Alabasters in Piccadilly, famous for
their 'Straw and Fancy Hats'.

George Chancellor was one of the many small scale operators of the
1830's who were licensed to run omnibus services. His route was from
Chelsea to Mile End, and he ran nine two-horse omnibuses. Breeze and
James of 32 Kensington High Street, was established in 1810 and
'enjoyed the distinguished patronage of H.M. the Queen when she was
Princess Victoria and made her home at Kensington Palace'. As a

IX

Fashion Showroom at Caley's of
Windsor, *c.* 1905.

Pratt's of Streatham in 1880.
The window display at left is
typical of the period.

X   Cavendish House, Cheltenham, in 1897.

Fenwick's, 37 and 39 Northumberland Street, Newcastle, in 1885.

gesture of loyalty, they named their business Coburg House after the Queen's marriage to a prince of the House of Saxe-Coburg. Later, Coburg House was owned by Moss & Cooke, and later again by John Bell & Co. Another of the little shuttered shops in Kensington High Street belonged to Joseph Toms, and was listed in the London Post Office Directory of 1854 as a 'Toy and Fancy Repository'. In 1862, Joseph Toms took Charles Derry as a partner, and so began the long history of Derry & Toms.

The Great Exhibition of 1851 was held in the Crystal Palace erected in Hyde Park near the Knightsbridge Barracks; and it was followed by a great deal of middle-class development around Kensington which, like Bayswater, became a favoured residential district owing to the westward migration of the well-to-do. Kensington was never quite so smart as Bayswater; but Knightsbridge, nearer town, was the smartest of all the new residential districts. In Knightsbridge, the little linen draper's shop founded by Benjamin Harvey in 1813 in what was then called Lowndes Terrace had benefited from its proximity to the Crystal Palace in Hyde Park, which drew throngs to the district all summer.

When Benjamin Harvey died in the late 1850's, he left his thriving business to his daughter Elizabeth, with the recommendation that she take the silk buyer, Colonel Nichols, into partnership. This unexpected appearance of a drapery Colonel is puzzling, since it was a time of sharp social distinctions; the Army and Trade were in completely different strata. Had there been any 'temporary gentlemen' in the Crimean War, as there were in the 1914–1918 War, that could have been the explanation—but the Crimea was left to the mishandling of the professional military. There could be a possible explanation of Colonel Nichols in the 'Volunteer Movement', started in the 1840's when invasion was feared from France owing to the rumours of revolution which resolved themselves in the abdication of Louis-Phillipe in 1848. Nichols may have achieved his rank through voluntary service to his country after work in the summer evenings, and on the all too short holidays he would have had in the drapery trade.

And did Miss Harvey marry her gallant military silk buyer? That also is purely a matter of speculation, since there is no record one way or another. But it is pleasing to think of it as a partnership of bed as well as Board. Whether romance was included in Colonel Nichols' partnership contract or not, it would certainly have been a marriage of convenience from the administrative point of view and would have kept the money in the family. It would also explain why the firm is known as Harvey Nichols—not Harvey & Nichols, or Harvey, Nichols.

The second great Exhibition, that of 1862, was held in South

Kensington on the site destined for the erection of the Natural History Museum, financed by some of the profits from the 1851 Exhibition. South Kensington itself was at the same time being residentially developed, and the family draper's shop of William Hatch, founded at 23 Gloucester Road in 1860, did well. Good trade was done with 'colonists and Americans' visiting London during the Exhibition, and their custom was continued by mail after they had returned home. But William Hatch built up his reputation chiefly as 'a reliable household caterer, children following their parents in patronising the house, which results from the perfectly persistent manner in which Mr Hatch has year by year maintained and enhanced his reputation'. By the 'eighties, he had bought the adjoining property at 21 Gloucester Road. Fashion goods of all kinds were sold on the ground floor, the upper floors had dressmaking departments, fitting rooms and household furnishing; in the basement there were upholstery workshops. A large cleaning department was 'devoted to the beating of carpets, cleaning of bedding and curtains, dyeing and cleaning of furniture, fabrics, feathers, dresses, dress goods, and gentlemen's clothing'.

Gloucester Road seems to have had rather a reputation for cleaning and dyeing, as Elton's, founded in 1827 in Sloane Street, moved to 113 Gloucester Road, where it was announced that 'long years of experience in what may be fairly termed an art, have enabled Messrs. Elton to bring their dyeing processes to a state of unsurpassed perfection'.

Gore House, midway between Knightsbridge and Kensington, was pulled down in 1860 and its site used for the Royal Albert Hall. And in the Gore House garden new residential buildings reared up, including great cliffs of gloomy terracotta 'mansion flats', the last word in Victorian-Gothic modernity. Further westwards, Kensington High Street was still a narrow, rather twisted stretch lined with little shops and dwelling houses, with no fewer than twenty-two public houses. In the opinion of the new Metropolitan Board of Works, it was ripe for development; and the Kensington Improvement Scheme was launched in 1867. The road was to be widened and 'A Handsome Range of Shop Property' was to be built on the south side. By 1870, a 'noble roadway' had taken the place of 'the inadequate and cramped approach to Town', and fifty-five superior houses and shops had gone up in High Street, King Street (now Derry Street), Young Street, Ball Street, and Burden Mews.

It was to this 'noble roadway' that John Barker turned his ambitious footsteps when he refused William Whiteley's offer of £1,000 a year. He took the lease of Nos. 91 and 93 in the High Street, described in the

52. 'An impressive example of the structural dimensions and commercial magnitude which a mercantile establishment is capable of attaining under the beneficial influences of unremitting enterprise and an able and energetic directorate.'

Modern London, 1887

prospectus as 'A Splendid Large Shop, with Plate Glass Front—Three Floors of Rooms, with Lofty Basement'; and in October 1870 started business as a general draper in partnership with Mr (later Sir James) Whitehead, a wealthy Bradford Merchant in the City, who became Lord Mayor of London. About a dozen assistants were engaged, a number which showed considerable confidence in the new enterprise; and trading was to be 'on the new system of supplying goods direct from the manufacturers at a small rate of profit for cash payments, thus saving the profit of the middleman'. The indications are that Whiteley had been following this system. With most of his early training in the great wholesale houses of the City, it would have been a revolutionary, almost anarchical thing for him to do, but that would not deter him.

The new system certainly paid John Barker. Before the first year was out he had bought two more shops for the development of the millinery, dressmaking and under-clothing departments. The next year he acquired 87 High Street for men's mercery, tailoring, and juvenile clothing; and the following year bought the stock of another draper and took over two new premises at 89 High Street and 24 Ball Street. Already he had begun to stock merchandise other than drapery; and in 1873 he bought some vacant land to build a block which would enable him to enlarge the bookselling, stationery and fancy-goods branches of his business. But drapery was still the main stand-by. On his Christmas Calendar for 1877, Barker was able to publish the commendation of the *Queen*, that successful magazine founded in 1861 by Samuel Beeton, husband of *the* Mrs Beeton: 'For good Drapery at moderate price there is no better establishment in London than Barker's.' We see from this that Kensington was now regarded as part of London, no longer a separate entity. People were now travelling to Kensington to shop from other districts of London and the suburbs.

The same year that John Barker came to Kensington High Street, another ultra-modern shop was taken by Seaman, Little & Co., Silk Mercers, Linen and General Drapers. Although this firm has not survived the vicissitudes of the years as has John Barker, it began as a fine progressive business with advanced ideas about services to shoppers: for instance, it had handsomely appointed lavatories for customers' convenience. These were situated beyond the three 'perfectly equipped fitting rooms for dressmaking, millinery, etc.'. On the floor above were dressmaking workrooms where over ninety hands were employed; and at the top of the building was a large kitchen 'from which the food descends by lift to the staff dining-room in the basement'. It must have been considered very revolutionary, in Victorian times, to have a kitchen on the top floor; but they evidently had not got so far as planning the dining-room alongside. Apart from workroom hands, Seaman, Little & Co. employed one hundred and fifty assistants, all living in, so it must have been a shop of some size. Not only big, but handsome: 'Two broad solid oak staircases lead from the ground floor shop, and give access to what is admittedly the finest showroom in the metropolis devoted to its purpose—a magnificent saloon, 200 feet by 50 feet, richly carpeted, and elegantly furnished throughout in solid mahogany, ebonized, and having walls lined with large glass show cases, relieved at intervals by glittering bevelled plate-glass mirrors'.

Seaman, Little & Co. issued a catalogue twice yearly, had two sales a year, and claimed large and important American contacts. There must have been great rivalry between them and Derry & Toms, who by this time had acquired seven shops in a row, and a separate shop as a Mourning Department. Derry's had about two hundred living-in assistants, for whom they provided 'a fine library and other advantages, the result of special study made by the proprietors for the comfort and social advancement of their little army of busy and efficient employees'.

Meanwhile, the Pontings had arrived in Kensington High Street. Four brothers, William, Tom, John, and Sydney Ponting had left

Gloucester to seek their fortunes in London. Tom Ponting started on his own in Westbourne Grove, putting his little bit of money on the district that William Whiteley had made so fashionable for shopping. The other three brothers foresaw an even rosier future in Kensington, and time has proved them right. They bought just one property, 125 High Street, and opened as drapers and milliners. They expanded by acquiring property on either side, and by the end of the century owned 123, 123a, and 127 High Street, and also Scarsdale House, formerly the mansion of the Curzons of Kedleston, who held the barony of Scarsdale. At first the mansion was 'adapted and co-ordinated with the shop premises', and much later pulled down to make way for a new modern store building. This must, surely, have been one of the first examples of a stately home being acquired for retail trade.

The purchase of Scarsdale House marked the peak of Ponting's prosperity, when according to a contemporary trade directory, their reputation was at its highest as 'the largest retail fancy goods and silk business in London'. Ponting's great speciality was 'supplying everything for the practice of art needlework in its myriad branches, especially Church work; wools, silks, cotton, card mounts, plush goods, cloths and specimens of commenced work in toile-crosse, cross-stitch, and Roman work, with all required for finishing the same . . . devices and designs supplied for book marks, alm bags, pulpit hangings, altar clothes, etc. Such work prepared, executed, and mounted'. One can see it was a favourite shop with the ladies of St Mary Abbots, Church Street. Moreover, Ponting's claimed to have royal patronage from Kensington Palace.

Ponting's also ran a school of needlework, 'under the direction of a lady of high attainments and long experience, which affords full instruction at moderate rates to pupils in all branches of this desirable art'. This, surely, was a splendid piece of business acumen, creating the demand for your goods on your own premises, and getting money for so doing. Nevertheless, something went wrong somewhere. Perhaps, in the gay, gadabout Edwardian days ladies became less industrious over their church needlework. At any rate, Ponting's had to go into liquidation in 1906, and were glad to accept an offer from John Barker & Co. to purchase the whole of the assets for £84,000.

❦ ❦ ❦

If Kensington of the 'sixties still had the atmosphere of a small country town, Streatham not only had the atmosphere of a little country village, but was still called a village. Up till 1839, it had not even been large enough to boast a draper's shop; but then a linen draper called William

Reynolds opened a small business, and to his shop in 1840 came thirteen-year-old George Pratt from Silchester in Hampshire to serve his apprenticeship. In ten years time, the former apprentice had bought out his employer, and G. Pratt, Linen draper, was in business on his own at 5 Bedford Row, on the High Road. This little shop became too small as Streatham grew; and in 1868 Mr Pratt built himself two new shops on the other side of the High Road and grandly called them Eldon House. There were two sons, Henry and Charles, who followed him into the business and gradually expanded it by buying neighbouring properties.

In the North London suburb of Holloway, much closer in than Streatham and therefore not so select, William Pearce Jones arrived in 1867, having run away from his home in Caernarvon. He acquired an ironmonger's shop in Pear Tree Terrace and sent for his brother from Wales to help turn it into a drapery business. Within four years they had bought the shop next door, and picturesque Pear Tree Terrace had become plain Holloway Road. After ten years, the Jones Brothers had a row of four little shops side by side, carrying ladies' underwear, men's wear, and a bazaar of fancy goods, bonnets, and music. Jones Brothers also supplied entertainers for parties—a service that not even the Universal Provider had thought of at this time, although later he was said to supply lonely ladies with evening escorts. For some time the four shops were kept quite separate with their own entrances, but 'spacious doorways' were knocked in the intervening walls and an 'elevated railway' carried money from all four to a main cash desk.

Before the end of the 'eighties, *Modern London* was extolling the wonders of the Jones's 'GIGANTIC EMPORIUM

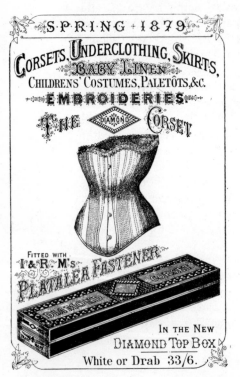

SPRING · 1879

CORSETS, UNDERCLOTHING, SKIRTS,
BABY LINEN
CHILDRENS' COSTUMES, PALETÔTS, &c.
EMBROIDERIES

THE DIAMOND CORSET

FITTED WITH
I & R M's
PLATALEA FASTENER

IN THE NEW
DIAMOND TOP BOX
White or Drab 33/6.

53. The attraction of the pack in which the product is presented begins to be offered as an inducement to stockists.
I. & R. Morley's Price List to the trade, Spring 1879.

166

. . . it is scarcely possible in writing to do justice to the beauty and elegance of the showrooms, the sumptuous manner in which they are fitted and upholstered, and the taste displayed in the various decorations.' There was 'every Parisian and Continental novelty' in the fashion rooms, where the showcases were 'perfect works of art by the well-known firm of Frederick Sage & Co. of Gray's Inn Road'; and there were also china, glass, grocery, and ironmongery departments—and an 'elegant buffet, where light refreshments can be obtained at extremely low prices and supplied with a promptness and politeness which might well be copied by other establishments'.

Holloway was never as fashionable a suburb as nearby Islington, and never had the village atmosphere of Streatham, which after all was five miles out from London. Streatham remained charmingly countrified even when Pratt's had become quite a large store. But there was plenty of good trade to be done in the district, since it was a great favourite with wealthy City merchants and successful tradesmen who built themselves fine spacious houses in big grounds up white-barred Private Roads. All the famous names in drapery were beginning to acquire properties outside London. William Edgar, founder of Swan & Edgar, had bought Eagle House on Clapham Common, where he lived until his death in 1869. It was a successful situation from the social point of view, because one of his six children married a baronet, a decided step up for a girl whose father had started business with a market stall. William Edgar's son, William Schindler Edgar, lived at Combe Warren, Kingston Hill, and used to ride to town on horseback. John Barker bought The Grange, Bishop's Stortford, and became quite the landed gentleman, breeding Syrian sheep and polo ponies on his 300 acres.

James Marshall, founder of Marshall & Snelgrove, was the trades-man with the biggest country property. In 1859 he bought Goldbeater Farm at Mill Hill with a thousand acres. When the Midland Railway was constructed to pass through his estate, Marshall was allowed to choose the site of Mill Hill station, and had the right to stop any express train to suit his own convenience. He gave staff parties and cricket matches at Goldbeater Farm; his youngest son, Charles Marshall, was an all-England cricketer. The elder son, James C. Marshall, took over the management of the business in 1871 when his father retired, and conceived the philanthropic idea of founding the Linen & Woollen Drapers Cottage Homes for retired members of the trade. On the death of his father in 1893, he gave a great part of the Gold-beater Estate to the project and financed the construction of the main buildings and some of the cottages.

Even further out from London than Mill Hill, Esher seems to have been a much favoured spot by successful drapers. The second Peter Robinson built Brookleigh at Esher and lived there until he died in 1895; and Mr C. D. Harrod, son of the founder of Harrods, moved his home and family to Esher in 1868. Perhaps he found fifteen miles from London too fatiguing for a daily journey, because sometime about 1874 they moved again to Sydenham, a fashionable suburb with the attraction of the Crystal Palace and its grounds. William Whiteley had his residence at Finchley, within easy reach of Westbourne Grove. Mr Liberty moved right out to Lee Manor, near his native Chesham, gradually acquiring 3,000 acres, with farms and cottages. John Lewis built a large, turreted house at Hampstead in four acres of grounds adjoining the Heath and Kenwood. He named it Spedan Tower, after the Aunt who brought him up in Shepton Mallet—Miss Ann Speed; and his eldest son was christened John Spedan.

Clapham was the suburb which Mrs M. E. Braddon chose in her novel *The Rose of Life* for the handsome residence of the father of her heroine. Thomas Dowden was the senior partner in the old-established firm of retail drapers called Dowden and Plowden, and he was rich enough to give his daughter thirty thousand pounds for her marriage portion:

Mr Dowden's hot-houses were the draper's chief pride. He had more glass than his partner Plowden, and prettier daughters; but the Plowdens, who lived in Bayswater, gave themselves more airs, and cultivated professional society. The Dowdens revolved in a circle of other shop-keepers and their families, keeping company with jewellery and fur, with silver and plated goods, with books and stationery, but not with butcher's meat, pastry, or poultry; and in this commercial circle there had sparkled occasional stars from the professional sphere—a barrister not over-proud, a genial young doctor, a journalist, something of a Bohemian, whose wit had kept the Clapham table in a roar.

But Clapham became unfashionable some time before Streatham lost its social cachet:

'It's a pity the tide of fashion has ebbed away from Clapham Park,' said Mr Dowden.
'Oh, father, Clapham Park was never fashionable,' Sally murmured.
'What, not when the Gaylords and the Trowmongers, and the Harlepools all had houses here?' protested her father, naming three well-known firms in Regent Street and Piccadilly. 'Your mother and I used to dine out three or four times a week in the season; and some of the finest run-outs in Hyde Park came from Clapham.'

SHOPWALKER.—Yes, Madam.
LADY.—I want to see something handsome and cheap.
SHOPWALKER.—Certainly, Madam. Mr. Jones, step forward.

54. A typical provincial draper's shop, with the traditional bent-wood chairs.

Mrs Braddon was a novelist with a very keen eye for the finer shades of social differences. But she can scarcely have heard, or surely she would have quoted, Thomas Carlyle's description of suburban society as 'retired wholesales looking down upon retired retails'.

❦ ❦ ❦

Only a few miles from Streatham, but more than a million miles in social grading, lay Brixton. And it was in Brixton that the first shop in England to be built from its beginning as a department store was opened in 1877. Mr James Smith of Tooting, a printer by trade and proprietor of the *Sportsman* newspaper, owned a horse called Rosebery which pulled off the first double event of its kind by winning the Cesarewitch and the Cambridgeshire Stakes at Newmarket in 1876. The prize money was £80,000. His owner, thereafter known as Mr Rosebery Smith, decided to invest his winnings in commerce in order to provide a secure future for his sons. He bought some land by Brixton Hill which for years had been a nursery garden, and erected a great new emporium which he named the Bon Marché after the famous Bon Marché in Paris.

An article in *The Builder* hailed it as 'a novelty in market accommodation in the metropolis, embracing the sale of almost every imaginable article in food, furniture, and dress, under one management, the whole of the employees residing on the premises in a large block which has been especially erected for them.' *The Builder* estimated that the buildings, which took eight months in construction, cost Smith over £70,000 —only £10,000 less than his prize-money. Something of its size can be imagined when it is said that the assistants' dining-room could hold three hundred at a sitting.

Trading was strictly on the ready money principle. This was in accordance with what had become the usual practice at all those shops which had by this time expanded into department stores, and was in fact one of the chief reasons why the stores could offer more advantageous prices than the smaller shops with whom it was customary to give customers extended credit. The small shopkeepers dare not offend their old customers by asking for prompt payment. One local tradesman at Brixton was said to have been so afraid that he would lose his customers to the Bon Marché with its low prices that he committed suicide . . . an unnecessary gesture, as it turned out, since the Bon Marché did not flourish.

Mr Rosebery Smith may have over-estimated the trading possibilities of the area—never a prosperous or fashionable one like nearby Streatham. Or perhaps it was because he was not, after all, a retailer, but was a printer and publisher. All the successful retailers of the nineteenth century started the hard way by being apprenticed to their trade at an early age. The failure of the Brixton Bon Marché was probably a case of inexperience rendered more dangerous by the over-optimism of a gambler. At any rate, within fifteen years of the opening day, Mr Smith was in the Bankruptcy Court with debts of £71,000, saying that he had not had sufficient capital to take advantage of trade discounts. The store was saved by five businessmen who made it a public company. One of them was Owen Owen of Liverpool who had, and still has, his own group of shops. Another was Edwin Jones, who became Chairman until he died in 1916.

The store these five experienced retailers acquired in 1892 had twenty-six departments to which they soon added new fashion departments and fitting rooms and a tea room. The Bon Marché might be in Brixton, but it was bringing itself up to Kensington standards; *all the departments were carpeted.* The Victorian pillars are still there—plain in the basement, and getting curlier as you go up; and so is the handsome arcade which they built in 1908. In another three years, they had bought Pratt's of Streatham, and the following year acquired the business next door to them in Brixton Road, Quin and Axtens. By 1924 there were forty-eight departments, including a soda fountain, and the Company was able to buy Laleham House in Clapham Park for use as a staff club and sports ground. Two years later, Selfridges acquired Pratt's, the Bon Marché, and Quin and Axtens; and sixteen years later they came into the John Lewis Partnership with the other Selfridge Provincial Stores. John Lewis closed the Brixton Bon Marché in 1975.

�   ✼   ✼

It was nearly always from little drapery shops that the big stores grew, Harrods being an exception in starting from groceries. Frank Bentall gained experience in his father's drapery business at Malden, Surrey, before opening his own small shop at Kingston-upon-Thames in 1867. He worked thirteen hours a day, served the customers himself, and guaranteed a cash refund on any purchase that proved unsatisfactory. In 1893 his sons George and Leonard joined him, and by 1900 they had acquired four adjacent properties. More new departments in 1908 included a tea-room with the then sensational feature of a door that opened automatically when you stepped on the mat. As Kingston grew, so Bentall's grew, but it remains a family firm. When Leonard Bentall succeeded Frank as chairman, his own son Gerald was waiting in the wings.

The first Bentall shop, and all the other little drapers' shops of the 'sixties and 'seventies which gradually expanded by acquiring the properties on each side of them and later rebuilt as great department stores, must have more or less resembled the drapery shop of Baines in Bursley, which is described by Arnold Bennett in the early chapters of *The Old Wives Tale*. He sets these chapters in the early 1860's, and in the preface says that he himself, having lived the first decade of his life (the 1870's) in the original of Mrs Baines's shop, remembered it 'as only a child remembers'.

Three dwelling houses had at intervals been thrown into one to make Baines's drapery shop, which was on the Square:

> The showroom was over the millinery and silken half of the shop. Over the woollen and shirting half were the drawing-room and the chief bedroom. When in quest of articles of coquetry, you mounted from the shop by a curving stair, and your head gradually rose level with a large apartment having a mahogany counter in front of the window and along one side, yellow linoleum on the floor, many cardboard boxes, a magnificent hinged cheval glass, and two chairs.

Downstairs, there was a central cash desk—the conning tower from which Mrs Baines could survey the whole shop. There were worn

171

polished counters with brass yard-measures nailed along their edges, great piles of shirtings and linseys near the entrance, and in the entrance itself, the opened doors were always hidden by displays of cheap lines. The lady assistants, on cold winter evenings, sat sewing around the central stove until a customer came in, when they unobtrusively turned higher the central gas, according to the *regime* of the shop. At eight o'clock, if the shop were empty, there was the formal order for dust sheets. Everything in the windows and displayed in the shop was ticketed:

> Heavy oblong tickets for flannels, shirting, and other stuffs in the piece; smaller and lighter tickets for intermediate goods, and diamond-shaped tickets (containing nothing but the price) for bonnets, gloves and flim-flam generally. The words 'lasting', 'durable', 'unshrinkable', 'latest', 'cheap', 'stylish', 'novelty', 'choice' (as an adjective), 'new', and 'tasteful', exhausted the entire vocabulary of tickets.

But Mr Povey, who was acknowledged to be the best window dresser in Bursley, began to design such *avant-garde* creations as 'Unsurpassable', 'Very Dainty', or 'Please Note'. His culminating expression of modernity was the word EXQUISITE pinned on a piece of broad tartan ribbon. This seemed to him and to Constance Baines to be the finality of appropriateness, but Mrs Baines thought it would not quite do.

'But why not, mother?'

'It's not suitable, my dear.'

EXQUISITE was consigned to the fire.

55. MILLINERY MODELS:
one hat, two bonnets, from
Debenham & Freebody's
Spring Fashion Book, 1886.

CHAPTER XVI

THE AESTHETIC MOVEMENT

*Liberty's of East India House. The Influence of Aestheticism on
Textiles and Costume. The Silk Association. Samuel Courtauld
and Black Crape. Art Nouveau. The first 'Shop within a Shop'.*

'I WISH you could see Mrs Sellar's drawing-room', wrote Lady
Jebb from Edinburgh on March 6, 1880, to her sister in America.
'So pretty and so comfortable. Morris papers on the walls, Burne-
Jones' photographs, old china, old carvings, Indian silks everywhere.'
In other words, the Aesthetic Movement had reached Edinburgh.

In London, the most fashionable shop for the diffusion of aestheticism
was Liberty's in Regent Street. It was 1875 when Arthur Lasenby
Liberty left the oriental department which he had originated and
directed at Farmer & Roger's Great Shawl and Cloak Emporium, and
opened his own shop at 218a Regent Street; but his admiration for
oriental art had first been fired at London's second great International
Exhibition held in 1862. That was the year when he joined Farmer &
Rogers at the age of eighteen. He had been born in Chesham, Bucking-
hamshire, where his family had a small draper's shop. But they moved
to Nottingham, and on leaving school he was apprenticed to a relative's
lace warehouse, and then to a draper in Baker Street, London.

A section of the International Exhibition was devoted to Japanese
art, which a few years earlier had come upon Paris like a revelation
from the East. Liberty was so excited by it that he persuaded Farmer
& Rogers, who already traded in shawls from India, to open an oriental
department to sell Japanese prints, lacquer, porcelain, bronzes, silks,
fans, and bric-à-brac. When he left to open his own shop twelve years
later, which he grandly named East India House, he had no capital
behind him but was driven by a burning enthusiasm for all things
oriental and possessed by an almost missionary zeal to encourage
craftsmanship and improve the public's taste.

The Aesthetic Movement was a revulsion from the brash products of the Industrial Revolution, from the crude aniline dyes which had been introduced in 1859, from machine-made finishes, false veneers, over elaboration, and all the pompous ugliness of urban Victorianism. Liberty's chief part in the Movement was the importing of soft oriental fabrics, exquisitely different from the stiff silks, thick woollens, and hard cottons which had encased the Victorians for so long. He believed there to be an essential superiority in oriental colour and design, and that their introduction, helped by Western mechanical resources, would improve the nation's taste as a whole. Unlike William Morris, Liberty was convinced that machines could be brought to the service of art; and that the weaving processes of the East could be adapted to the machine-woven fabrics of the English Midlands. Some of the Eastern fabrics proved too delicate, or the dyes too fugitive, to make up into garments for the European market; so Liberty set about persuading British manufacturers to reproduce in correspondingly soft fabrics both original oriental designs and new designs, reviving some of the ancient dyeing techniques, notably those of Persia. For those designs which required hand-printing, he set up his own printing works at Merton Abbey. Hand-printing continued there until the 1960s, when screens from some of the original blocks were made for screen-printing.

Customers at Liberty's new shop soon included William Morris (who founded Morris & Co. in 1861), Thomas Carlyle, Ruskin, Charles Keen, Watts, Burne-Jones, Leighton, Millais, Alma Tadema, and all the minor apostles of the Aesthetic Movement. The more precious attitudes of these frail Beings were mercilessly cartooned by du Maurier in *Punch*, with his Cimabue Browns who lived in Passionate Brompton and collected blue-and-white china. They were also satirised by Gilbert in *Patience* (1881) with his 'Greenery-yallery, Grosvenor Gallery, Foot-in-the-grave young man'. The peak year for both fashionable and intellectual aestheticism was 1877, the year of the opening of the Grosvenor Gallery, which brought the paintings of Whistler to public notice for the first time. Whistler was a friend of Arthur Liberty's, and influenced him considerably, as did other friends such as Dante Gabriel Rossetti, and Albert Moore. He was also, surprisingly, influenced by Kate Greenaway. He never met her but admired her as an early popular educator in his colour theories with her simple little outline drawings and pure, pale colourings. When a reporter asked Arthur Liberty if he had influenced Oscar Wilde, he replied: 'Indeed, yes. My art fabrics were produced before he became a celebrity. I gave him his opportunity, and he helped me mightily with mine through the publicity he commanded.'

56.
The Aesthetic and
the Oriental are
combined in both
dress and furnish-
ings. Teagowns by
Liberty & Co.,
featured in the
Lady's World,
July 1887.

The dressmaking department at Liberty's produced 'aesthetic gowns' in softly draping fabrics, offering suggestions for 'complete costumes designed and executed on artistic lines, and based upon a close and intimate study of the history of costume and a definite knowledge of modern requirements'. The important thing was that they were absolutely different from the fashionable dresses of the day which were tightly fitted, bustled and trained. Ideals of feminine beauty were also challenged. Mrs Haweis wrote in *The Art of Beauty:*

> Morris, Burne-Jones, and others, have made certain types of face and figure, once literally hated, actually the fashion. Red hair—once, to say a woman had red hair was social assassination—is all the rage. A pallid face with a protruding upper lip, is highly esteemed. Green eyes, a squint, square eyebrows, whitey-brown complexion, are not left out in the cold. Now is the time for plain women. Only dress after the pre-Raphaelite style, and you will

be astonished to find that so far from being an 'ugly duckling' you are a full-fledged swan.

Reading between the lines, one can guess that Mrs Haweis herself had that healthy, pink and white type of beauty which was being out-dated. Nothing is more infuriating to the woman of ordinary prettiness than to find those she considers ugly extravagantly admired. *Sylvia's Home Journal* had an article in 1879 on 'The Influence of Aesthetics on English Society', which spoke of their advantages to plain women, and again one suspects a grievance:

There is always a subtle charm in character more potent than that of simple prettiness . . . but there, however, begins the danger of aesthetics in dress— exaggeration, without a restraining taste. We have seen odd figures, with frizzed, dishevelled hair, distended sleeves, draggle-tail garments, wearing no dainty rim of white about neck or wrists. On the Continent, aesthetic dress-ing is, in any distinct degree, inadmissible. We remember the sensation produced by the appearance of an English damsel at fashionable places in Normandy. Her trailing, narrow skirts, her short-waisted, square-cut bodice, her puffed sleeves, her frizzed hair ensconsed in an immense Mother Shipton bonnet, struck the tasteful, somewhat conventional French women as the most extraordinary get up they had ever beheld.

Nevertheless, the mad Englishwomen were not deterred by French ridicule—in fact, as far as the intellectual section of aesthetic society went, it probably goaded them on. Lady Jebb's niece Maud wrote to her family in America that there were quite a number of aesthetic dresses at a Newnham Garden Party, but that she and Aunt Cara considered them affected and ridiculous. She added: 'Aunt C. has a simply perfect tea-gown, not aesthetic, but so graceful and lovely'. High Society also had its aesthetic adherents. Lady Diana Cooper describes her 'pre-Raphaelite mother' in *The Rainbow Comes & Goes*:

My mother had great beauty. She was tall and frail with a complexion as delicate as the palest anemone. Her hair was just auburn and she wore a cloudy fringe like Sarah Bernhardt and a classical handle of hair pinned where the Grecians pinned theirs . . . She had in her day despised fashionable bustles. She was greenery-yallery rather than the Duchess of Towers, with very high-heeled pointed shoes, with buckles, to increase her height, beauti-ful slim legs and ankles, a small waist drawn tightly into a silver-buckled petersham belt, a creamy flimsy open-necked shirt, free-wristed, with numberless little cream lace scarves draped round her neck and elbows. Always a sprig of bay was pinned high up to her neck by a green enamel tortoise. In London for out-of-doors there were face-cloth clothes (greenish-greyish-bluish-fawnish) with tabs and smoke flat pearl buttons, and three-cornered hats with panaches of cocks' feathers.

One can see that the lovely Duchess of Rutland achieved her own especial symposium of fashion, blending the aesthetic mood with the ultra-feminine mode, the quintessence of which was the tea-gown. She had been painted by Watts and had sat to Millais for the nun in St Bartholomew's Day. She had her daughters' schoolroom walls papered in William Morris's olive leaves, and hung with photographs of Italian masters framed in arty green wood. And every summer the drawing room curtains were laid out on the lawns to fade their in-artistic brightness.

The Aesthetic Movement was not just the passing craze of a season or two. House-furnishings necessarily have a longer fashionable life than clothes; but even aesthetic costume lasted a surprisingly long time. In 1881, *Sylvia's Home Journal* wrote:

Truly the rage for aesthetic dress is on the increase. A little while ago it was (and even now it is) ridiculed and laughed at, but nevertheless it is more sought after than hithertofore. With the taste employed in its arrangement, and the rich and costly materials used, commend me to it for indoor attire where the surroundings of stained floors, art embroidered hangings, and quaint carved oaken furniture seem to harmonize with it perfectly; but for outdoor attire its peculiar colours look anything but well amongst the bright fresh tints of spring; and for ball dress the modern colours are, I think, by far the prettiest under the brilliant light.

Some of the simply made long straight gowns of rich materials and quaint design form very effective toilettes, that are extremely becoming to some people; and we see now dresses most faithfully copied from pictures of those of the 13th and 14th centuries, that contrast forcibly with those of modern French taste which is struggling just now to supersede the aesthetic style both in furniture and dress.

Needless to say, many other shops had followed Liberty's pioneering work and were cashing in on the oriental craze. William Whiteley had, as a matter of fact, opened an Oriental Department in 1875, the same year that Liberty left Farmer & Roger's Oriental Warehouse to open his own shop. Swan & Edgar and Debenham & Freebody both had oriental departments at least by 1880. The Japanese Exhibition held in 1883 at the Humphrey Hall in Brompton Road gave the movement fresh stimulus, and every year at Christmas time Liberty's held an Exhibition of Oriental fabrics and other artistic embroidery on their premises at East India House. A critic of the Exhibition of November 1886, wrote in *The Lady's World:*

The quaint examples of antique work from China and Japan were of more than usual interest this year; and in addition to the usual exhibition of embroideries, two rooms were devoted on this occasion to the latest productions in aesthetic dress. The adaptations of Chinese embroidery to modern tea-gowns had an effect more remarkable than satisfactory.

A firm called A. Stephens & Co., which had established itself at 326 Regent Street in 1885 as importers of Indian Silks, fine Cashmeres, and Oriental Fabrics, decided to 'promote the use of these fabrics for tasteful and artistic costume purposes'. They acquired 291 Regent Street, and opened a suite of showrooms 'wherein are exemplified some of the daintiest phases of artistic costuming of which the metropolis affords an instance'. They furnished original designs, formulated by their own artists on the premises, and made a special study of colour in their practise of the art of costuming . . . 'all present evidences indicate that Messrs. Stephens have accomplished *nothing less than the inauguration of a new epoch in the construction of ladies' costumes and children's dresses*, in which perfect taste and graceful design are destined to play more important parts than hitherto.' The new epoch had, surely, already been inaugurated by Liberty's aesthetic gowns designed in their dressmaking workrooms.

In Debenham's *New Fashion Book* of Spring 1877 (No. 15 in the series), the influence that Liberty's softer fabrics had already had on fashion is apparent—even on those fashions which were very far from being pre-Raphaelite:

> The distinguishing feature of the present style of silk costumes is the mode in which they cling to the figure. All the various modifications of the Princess cut serve to give an appearance of slimness; and either four or six seams at the back of the bodice are universally adopted. The fault of the Princess cut is that its exceeding plainness is often suggestive of a dressing-gown, and to obviate this, various trimmings are planned for the back of the skirt. Distinct trains are also worn, sometimes kept in place by a drapery bordered with fringe.
> Fashionable evening dresses cling closely to the figure, and with exceeding long trains, which are tied back with a multiplicity of strings. Japanese silks make inexpensive evening dresses.

Under the heading of UNDERCLOTHING DEPARTMENT came 'Morning and Dressing-gowns . . . the fashion of wearing loose dresses for five o'clock tea has given an additional impetus to all this class of garments, and some very tasteful ones are the result. For example, a light blue cashmere, trimmed with diagonal bands of oriental galon and cream lace. Other robes in white cambric are richly trimmed with torchon lace.' In this guise did the tea-gown begin its long and languorous era.

✻　　　✻　　　✻

The Aesthetic Movement

There is no doubt that the influence of the Aesthetic Movement upon the textile trade of this country was entirely good. Crude colour had predominated since the introduction of aniline dyes in 1859; and the fashions of the 'sixties and early 'seventies, which mixed many bright colours together, were particularly displeasing. The Aesthetic Movement encouraged a return to the softer, more subtle shades of vegetable dyes. Thick woollens, stiff silks, shiny alpacas, and hard cottons lost favour when fashionable people began to buy soft, fragile, hand-woven silks imported from India, cashmere from the Persian border, honans, shantungs, and shanghais from China, crapes and satins from Japan. Liberty silks were imported undyed, and then dyed and printed in England. The irregularity in the threads produced by primitive weaving in India gave them an accidental play of light and shade which was one of their chief charms. In woollen fabrics, one of Liberty's greatest successes was an adaptation of the soft but rather loose cashmere woollens, so long popular as shawls, to make a cashmere dress material which Liberty named 'Umritza'.

English textile design during the next fifteen years was changed out of all recognition—as was demonstrated in the First Silk Exhibition held in 1890 by the Silk Association of Great Britain and Ireland. This Association was formed in an attempt to encourage the use of silk, the silk industry having fallen upon very hard times. Not the least of its misfortunes had been the introduction of alpaca, invented in 1838 by Sir Titus Salt as a substitute for silk, and royally endorsed in 1844 when Queen Victoria ordered some alpaca for herself. Originally it was made of the wool of the alpaca goat and silk; later, cotton was substituted. Shiny and springy, alpaca gave the rustly frou-frou of silk at much less cost, and provided the important stiffness to skirts, underskirts, and linings. Then after Cobden's Free Trade treaty of 1860 English silks suffered a further set-back.

Liberty and many other shopkeepers, manufacturers, and wholesale silk merchants exhibited at this First Silk Exhibition. One of the advertisers in the catalogue was The Aesthetic Gallery of 155 New Bond Street, whose proprietor was F. B. Goodyer, a former partner with Liberty & Co. . . . 'English silks, cashmeres, velveteens, fans, cushions, handkerchiefs, table covers, and other dainty manufactures.' The 'dainty manufactures' sound out of key in the Aesthetic Gallery, and one cannot think that Mr Goodyer picked up the phrase when he was at Liberty's. Could it be that he was one of the debasers of the movement into the kind of orientalisms represented by bric-à-brac and 'gifts'?

Other advertisers in this First Silk Exhibition catalogue were Lewis & Allenby, featuring Irish Silk Poplins from Dublin, and J. Roberts &

Son of Bradford, Plush Manufacturers: Silk plushes, silk seals, and imitation beavers. Tootal, Broadhurst, Lee were in the oriental swim with silk-bordered Indian Dhooties. Jay & Company of the General Mourning House must have had a very striking display, as theirs was an all black stand, dramatised by the contrast of some black and white striped materials. The Norwich Crape Co., which specialised in black silk rainproof crape so indispensable to widows (the rain falls upon the bereaved as well as the unbereaved) rivalled that of Samuel Courtauld & Co., 19 Aldermanbury, London, who had long been famous as crape manufacturers of Bocking, Essex.

That Courtauld's were able to build the foundations of their great world-wide business on this one fabric alone is quite understandable. Every draper's shop of any size had its mourning department, quite apart from those shops, like Jay's and the other Mourning Warehouses, which sold nothing else but the trappings of grief. From Debenham & Freebody's *Fashion Book* of 1877 we get a good idea of the amount of trade there was in black crape. It gives these instructions 'in answer to numerous enquiries respecting the duration and depth of Mourning':

A widow wears a Paramatta covered with Crape for nine months, and then slightly alters the depth of Crape; a Paramatta mantle trimmed with Crape, and Crape bonnet for six months. Afterwards Silk and Crape; this is slightly lightened for three months, and is succeeded for three more by plain Black.
  The length of mourning for a parent is one year—three months in Paramatta and Crape, three Silk and Crape, six without Crape. For a brother or sister, six month's mourning, three in Crape, two in Black, and one in half-mourning. For an aunt, uncle, niece, or nephew, three months, and no crape is worn. For a first cousin, six weeks—three weeks only slight. A husband's or wife's relations require the same length of mourning as blood relations.

So what with the aunts by marriage as well as the blood aunts, and all the cousins on both sides of the family, mourning clothes came into use over and over again even if one's immediate family kept both feet out of the grave. Debenham & Freebody pointed out that 'in no department is the economy of having good materials more thoroughly substantiated than in regard to Mourning. Inferior crape may reduce the first outlay; but it becomes shabby and loses colour so quickly that the price of replacing it should

57.

403.—CRAPE BONNET.

180

be added to the original cost'. Samuel Courtauld, of course, made superior Crape.

It is doubtful whether aesthetic costume was ever worn when in mourning. Although the pale, soulful, yearning face would go well with the apparel of grief, black was never an aesthetic colour. Pre-Raphaelites proper would all have been admirers of that bitter-sweet poetess Miss Christina Georgina Rossetti, and would follow her admonition:

> Better by far you should forget and smile
> Than that you should remember and be sad.

That would seem to preclude wearing mourning, since one could not possibly *forget and smile* in black crape.

⚘   ⚘   ⚘

Definitely there was no mourning department at Liberty's, where all the time business was expanding. By 1883, more space was needed; and since no adjoining premises were available they took 142 and 144 Regent Street, called the premises Chesham House, and transferred the furnishing and decoration departments there leaving the fabric and dress departments at East India House. The great success of the Liberty stand at the Paris Exhibition of 1889 led them to establish a branch at 38 Avenue de l'Opera. The *British Warehouseman* wrote, 'These premises have become the centre of a Parisian social craze for Liberty costumes and decoration which is spreading every day'. This was in an article in the issue of February 1895 entitled *The 'Liberty' Art Movement*, based on an interview with Mr Arthur Lasenby Liberty. Mr Liberty was introduced to the readers as the Man of the Moment in West End trade quarters, having recently converted his unique business into a limited liability company. The uniqueness of the business was that it had created an entirely new taste in fabrics, dress and interior decoration, the word Liberty having become descriptive of the style ... 'I was determined,' Mr Liberty said, 'not to follow existing fashion but to create new ones.'

His interviewer had arrived at what he called the *sanctum sanctorum* through a labyrinth of rooms in which 'the employment of electric light has developed a use for every turn and out-of-the-way corner one traverses, for each is utilised to display some rich or curious effect of oriental drapery and decoration'. He was invited to sit in a chair resembling a bishop's canopied throne, from which he observed a Sicilian Madonna enshrined above the chimneypiece, a Delft tiled mantel, an open box of Russian cigarettes on the desk, and a little dial of enamelled metal 'with a needle indicating whatever part of the

FELICITOUS QUOTATIONS.

Hostess (of Upper Tooting, showing new house to Friend). "WE'RE VERY PROUD OF THIS ROOM, MRS. HOMINY. OUR OWN LITTLE UPHOLSTERER DID IT UP JUST AS YOU SEE IT, AND ALL OUR FRIENDS THINK IT WAS *LIBERTY!*"
Visitor (sotto voce). "'OH, LIBERTY, LIBERTY, HOW MANY CRIMES ARE COMMITTED IN THY NAME!'"

58. *Punch*, October 20, 1894

house Mr Liberty desires to electrically communicate with'. This splendid split infinitive was no doubt contributed by the journalist, not by the Man of the Moment.

By the turn of the century, Liberty's had passed through a vogue for Arab-style décor with brass trays, Moroccan rugs, incense burners, and tables inlaid with mother-of-pearl. Afternoon tea was served in the Arab tea-room. When Art Nouveau burst upon a startled Europe, first at the Dresden Art Exhibition of 1897 and then at the Paris Exhibition of 1900, Liberty's workshops made carved settles, side-boards, and chimney-pieces with inserted Dutch tiles, beaten brass panels, enamel bands, and carved scrolls. Water-lilies, lotus flowers, and convolvulus asymmetrically writhed on fabrics and wallpapers. The original 'Liberty style' was eclipsed by Art Nouveau in the most *avant garde* circles, but still, according to *Punch*, flourished in the outer circles of Upper Tooting . . . 'Oh, Liberty, Liberty, how many crimes are committed in thy Name!'

Crimes were also being committed on the Continent in the name of Liberty. The success of their Paris branch led to the name of Liberty being applied to goods in many European countries for which Libertys had no responsibility. In the *Algemeen Handelsblad* of November 8, 1902, there is an advertisement by Liberty & Co. announcing that Metz & Co. of Amsterdam had opened a separate Liberty department, which was the only place in Holland where Liberty art fabrics and specialities were obtainable . . . 'Particular stress is laid upon this point, as on the Continent Liberty & Co.'s name appears to be mis-leadingly applied to, and too generally identified with, a certain class of silks and materials WHICH ARE IN NO WAY EQUAL TO THE GOODS SUPPLIED BY THEM, being inferior imitations of the original Liberty productions'. The Liberty specialities at Metz were listed as: Liberty silk, satin, velveteen, dress silks, dress velveteens, cushions, etc., art brocades, centres, cosies, art muslins, art tapestries, art furniture. The connection between the two firms continued until 1973, when their long friendship was consummated in marriage: Liberty & Co. took over Metz with its shops at Amsterdam, The Hague, and Schipol Airport.

It was not only abroad that Liberty agencies were set up during the Edwardian period. Although Liberty's themselves have no record of their agencies in provincial shops, the Sale Catalogue of Cavendish House, Cheltenham, Winter 1909, had a whole page devoted to their 'Liberty Department'. This was even more comprehensive, it seems, than at Metz in Amsterdam, for it included Liberty cushion squares, table covers, Indian printed covers, bed coverlets, etc., Liberty lacquer trays, Japanese inlaid tables, draught screens, Liberty garden and summer hats, and imitation panama hats, Liberty scarves, and 'About 30 Liberty Felt Hats, all of new shapes and artistic colourings, to be cleared at half price.'

This Liberty Department must be considered as an early example of the 'shop within a shop' idea, which is such a feature of modern department store trading.

59. Very handsome Polished Brass Door Lamp, with bevelled plate glass sides. Harris & Sheldon, 1902.

CHAPTER XVII

THE WOOLLEN MOVEMENT

Dr. Jaeger and Sanitary Woollen Underclothing. The Rational Dress Society and Hygienic Wearing Apparel. Chamois Leather Underwear. Knitted Outerwear; Parcels for the Poor and for Servants, Welsh flannel. Tennis clothes.

WHILE aestheticism was pulsating in Passionate Brompton and in the artistic ambience of the Grosvenor Gallery, in Germany a very different kind of culture was becoming news. In 1870, Dr Gustave Jaeger published a volume called *Health Culture*, and this was the beginning of what became known as the Woollen Movement. Dr Jaeger's ponderous work expounded his theory that the human race, being animal, should use the products of animals for clothing instead of vegetable products . . . 'wool is meant by nature to protect animal life; and instead of preventing, it assists the evaporation of the emanations coming from the body. It is therefore warm in winter, cool in summer, healthy at all times'. The word 'sanitary' was used to sum up all these virtues.

Dr Jaeger's Sanitary Woollen Clothing was extremely comprehensive, from stockinette combinations to digitated hosiery, consisting of woollen stockings with a compartment for each toe. Even the pocket handkerchief of the out-and-out 'Woollenite' had to be made of wool. Faithful followers of the gospel according to Dr Jaeger were called 'Woollenites' or 'Woolleners'; and one of the tenets of their faith was that no wool should be dyed. The raw material must be left in its natural state—hence the very unattractive greyish-cream colour of the original Jaeger underwear.

An Englishman who was staying in Germany at the height of the woollen crusade became completely converted. This was Mr L. R. S. Tomalin. He came back to England determined to convert his fellow countrymen to the sanitary way of life. He obtained the sole agency for

Dr Jaeger's made-up garments, and set up a small shop in Princes Street, near Oxford Circus. Within a few years he moved the shop to Fore Street in the City, which was then a very busy street for wholesale and retail drapery and outfitting. In 1883, Mr Tomalin and two cousins formed the Jaeger Company, and very soon the carriages of fashionable women formed queues outside the shop in Fore Street. Amongst the most distinguished male customers were Oscar Wilde and Bernard Shaw. Oscar Wilde provides a very unexpected link between the Aesthetic Movement and the Woollen Movement—Dr Jaeger's Sanitary Woollen Clothing would seem to be the very antithesis of Oscarism. One can only assume that Wilde became a 'Woollener' simply because it was the latest craze, and perhaps to please his wife who was a very active member of the Dress Reform Society. Bernard Shaw, on the other hand, took it very seriously, and ordered a complete suit of natural, undyed Jaeger wool stockinette. In this he has been recorded as walking down Regent Street looking, with his tall leggy figure and red hair, exactly like a forked radish.

Dr Jaeger's doctrines fell upon fertile feminine ground in the England of the early 'eighties because dress reform was in the air. Led by Viscountess Harberton, a distinguished body of women 'in the best Society' were rebelling against the tyranny of ladies' fashions. They were making much greater headway than Mrs Amelia Bloomer had done thirty years earlier . . . but then Mrs Bloomer was not only an American, but was what was even worse—she was middle-class. Even worse still, she was a temperance reformer, and was thus subject to ridicule on a double count. Mrs Ada Ballin, lecturer to the National Health Society, published an invaluable book in 1885 called *The Science of Dress*. In this she explains further the failure of the Bloomer costume:

> The feeling against the Bloomer costume was very strong, for although it had many good points about it, it represented too violent a change from the fashion of the time, and ladies would not adopt it for fear of appearing ridiculous. Reform, to be effective must be gradual, and it takes some time for the public to become accustomed to a new idea even in dress.
>
> Ever since the Bloomer costume, however, the idea has been gaining popularity, although but slowly, and at the Health Exhibition at South Kensington several divided dresses of the most pronounced type were shown, and met with favourable comment.

Mrs Ballin particularly recommended the Trouser Dress designed by Mrs Louisa Beck of 24 Connaught Street, Hyde Park, from whom it could be obtained.

A Rational Dress Society had been formed in 1881, and in 1882 a Hygienic Wearing Apparel Exhibition was held in Kensington Town

Hall, its object being 'to promote the adoption, according to individual taste and convenience, of a style of dress, based upon considerations of health, comfort, and beauty; and to deprecate constant changes of fashion which cannot be recommended on any of these grounds. The Society seeks to promote these objects by means of drawing-room meetings, advertisements, circulating pamphlets, leaflets, etc.; and also by issuing patterns which meet the approval of the Committee. (Anyone wishing to submit costumes is invited to forward them to the Hon. Secretary.)'

The costume which excited the most comment at the Hygienic Wearing Apparel Exhibition was Lady Harberton's Dual Garmenture. Dual garmenture consisted of a divided skirt worn underneath an ordinary skirt of almost the same length—in fact, a divided petticoat. There were divided opinions about its modesty and there is no evidence that it was ever worn except by members of the Rational Dress Society. Even they were not all sufficiently strong-minded. As a writer in *The Rational Dress Society's Gazette* of September 1888 complained: 'The effect of singularity in attire is to incur a social martyrdom out of all proportion to the relief obtained. It is vain to be comfortably and modestly attired if one is made an object of observation or ridicule.'

A year after the English Jaeger Company had been formed, there was held the International Health Exhibition at South Kensington to which Mrs Ballin referred in her book. The Jaeger Company had a Stand, and *The Times* published a long article on October 4, 1884 under the headline 'Sanitary Clothing'. The final paragraph read:

Such briefly is the reform in clothing approved, and carried out by thousands of Germans, not a few Russians, and some Englishmen, and which has been introduced in our midst at the South Kensington International Health Exhibition and by the opening of a depôt in Fore-street, where articles of every description in connexion with the system are to be seen. Already Dr Jaeger's sanitary woollen system has been adopted by some of our most eminent sanitary reformers; while, in Germany, it has not only revolution-ized the trade of Stuttgart, where its founder practices, but the clothes are worn and highly appreciated by such men as Count von Moltke, who may be expected to apply the principles in question to the German army.

Georgiana Hill in her *History of English Dress* published ten years after Jaeger clothes were introduced to England, wrote:

The soft, warm, natural wool was hailed with delight . . . it was just what people wanted. Every article that could be procured was sold directly. The goods could not be made fast enough to meet the demand. People went mad about wool. They slept in woollen sheets and clothed themselves from head to foot in wool. Regular 'woolleners' who abjured silk, satin, muslin, and velvet gowns, had to renounce all festivities at which it was impossible for them to appear in wool. No 'woolleners', for instance, could go to Court. The majority were, however, content with woollen fabrics for underwear. There was such a rush for these garments that ladies would drive up in their carriages to the emporium in Mortimer Street, where the first agency was established under the management of Miss Franks, and carry off the precious bales without waiting for them to be wrapped up.

This Miss Franks of Mortimer Street was mentioned in the *Lady's World* of February 1887 as manager of the depot of the Rational Dress Society at 23 Mortimer Street; and the depot was also mentioned by Mrs Ada Ballin in her *Science of Dress* as selling 'the Girton Stays', which were designed by students of Girton and Newnham and were known as the *Corsets sans arrête* after the boneless sardines of that name. Mrs Ballin also says that Mrs Addley Bourne of 174 Sloane Street (whom we have met before in the crinoline era, when her shop was at 37 Piccadilly) had agreed to stock all the children's and ladies' underclothing advocated in her book. It would seem almost certain that the Rational Dress Society depot in Mortimer Street was an agency for Dr Jaeger's Sanitary Woollen Clothing. The Jaeger Company itself has no record of this—only of their original premises in Princes Street, and then the Fore Street shop; nor have they any record of when they began to appoint drapers as Jaeger agents. But Cole Brothers of Sheffield advertised in 1893 that they were agents for Dr Jaeger's Sanitary Woollen System. In 1900 Browns of Chester were advertising Sanitary Woollen Underwear and had a display of Jaeger articles. Alison Gernsheim in *Fashion and Reality* says that E. M. Ward & Co. of Bradford were agents for Dr Gustave Jaeger's Sanitary Woollen Clothing, but does not give a date.

❦   ❦   ❦

English and Scottish manufacturers had risen to the German challenge of the 'eighties. Only four years after the Jaeger Company was established in Fore Street, the Winter Fashions Catalogue of Cavendish House, Cheltenham, included these entries:

Bodices for Winter wear in the new sanitary undyed wool.
Ladies Hand-wrought Natural Undyed Sanitary Wool Vests and Combination Under Garments, in all shapes and sizes, of the best English and Scotch manufacture; superior in texture and finish to the German make, and fitting much better.
Ladies Natural Undyed Cashmere Wool Sanitary Hose, 2/11 a pair.

In their Sale Catalogue of the following summer they offer:

Natural Sanitary Wool Combination Under Dresses, with high necks and short sleeves, or high necks and long sleeves.
Natural Sanitary Wool Summer Vests and Drawers.

The wearing of 'drawers' by girls and women was by no means universal at this time. In 1879, *The Lancet* wrote: 'We consider this article of dress unnecessary, and in many ways detrimental to health and morals'. Unfortunately, it did not go on to explain their moral view point. Mrs Ada Ballin preferred combinations to vest and drawers. Unlike *The Lancet* she explained her reasons, and in doing so has given us some intriguing glimpses of the sleeping habits of the period:

The combination garment, with the addition of woollen stockings, forms a complete and most sanitary costume. If any objection is raised against combinations, on the score that it is dangerous to change them at night and unpleasant to sleep in drawers, woollen vests may be worn, and drawers of the same material fastened to the stays or bodice. The vests can then be retained for nightwear, and the drawers taken off with the other clothes. Many people, however, think it is advisable to change the underclothing at night. If this is done, great care is needed in order to prevent chill. If the woollen vest is changed, its place must be supplied by one of equal thickness and warmth.

HARBOROW

15. COCKSPUR STREET.
S.W.

SPECIALITY

BRITISH WOOL
UNDERCLOTHING

It would be fascinating to have the opinions of *The Lancet* and of Mrs Ballin upon chamois leather underwear. This was introduced towards the end of the 'seventies, for those who wished for an excessively svelt figure under the exceedingly tight dresses. It could come under neither the heading of 'sanitary' nor of 'hygienic'. As for laundering, it must have been the very antithesis of drip-dry.

60. '*Harborow's have a world-wide reputation for their pure British wool underclothing for gentlemen. They made the gloves worn by Queen Victoria at her Coronation, and those she has worn for the last half-century.' Modern London,* 1887.

There had been chamois leather equestrian pants before, and also chamois leather knickerbockers to wear under skating skirts; but the new chamois underwear was in the shape of everyday drawers, combinations, vests and bodices. Madame Aldegonde, whose Regent Street shop was *Punch's* imaginary high-society dressmaking establishment, is in 1879 depicted asking two clients if they wore chamois leather underclothes. 'No?—very well . . .' Madame allocates them to her *second* dressmaker. In I. & R. Morley's catalogue of that same year, chamois vests and 'bodies' appear, and continue in the catalogues up to the mid-1880's. In the later years, the 'bodies' are perforated and covered with silk or flannel. By 1909, chamois vests have been dropped and 'bodies' have become bodices. They are all perforated and covered with scarlet flannel, and cannot have been very different from the chamois chest protectors covered with scarlet flannel which were also listed.

❧   ❧   ❧

Before the Woollen Movement, the majority of people wore cotton underwear of cambric or nainsook, reinforced by flannel petticoats and flannel bodices; but it would be wrong to give the impression that there was no woollen underwear before Dr Jaeger's. As far back as 1835, H. Thorn's Patent Merino Underwear was advertised in the *Morning Herald* and sold at his Hosiery Warehouse at 23 Ludgate Street, 'three doors from St Paul's'. It is very likely that Mr Thorn was exclusively a men's outfitter; but at least by the beginning of the 1880's, and before Jaeger was obtainable in England, Mr Bill of Tenby was selling hand-knitted underclothes. This was the William Bill who set up as a 'Homespun Merchant' in Mold, Flintshire, in 1846 and moved to the fashionable Pembrokeshire spa later. His products were written about in the editorial columns of *Sylvia's Home Journal* in 1881:

'Light, elastic, inexpensive, including Jerseys, Cardigans, Vests, Spencers, Combinations, etc. This Shetland underclothing owes its immense superiority over other productions to the fact that Shetlanders spin their own yarn. The fleece is glossy and fine, and makes especially valuable underclothes for invalids who cannot bear thickness or weight'. Mr Bill kept 'the largest stock in the kingdom of hand-knitted socks and stockings—Welsh fingering, Wheeling, Shetland, Cashmere, Welsh Turnovers—charming little shawls in pale tint of grey homespun with fringed edges. The Whittles are even prettier white; they are fringed and make comfortable and becoming wraps. Also, old-fashioned hand-loom Welsh flannel, Velvet Flannel, soft and white.'

61. Mr Bill, originally '*Homespun Merchant of Mold, Flintshire, selling Welsh flannels and hand-knitted underclothes in Welsh fingering*', goes over to the more fashionable products of Scotland and Ireland.

Perhaps *Sylvia's* handsome write-up brought Mr Bill a great many enquiries from the metropolis. At any rate, something encouraged the family to transfer their business to London about 1892, where at 31 Great Portland Street they sold wholesale as well as retail, and built up an overseas trade. In 1910, they acquired additional premises at 93 New Bond Street, under the name of W. Bill, Homespun Merchant, and began to sell knitted outer-garments as well as woollen cloth and underwear. There are now four Mr Bills in the business, and they still occupy their Old Bond Street and New Bond Street shops. What is more, there is a young generation of Bills growing up, who will carry the family firm into the twenty-first century.

Two years before the English Jaeger Company was formed, Edmonds, Orr & Co. opened a shop at 47 Wigmore Street to sell Patent Ladies' Woven Undervests and Combination Garments 'designed to prevent creases under the corsets, and thereby reduce the size of the waist and improve the figure. In wool, merino, or silk'. This merino, since it is differentiated from wool, would be a wool and cotton mixture—which was, in fact, what merino had come to mean. Originally it was simply wool from Spanish merino sheep, which were naturalised in Australia by the 1820's. This short staple wool was found to spin very well with cotton, and this mixing process was invented by William Hollins's hosiery firm about 1847. Much later, in 1894, Hollins used the same cotton and wool yarn to make a cloth, and registered it under the name of 'Viyella' which they say was the first fabric with a registered name. Fifteen years earlier, Thomas Burberry in Basingstoke had registered the name 'Gabardine' for his proofed cloth made of Egyptian cotton proofed before weaving; but it was not sold over the counter as piece goods. Burberry allowed his patent to lapse, and gabardine has become a generic name for a material, while the name Burberry has been immortalized with a small 'b' in the English Dictionary, meaning raincoat. 'Viyella', on the other hand, has remained a brand name and become more widely known than the name of its makers, William Hollins.

The Don Association of Woollen Manufacturers was founded in 1877, when there was a depression in the wool trade, before the German Woollen Movement spread to this country. They sold general outfitting for men and boys, with special offers to 'clergymen and professionals'. Their black superfine cloths were 'all of woaded colour and guaranteed to stand the test of downright hard-wear'. In the 1880's, the Don Association had two London shops at Holborn Viaduct and at Cheapside, two shops in Birmingham, one in Manchester, three in Liverpool, and one in Bristol—in fact, a multiple chain.

Fleming Reid also began a retail chain, only a little later. They opened their first Scotch Wool Shop in Greenock in 1881, and by 1889 their branches numbered fifty-three. By 1910 there were over two hundred, and their peak year was 1939, when they totalled four hundred and twelve shops. The original Fleming Reid mills produced worsted weaving yarn for Glasgow and Bradford manufacturers, and their development into knitting wools was due to one of those accidents of commerce which have so often led to business development in hitherto unthought-of directions. A parcel of Single Tweed Yarn returned from the manufacturers as not correct to shade was twisted four-fold into knitting wool and sold to their own mill workers. According to an early leaflet of Fleming Reid's, 'Success was immediate. The towns-people quickly learned of the wonderful wearing qualities of this new knitting wool and the firm had to open a retail shop in West Burn Street, Greenock in 1881 to meet the demand which resulted from this trivial beginning.'

The opening of the first Scotch Wool Shop coincided happily with the Woollen Movement stemming from Germany, and also with the 'Buy British Wool' campaign which was launched by the Marquis of

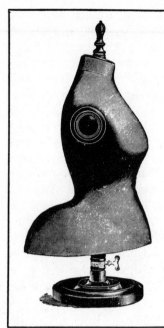

NEW SHAPE JACKET
OR JERSEY STAND.

Just introduced to meet the requirements of the present fashion. It is of
an improved shape and has been submit-
ted to and approved by the LONDON
MANTLE HOUSES.

Price on Stand complete   12/6 each
If Stand to Telescope   13/6 each
If made to Suspend   9/6 each

62.

Salisbury at a meeting in the Mansion House to counter the depression
in the British woollen industry. For a time the shop windows were full
of materials labelled British, and Georgiana Hill commented some
years later:

> How merry the Press were over the new craze, and the patriotism that would
> voluntarily make use of articles which were BRITISH, INFERIOR, and
> OBSOLETE.

The Scotch Wool Shops also benefited from the introduction to
fashion at this time of women's knitted outdoor garments. Hitherto
the cardigan had been an exclusively male garment. Invented by Lord
Cardigan to keep him warm in the Crimean campaign, it was originally
known as the Cardigan Bodywarmer. Knitted garments for ladies were,
until almost the end of the 'seventies, confined to spencers, petticoats,
shawls, wraps, and bed jackets. But in 1879 *Sylvia's Home Journal* was
writing: 'To wear fishermen's Jerseys is the latest freak of fashion for
ladies. With very little contrivance they fit very closely to the figure
and when it is good, they are not unbecoming.' That same summer,
Redfern's introduced the 'Jersey Costume'.

The Jersey Costume became immensely fashionable because it was
worn by Lillie Langtry. Since Mrs Langtry was known as The Jersey

XI Woolland Bros. of Knightsbridge: the new building of 1899, which replaced a row of three-storey yellow brick houses.

Marshall & Snelgrove's of Oxford Street and Vere Street: the new building of 1876 replaced an irregular assortment of houses, and still remains today.

XII   Regent Street at 5 o'clock on a summer afternoon of the late 1890's, showing Liberty's, East India House: *above*, on the corner of Great Marlborough Street; *below*, the windows on Regent Street.

Lily (she was the daughter of the Very Rev. Corbet le Breton, Dean of Jersey), it may have been her flair for publicity which led her to adopt the fashion; and no doubt her famous figure could wear it better than most. It consisted of a close-fitting long-sleeved garment of knitted silk or wool, which swathed the figure from a high round neck to well below the hips, and was worn over a tight tie-back skirt, which was usually pleated all round from the knee. It was described in *Punch*:

> Then she wore a jersey fitting
> Like an eel-skin all complete,
> With a skirt so tight that sitting
> Was an agonising feat.

Yes, the Jersey Costume was a struggle; in fact, it was the first outer garment not to have some form of fastening. The difficulty of getting in and out of it may partly account for its short life in fashion.

Nevertheless, knitted fabrics had come to stay. By 1887, Nicholson's of St Paul's, in their Jubilee Sale Catalogue, were offering any amount of garments in Stockinette: 'New jersey jacket in Stockinette; the Habit Jersey in Stockinette; richly braided or beaded jackets in firm Stockinette. Also the Garibaldi Jacquette in fashionable striped Jersey cloth, with silk collar and cuffs, suitable for boating, tennis, etc.' The outdoor sports girl had arrived. And by the end of the century, Monro's of Edinburgh, who were among the first manufacturers to see the possibilities of outer knitwear for women, were selling it in the United States, Russia, Scandinavia, Germany, and France, a Monro warehouse being established in Paris in 1908. Home-knitters, who hitherto had confined their industry to socks, stockings, spencers, bed-jackets and shawls, began to yearn to create outwardly visible garments. And it was in 1899 that John Paton produced *The Universal Knitting Book*, which gave home-knitters patterns of fashionable garments for the whole family, price one penny—an immediate and phenomenal success. It was not the first knitting pattern book. In the 1840's, Mrs Gaugain, a gentlewoman of Edinburgh who had come upon hard times, produced three slim knitting books for the daughters of the Nobility. During the Crimean War, lady's magazines began to give knitting patterns of Balaclava helmets, scarves, and other comforts. But John Paton's book was the first family knitting book.

It is significant of the great vogue for wool that even the National Linen Company (established in Fleet Street 1845, and later at 130 New Bond Street), made a speciality of Shetland Goods in the 1880's:

Shetland combination suits and jerseys for ladies' wear, cardigans for clergymen's use, to be worn under the surplice, sleeping gowns, socks, stockings, underclothing, respirators, and hosiery of all descriptions, made from natural wools, grey and white—all made specially for this house in the Islands, and strongly recommended by the medical profession.

The National Linen Company made a great feature of offers to charitable organisations at Christmas, when their goods were 'largely purchased and given away by customers benevolently inclined'. A contemporary directory says: 'They also tender for workhouse supplies, in which they enter into fierce competition with many wholesale houses in their line'.

There was still no very clear cut demarcation between wholesale and retail in the drapery trade, and whenever there was a possibility of large orders, most shops were prepared to give keen trade prices. Hospital, workhouse, and charitable orders were well worth getting. There was also the immense yardage of flannel and calico supplied to working parties of ladies who met in each other's drawing-rooms to sew garments for charitable institutions, fallen women, orphans and the aged. These ladies also cut out materials to supply needlework to the 'Respectable Poor'—presumably, to keep them respectable.

Fashionable philanthropy was at its height, and in 1884 the word slumming changed its dictionary meaning from 'to go into or frequent slums for discreditable purposes; to keep to back streets to avoid observation'. It now became 'to visit slums for charitable or philanthropic purpose, or out of curiosity, especially as a fashionable pursuit'. There was, as a matter of fact, a very genuine wave of compassion in the air, and the London Society for the Prevention of Cruelty to Children was founded in 1884. Lord Shaftesbury, Lord Aberdeen, Dr Barnardo, and the Baroness Burdett-Coutts found many hard workers to help their own untiring efforts. But many people, including Mr Punch, took a very cynical view of 'Slumming': 'It is the new way to climb the social ladder, because you meet so many Duchesses in the East End now'.

Christmas parcels for the poor were another profitable line for drapers. These were advertised every year by Lewis's of Liverpool, who now had a second Liverpool shop called the Bon Marché, and another in Manchester and in Birmingham. The parcels were bought by Lady Bountifuls who probably only condescended to patronise such popular emporiums for this particular, beneficent purpose.

Domestic servants were only one degree higher than 'the poor', and were generally regarded as rather less deserving. Lewis's sold gift parcels for servants which consisted of 'Seven yards of double-width black merino, two yards of lining, one striped skirt, and half a dozen linen handkerchiefs'. Thus employers gave their servants as

Christmas presents the materials to make their own uniforms—with some handkerchiefs thrown in to promote good-will at the festive season. Even as late as the 1920's, the business to be got in Christmas parcels for servants was considerable, and the presents were still very utilitarian, although perhaps rather more acceptable. Mr Cecil Mills, who joined Gorringes in 1926, remembers the days when ladies would come in and order two to three hundred pairs of socks and stockings for the servants . . . 'We also used to get orders for a dozen cardigans at a time. These were for the stablemen and gardeners. They were bought in large lots of the same colour, because each family had a different coloured livery for their servants'.

In the mid-century there were shops in London and the bigger cities called Servants' Bazaars, where servants could buy their own uniforms and other needs. The London Post Office Street Directory of 1859 listed two 'Servants Bazaars' in Oxford Street: Archibald Thompson's at 252, and William Mills's at 309. Woollands of Knightsbridge was established in 1869 as a shop for servants—and it is surprising that in such a class-conscious era Woollands became by the turn of the century one of the most elegant shops for ladies of fashion, famed particularly for that symbol of useless beauty and idleness, the tea-gown. Garroulds, 61 Edgware Road, specialized in nurses' and maids' uniforms.

Shops liked it to be understood that they made virtually no money out of the goods they sold for charity, and it is possible that some of them kept their profit margin very low. An announcement of Browns of Chester in 1878 reads:

Important Being connected with the Manufactory of Real Welsh Flannels, we supply them at exceptionally low prices. Blankets, Homespuns, Calicoes, Shirtings and all kinds of goods suitable for Charities are obtained direct from the looms and sold at a nominal profit.

William Brown was Chairman of the North Wales Flannel Company which amalgamated two large mills at Holywell, and this was a time when Welsh flannel had become so out of fashion that it was usually advertised as 'suitable for Charities'.

The Welsh Woollen Industry, like so many other textile industries in these islands, can be traced back to workshops set up by Flemish weavers. A party landed in Pembrokeshire in the fourteenth century, when the existing industry was a very humble home-craft. The Flemings helped to build up the reputation of Welsh woollen products until it was second only to that of the Spitalfields silk weavers. The decline of the industry in the second half of the nineteenth century was due to three factors: English woollen districts began producing an 'Imitation Welsh Flannel' which was softer and finer; Welsh mills, dependent upon water-power, could not expand like the Yorkshire mills which had gone over to steam power; and the final blow was the revolutionary change in women's underwear which took place during the Woollen Movement of the 1880's. Flannel petticoats and bodices, which had for so long been women's bulwarks against the cold and other less constant perils, went out; and everybody wore garments made of knitted wool or merino mixture yarns.

Fashion, which was so largely responsible for ruining the flannel industry, can be defended in that it brought comfort and hygiene. Flannel shrunk and went hard after washing, and therefore flannel was not washed. Mr Bernard Roth, F.R.C.S., is quoted by Mrs Ada Ballin on this point:

> No doubt many of the objections which medical authorities have raised to flannel being worn next to the skin have arisen from observations on the poor, who often will put on a flannel shirt or vest and keep it on till it almost falls to pieces. When I was house surgeon to a London hospital I have more than once noticed an expression of surprise when a patient suffering from a skin affection was asked when his flannel shirt was last washed, the idea that a flannel shirt required washing never apparently having occured to him.

We are not, here, concerned with the habits of 'the poor'; but it is fairly safe to say that the flannel petticoats and bodices of the rich were infrequently washed. They did, however, wear chemises of cotton or fine linen next to their skin. The most exquisite of these were made by Irish peasants and nuns, both qualifying to belong to the unwashed category of the community. They had a rare reputation for needlework, and no doubt were not paid much for their handwork by the shops which proudly advertised underwear especially made to order by Irish peasants and nuns.

The balance was in some part redressed for the manufacturers of flannel by the increasing involvement in outdoor sports of ladies who hitherto had been spectators except at croquet. Lawn tennis swept the country from its introduction by Major Wingfield in 1874. Three years later the All England Croquet Club became the All England Croquet and Lawn Tennis Club, and the first championships were played. The first ladies' championship was in 1884; but ladies played garden-party tennis from the very beginning.

Even middle-aged ladies took up lawn tennis with enthusiasm. Lady Jebb was forty years old, very definitely middle-aged by Victorian standards, when she wrote to her sister from Cambridge in 1877:

63. Lawn-Tennis Dress
from Peter Robinson.

'*In lawn-tennis costumes,*
beauty has to cede so wide a
place to convenience, that when
the latter has been attained,
ardent players often rest
satisfied to forego what is
distinctly more becoming.'

Lady's World, July 1887.

At garden parties you always have games of some kind, either croquet or lawn tennis. The latter is most played now, and is the nicest of all. I am just learning and it is certainly a livelier movement than I have indulged in for many a day.

Strange that for a game of such lively movement, Mrs Ada Ballin, that pontificator upon rational dress, says in her *Science of Dress:* 'For Lawn Tennis no special dress is required, but jerseys are very comfortable to play in, and on the whole the prettiest tennis dresses are those made in white flannel with loose sailor bodices.' These fairly sensible suggestions were evidently not widely taken up. The Hon. Mrs Peel describes tennis of the 1880's in *Life's Enchanted Cup:*

For tennis we wore long skirts with bustles, washing shirts with stiff white linen collars, ties, and mannish straw hats. The meeting place of shirt and skirt was hidden by a Petersham belt, and kept in place at the back by an ornamental safety pin stuck through the belt.

Ready-made Lawn Tennis Costumes were offered by Brown's of Chester as early as 1882; and in 1887 Dickins & Jones's Summer Catalogue included 'a very large assortment of the New Unshrinkable Lawn Tennis Flannels. Also the Tennis or Boating Jacket, in fancy striped flannel and plain cream and colours, well-shrunk and tailor-made.' An illustration of this jacket shows it worn over a shirt-blouse

64. Regatta Costume
designed by Miss Dust,
5 Brook Street, W.

*'The week of Henley Regatta
is a time when beauty and
fashion are expected to don
their smartest dresses and
most brilliant parasols, and
awaken animation in one of
the dullest little towns in
England.'*

Lady's World, July 1887

with high starched collar; ground-length skirt with bustle, and a straw
boater hat complete the sporting outfit—which is, in fact, the perfect
illustration to Mrs Peel's description. A year later, Cavendish House
Cheltenham has Girton Tennis Cloth of best Egyptian Cotton, and
Lawn Tennis Woollen Materials in Fancy Checks and Stripes with
plain to match. Also tennis jackets of striped flannel with loose fronts—
the forerunner of the blazer.

Not all women were enthusiastic about exhibiting themselves on the
courts. *Sylvia's Home Journal* in 1877 wrote that there was a leaven of
truth in the criticism which appeared in a contemporary weekly upon
the prevalence of the game of lawn tennis:

The woman or girl who is properly alive to the effect of her appearance
should never think of playing lawn-tennis in public. A woman taking an
active part in a lawn-tennis competition may be compared to a swan wad-
dling on a bowling green, for women clad in the dresses of the present day
were never intended by Providence to run.

Some alert member of the Dress Reform Society must surely have
retorted that Providence never intended women to be clad in tight
bustled dresses and starched collars.

CHAPTER XVIII

SHOP FITTINGS AND SHOPS OF THE 'EIGHTIES

*South Coast Drapers. Display Stands and Mannequin Figures,
Fenwicks of Newcastle, Jessops of Nottingham. Dressmaking
Departments. Lace and Fans, Furs and Furriers.*

I N 1881, when H. G. Wells was fifteen, he was apprenticed to Edwin
Hide's Drapery Emporium at Southsea. The opening chapters of
Kipps are set in this shop, which Wells only slightly disguised by
calling it Edwin Shalford's Drapery Bazaar at Folkestone. Mr Shalford
is showing his new apprentice round the shop . . .

They crossed a large room full of the strangest things Kipps had ever seen.
Lady-like figures, surmounted by black, wooden knobs in the place of the
refined heads one might have reasonably expected stood about with a life-
like air of conscious fashion. 'Costume Room,' said Shalford. They discovered two young ladies, taller and fairer than any of the other young
ladies, and with black trains to their dresses, who were engaged in writing
at a little table.

It was only the superior young ladies in the Costume Room who
would have worn trains. Downstairs, in the main shop, where there was
'a long vista of gloves dangling from overhead rods', the lady assistants'
attire was not described, beyond that they wore black mittens. The
male shop assistants were also distinguished according to seniority by
their clothes. By the time Kipps had been promoted from running
errands and cleaning windows to serving the less important customers
and taking goods out on approval, he had grave sartorial discussions
with his immediate senior, who was by way of being a 'Masher'.
They talked of collars, ties, the cut of a trouser-leg and the proper
shape of a boot-toe; and in due course Kipps replaced his short jacket
by a morning coat with tails, and high stand-up collars replaced his
former turn-down ones.

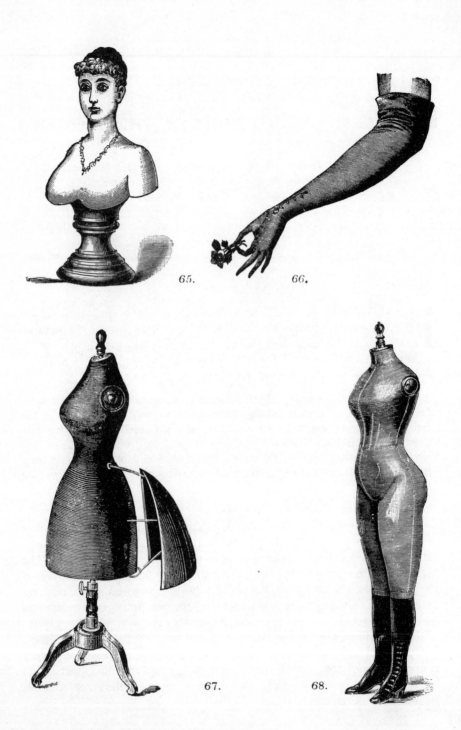

65.   66.

67.   68.

Kipps served in the Manchester Department, that is the department for cotton goods and materials . . . 'they came round a corner into a new smell which was destined to be the smell of Kipps's life for many years, the vague distinctive smell of Manchester Goods'. Mr Edwin Shalford was very proud of his overhead change carrier which, he calculated, through the 'fishency of the system', saved him pounds and pounds a year.

Lamson's Cash Balls were an ingenious invention of the early 1880's. They were hollow wooden balls which came into two parts like an Easter egg, so that the money and the bill could be placed inside. They rolled along inclined tracks from above each counter to the desk, and back along another track with the receipt. Later on, the inclined tracks were changed for overhead 'railways'. These, with their hanging wooden cash containers like miniature cable cars on a Swiss mountain railway, were impelled along by the assistant pulling a cord. They went PING! . . . and shot off on their journey round the ceiling. Children shopping with their mothers were entranced as they watched them scudding about and turning corners. Overhead railways continued to be used by small-town drapers well into the 1930's, and it is very possible that some are still in use. The firm of Lamson's, which originated the cash balls and then the overhead railways, were by 1900 making pneumatic tubes for the same purpose.

Also in the early 1880's, certain developments took place in the shape of the lady-like figures with wooden knobs for heads described in *Kipps*. Stockman's Busts, still one of the leading makes, originated in the French Bust Factory of Stockman Frères, established in Paris in 1869. A Mr Valentine of Great Portland Street became sole agent in

65. New handsome Fichu Stand with wax head. 1888.

66. Glove hand and arm with Mousquetaire . Suède gloves. 1879.

67. Long Mantle or Jacket stand with adjustable improver. French body, best make. 1888.

68. Lady's Figure, with polished Wood Legs to knee. 1902.

69. Wire Cape Holder. 1902.

69.

201

the United Kingdom and the Colonies, and an early twentieth century catalogue of his proudly announces that at the Great Exhibition of Moscow 1891, Chicago 1893, Paris 1900 and Hanoi 1901, Stockman's Busts were *hors concours*, signifying 'above competition'. They were allowed to exhibit only, not to compete, in order to give other exhibitors a chance.

In the late Victorian period, Sydney Harris, who had a Shop Fitting Works in Birmingham, probably did the greatest business in mannequin figures in England. It was evidently considered highly desirable to have a French body, since an early catalogue of his claims 'French Bodies' for most of his dress stands. This was in the 1880's, and there are some truly breath-taking Ladies' French Body Costume Stands, with skittish wire skirts and provocative Improvers. The Improver was the bustle, and was adjustable so that it could be shot out at the back to any desired distance. The firm became Harris and Sheldon about this time, and a Jersey Stand with adjustable Improver was illustrated in their catalogue of 1877—that is, eight years after the launching of the Jersey Costume by Redfern, which was the beginning of outer-knitwear for women. Jerseys had in those eight years become well-established garments, on display in all elegant shops equipped with Harris & Sheldon's mannequin figures.

This particular jersey stand was finished with a wooden knob, and no doubt headless figures were, so to speak, the backbone of the trade. Nevertheless, Harris & Sheldon also traded in lovely creatures with wax heads and velvet bodies. One particularly expressive full-length figure had not only a wax head but wax hands and moveable arms. Also illustrated was 'A New Handsome Fichu Stand'. This was a wax bust and head, completely naked, but cut off in the prime of her youth, just where the most appealing curves are beginning to take shape. She was described as 'suitable for Hairdressers, Milliners, or Lacemen'. She was less expensive in washable composition and this might have had certain advantages over wax, although 'The Best Quality Wax-work' was said to stand a hot climate.

Besides 'Special Attitude Figures' of all descriptions, the catalogue of 1902 illustrated an exciting 'Cycle Figure', a daring young lady with wax head and real hair, riding a bicycle unclothed. She was available with a choice of wax, gloved, or articulated hands, and had ball joints. Ladies' Habit Figures sat side-saddle on a wooden horse without their habits. There was the same choice here between wax, gloved, or articulated wooden hands, and their legs were jointed. Milliners' hat stands had heads with elaborate coiffures, and hairdressers' busts had specially implanted hair all one way. These appear very much as those described by Osbert Sitwell in *Before the Bombardment*, in the window of the chief hairdresser of Scarborough. This hairdressing shop was in the Winter Gardens, which had been closed since the end of the Season:

> . . . imprisoned behind their glass walls several coquettishly mildewed wax ladies were coyly grimacing. One or two of these were cut off prematurely, like the effigy of the Sovereign on coin or postage stamp, but others did not forbid a glimpse of alluring rotundities, for the full figures of the last century were still in vogue. It seemed as though these ladies had been the victims, several years previously, of that strange fate so often predicted for children by their nurses: they must, surely, have been rehearsing these pouts and dimples, when suddenly the wind had changed, and they had remained ever since caught fast in the arch posture of the moment. Wax figures, perhaps because they are moulded and set in the very breath of an instant, age more rapidly, more obviously, than anything in the world. It is as possible to put a date to them as it is to a fashion plate. And it added to the mad indecency of the spectacle, that these abandoned females, by their style of hairdressing and of such drapery as they possessed beside the natural shelter of their tresses, had obviously been disporting themselves in the window for several years.

There was, of course, a great variety of shop equipment other than lay figures for displaying drapery goods. Harris & Sheldon's catalogue lists Muff Stands and many-branched Millinery Stands; Fancy Brass Fan Stands, and Sunshade Stands for opened parasols. There was a Circular Show Stand to display thirty-six umbrellas. For footwear there were Fancy Brass Boot Stands, Elegant Boot Brackets, Handsome All-brass Boot Arrangements, Telescopic Boot Stands, and Enamelled Paper-maché Legs and Feet for Shoes and Hose. For the convenience of customers trying on shoes, there were Polished Brass Foot Stands with Bevelled Plate-glass Mirror in Centre; for trying on clothes, there were Mahogany Silvered Plate Cheval Glasses. There were Mantle Horses, Mantle Shoulders (now called coat-hangers), Cape Stands, Fichu and Visite Stands, Flower and Feather Stands, and Glove Hands.

There were also the bent wood chairs which were the traditional seating for customers in drapery shops (Fig. 54)—two to each counter, or even more. Some shops still have these high bent wood chairs. Very occasionally encountered, they are an unexpected but much appreciated service to the customer of this generation, resigned as she is to stand while being served and while waiting to be served. It took an Act of Parliament to assure that shop assistants were provided with chairs behind the counter . . . perhaps in the not too far distant future there will be another Act to make compulsory the provision of chairs for customers.

70. Bobby & Co. of Margate in 1902 (established 1887)—the first of the
Bobby shops.

Edwin Hide's Drapery Emporium at Southsea had a long established
rival in the firm of Knight and Lee. As far back as 1831, there was a
Laceman called William Wink in Queen Street, near the Portsea
docks. After Mr Wink's death, his business was carried on by his
widow, Sarah Wink, who described herself as 'Lace Manufacturer,
Milliner, and Dressmaker'. Queen Street, however, was too near the
docks to be a fashionable shopping district, and by the time the business
had become Wink & Co., Silk Mercers and Ladies' Outfitters, First-
class Dressmakers, Furs, Costumes, Mantles, Sunshades, Lace Curtains,
and Blankets, it was removed to the more prosperous atmosphere of
Palmerston Road. Here the drapery store of J. D. Morant enjoyed a
high-class trade. Morant's, indeed, were there until bombed out in the
Second World War. The business reopened in Chichester and was
acquired in 1956 by the Army & Navy Stores. Wink & Co. prospered
in Palmerston Road and by 1877 had expanded into two more houses.
Ten years later two go-ahead young men from London, Knight and
Lee, bought what was a splendidly thriving business.

Jesse Knight and Edward Herbert Soden Lee were friends who
became brothers-in-law when Knight married Lee's sister. They had
worked together at William Whiteley's, where business was operated
on lines which were considered unconventional, if not down-right
unethical, by the old-fashioned tradesmen who found themselves being
undersold. Within three weeks of arriving in Southsea, Knight and

Lee were advertising a special purchase of ladies' mackintoshes direct from the manufacturer. By cutting out the wholesaler, they were able to undercut other retailers.

Clearly, Knight and Lee were out for quick turnover, small margins, and the attraction of keen prices. One does not get the impression that these South Coast shops—Edwin Hide's, Knight and Lee, and the fictional Edwin Shalford's Drapery Emporium—were very 'exclusive' in the sense which implied so much in shop-keeping. And the shop that Mr F. J. Bobby bought in Margate in 1887 would have been run on much the same lines. But when Mr Bobby set up a branch in Leamington (1904), Folkestone (1906), Eastbourne (1910), Torquay (1913) and Bournemouth (1915), all fashionable resorts, he raised the level of his trading accordingly. Three other South Coast shops which came within the Bobby group in more recent years go back to Victorian times: Handleys of Southsea, founded 1867; John K. Hubbard of Worthing, 1870; and William Hill of Hove, 1898.

In Newcastle upon Tyne, an exceptionally elegant and exclusive establishment was opened in 1882. This original shop of Mr J. J. Fenwick was at 4 Northumberland Street, which in those days was mainly residential, Newcastle's main shopping area being in Pilgrim Street. Two of the Northumberland Street residences, 37 and 39, were owned by doctors; and when they moved out Mr Fenwick bought their imposing stone-built houses. They had originally been built for the grandfather of the actress Dorothea Baird, who became Mrs Henry Irving; and when Miss Baird played Trilby in Du Maurier's play (the play which gave the name to the hat), Mr Fenwick was called to London to design her gown—on the strict understanding that it was to be made in the old premises in Newcastle built by her grandfather.

Mr Fenwick took the unusual course, for those days, of having his new shop-front designed by an eminent architect: W. H. Knowles, who designed much of Armstrong College, Newcastle, which is now King's College. The beautiful shop-front caused a sensation . . . two large display windows each had seven graceful supporting pillars with fluting picked out in gold leaf. The windows were advanced from the building, and curved round to the centre entrance in which stood a metal statue supported by a large gas lamp. Above, there was an elegant balustrade.

In these distinguished windows Mr Fenwick allowed no crowded display of merchandise such as customarily choked the windows of drapery shops. Just a few handsome costumes and furs set the character of his high-class dressmaking establishment, which was everything implied by 'exclusive'.

Mr J. J. Fenwick's

SUCCESS IN LONDON.

WINTER SALE

MR FENWICK'S immediate success at 62, New Bond-street is without parallel, and in order to further its continuance he purposes to effect a clearance of his entire Stock, thus allowing adequate time for the Creation of New Toilettes for the Spring. The Sale will be held during the month commencing

THURSDAY, DEC. 1.

This Sale will afford MR FENWICK'S own clientele an opportunity *before they leave town* of purchasing his MODEL GOWNS, COATS, and MANTLES at irresistible prices.

☛ A LARGE ASSORTMENT OF SEALSKIN AND FUR-LINED COATS INCLUDED IN THE SALE

MR J. J. FENWICK, 62 & 63, NEW BOND ST., W.

71.

This exclusiveness was kept unsullied by the trend of progressive retailing. When Mr Fenwick decided that he must take advantage of the increasing demand for ready-made clothes, and also develop the variety of his stock, he bought another shop on the other side of the street, where its proximity would not detract from his other establishment by actually adjoining it. The very name of Fenwick was held aloof. When he extended his original premises by buying a building which did adjoin them, he traded there as the Eastern Art Store. By 1891, Mr Fenwick felt able to take the bold step of opening a London branch in New Bond Street.

Meanwhile, he had sent his two sons abroad to be trained in various Paris stores. They returned eager to try out Paris department store methods in Newcastle. They built a new shop-front capable of displaying a much larger selection of merchandise than the elegant windows had ever done, and they urged people to come and walk round, assuring them that they would not be importuned to buy— which was still the case in some North Country shops. An advertisement in the *Newcastle Journal* of November 27, 1902 read: 'Assistants are not allowed to speak to visitors. Walk round today, don't buy. There is time for that another day.' This resulted in a rival shop replying: 'We have fine displays of fancy goods and toys, including the new non-speaking shop assistants'.

꭛   ꭛   ꭛

Before this popularizing of the Newcastle Fenwick's and its development into a department store, the business must have been conducted on very similar lines to those which obtained at Jessops of Nottingham, which had an equally high reputation for dressmaking. The original founder of this business was a John Townsend from London, who announced in October 1804 his resolution to keep nothing in his newly opened shop but articles of the most *superior quality*; and through all the changes of the shop's first sixty years, the same standard was maintained. Townsend took a William Daft into partnership in 1832, and Daft was joined in 1860, six years before he died, by Zebedee Jessop from Swineshead in Lincolnshire. Jessop developed the business to take in different departments of fashion; but he always maintained a certain aloofness towards popular trends. Fortunately there exists a detailed description of the way this business was conducted, written by Mr Gee who joined Jessops in 1897 as sole clerk.

The shop opened for customers at 8.30 in the morning, but Mr Gee used to arrive at 7.30; and always he found Mr Jessop was there before him. Trade was mainly in ladies' coats, dresses and underwear, most of which were made to order. Dressmaking rooms took up about half the premises. It was unusual to give, or to be asked to give, any estimate of the final price when the order was given. About eighty per cent of the shop's trade was done on credit, and customers might not know what they had spent until the bill arrived six months later. There were about a thousand accounts, and Mr Gee entered all credit transactions in a ledger from word of mouth descriptions. Sales checks were used only for cash sales. At stocktaking, Mr Jessop called out all the nine or ten thousand pounds worth of stock himself. He and his eldest son William wrote out by hand all letters to customers and all orders to suppliers. The first typewriter was not acquired until after the First World War. In 1933 the John Lewis Partnership acquired Jessop's as the first of its provincial branches.

❧   ❧   ❧

In London, the dressmaking departments and workrooms of the expanding stores continued to maintain an aura of exclusiveness. Many were still conducted in much the same manner as in Mr Gee's description of Jessop's, with very long credit facilities. The Model Costume rooms of such shops as Marshall & Snelgrove, Debenham & Freebody, and Jays were still very considerable, but were no longer the most important departments. They shared with piece-goods the largest turnover; but new departments for ready-made clothes were being set up and expanding all the time, and the really high-class clientele for made to measure clothes was beginning to be drawn away by a new development in London shopping.

This development was the emergence of handsome dressmaking establishments from what had been relatively small 'court dressmakers', known only to their own clients. These dressmakers never advertised, but were recommended by word of mouth; their names were no more known to the public than were those of the men's tailors in Savile Row. But now they were beginning to be run on the lines of Parisian couture houses, they were being written about in the ever more widely read fashion magazines and fashion columns in the newspapers; and their names were becoming famous.

Thus it became the snob thing to patronize these couture houses—and the dressmaking departments of the stores felt the draught as their doors closed behind these departing customers. Peter Robinsons still have many old ledgers of their department returns, and for the year 1885 to 1886 takings in Silk Costumes (ready-made) were £12,798, and in Silk Dressmaking only £575. Stuff costumes, ready-made, sold £16,789 worth; stuff costumes made to order took £14,125. Five years later, the ready-made stuff costumes took £18,641, the made to order only £12,729. And the gap went on widening each year.

A newcomer to Oxford Street at this time was D. H. Evans, who in 1879 bought 320 Oxford Street, just on the west side of Old Cavendish Street. Dan Harries Evans was the son of a farmer, who had left his native Llanelly with £400 in his pocket two years earlier and acquired a small draper's shop in Westminster Bridge Road. He was helped in the shop by his wife, who did the dressmaking, and by her brother and sister. It was very much a family business. Dan Evans built up the chief part of his trade around lace flouncings and general lace goods, in which he specialized.

It was a great period for lace, and it did not deter D. H. Evans, when he moved to Oxford Street, that there were already so many shops dealing in lace. The most famous was Hayward's, who were established at 73 Oxford Street in 1770. In the mid-century the name changed to D. Biddle, but by the 1870's it reverted to being Hayward again. Of the general drapers, Peter Robinsons were particularly famed for their lace department. Their lace buyer travelled Europe placing his orders, and was a connoisseur of every kind of handmade lace. The ever-increasing use of lace in fashion and furnishings—boudoir hangings, bedspreads, d'oyleys, antimacassars, tablecloths, and mats—can be followed in the old sales ledgers which still exist at Peter Robinson's. For the year 1885, sales in the lace department were £15,964; ten years later, they were £25,958. In 1901 they were £31,548; and in 1906, the crest of the ultra-feminine Edwardian period, lace sales peaked at £33,193.

Four years after D. H. Evans opened in Oxford Street, Frederick Penberthy arrived. Mr Penberthy, in that year of 1883, announced himself as British and Foreign Lace-man, Court Glover, English Hosier, and Importer of Viennese and Paris Fans. This was a great fan period as well as a great lace period. Never had fans been larger than in the late 1870's and 1880's. Lady Jebb wrote to her sister in America in December 1874:

Dick gave me an immense painted black satin fan for my birthday. These big

72. Lace Fichu by Hayward's of Oxford Street . . . *'In Blonde de Seville, it falls into cascades and rivières without any manipulation—the only, yet all-sufficient ornamentation of the simple dress.'* 1886.

fans are all the fashion in London, nobody carries anything else. He wanted to give me a sealskin jacket, but I would not permit the extravagance.

It was quite logical for Frederick Penberthy to be a laceman and specialist in fans. At the Paris Exhibition of 1878, fans made of lace were far and away the most numerous amongst the fans exhibited. Ten years later, huge feather fans were all the rage, ostrich feather fans being, of course, the most monstrous: 'Leaders of fashion prefer about sixteen magnificent ostrich feathers mounted on tortoiseshell' wrote the *Lady's World* in 1887; and ballroom fans became so preposterous that they were known as fire-screens: 'One sees drawings of them,' wrote Julius Price, 'which almost give the impression of caricatures, so absurd are their dimensions.'

By the mid-'nineties, these vast status symbols had become démodé. Small fans with mother-of-pearl sticks, usually referred to as 'Empire Fans', were all the rage; and needless to say the vogue for Japanese art, which began with the Aesthetic Movement in the 1870's and continued for so long, included a penchant for Japanese fans. These could be very beautiful since in Japan, as in China, the painting of a fan was not considered beneath the dignity of even the greatest masters. But such collectors' pieces were few in number compared with the inexhaustible importation of inexpensive Japanese fans. These, with their slim sticks and painted paper leaves, became cheaper and cheaper as the oriental vogue descended the social scale.

᪥ ᪥ ᪥

Professor Jebb's offer of a sealskin jacket, which his wife so self-sacrificingly declined in favour of the less extravagant gift of a fan, was probably activated by the fact that nearly everybody's wife who was anybody's wife had a sealskin jacket. They came into fashion about 1865, and remained in fashion until the end of the century, which must be a record for the duration of a mode. Previously a sealskin cloak had been every woman's heart's desire—but a desire beyond hope of fulfillment except for the moneyed few, since they required such a lot of pelts. In 1860 H. J. & D. Nicoll of Regent Street announced 'The new seal-skin cloak for ladies, so very rich and costly that the price, which is of necessity high, cannot be regretted.'

At the beginning of the century, fur was chiefly used for linings, and was more worn by men than women. Oxford Street was the favourite street of furriers: John and George Poland of 90 Oxford Street were one of the very early 'fashionable' Fur Manufacturers; Sneider's at

No. 92 Oxford Street were established in 1785, and Nicholays at 170 five years earlier. Sneider's, advertising Russian shawl cloaks in the *Morning Herald* (1835), claimed to be the furriers who had introduced kolinsky to this country. Charles Russ, Court Furrier of 70 New Bond Street, specialized in fur seal mantles, fur-lined travelling cloaks and coats, and carriage wrappers.

The Fur Company of the Argyll Rooms, Regent Street, stored furs free from moth for their customers during the summer without charge, and had perhaps the most extensive West End business in 'the Sale of Russian and Hudson's Bay Furs . . . Coronation Robes, Victoria Shawls, and Russian Shawl Cloaks made entirely of fur . . . also a variety of Esquimaux and Squaw dresses'. Were these intriguing garments actually worn by fashionable ladies? Looking at the fashion plates of the 1830's, it is impossible to imagine squaw dresses even at fancy dress balls.

The neat little, sweet little, sealskin jacket was the first *fitted* fur garment, and the first fur garment designed for *walking* instead of for carriage wear. Comfortable, cosy, and convenient, they sold like hot cakes. In 1866, Sewell & Co. of Old Compton Street and Frith Street advertised a stock of five hundred sealskin jackets; and milliners were not slow to see their chance . . . 'All Ladies wearing sealskin jackets should see Mrs Harriet Roper's seal bonnets to match, 25/- in Golden and Lustre Sealskin. The famous, or notorious, Madame Parsons of the Burlington Arcade and Regent Street went one faster and advertised sealskin hats—more bare-faced than bonnets behind whose jutting wings young ladies, and married ladies too, were supposed to blush unseen.

There are very few women in the fur trade, even today; but at No. 2 Soho Street in the 1880's there was a retail fur business run by two sisters, the Misses F. and E. Ford, who had 'a show of skins and furs of rare value, and enjoyed a very large and more than local business'. The business was established thirty years earlier by a Mr Edwards. The Misses Ford cannot have been his daughters; but they may well have been his nieces, since it is a profession that tends very much to run in families. There is an inherited instinct for understanding fur. In *The Book of Fur*, J. G. Links tells how his father, a master furrier, used to bring home skins, which he would work on in the evenings in a shed in the garden . . .

I think it was the pleasure of exercising his craft which accounted for his industry rather than the additional production which could not have contributed very much to the output of Calman Links of Golden Lane. It did, however, implant the smell of fur in my nostrils. I did not realise at the time that it was there; I noticed only that there was something missing when it was not. I was on my way to becoming a furrier myself.

Moreover, he was on the way to becoming the Queen's furrier and a Director of the Hudson Bay Company. Later in his book, Mr Links shatters the illusion that the wages of sin is fur coats . . . 'In his dealings with men the furrier sees life through rose-coloured spectacles. For one thing they are all happily married; in a life-time of supplying furs for wives I could count the mistresses who have been bought for on the fingers of one hand.' Yet, even deprived of the *goût de scandale* with which imagination likes to flavour them, furs still cannot be viewed with entirely dispassionate appraisal. They are not, and never will be, just a branch of the clothing trade: as wine is to groceries, so furs are to drapery. All through the centuries furs have been associated with pride and prejudice, pomp and circumstance, and kings have decreed what fur must be worn and by whom. Had Mr Links been furrier to Elizabeth I instead of Elizabeth II he would have been Sergeant of the Peltry and received twelve pence a day; even more picturesquely in Henry IV's reign, he would have been Skinner to the Great Wardrobe.

The most prolific family in the fur trade must surely be the Barder family. Louis Barder, a mid-nineteenth century furrier, had seven sons who all became furriers. Instead of working in their father's business, each one set up on his own. Thus they all became deadly rivals in business, although it was a devoted family in every other way.

All the brothers chose grand titles for their companies. The one which is still known today is the National Fur Company, which Arnold Barder established in Sloane Street in 1878, and moved to Brompton Road shortly afterwards. By the mid-1920's, only two other Barder brothers were still in the fur trade, their companies being the London Fur Company and one trading in Bristol. In 1926, the London Fur Company was bought by Swears and Wells, and by 1945 the Bristol company was also sold. But the National Fur Company went from strength to strength, and expanded into a concern with seven branches, four of them in Wales. The great grandson and great-great grandson of the original Louis Barder now run the business. The main shop is still in Brompton Road, and there are three branches in Wales, and one in Leicester. It is the only retail fur business on this scale still to remain under private ownership.

It would almost seem that the Barder family must have appropriated all possible imposing titles for a fur business . . . yet the International Fur Store of 163 and 165 Regent Street was nothing to do with the Barders. It was established in 1882, under the management of Mr

A SNUB.

"Fifty Guineas for a Boa and a Muff! That's rather dear, isn't it!"
"We don't keep Catskin, Madam!"

73. *Punch*, February 11, 1893.

T. S. Jay, maybe a descendant of W. C. Jay, founder of Jay's General
Mourning Warehouse. The International Fur Store evidently set out to
be popular rather than exclusive, as this extract from *Modern London*,
1887, indicates:

The object of the International Fur Store is the supply of the very best and
most stylish furs for ladies' and gentlemen's wear at the very lowest possible
prices for cash. The credit system is non-existent; ready money is the sole
purchasing medium, and by this means Mr Jay is enabled to take the fullest
advantage of his exceptionally close connection with the best sources of the
fur supply. All goods are marked in plain figures, and 'prices in pairs' are
conspicuous by their absence. Mr Jay buys all his skins for cash in the best
European and American markets, which are all dressed under the direct
personal supervision of this experienced gentleman. Fitting rooms, skin-
rooms (for storage purposes), quilting and finishing rooms, and other
workshops, with 100-150 hands, according to the season. Mr Jay exhibited

213

at the Health Exhibition of 1884 and won the only medal awarded to an English furrier. Extensive business connection among Americans, and trade connections throughout the world.

By the 'eighties, most big drapery stores had fur departments; and Sélincourt & Colman were the leading wholesale furriers supplying the stores. But stores concentrated mainly upon 'small furs', since to carry a comprehensive stock of fur coats in different sizes, and employ staff sufficiently expert upon furs, meant too great an outlay. An idea of the stock of the Fur Department in a high-class drapery store of the 1880's is given on one page of a catalogue of Cavendish House, Cheltenham, in 1886 . . . a strange assortment, of which a Vigogne Cashmere cloak, lined with squirrel and trimmed oppossum, was the only full-length garment, and the Wagram Sealskin Jacket, 23" long, the only other actual garment—all the rest were 'small furs'. There was a very long, very thin squirrel tail boa; and a Magicienne Fur Bag Muff. The 'Alert Fur Tie' consisted of a squirrel with tail in mouth, and a fur muff was ornamented with no less than three animals' heads.

This fashion for going the whole animal, heads, tails, and paws may have started an anti-fur movement; but the main incentive for producing imitation fur cloth was, and still is, to produce cheap 'fur' coats. In 1879, Spence & Co. of St Paul's Churchyard had a new kind of circular cloak called the Polarium; made of cloth that 'faithfully imitates fur'. That same year, *Sylvia's Home Journal* wrote approvingly of 'Sealskin Cloth': 'a material now much used for jackets and dress trimmings. It resembles real seal so closely that at a short distance it could not be distinguished from it'.

The Age of Imitation had come. Lewis's velveteen department was, during the 1880's, the biggest department in their Manchester store. In 1894, the first flannelette appeared. The first commercially successful viscose rayon was to be manufactured in Courtauld's factory at Coventry in 1905, some fifty years before man-made fibres brought the imitation of animal pelts to a fine degree of simulation—far, far beyond that of those coats of the 1880's which so 'faithfully imitated fur'.

CHAPTER XIX

CO-OPERATIVES AND TAILORING HOUSES

Civil Service Supply Association and Army & Navy Stores.
Couture Houses and Ladies' Tailors. Bustles. Dress Labels and
Name-tapes.

ALL the shops which had by the 1880's grown into sizeable stores
had begun as small linen drapers, silk mercers, or haberdashers.
The only exception was the Bon Marché at Brixton, which was
conceived and built as a department store. Harrods at this time still
dealt mainly in food stuffs, although china had been added in 1874.

Henry Charles Harrod was first a miller at Clacton, and then a tea
merchant in the City. He was nearly fifty when, in 1849, he took over
a little grocery shop belonging to a friend in the Brompton Road. His
son, Charles Digby Harrod, took control twelve years later. Expansion
in the late 'eighties added carpets, furniture and household merchandise,
but drapery and fashion goods came last of all. Fortnum & Mason,
established as a grocery shop in 1707 by two footmen from the court
of Queen Anne, did not branch out into other merchandise until well
on in the twentieth century.

The co-operative stores also started with grocery and moved into
drapery. Co-operative retailing, originated by a group of working
people in Rochdale during the 'Hungry Forties', was in the main a
working-class movement and as such does not come within the scope of
this book. There was, however, a middle-class co-operative movement
which influenced the development of department stores in general.
Both the Civil Service Supply Stores and the Army & Navy Stores were
nearer to the modern department store by the late 'seventies than any
privately owned shops; and the competition of these co-operatives was
to some extent responsible for the form of development taken by such
stores as Whiteley's and Harrods, although they made less impact

upon shops dealing only in fashion goods. At one time, Harrods was advertising 'Co-operative prices' in order to prevent customers being lured away.

The first of the middle-class co-operatives was the Post Office Supply Association, which was founded in 1864 and changed its name during 1866 to the Civil Service Supply Association. It was started by a group of clerks in the General Post Office, who clubbed together to buy a chest of tea, and thereby saved themselves ninepence a pound. Two years later the group opened a retail shop in the Strand. Groceries were the main stock; but very soon a wide range of clothing and household goods were added, supplied by affiliated private traders. By 1870, the groceries accounted for only a small part of the business, which by then covered almost all the things which people buy from day to day. For its members, the Civil Service Supply Association was in fact a universal provider rather before William Whiteley was boasting of providing 'anything from a pin to an elephant'.

In 1871, a small group of officers of the Armed Forces combined to buy a few cases of wine at wholesale prices; and this led to them forming a society to buy other commodities in bulk . . . the way had already been shown by the Civil Service Stores and other co-operatives. There is surely something very appropriate about the Civil Service Stores having started with tea, and the Army & Navy with wine.

The Army and Navy opened their retail shop in Victoria Street in 1872 on a site which still forms part of the Army & Navy Stores building. By no means a fashionable shopping street, it was nevertheless quite convenient for the residential districts of Belgravia, and a pleasant walk across St James's Park from clubland. The immediate success of the shop was, in the words of a contemporary writer, 'little short of phenomenal'. By 1887, it had 5,000 employees; 50,000 life members and subscribers made over 8,000 purchases a day. Letters arrived at the rate of 4,000 a day from all over the country and from overseas . . . 'Practically speaking, the Society supplies its members with everything, and there is hardly a demand possible—or, at least probable—which it would be beyond its capacity to meet.'

The Stores ran a catering department, and rejoiced in an 'elegantly appointed refreshment room, wherein are served breakfasts, lunches, and all kinds of hot and cold refreshments of a light character to members visiting the stores'. It may be presumed that the refreshment room, unlike that of William Whiteley, was licenced . . . after all, the Army & Navy Stores started with a case of wine. And it was much more than a shop: spiritually it was a club. Serving officers and their wives in far-flung places spoke of the Army & Navy with the same sentimental

74. Junior Army & Navy Stores, York House, Waterloo Place, in the 1880's.

attachment as they spoke of 'home'. And when they visited it on their leaves, they were always remembered by name and greeted warmly by the assistants, even if it was years since their last visit.

A dispute over policy between shareholders and management led to the formation in 1879 of the Junior Army & Navy Stores and its establishment in York House, Waterloo Place . . . 'one of the most stately buildings in Regent Street'. Its aim was 'to work in the interests of the auxilliary forces as in those of the regular military and naval branches, to supply the best articles of domestic consumption and general use at the lowest remunerative prices'. In York House there were boot and shoe departments, a tailor's shop, linen, general drapery and outfitting. Facilities for members included a hairdressing department for Ladies and for Gentlemen, cloakrooms, and two passenger elevators. These may well have been the first passenger lifts in any English store. Soon the Junior Army & Navy opened branches at Dublin and Aldershot, and had five branches in London.

The senior Army & Navy Stores opened branches at Aldershot, Chatham, Plymouth, Bombay, Calcutta, Karachi, and Delhi; and in Victoria Street, the store expanded all through the 'eighties and 'nineties until, before the end of the century, it occupied the whole of its present site. Display windows were not put into the existing building until the 1920's, and from the outside it looked no more like a shop than the Junior Army & Navy in Waterloo Place (Fig. 74).

Perhaps no other store has commanded quite the same family loyalties as the Army & Navy, from generation to generation. Even those who became account customers after it was made into an ordinary retail store and membership was no longer necessary—many of whom had no connection at all with the armed forces—looked upon 'The Stores' as part of their family life. However far away from Victoria Street time and tide might take them, they kept in touch with the Army & Navy through its enormous clothbound catalogue.

⚘   ⚘   ⚘

Although the Army & Navy Stores and the Civil Service Supply Association stocked every garment that a lady of the middle-classes could require, no-one would suggest that they represented high fashion. At the same time as they were building up their loyal clientele, and while the other stores were increasing the number of departments for ready-made clothes, some of the exclusive dressmakers (usually styled 'Court Dressmakers') were developing into large establishments run upon the lines of French couture houses. Their names were becoming known to the readers of fashion magazines. Most of these readers would not be able to afford to be dressed by them, but they liked to be *au fait* with what Society was wearing. The names which most often occurred in the magazines of the later 1880's, were these:

Redfern & Sons, 26 Conduit Street (also in Paris).
Redmayne, New Bond Street.
Rouy & Felix, 31 St George's Place, Knightsbridge.
Russell & Allen, Old Bond Street.
Hulbert Beach, 27, 28 and 29 Sloane Street.
H. J. & D. Nicoll & Co., 114 Regent Street.
Madame Philippe, 12 Princes Street, Hanover Square.
Mr F. Robins, Maddox Street.
Madame Jeannette, Regent Street.
Miss Metcalfe, 111 New Bond Street.
Madame Sear, Old Bond Street.
Mr Winter, 56 Brook Street.
Miss Dust, 5 Brook Street.
Worth et Cie, Bond Street.

This Worth, a branch of the Paris house, moved from Bond Street to Grosvenor Street in 1926. It was the first house in Grosvenor Street to become business premises, and there was a stipulation that the front

BUSINESS IS BUSINESS.

Rector's Wife. "Oh, Mr. Dosset, we have not seen your Assistant, who has such a very nice Tenor Voice, in the Choir lately."

Country Grocer. "No, Ma'am; I've parted with him owing to the Rector and other Gentlemen getting their Supplies from the Stores in London!"

75. *Punch*, September 28, 1878.

door must be kept shut, and that the lettering on the brass plate should not be higher than two inches nor longer than six inches. Today, there is not one private house left in Grosvenor Street.

Apart from the celebrated dressmaking houses, there were still an immense number of small establishments and private dressmakers in the West End. Even those Society ladies who patronized well-known couture houses had 'small dressmakers' for their less important clothes. When Princess May of Teck (later Queen Mary) was a girl of eighteen living at White Lodge, she had only a small dress allowance. The clothes she wore at home were made by the local dressmaker at Kingston-on-Thames. For London clothes she went, like her mother, to Madame Mangas, whom she described as a 'first-rate' Parisian dressmaker who did not, however, charge 'tip-top prices', and who came over regularly to London where she had 'a tiny *pied-à-terre* in Mount Street'. This she shared with Madame Valentine Meurice, a milliner whom the Duchess of Teck considered an admirable bonnet maker.

James Pope-Hennessy in *Queen Mary* quotes a letter recommending her:

'Her bonnets . . . I think remarkably pretty and am sure you will not consider outrés or ruinous,' she wrote in 1888 to her Petersham neighbour, Mrs Masters. 'Her prices run from £2.8. to £3.3. or thereabouts, £4 representing her highest figure and are only charged for a very handsome confection with feathers and embroidery! If you want a black bonnet make Madame Meurice show you one similar to the bonnet May has just bought of her, for it is made of a particularly pretty stuff, and cost £2.8.; or should you prefer a jet bonnet, I can recommend one after the pattern of *mine* at £3.3.'

When Princess May married the Duke of York in 1893, tea-gowns and matinée gowns played a large part in her trousseau, as well as travelling capes, travelling wraps, and driving capes. The clothes were all made by English dress houses: Linton and Curtis, Scott Adie, and Redfern. Letters to her mother after her marriage include many descriptions of the clothes she wore at various functions, and show that Madame Mangas and a Mrs Mason also made for her trousseau— maybe Mrs Mason was the 'little dressmaker' at Kingston-on-Thames. There were plenty of wedding presents with which to dress up her evening gowns. The newly-wed Duchess of York wrote to her mother that at dinner on her first evening at Osborne 'I wore my white brôché satin low with the Iveagh's tiara, Gdmama's necklace, the Kensington bow in front of the bodice, and the Warwicks' sun on the side. I wish you had seen me, I think you would have thought I looked tidy.' Perhaps 'tidy' was a family joke . . . if not it was the understatement of all time.

The rise of London dressmaking and tailoring establishments to something of the status held by the couture houses of Paris was helped by the fashion for tailormade dresses and costumes which, uniquely in history of fashion, had its origin in England instead of France. Paris fashion lost ground during the unsettled years following the fall of the Second Empire in 1870. Englishwomen did not go to Paris for their clothes, and the travelling backwards and forwards of English trade buyers and dressmakers with Parisian connections was to a certain extent curtailed. Tailormades were in the mood of the moment, because Englishwomen were becoming more independent—going about in horse omnibuses and horsedrawn trams (the first tram was 'launched' in 1870), working on committees, demanding higher education and the vote. Queen's College, London, was founded in Harley Street in 1848 as a 'College for Governesses'. Newnham College was founded in 1871; Bedford College, attached to the University of London, 1879. Somerville and Lady Margaret Hall, Oxford, 1884. The first ladies' club was opened in London in 1884—the Alexander Club—then two years later the University Women's Club, which is still in Audley Square.

It was the blue serge yachting costume which really touched off the vogue for tailormade clothes; and the earliest exponent of this classic was John Morgan of Cowes, tailor to the Royal Yacht Squadron. John Morgan was established in 1820 in High Street, West Cowes. By the 'eighties there were branches at Ryde, Southampton, and Southsea. At the height of their fame, Morgan's had an output of four to five hundred outfits a year, making for the officers and crews of yachts belonging to nearly all the famous yachting clubs. They had probably been making costumes for ladies for a good many years before they opened a London branch in 1883. At that time they held an appointment from the Master of the Horse of the Queen's Household for royal liveries.

The fashion of wearing tailormade dresses or costumes for ordinary morning wear must have reached the provinces before the 'eighties, since Browns of Chester were advertising tailormade costumes in 1879. And within a few years, tailormades were even worn for afternoon visiting and smart occasions. In 1887, the *Lady's World* reported: 'At the wedding of Miss Gertrude Mills to Viscount Stopford, tailormade frocks were very much worn, especially by the younger girls, who depended upon Redfern, or his imitators, to show to advantage their pretty figures.'

By some authorities, Redfern is credited with the introduction of the man-tailored ladies' costume. He, like John Morgan, began in Cowes, but he never had Morgan's reputation as a tailor for yachtsmen. He seems to have pulled out of Cowes completely and concentrated, with singular success, upon women's clothes. Redfern's became famous, not just as a tailoring house, but as a creative dressmaking house, producing new models every season. Branches were opened in Paris, Edinburgh, and New York. But

76. Costumes for the Moors, designed by Redfern, August 1887.

always the tailoring background was there, and Redfern's were particularly noted for costumes for fishing, hunting, shooting, and driving. His premises at 26 Conduit Street, communicating with 27 New Bond Street, were like the Palm Court of a Grand Hotel.

Yet another fashionable tailor had his origins by the sea. Joseph Smith began his business in Hastings and then moved to Glendower Place, Kensington. But Hastings was not a yachting place, and Smith's reputation had been built up upon ladies' riding habits. Ladies' riding habits had always been made by men's tailors, but Joseph Smith's establishment at Kensington was quite different from the small, modest tailoring houses which ladies were accustomed to visit when they went to order a habit from their father or husband's tailor. During the time he was in Glendower Place, he was known as Smith of Kensington; and wherever Englishwomen rode—particularly when they rode the gauntlet of social appraisal in the snobbish hill stations of India—it was said that 'the hall-mark of Joseph Smith is an almost indispensable attribute to any riding habit of fashionable pretensions.' Smith's was a most palatial establishment for a tailor. All the rooms were panelled in old oak, the hall was magnificent with tessellated pavements; messengers and liveried pages scurried about as though it were an hotel. There was a library, writing room, waiting room, dressing rooms and lavatories for the convenience of patrons.

Joseph Smith became a frequent contributor to journals and reviews and a well-known figure in London. He moved to South Molton Street and then Bond Street in order to be more central. In Bond Street he had a staff of fifty, and three fitting-rooms equipped with life size horses for ladies to mount when trying on habits. He patented a habit safe-guard for the prevention of riding skirts catching on the pommel when the rider dismounted or became unseated—a similar invention to that of C. W. Davis, a habit-maker of Great Portland Street, who patented the *Sans Gêne Riding Skirt*. Once well established in Bond Street, Smith branched out into other clothes for ladies: costumes for walking and visiting, jackets, ulsters, furs. In fact, he became a rival to Redfern.

But Redfern by now had a Paris branch, which gave them additional prestige. According to Paul Poiret in *My First Fifty Years*—and who should know better than Poiret?—the great Parisian Houses of the 'nineties were Doucet, Worth, Rouff, Paquin, and Redfern. Of these, Worth was founded by an Englishman and carried on by his sons; and Redfern was a branch of an English House. Another famous exponent of *le style Anglais* was Henry Creed, Queen Victoria's tailor, who had

77. Hunting Jackets, Driving Coat, and Tailor-made Costumes, designed by
    Redfern, March 1886.

established his Parisian House in 1850 on the Place de l'Opéra, and had
become tailor to the Empress Eugénie. English influence upon dress
had become very strong even in the City of Fashion. In every European
capital, the English tailormade was every woman's social passport.

Rivalling both Redfern and Smith in the magnificence of his salons
was another ladies' tailor, Mr Hulbert Beach of 27–29 Sloane Street. In
a contemporary trade directory his establishment was described as 'a
sumptuously appointed saloon, carpeted and decorated with oriental
magnificence. The display of ladies' habits, walking, and yachting
costumes is the first in London. Patronized by royalty, Queen's family,
all the leading courts of Europe, and all the best families in the West
End of London.' The immense size of Queen Victoria's immediate
family and the vast network of her less immediate but no less clinging
relatives meant that the chances a London shopkeeper had of a royal
appointment were pretty good. Nevertheless, one is constantly sur-

prised by the number of Royal Appointments that the Queen herself liberally bestowed. In Cowes, it seems that every shop of every kind had its Royal Appointment—except one butcher, who displayed the notice 'By Appointment to Her Majesty's Subjects'.

Mr Hulbert Beach was not an initiator of fashion, like Redfern, but he followed the mode much more closely than most tailors, A contemporary wrote:

> To fulfill the requirements of fashion now, in the latter part of the 19th century, requires not only a considerable amount of ability, but a thorough appreciation of the prevailing taste in the style of dress and materials, so as to anticipate, in a certain degree, the ever changing phases of public taste. In this connection, the long-established house of Mr Hulbert Beach is in an eminent degree conspicuous.

Some time early in the Edwardian period, Hulbert Beach and another dress house called Elfrida were bought by Charles Lee, who continued in Mr Beach's premises in Sloane Street. To Mr Beach's skill with riding habits, coats, and tailormades of all kinds, was added Elfrida's feminine touch with dresses, blouses, millinery, lingerie. There was also a shoe department. Clients included the elegant Heather Firbank, a collection of whose clothes is at the Victoria & Albert Museum.

❧   ❧   ❧

The bustle or 'dress improver' came in at the beginning of the 'eighties, and it reached its maximum size in the year of Queen Victoria's Golden Jubilee. Catalogues, fashion magazines, and illustrated journals such as *Punch* and *Pick-me-up*, all show costumes with bustles which, if they were not so unanimous and were not confirmed by contemporary photographs, one would imagine to be caricatures. The bustle in that year of 1887 stuck out behind like some monstrous deformity. And it was not only worn with evening gowns and afternoon visiting toilettes, but also with tailored costumes. Presumably the bustle was intended to emphasise femininity; and presumably it succeeded since fashions, however unattractive they may seem to later generations, are infallible in fulfilling the current laws of attraction. Young girls adopted bustles the day they 'came out', if not before—it was their symbol of maturity. The Hon. Mrs Peel wrote this description of the clothes she wore when she came out in the 'eighties:

> I tried to smarten up my few frocks and tied the strings of my bustle so tightly that it stuck out aggressively and waggled when I walked. It was the sort of bustle which was made of steels run into some kind of stout material, and sometimes the steels wore through and poked out. The cushion bustles came in later.

XIII   Pencil sketch of design for a gown (original 15 in. × 10½ in.) sent out by Reville & Rossiter to Miss Heather Firbank—who did not return it as requested.

Rich silk combinations, 'Empire' shape, for evening wear; chemise in Anglo-Indian gauze, trimmed torchon lace. From Woven Underwear section, Debenham & Freebody's Catalogue of Lingerie, 1912.

The famous 'straight-fronted corset', which shaped the Edwardian swan silhouette. Displayed on a shop bust by Stockman Frères.

ENTRANCE TO THE ARCADE, OLD BOND STREET.   INTERIOR VIEW OF THE ARCADE, OLD BOND STREET.

78. The Royal Arcade, leading from Old Bond Street into Albemarle Street, in the 1880's.

We wore high-boned collars which rubbed raw places on our necks; and stiff stays; and we skewered our hats through our hair with long bonnet pins, our gloves were tight and our boots buttoned.

When the bustle began to shrink, the sleeve began to swell; by 1893 the bustle had completely disappeared and leg of mutton sleeves had blown themselves out into balloon sleeves of even greater size. These, by contrast, gave the illusion of a tiny waist—a tiny, tiny waist pulled in by a broad petersham belt with silver clasp.

English dress houses, and the more fashionable of the big shops such as Peter Robinson, Jay's, Marshall & Snelgrove, and Debenham & Freebody, had begun to put woven silk name labels into the clothes they made. Mrs Doris Langley Moore dates the beginning of French dress labels at 1870, with those of Alexandre and Elise as the first. Dr Willett Cunnington writes that labels were not attached by English dressmakers until the end of the 1870s; but the Museum of London has an evening dress of 1869 with the label sewn in of Philips & Co. in impressed gold lettering. And the trade paper *Milliner & Dressmaker* carried in November 1872 an advertisement for Thomas Lomas of Manchester for dress-bands, labels, etc., woven with addresses.

225

I. & R. Morley's trade catalogue of 1879 lists Mantle and Coat Hangers in cotton or silk, the price being according to whether the shop or dressmaker has one, two, or three lines in the name and address. It is not stated whether these were woven or printed; whereas their catalogue of 1883 has: 'Woven ingrain red initial letters, old English style; whole names in old English or script; woven shirt labels in black or red with coloured borders or scrolls. Prices by the gross, with special quotations for large quantities.' These would be ordered, not only by shops and dress-houses, but also by those manufacturers who were beginning to mark their goods with woven names or trade-marks. Some of the first underwear to carry a trade-mark was that made by Stapley and Smith of London Wall, who made the 'Hibernia' and 'Sterling' brands of woollen underclothes.

The weaving of dress labels was a development from the Stevengraphs, or woven silk pictures. These were invented by a jacquard ribbon weaver, Thomas Stevens of Coventry, during the great depression in the ribbon industry that began in 1860. Stevens first made flowered and fancy ribbon bookmarks with poems, texts, and nursery rhymes, and later made very charming and detailed woven-silk pictures. These were originally sold on barrows in the market as souvenirs. As they became well-known they were mounted and sold framed in shops. These have now become collectors' pieces. Many other ribbon firms copied the idea of Stevengraphs to see them through the depression, which was caused chiefly by the repeal of import duties at a time when ribbons were fashionably out of favour. The firm of J. & J. Cash, which has recently revived the skilled craft of weaving silk pictures (a very beautiful example being one executed for the Silver Jubilee of 1977), turned to cotton frillings for underclothes and pillowslips, and all kinds of insertions and embroidered edgings. A further development of Cash's in 1889 was the idea of personal woven name-tapes ordered at haberdashery counters of drapers' shops—those name-tapes which we all know so well from our schooldays onwards. A memory of an additional service which shops used to offer their customers who bought school uniforms or trousseau linen from them is revived by a letter written to Gorringes. . . . 'I shall always be grateful for all the name tapes you have sewn on for me.'

CHAPTER XX

THE NEW WOMAN AND
THE NEW SHOPPING

The tailor-made costume. Tricycling and Bicycling. Attractions of a day's Shopping in Town; Display Advertising, Bi-annual Sales, Country Orders, Shopping by Telephone. Harrod's Moving Staircase. The Ethics of Shopping. John Barnes of Hampstead. Family Businesses become Limited Companies.

꙰꙰꙰꙰꙰꙰꙰꙰꙰꙰꙰꙰꙰꙰꙰꙰꙰꙰꙰꙰꙰꙰꙰꙰꙰꙰꙰꙰꙰꙰꙰꙰꙰꙰꙰꙰꙰

THE tailor-made costume of the 'nineties was the outward and visible form of the New Woman. It was hardly an emancipated costume, with its stiff collared shirt blouse and tie, tight waist, long skirts and underskirts which were often bound with leather since they trailed in the mud. But there was an efficient look about it which expressed the mood of the young women who were determined to show that they were the equals of men. The 'nineties saw the first international ladies' hockey match (1897), the formation of the Ladies' Golf Union (1893), and of the Original Lady's Cricketers' Club (1890); but above all it was the time of the great bicycling craze. Bicycles did more for the social emancipation of women than anything else, because the chaperons could not keep up.

Previously there had been tricycling. In 1885, Mrs Ada Ballin wrote:

Tricycling has become quite fashionable for men, and there is every reason to believe it will soon become so for women, if only ladies living in towns will cast off the fear of being stared at, and bravely mount the iron steed in public. Ladies in the country already largely patronize the tricycle. The ladies of the Royal Family have set a good example. The Princess Mary, Duchess of Teck, took the initiative; then the Queen presented machines to her young grand-daughters, the Princesses of Hesse; the Princess of Wales next gave her eldest daughter one for a birthday present; and the Princess

Louise rides one herself. In Manchester it is quite usual for a lady to do her marketing on a tricycle, or make a round of visits, and I cannot see why the same thing should not be done in London and other great towns. To ladies not accustomed to go out alone the 'Sociable' should prove a great boon. I have often seen husbands and wives bowling along on these double machines, and noticed how happy and comfortable they looked. The same sort of machine would be delightful for two ladies.

In the dress department of the International Health Exhibition were several dresses adapted for the tricycle. The special dresses would be exceedingly comfortable and suitable, but these could hardly be worn in towns unless the wearers were hardened to a considerable amount of staring and comment from the younger and dirtier portion of the community.

The costumes for the Ladies' Cyclist Touring Club were made by a tailor called Mr T. W. Goodman of 47 Albemarle Street and consisted of fitted jacket, long skirt covering knickerbockers, and a hat to match. Mr Goodman also designed three other costumes for tricycling, walking, or travelling, all of which won medals at different Health Exhibitions. Mrs White of 63 Jermyn Street designed and made the hats to go with Mr Goodman's outfits . . . an early example of a combined promotion.

In spite of royal example, tricycling was considered rather more freakish than fashionable, and soon went out after the 'Safety' bicycle was invented in 1885. The 'Safety' bicycle had wheels almost the same size and was an altogether different proposition from the original penny-farthing which was only ridden by men. After Dunlop invented his pneumatic tyre in 1888, there was no stopping the ladies. In France, they did not even wait for a feminine model, but put on knickerbockers and rode the same bicycles as men. Englishwomen more prudishly, or prudently, waited until a model was designed which did not require them to sling a leg. The first lady bicyclist appeared in *Punch* in July 1894; knickerbockers, Norfolk jacket, Trilby hat, black stockings, shirt and tie. In the same year, there was published George G. Harper's *Revolted Woman*:

Rational Dress seen on the flying female who pedals down the roads today is only Bloomerism with a difference: legs clothed in roomy knickerbockers down to the knees and encased in cloth gaiters for the rest, buttoned down to the ankles. These in place of the Turk-like trousers, tied round the ankles and finished off with frills, of over forty years ago. As for the attenuated skirts of the Prophet Bloomer, Rational Dress replaces them with a species of frantic frock-coat, spreading its ample skirts, but tightened round the waist. A 'Robin Hood' hat, even as in bygone years, crowns this confection.

By the mid-nineties, the bicycling craze was at its height. Battersea

TRICYCLING COSTUME
by
Mr T. W. Goodman,
47 Albemarle Street,
tailor to the Ladies' Cyclist Club

HAT TO MATCH
by
Mrs White, 63 Jermyn Street.

'Lined with flannel, it is worn over woollen combinations and flannel body instead of stays, to which knickerbockers to match dress are buttoned . . . of course these unmentionables do not show', but a lady clothed in this way is better able to face the risks of accidents.'

Mrs Ada Ballin, *The Science of Dress*, 1885.

79.

Park was the chic venue, and noon on Sunday the modish hour. Elegance and beauty, masculine and feminine, arrived in carriages, their iron steeds being brought by servants, who held them for mounting. When in 1896 Hyde Park was opened to bicycles, William Whiteley ordered a consignment of five hundred machines and sold them in a matter of days. Maybe that was the moment when Society, ever sensitive to their rages becoming too popular, dismounted in favour of the motor-car. When the fashionable furore had died away, Max Beerbohm wrote: 'On her bicycle, for all the devices of her *couturier*, Fashion never looked anything but her worst'.

In the matter of bicycling costume, the provinces were, as in most things, more prudish than the metropolis—although we must not forget those advanced tricyclistes of Manchester. In *Period Piece*, Gwen Raverat writes of bicycling in Cambridge as a child in the 'nineties:

We were promoted to wearing baggy knickerbockers under our frocks and over our white frill drawers. We thought this horridly improper, but rather grand . . . I only once saw a woman (not, of course, a *lady*) in real bloomers.

Small girls and young ladies were still excessively modest . . . far too bashful to be seen even by a school-friend in anything nearer the skin than a petticoat. Mrs Raverat recalled. . .

as a consequence, decent women did not take very much trouble about their underclothes, which were apt to be rather Jaeger and patched; but they were often extremely complicated. This is what a young lady wore, with whom I shared a room one night—I watched her under my eyelashes as I lay in bed. She would have been horrified if she had known that I was awake:

1. Thick, long-legged, long-sleeved woollen combinations.
2. Over them, white cotton combinations, with plenty of buttons and frills.
3. Very serious, bony, grey stays, with suspenders.
4. Black woollen stockings.
5. White cotton drawers, with buttons and frills.
6. White cotton 'petticoat-bodice', with embroidery, buttons and frills.
7. Rather short, white flannel petticoat.
8. Long alpaca petticoat, with flounces round the bottom.
9. Pink flannel blouse.
10. High, starched, white collar, fastened on with studs.
11. Navy-blue tie.
12. Blue skirt, touching the ground, and fastened tightly to the blouse with a safety-pin behind.
13. Leather belt, very tight.
14. High button boots.

A young lady thus dressed to kill, can hardly have been in much danger herself, even from the most passionate advances. The chaperons who were being left panting behind the young men and maidens on bicycling expeditions can scarcely have feared anything like the worst. The New Woman might be emancipated, but she had not yet loosened her sartorial shackles. And once safely married, she was apt to relapse into the mental and emotional security of the conventions. M. Vivian Hughes writes in *A London Home in the Nineties* of a visit to her sister-in-law in Guernsey, where she imagined a simple life would be led:

I think she had made life complex by importing some Guildford notions, for Guildford is one of those provincial towns where people know what's what. For breakfast she had a pretty flowered dressing-gown. At ten she put on a simple business-like tailor-made costume for shopping in Peterport. On returning she changed into a workaday dress and an overall for kitchen operations. The overall was removed for lunch, and then, for afternoon, a really good dress was put on for paying calls. When we came back a little exhausted from this strain of looking well and being polite, a loose tea-gown was the thing, and this remained on until it was time to dress for dinner.

It is not surprising that shopping and dressmakers took up a large part of a woman's life—and no wonder that would-be emancipated young women began to grudge so much time and money spent the very reverse of profitably. For their mothers, who had nothing else to do, it was a way of filling the time; but the new generation were busy with new occupations. Thus the department stores, with their variety of ready-made clothes and accessories at reasonable prices, played an important part in the emancipation of women. One could go to town for a day and get everything done in one store; and more and more, the stores in London and the big cities set out to attract shoppers from a distance by offering auxiliary, non-selling services such as restaurants, banking facilities, and exhibitions—and cloakrooms. These last were particularly appreciated. The Ladies Lavatory Company opened its first establishment at Oxford Circus in 1884, but there were few such facilities, and one feared to be observed entering them.

In the 'seventies, Lady Jebb used to go to London for a day's shopping by train from Cambridge, fifty-four miles each way, as did her niece Maud Darwin in the next decade. Railway services were more frequent, very much cheaper, and less crowded than they are now. Indeed, shoppers travelled to London for the day from much farther afield than Cambridge. The shops were open so long that you could fit in a great deal. When West End shopkeepers gave evidence before the Select Committee on Shop Hours in 1886, the hours of opening, which varied from shop to shop, were around 8.15 a.m. to 7.30 p.m., some a little longer, some a little less, six full days a week. That same year, the *Lady's World* wrote:

Now that the train service is so perfect between London and Bath, it is quite possible to spend a day in town and return to Bath the same evening. This is no small advantage when you have a day's shopping to get through, or winter gowns and mantles to be tried on at your favourite London modiste's.

This was in spite of the fact that Bath had exceptionally good shops of its own.

Those stores which had restaurants gained tremendous pulling power. Until the opening of the ABC tea shops in 1880, there was nowhere a lady could have a meal by herself, nowhere for women to meet their friends outside their own homes; it was inconceivable for them to go to a public restaurant unescorted by husband or brother. The ABCs answered a great need of the new professional and business women: Roger Fulford in *Votes for Women* contends that the tea shop was an integral part of the Women's Suffrage Movement. The first Lyons' tea shop opened in Piccadilly in 1894. Also in the 1890s more gracious surroundings were offered by Fuller's tea shops, started by Mrs Fuller, an American lady who deplored London's lack of nice places for leisured friends to meet. The department store restaurants were designed to pull in shoppers in town for the day. Dainty teas and luncheons, perhaps with music by a pianist or even a ladies' string quartette, seduced them into a spending mood.

       ✿   ✿   ✿

The increasing use of display advertising, with illustrations, was another factor in attracting customers from a distance. Hitherto, shops had advertised almost entirely in the classified columns of newspapers and magazines. Many had eschewed advertising altogether, considering it undignified. William Whiteley never advertised, not through excess of dignity, but because he had the gift of attracting free publicity in the editorial columns . . . there was always something newsworthy happening at Whiteley's. Now, in 1894, Harrods took a full page in the *Daily Telegraph*; and two years later, Swan & Edgar took space on the front page of the first issue of the *Daily Mail*. Fenwicks took a large space on this front page, the most expensive of advertising media, to advertise a sale of model gowns in the summer of 1903. Provincial stores began to make much greater use of their local papers to pull the customers in. The newspapers themselves now had far more women readers.

The bi-annual stock-taking sales were much advertised both in the provincial and the national press. The white sales, first introduced by Dickins & Jones, were also occasions for big announcements. Sales were an excitement that even wealthy women could not resist . . . 'the carriages which fill up the streets during the sales are a serious impediment to locomotion' wrote one spoil-sport contemporary; and in July 1897, Swan & Edgar published this announcement:

AN APOLOGY—THE GREATEST SALE OF THE SEASON
Swan & Edgar beg to express their regret to the many thousands of customers who were unable to get properly served yesterday (owing to the crush and dense overcrowding on their opening day) and respectfully invite another visit during the week.

The custom for shops to buy in cheap goods especially for their sales is not a modern one. H. G. Wells makes Kipps's employer, Mr Shalford of the Great Drapery Bazaar at Folkestone, go up to London to buy goods for the January Sale. And it is clear from catalogues of the period that consignments of new goods were bought direct from manufacturers or wholesalers to be offered at 'drastically reduced prices' during the period of the sale. It was not, any more than it is today, the universal custom to confine the sales to genuinely reduced existing stock. An old deceit, much used by city shops earlier in the century, was to advertise the purchase of a bankrupt's stock or of stock damaged through fire, to be sold at Sacrificial Reductions.

In spite of the wonderful travel facilities which brought more people to shop in the city centres, mail order was still a vastly important part of store business. In 1888, Marshall & Snelgrove received about 1,000 letters daily, and the sample department had to install machinery to cut the fabric patterns. Their Country Rooms employed upwards of a hundred clerks and accountants, and there were Examining Rooms where every garment or other order was inspected before despatch. Altogether, at this date, Marshall & Snelgrove employed 2,000 workers, of which 700 boarded on the premises, with library, and sitting rooms, smoking rooms, committee rooms, reading rooms.

Although the domestic telephone came into use in 1878, it was a long time before it became a customer service. *Modern London*, published in 1887, gives Warrin & Craik, Court Florists of 43 Jermyn Street, as being 'in connection with all the Telephone Exchanges in the kingdom, thereby allowing their customers the privilege of communicating direct with the firm'—but this trade directory does not mention the telephone in any other of its detailed descriptions of retail shops, their premises and services. William Whiteley's biographer, Richard Lambert, says that Whiteleys acquired a telephone 'about 1885'; but *Modern London*, which gives Whiteley a fulsome write-up, does not include this novel service. Neither Nicholson of St Paul's catalogue of 1887, nor Dickins & Jones's of 1890, gives a telephone number. But Peter Robinson installed the instrument in 1892, telephone number London 3557; and in 1894, Swan & Edgar's was London 3586.

Fashions for February.

80. Beaver hats designed by Mr Henry Heath, 105–109 Oxford Street. 1887.

Shops and Shopping

Cole Brothers of Sheffield were considered very progressive in 1893 since they were 'to a large extent lighted by electricity, had a passenger lift upon the most approved principle, and were on the telephone: National Telephone No. 224. Harrods instituted a day-and-night telephone service about 1905.

Most drapers' shops and department stores used Lamson's overhead railways for carrying customers' money and change to and from a main cash desk. But for some reason Charles Digby Harrod, son of the founder of Harrod's, would not install them. Equally he was opposed to wasting staff time by having boys as runners from counter to cash desk. His department managers declared it would never do to expect customers to fetch their own change, but against their advice Mr Harrod installed, in 1884, several cash desks at different points, and a PAY AT THE DESK notice on every counter. Surprisingly, this peremptory request was obeyed without a single customer objecting. The following year, Mr Harrod decided to reward their docility by allowing limited credit to approved customers. Hitherto every customer, wholesale or retail, was obliged to pay cash before delivery—it was a system that department stores considered essential to offering low prices. The first list of those allowed credit at Harrods included the names of Lillie Langtry, Ellen Terry, and Oscar Wilde . . . none of whom, in the light of latter-day biographies, would seem to have been customers to inspire implicit confidence in their bank balance. However, their fame was their fortune, and they no doubt shed lustre upon the emporium.

Harrods became a Limited Liability Company in 1889, and Charles Digby Harrod retired in 1891, when Richard Burbidge was appointed General Manager. Burbidge had earned a considerable reputation at the Army & Navy Stores, Whiteleys, and the West Kensington Stores and was full of progressive ideas when he joined Harrods at the age of forty-four; but he too, like Charles Harrod who had objected first to electric light and then to overhead cash carriers, had an oddly stubborn streak. Burbidge's particular bugbear was that most desirable customer service a lift. His refusal to install lifts at a time when they had become an expected facility in the larger stores could have led to the loss of much trade. In the outcome, however, it led to installing a piece of equipment which gave Harrods a magnificent burst of publicity. This was a pioneer moving staircase, which ran for some forty feet up a gradual slope between the ground floor and the first floor, and consisted simply of a conveyor belt between two handrails, installed in 1898.

On the day of the great opening, an attendant was ready at the top to revive customers fluttered by the experience with free doses of sal volatile or cognac. But the British are an unflappable race. There was no panic or alarm, only a wide-eyed wonder. Even the reporter of the dignified *Pall Mall Gazette* seems to have been like a child at a panto-mime: 'Such a getting upstairs there was yesterday as has not been hitherto attempted in this country. The novelty consists in an adaptation of the magic carpet of the fairy tale to the prosaic purposes of stairs'. The *Daily Chronicle* reported: 'The "traveller" puts his feet on the moving staircase, his hand on the rail, and is "wafted" by imperceptible motion to the place where he should be.' The *Sketch* was even more lyrical:

> By a delightful movement which is both exhilarating and fascinating, you are carried from floor to floor without the least effort, and without any of those unpleasant thrills which lifts always succeed in giving to nervous persons.

The *Sketch* correspondent certainly seems to have been carried away, since this first escalator only went up one floor.

⚥ ⚥ ⚥

In the *Fortnightly Review* of January 1896, Lady Jeune wrote an article called 'The Ethics of Shopping', from which extracts were quoted in Chapter XIII of her recollections of shopping as a young woman in the 'seventies. These recollections she contrasted with shopping in the 'nineties—which she considered less tedious, but far more dangerous:

> We are not able to stand against the overwhelming temptations which besiege us at every turn . . . We go to purchase something we want; but when we get to our shop there are so many more things that we never thought of till they presented their obstrusive fascinations on every side. We look for a ribbon, a flower, a chiffon of some sort or other, and we find ourselves in a Paradise of ribbons, flowers, and chiffons, without which our life becomes impossible and our gown unwearable. There are many shops in London into which one cannot safely trust oneself. There are the drawbacks of noise, heat, and overcrowding, but they are more than counterbalanced by the brightness of the electric light and the brilliancy of the colours, and the endless variety on either side. There are two very important changes which have contributed to the temptation of spending money nowadays. One is the gathering together under one roof of all kinds of goods—clothing, millinery, groceries, furniture, in fact of all the necessities of life . . . nearly all the great shops in London are becoming vast stores, one of which, more enterprising than the others, is said to supply young men for dancing and coffins to bury them in. (*This was William Whiteley.*)

Many more people than formerly come to London, and to the large centres, to do their shopping; they prefer to make their purchases where they can concentrate their forces and diminish fatigue. The shops which still cling to the old-fashioned way of carrying on business are being pressed out by the keen competition which increases so rapidly. What an amount of trouble and expense is avoided where one can order one's New Zealand mutton downstairs, buy one's carpet on the ground floor, and deck oneself out in all the glory of Worth or La Ferrier, on the top floor, to all of which one is borne on the wings of a lift, swift and silent.

The other reason for the increased temptation to spend money is the large numbers of women which are now employed . . . women are so much quicker than men, and they understand so much more readily what other women want; they can enter into the little troubles of their customers; they can fathom the agony of despair as to the arrangement of colours, the alternative trimmings, the duration of a fashion, the depths of a woman's purse, and, more important than all, the question of the becomingness of a dress, or a combination of material, to the wearer.

The trend to have women shop assistants was greatly accelerated by the First World War. Before 1914, Peter Robinson's had 300 men to a hundred women assistants—after 1918, women predominated, even working on the delivery vans in smart grey uniforms.

The working conditions of shop assistants had been slightly improved by the Shop Hours Regulation Act of 1886, but it seems that their servile status was still abused by many customers. Lady Jeune wrote:

The complaints which have lately appeared in many papers about the rudeness, the insolence, and discourtesy of customers to shop-women are not really exaggerated. One very rarely hears 'please' or 'thank-you' and no expression of gratitude for trouble taken is vouchsafed by many an over-dressed and moneyed boor. Many people complain that the shop assistants bore them by their persistent appeals to buy things they do not require . . . but many women go to shops for no reason beyond the desire to look round. The ingenious entrepreneur of today has, however, hit on the scheme which offers the greatest seductions to the shopping women, in the sales which take place twice every year. At these times women can walk about unmolested, turning over laces and ribbons and finery of all sorts without being pressed to purchase, though they are possibly tempted and succumb before leaving.

Clearly, the department stores did not all live up to the ideal of 'free circulation without obligation to purchase', and the customer still felt a moral obligation to buy. Where there was no importuning from the assistants, there was apt to be so much obsequiousness that retreat was difficult without making a purchase. The general custom well into the twentieth century at shops which catered for the carriage trade was that of 'shopping through'. The honoured customer was met at the main entrance by the principal shop-walker wearing dignified morning dress (often it was the proprietor himself) who enquired what department she required. He then called another shop-walker forward, who escorted her to the appropriate counter and offered her a chair, summoning an assistant to attend to her needs. If she could not be suited, the shop-walker was signalled for. When she had completed her purchase at the first counter, she was escorted to the next . . . and so on until she was finally escorted to the main door and handed into her carriage. A few tiny parcels might be taken in the carriage, but anything at all large would be delivered.

It was all very flattering and courteous, but it did not give her a chance to look round for herself and compare the goods and prices at one shop with those of another. In some shops, particularly in the provinces, the most valued customers were not even taken from counter to counter . . . everything Madam wanted to see was brought to her at the first counter she sat down at. This was recalled by a resident at the Linen and Woollen Drapers' Cottage Homes for retired members of the trade, who was first apprenticed to Burberry's in Basingstoke when she was twelve years old, and joined Edwin Jones at Southampton while Queen Victoria was still on the throne. It would not seem from her account that any customer, however humble, was ever treated anything less than deferentially; and at Gorringe's it was the rule that no assistant must ever say 'Good Morning, Madam', unless first addressed by the customer.

This reverential atmosphere struck Mr Gordon Selfridge as absurd when he visited London in the 1890's, while still an employee of Marshall Fields, Chicago. His biographer, Reginald Pound, wrote:

81. Boots and shoes by Sparkes Hall, Regent Street. 1886.

He was amused by the ridiculous deference of the shopwalkers. 'The stores and larger shops tried to reproduce the subdued and disciplined atmosphere of the gentleman's mansion.' The initiative, he found, was with the customer. 'It was no part of the function of the store to create a demand. That would be presumptious, entirely out of harmony with the dignity of the house'; and in reporting his impressions of the London retail scene of that time he dwelt largely on the snobbery of it, the notion that 'it was better to do an exclusive trade than a big trade', to serve the customers only with what they asked for, to expect them to say not only what they would like but also how much they were prepared to pay. He found Harrods, Whiteleys, Gorringes, Marshall & Snelgrove, Dickins & Jones, Debenham & Freebody, John Lewis, Peter Robinson, D. H. Evans and Libertys 'all soundly established', but not qualifying for his respect in much else but tradition and the vaunted stability. Harrods, Whiteleys and Debenhams came nearest to his ideas of what a modern department store should be, but they were elaborations rather than original conceptions. The others, chiefly, were agglomerations of shops, and from his point of view, formless and inefficient.

❧   ❧   ❧

Nevertheless, before the turn of the century, a new enterprise was conceived which would not be what Mr Selfridge so scornfully called an 'agglomeration of shops', but a fine departmental store built for its purpose. In July 1898, John Barnes & Co. Ltd. was set up with a nominal capital of £125,000 by six ambitious retailers who subscribed all the capital themselves. John Barnes was a director of John Barker & Co. Ltd.; the others were Owen Owen of Liverpool, William P. Jones of Jones Brothers Holloway, John P. Jones of Dickins & Jones, John Francis of Francis & Sons, grocers, in Brixton, and the same Edwin Jones who had six years earlier saved the Bon Marché in Brixton from liquidation.

Less than a year after the Company was floated, John Barnes was drowned when the steamship *Stella*, carrying Easter holiday-makers, ran aground in fog off Guernsey and sank in fifteen minutes. Thus, John Barnes never saw the building which still carries his name in Finchley Road, Hampstead. Edwin Jones was made Chairman of the group after the shipwreck, and work continued on the building which was going up on a piece of land which had formerly held fourteen shops and some private houses. It was planned as an ultra-modern store, with fifty different departments under one roof. The General Manager, John Lawrie, had spent seventeen years learning the trade at Swan & Edgar. Almost exactly a year after the *Stella* disaster, on

March 29, 1900, the doors of John Barnes opened to the public. The following week the *Hampstead Advertiser* carried this announcement:

> John Barnes and Company Ltd. beg to express their regret and to tender sincere apologies to the many hundreds of customers who were inconvenienced by the non-delivery of their goods during the first three openings days. The Directors have to acknowledge that the large staff of assistants which they had considered sufficient proved totally inadequate to cope with the immense volume of business.

No expense was spared: Axminster carpeting in all the fashion departments, a central passenger lift to the second floor—safety regulations did not permit it to go further—and Lamson Pneumatic Tubing in all departments to save delays at cash desks. At that time, only three other London shops had this system: the Bon Marché in Brixton, Robinson and Cleaver, the Belfast linen-drapers who had opened a branch in Regent Street in 1894, and Roberts of Stratford. Harrods installed it very soon after. There was accommodation for four hundred assistants to live in the building, with three dining-rooms, one for each sex of the rank and file, and one for the buyers. An article in *The Draper's Record* commented that, given a good locality, there was 'no reason why a big trading establishment should not be a mammoth establishment from the start, without undergoing the laborious and time-wasting process of the gradual addition of department on department' which, it added, was the British method and had the crowning merit of safety.

Perhaps *The Draper's Record* was in some way correct in sounding this grudgingly cautionary note, since the building expenses had been nearly £125,000, and in the first year the trading loss was £10,000. It was 1911 before John Barnes really began to make profitable progress. When Selfridges took it over in 1926, sales were well past the quarter million mark. They rebuilt in 1935, adding a five-storey block of flats above the selling floors in place of the old staff rooms, kitchens and servants' rooms, and putting in an arcade and bargain basement. Five years later, John Barnes came into the John Lewis Partnership with the other Selfridge Provincial Stores. Hardly a *provincial* store, John Barnes flourished as a neighbourhood shop for prosperous Hampstead and other northern suburbs.

✻   ✻   ✻

By the end of the century, most of the drapery shops which had expanded into department stores had become limited liability companies. This did not necessarily mean that they were passing out of the hands of their founders' families, but simply that their expansion and rebuilding programmes called for considerable capital outlay. Nevertheless, devoted customers were frightened that their favourite stores would never be the same again . . . a columnist in a ladies' magazine wrote in April 1898: 'There seems to be a small scare amongst certain numbers of my correspondents who imagine that their dearly beloved Marshall & Snelgrove's is going to be altered out of all recognition simply because it has been turned into a limited liability company'. And the fashion historian Georgiana Hill, writing in 1893, foresaw the end of the old order, the grinding of the individual trader between the wheels of the monoliths:

> Trade is now worked on totally different lines from those which served at the beginning of the century. The old methods are worn out. The fierceness of competition has developed an elaborate and expensive system of advertising, on which manufacturers and merchants are, practically, dependent for success. Consequently, few can stand alone. A business, as soon as it becomes large, passes from the hands of the individual to those of a syndicate or company. It is an age of big combinations, and those who either cannot or will not fall in with the new order of things are frequently left behind and crushed.

To us, it seems those words are more applicable to our own day than to the 1890's. But there were significant straws in the wind. Dickins & Jones had acquired Lewis & Allenby of Conduit Street, the most famous of all the silk mercers, and also Allison's of Regent Street. Later they acquired Balls and Flint, also of Regent Street, a well known house for baby linens. They took over Redmayne, renowned tailors and dress-makers of Bond Street, bought up the stock of Hilditch's, silk mercers in the City, acquired George Hitchcock's of St. Paul's, and started a silk-warehouse in Manchester. Dickins & Jones became a Company in 1900, but the family was still in control. There were still two Dickins, father and son, on the board; and Sir John Pritchard Jones was the first Manager and then the Managing Director of the new company. It was certainly still a family business.

In 1896, Debenham & Freebody acquired Nicholay, celebrated furriers, who had been in existence for more than a century and held the appointment of furriers to Queen Victoria and the reigning families of Russia, Austria, Prussia, Belgium and Spain. The good will of this firm, and its staff of merchandising experts and purchasing agents all over the world, formed the basis of Debenham's great fur department. And at about the same time, Debenham's absorbed the well-known linen house of Cappers, suppliers of linen to Buckingham Palace. A little later they acquired the Maison Helbronner, established in Oxford Street in 1834 and later at 106 New Bond Street. This house had an unique position as Ecclesiastical, Heraldic and Domestic Embroiderers, and for many years Debenham's held annual exhibitions of antique and modern embroidery. In 1900, this side of their activities was strengthened by the acquisition of Howell & James, whose stock included rare tapestries, embroideries, brocades, also antique silver, jewellery, glass, pewter and ceramics. Harrods was late in joining the acquisition game, but they took over Dickins & Jones in 1914, and after the war acquired Swan & Edgar.

In 1895, Peter Robinson's became a Company, but the family interest continued in the person of Ernest Robinson, son of John Peter Robinson and grandson of the original Peter Robinson. In 1900 Peter Jones of Sloane Square, which began as a little draper's shop in Draycott Avenue in 1871, became a Company. John Lewis acquired it in 1906, after Peter Jones's death, and in 1914 gave control of the ailing business to his son Spedan, who was straining at the paternal leash. At Peter Jones, Spedan introduced his progressive ideas about staff involvement and profit sharing which led to the John Lewis Partnership, most democratic of all retail empires.

Public Companies might be signs of coming times, but the gracious days of shopping were by no means over. The 'serving through' system still obtained in high-class stores and has been described by a pensioner of Dickins & Jones, who joined the firm about 1900:

'The trade in those days was steady and plenty to do. All the élite arriving in carriage and pairs, cabs, etc. were attended by commissionaires and page boys on every door in their white gloves. Flowers in season could always be seen over all the windows, and the Golden Lion which was the trade mark of the early days of Hanover House was on the North Side doorway.' An employee of Peter Robinson, in a conversation, described the departed grandeur even more nostalgically: 'Oxford Street was a superior shopping street until Bourne & Hollingsworth brought the general trade and then Selfridges. We were family drapers . . . the carriages would drive up and the duchesses would step out. Customers would discuss Sunday's sermon with you, give all their family news, and say their married daughter would be in during the afternoon.'

The recollections of this member of Peter Robinson's staff included a vivid picture of Black Peter Robinson's brougham, always ready harnessed to dash off at a message from a house of mourning: 'The coachmen were in black from head to foot, with crape hat bands and arm bands, and whips with crape bows. Two lady fitters, also clad completely in black, sat in the brougham, equipped with patterns and designs.' A thing to see!—as thrilling in its black and macabre melancholy as a fire-engine in its red and brassy urgency.

CHAPTER XXI

EDWARDIAN DRESSMAKERS

Mourning for Victoria. The Edwardian coiffure. Dressmaking
at Swan & Edgar. Maison Lucile. Diaphanous Underclothes.
Mannequin Parades. Mrs. Asquith and Fashion. Court Dress-
makers. Shopping at Woollands. Blouses in Bond Street.

'THE day Queen Victoria died, we were on the eve of the White
Sales. By the next morning everything was turned to black—it
was one of the biggest transformations in the trade. Everything
that could be dyed was used to meet the colossal demand.' This was
the most dramatic day in the history of drapery recalled in some notes
written by Mr J. B. Smith who joined Dickins & Jones a year or so
before. Ten months earlier, on March 4, 1900, news of the relief of
Ladysmith had been the occasion for very different displays in the
shop windows. A *Sunday Times* correspondent wrote:

Flags were flying. The omnibus drivers waved red, white and blue ribbons
from the whips, and the windows of Messrs Marshall & Snelgrove's well-
known establishments in Oxford Street and Vere Street were simply filled
with dress materials, silks, mantles, blouses, capes, and millinery, in the
national colours. In their principal window there was a small portrait of
Lord Roberts in a gold frame decorated with miniature Union Jacks, and in
front, a velvet pin cushion, painted to represent President Kruger. Right
through the President's venerable head, a long bonnet pin was thrust, and
from the crystal head of the pin there floated the English flag.

The hat-pins of those days were formidable weapons with which
to spear an enemy. Made of sharp steel, ten inches to a foot long, they
secured the monstrous hats, which were mounted upon the abundant
hair, or the apparently abundant hair. The fashion was for the coiffure
to be arranged 'big', which meant arranged in large swathed puffs,
the inner hair of which was fluffed up with a comb. Those without

sufficient hair of their own used frames to fill out the puffs, or pads which were often, according to Irene Clephane in *Ourselves*, made of their own hair combings. This makes one suspect that the 'hair-tidy' which hung by the dressing table mirror was not a receptable emptied by the maid every day, but a collection box for supplies of hair.

Numerous and various were the ingenious inventions to exaggerate one's crowning glory. In *Grace & Favour*, Loelia Duchess of West-minster wrote:

> Hair was first tied in bunches with little bits of tape and then pinned up in puffs and mounds and curls attached to long wires fixed on at the side. At least twenty minutes a day must be devoted to brushing it. When it was cut it had to be singed with a taper, otherwise it would split and bleed.

Those were great days for creative hairdressers; they literally created the coiffure. Unwin & Albert, a firm with branches in Regent Street, Waterloo Place, and Victoria, who claimed in Edwardian times to be 'a firm with 100 years' reputation', sold tresses to make the New Torsair Coil, 20–30″ long (pale and grey shades extra). Their Zaza Comb was sold 'for puffing hair without Frame or Frizette'; and their 'Simplex Transformations' were sent on approval (on receipt of deposit or London reference) and could be *supplied on the Instalment System to suit the convenience of customers.*

During the Boer War there was a young floorman at Swan & Edgar called Gilbert Clarke, who later became apprenticed to Lucile, and very much later became a dress designer for Metro-Goldwyn Mayer in the early days of Hollywood. Gilbert Clarke became acquainted with Somerset Maugham, who asked him to write down his experiences at Swan & Edgar as material for a novel. Clarke wrote about 6,000 words, for which Maugham gave him thirty guineas . . . 'Willie used my stuff practically word for word,' Clarke noted. Whether word for word or well worked on by Somerset Maugham, the material was used in three chapters of *Of Human Bondage* in which the narrator, Philip Carey, is employed at Lynn and Sedley. This novel was not published until 1915, but Maugham wrote it very much earlier, and it is interesting to know that Philip Carey's experiences are based upon first-hand accounts by a floorman at Swan & Edgar at the turn of the century. A good deal of it is about the living-in conditions at the Swan & Edgar hostel, which was an old house in Frith Street . . . 'filthy and disgusting' according to Clarke; but there is information also, about the kind of customers and the methods by which the store built up its dressmaking department:

> Lynn and Sedley received fashion papers from Paris once a week and adapted the costumes illustrated in them to the needs of their customers. Their

clientele was peculiar. The most substantial part consisted of women from the smaller manufacturing towns, who were too elegant to have their frocks made locally and not sufficiently acquainted with London to discover good dressmakers within their means. Besides these, incongruously, was a large number of music-hall artistes. This was a connection that Mr Sampson had worked up for himself and took great pride in. They had begun by getting their stage-costumes at Lynn's, and he had induced many of them to get their other clothes there as well.

'As good as Paquin and half the price,' he said. He had a persuasive, hail-fellow-well-met air with him which appealed to customers of this sort, and they said to one another:

'What's the good of throwing money away when you can get a coat and skirt at Lynn's that nobody knows don't come from Paris?'

It was a fairly usual thing for stage producers to commission the costumes for their productions from big stores, since the dressmaking workrooms were extensive and well staffed. George Edwards, the famous Edwardian impresario, commissioned the designing and making of about fifty dresses for *Our Miss Gibbs* from Harrods. In this musical, two scenes are actually set in representations of Harrod's departments.

The way in which Philip Carey in *Of Human Bondage* came to be a dress designer is almost certainly based upon what happened to Gilbert Clarke at Swan & Edgar:

After Philip Carey had drawn a successful design for Miss Alice Antonia, the well-known serio-comic, in a show at the Tivoli, the buyer began to treat him a little more deferentially and presently gave him designs to do for two of the country customers. They met with satisfaction. Then he began to speak to his clients of a 'clever young feller, Paris art-student, you know,' who worked for him; and soon Philip, ensconced behind a screen, in his shirt-sleeves, was drawing from morning till night. Philip's rise from shop-walker to designer of costumes had a great effect on the department. He realized that he was an object of envy. But he still received no more than the six shillings a week with which he started.

Clearly, being dress designer for a store was not a get rich quick job. Gilbert Clarke was lucky in finding, through his contacts with actresses at Swan & Edgar, a way onto the stage and greater independence. He was not an actor for long. Some figurines he dressed in eighteenth century costume as a birthday present for Violet Vanbrugh's little daughter, led him to make a figurine as a present for Lady Margery Manners when she married the Earl of Anglesey. It was seen by Lady Duff Gordon, the famous Lucile, who immediately signed Clarke to a seven year's apprenticeship, taking him with her to her branches in Paris, New York, and Chicago. In America, Lucile designed costumes for the Ziegfield Follies, and dressed some of the stars of the early screen, amongst them Mary Pickford. And it was doubtless through such contacts at Lucile's that Gilbert Clarke came to join Metro-Goldwyn Mayer as their chief costume designer.

Lucile was the first Englishwoman to become internationally famous as a dress designer. Other dressmakers, such as Miss Jane Clark in the mid-nineteenth century, had been known to Society as *the* dressmaker to have; but Lucile became a name known to thousands of people who could never afford to be dressed by her. She had the advantage of being well-connected. Lucy Christiana Sutherland had married James Stuart Wallace when she was seventeen and he was more than twenty years older. There was a daughter, but the marriage ended after five years. Divorce was a very serious social handicap, even though Mrs Wallace was the innocent party; and poverty was an even worse disgrace. The New Woman of the 'nineties had not yet emerged and it was still humiliating for a gentlewoman to have to earn her own living. Mrs Wallace had always made her own clothes and those of her little daughter, and now she began to make clothes for those friends who stood by her. Her undoubted talent was first seen by a big gathering when she made the bridesmaids' dresses and wedding gown for the marriage of her younger sister, Elinor, to Clayton Glyn at St George's, Hanover Square. This was the beautiful young woman who was soon to become famous through her 'scandalous' novels of Society life. The Hon. Mrs Peel recalls in *Life's Enchanted Cup* how she met the two sisters early in the 1890's:

I had met Mrs Wallace when we had organized a week's programme of amateur operetta at the Richmond Theatre in the cause of local charities. She was our star dancer, a pretty, graceful little woman with a talent for designing dresses and making them. With her she brought her sister Mrs Elinor Glyn, who a year or two later wrote *The Visits of Elizabeth*. It appeared in *The World*, and in book form was refused by one publisher and accepted by another who made a considerable sum of money out of his venture. Mrs Elinor Glyn, red-haired and extraordinarily striking, became a celebrity, but never again did she write anything to compare with those delicious 'Visits of Elizabeth'.

By about 1890, Lucy Wallace was doing so well that she was able to leave her mother's house and set up on her own as a dressmaker in Old Burlington Street. Here she put into practise her ideas about underclothes, as she relates in her reminiscences:

I was particularly anxious to have a department for beautiful underclothes, as I hated the thought of my creations being worn over the ugly nun's veiling or linen-cum-Swiss embroidery which was all that the really virtuous woman of those days permitted herself. With the arrogance which success was beginning to give me I vowed to change all that, and made plans for the day of chiffons and laces, of boudoir caps and transparent nightdresses.

So I started making underclothes as delicate as cobwebs and as beautifully tinted as flowers, and half the women in London flocked to see them, though they had not the courage to buy them at first. Those cunning little lace motifs let in just over the heart, those saucy velvet bows on the shoulder might surely be the weapons of the woman who was 'not quite nice'? But slowly one by one they slunk into the shop in a rather shame-faced way and departed carrying an inconspicuous parcel, which contained a crepe-de-chine or a chiffon petticoat, and although one or two returned to bring the new purchases sorrowfully back because a Victorian husband had 'put his foot down', the majority came back to order more.

Soon the Lucile operation became too big for the house in Old Burlington Street, and she rented Sir George Dashwood's house at 17 Hanover Square. The business was turned into a company, and in 1900 Lucy Wallace married one of her directors, Sir Cosmo Duff Gordon. Soon afterwards the owner of 17 Hanover Square returned to live there, and the Maison Lucile was moved to 23 Hanover Square.

82.

The Maison Lucile is said to have been the first dressmaking house to deliver orders to customers in decorative boxes—a smart green and white stripe—and the first house to be furnished with a sympathetic background for the viewing of clothes. This is how Lucile herself described the traditional dressmaking establishment:

In those days one paid a visit to one's dressmaker and was received into the uncompromising atmosphere of a shop, with hard chairs, a few unbecoming mirrors and a door, which opened on a little fitting-room. Nobody had thought of developing the social side of choosing clothes, of serving tea and imitating the setting of a drawing-room.

Even more of an historic innovation was Lucile's introduction of the mannequin parade:

In many of the then fashionable dressmakers' establishments the models were displayed on horrid lay figures—dreadful affairs of sawdust and wax faces. Then, greatly daring, some resourceful soul conceived the idea in Paris of having living models. But there was no parade, oh! dear no! nothing so frivolous . . . there must be nothing which might suggest that the poor little mannequin had a personality of her own, that she was capable of any more emotion than the sawdust dummy which she replaced. She must not show the glow of youthful flesh, or the curves of young ankles. So to prevent it they encased her in a garment of rigid black satin, reaching from chin to feet, which were shod in unappetizing lace boots. And as a guarantee of the respectability of the establishment the director could be relied upon to choose only the plainest of girls to show off his creations. I shall never forget being taken to see the models of a famous house in Paris and the positive shock I felt when I saw lovely evening dresses in pale shades being worn by girls whose arms and necks, in dingy black satin, emerged from the low-cut décolletés. I decided that nothing on earth would induce me to show such atrocities.

So Lucile engaged six beautiful girls, and prepared the *mise en scène* for the first dress parade: a soft, rich carpet, grey brocade curtains to tone with it, and a miniature stage hung with misty olive chiffon curtains. The invitations were sent out on dainty cards, keeping the illusion that she was inviting her friends to an afternoon party rather than a place of business. Guests included Princess Alice, Ellen Terry, the Duchess of Westminster, Lillie Langtry and Margot Asquith.

Mrs Asquith's interest in dress was an embarrassment to the Prime Minister upon at least one occasion. Paul Poiret, the sensational Parisian designer of this period, described in *My First Fifty Years* a visit paid to his *maison de couture* by Margot Asquith:

She entered my salons like a thunderclap, and while preparations were being made to show her my collection of dresses she explained to me how she was accustomed to dress; and she showed me that she was wearing knickers, which were of violet satin . . . 'Monsieur Poiret, Englishwomen must know your dresses. They are dresses for aristocrats and great ladies. I am going to organize a tea to which I shall invite my most elegant friends.'

And indeed she did—a tea at No. 10 Downing Street. Not surprisingly the Press was after her in full cry . . .

Not only does Mr Asquith refuse his own people the right of protection, but he facilitates the instrusion of foreign merchandise by organizing exhibitions in the residence which has been paid for by the nation's trade.

Mr Asquith was questioned in Parliament and called to order by his party; but everyone knew that neither Parliament nor Mr Asquith himself had any power to call Mrs Asquith to order. Later Paul Poiret recalled;

> I saw Mrs Asquith at a friend's in Paris, long after. The poor woman no longer dared to meet me. She had had to order dresses in all the shops in London to give them proof of her loyalty and fidelity.

From another source there is a story that it was Mrs Asquith who persuaded Jay's to become ordinary dressmakers, instead of specializing only in mourning, by insisting on a red sash to a black dress she ordered from them—the Poiret touch!

Lucile does not mention the Downing Street story in her reminiscences—in fact, references to Paul Poiret by Lucile, or to Lucile by Paul Poiret, are conspicuous by their complete absence in both autobiographies. They must have been deadly rivals. After all, Lucile invaded Paris; and both of them were egotistic, vain, and temperamental. We do not even know whether Lucile's first mannequin parade which Mrs Asquith attended was before the Poiret incident in Downing Street or after—one suspects after. Mrs Asquith was making amends! And perhaps it is significant that many years later Lucile had her first male guest at a dress parade: Mr Asquith. Lucile recorded, 'He sat calmly through the show, though I do not think he gave much attention to the models'. To sit calmly was surely the least he could do.

At that first fashion parade in the Maison Lucile, hats, gloves, shoes, jewels and parasols were all chosen to harmonize with the dresses—in the modern phrase, to co-ordinate. Another innovation

83. Electrolier for showrooms, in polished brass or bronze.
Harris & Sheldon, 1902.

was the naming of models. Previously dresses were simply referred to as 'the pink silk' or 'the black velvet', or sometimes by numbers. Lucile called her models 'Gowns of Emotion', and named them *Give Me Your Heart, When Passion's Thrall is O'er, Do You Love Me?*, and *The Sighing Sound of Lips Unsatisfied*—'a soft gray chiffon veiling an underdress of short pink and violet taffeta, shadowed and unreal'. Later Lucile successes were: *A Frenzied Song of Amorous Things, Red Mouth of a Venomous Flower*, and *The Meaning of Life is Clear*. Lady Duff Gordon was certainly sister to Elinor Glyn.

The Lucile mannequins also caused a sensation . . . Gamela and Hebe, Dolores, Phyllis and Florence. Not one of them weighed much under eleven stone and the six-footers considerably more. It was an era when 'big girls' with 'fine figures' were the ideal of beauty. Lucile took her mannequins to New York, Chicago and Paris, and they all married millionaires. Nowadays, millionaires seem to be small men, so it is fortunate that the ideal of feminine beauty is less physically dominating than it was then.

Mr Hiley, fashion dictator at Jay's in the 1890's, is credited by one authority as having been the first to use living mannequins in England; but the mannequins at Jay's wore black combination garments similar to the 'maillots' worn in the French couture houses. Swan & Edgar claim to have had a mannequin parade in 1869, but there is nothing about mannequins in *Of Human Bondage* in which there is so much first-hand information about the costume departments of Swan & Edgar. Once Lucile's lovelies had broken down inhibitions, it was not long before the more progressive stores saw that mannequin parades would be a great attraction in their dress departments. Harrod's Jubilee Booklet (1909) says:

A feature of the Costume Department (to which luxurious fitting-rooms are attached) is the displaying of gowns on living models, some of the smartest figures in London being specially employed for this purpose. Harrods is widely known as THE SHRINE OF FASHION. We adapt beautiful Continental Creations to English tastes and conditions, and supply the most exclusive creations in fashionable attire at moderate prices.

We may be sure that they were ten times as moderate as Lucile. But then Lucile did not adapt 'beautiful Continental Creations to English tastes and conditions'—she created a new English taste for extravagance.

Harrod's living models were employed in the costume department; but very soon the idea of giving fashion parades in the restaurants of the stores was conceived. By 1913, fashion parades had reached the provinces—Browns of Chester gave their first mannequin parade in the ballroom of the Grosvenor Hotel, Chester, in 1913. In 1915, D. H. Evans gave a children's frock parade, 'for the purpose of showing new style in juvenile dress'. These were probably the first child models to be employed.

        ❦   ❦   ❦

Like Swan & Edgar, some of the other large London stores probably drew many dressmaking clients from the rich manufacturing towns . . . women who had become 'too elegant to have their clothes made locally, and were not sufficiently acquainted with London to discover good dressmakers within their means' . . . or were too self-conscious to submit themselves to the dispraising eyes of supercilious *vendeuses* in the couture houses. The stores themselves could be very exclusive. Debenham & Freebody, for instance, had a special salon which was called 'Madame Pacard's Dressmaking Department', and one can be sure that timid customers would find a visit to Madame Pacard almost as terrifying as to a court dressmaker with her own establishment. But a shop with a constant flow of customers to all departments was never quite so alarming as the kind of dressmaking house which the privileged ladies of Society patronized. The great houses of the Edwardian period were Reville & Rossiter, Russell & Allen, Redfern, Mascotte of 89 Park Street (run by Mrs Cyril Drummond, herself a Society Woman), Fred Bosworth, famed for his sporting clothes and walking costumes, the Maison Lucile, Worth. Bradley's of Chepstow Place, the Arctic Fur Store, was beginning to branch out from furs only into tailoring and dressmaking—and were to become the largest London couture house in the period between the wars.

There were also innumerable court dressmakers—far more than made for court circles. The term was understood to imply ability to undertake presentation dresses. At 116 New Bond Street was the establishment of Madame F. G. Durrant, court dressmaker, where Hardy Amies' mother started working. The manageress was a Miss Gray, and when she left to start her own business, she took Mrs Amies with her, and one or two others of the staff—also some of the customers. That, in fact, is the traditional way for new couture houses to start.

Miss Gray's new establishment was in Brook Street, in premises now occupied by the development of Fenwicks. It was called Miss Gray, Ltd.—not Eva Gray Ltd. as it would be today. Hardy Amies wrote in *Just So Far:*

84.

85.

86.

87.

Miss Gray did not set herself up as a dress designer. She bought some models in Paris, and made others to her own design, which she never pretended were anything other than adaptations of Paris models, which she had either seen in reality or in the fashion newspapers. She did, however, call herself a Court Dressmaker, and in actual fact had the patronage of Court Circles.

Miss Fowler, the skirt fitter at Miss Gray Ltd., had an apprentice called Maud Beard, who became a fitter at Hardy Amies. So the court dressmaker's apprentice came to be the fitter responsible for many of the Queen of England's dresses.

Reville & Rossiter was an important couture house from the day it started. It was founded in Hanover Square in 1906 by William Wallace Reville Terry and Miss Rossiter, both of whom were at Jay's. He had been mantle buyer, and she the buyer of tea-gowns; at their new firm Reville was the designer and Miss Rossiter the administrator. They were court dressmakers in the most literal sense of the term, for they made costumes for Queen Mary. Later they made the trousseau of the Princess Royal. It was with Reville Terry that Victor Stiebel, himself to become a royal dressmaker, started designing in the late 1920's. Reville made the dress in which Sonia Keppel was presented at Court in 1919, and his salon before the 1914–18 war was probably the same as she described it in *Edwardian Daughter*:

> The personality of Mr Reville always intrigued me as, apart from being an expert dress designer, he was also an expert on Chinese art. As one came into the shop, a large part of the left side of it was divided off by curtains, sumptuously embroidered with Chinese dragons, behind which one had an occasional tantalizing glimpse of a large gilt Buddha and walls draped in black. Wild rumour had it that, behind the Buddha, Mr Reville had an opium den and Mamma told me never to accept an invitation from him to go behind the curtains.

The young Keppels had their riding clothes made at Swears & Wells . . . 'sitting erect on the girth section of a wooden horse, we both felt confident. Both of us were equipped with bowler-hats and covert coats, and thong-less whips. Violet, a riding-habit; me, some breeches.' When younger still they were dressed by Mr Nichols in Glasgow, and Woollands in Knightsbridge. They made four seasonal expeditions to Woollands each year . . .

> Early in the afternoon, my mother, Nannie, Violet and I would squeeze into the electric brougham and ping through Hyde Park . . . In those days, the 'Juvenile Department' at Woollands was situated on the 3rd or 4th floor. Grimly, the lift man shut his concertina-gates on us, and very, very slowly we ascended to our appointment with 'No. 10'. We never discovered whether

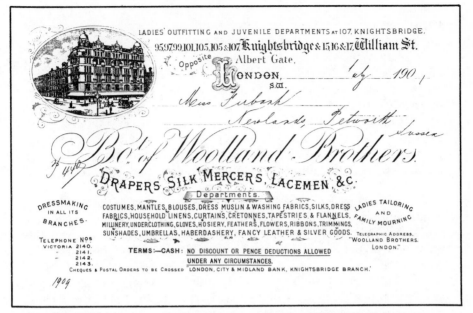

LADIES' OUTFITTING AND JUVENILE DEPARTMENTS AT 107, KNIGHTSBRIDGE.

95,97,99,101,105,&107 Knightsbridge & 15,16 & 17, William St.

Opposite Albert Gate,

LONDON,
S.W.

190

Miss Firbank

Newlands, Petworth

Sussex

Bo.t of Woolland Brothers

DRAPERS, SILK MERCERS, LACEMEN &c.

Departments.

DRESSMAKING IN ALL ITS BRANCHES

COSTUMES, MANTLES, BLOUSES, DRESS MUSLIN & WASHING FABRICS, SILKS, DRESS FABRICS, HOUSEHOLD LINENS, CURTAINS, CRETONNES, TAPESTRIES & FLANNELS, MILLINERY, UNDERCLOTHING, GLOVES, HOSIERY, FEATHERS, FLOWERS, RIBBONS, TRIMMINGS, SUNSHADES, UMBRELLAS, HABERDASHERY, FANCY LEATHER & SILVER GOODS.

LADIES' TAILORING AND FAMILY MOURNING

TELEPHONE NOS
VICTORIA 2140.
" 2141.
" 2142.
2143.

TERMS:—CASH: NO DISCOUNT OR PENCE DEDUCTIONS ALLOWED UNDER ANY CIRCUMSTANCES.

CHEQUES & POSTAL ORDERS TO BE CROSSED "LONDON, CITY & MIDLAND BANK, KNIGHTSBRIDGE BRANCH."

TELEGRAPHIC ADDRESS,
"WOOLLAND BROTHERS.
LONDON."

1909

88. Bill-head from an account sent to Miss Heather Firbank in July 1909. The items, which totalled £144 17s. 7½d., were all underclothes, and included twenty chemises and fourteen petticoats. There was an 'account rendered' of £82 12s. 8d., in spite of TERMS CASH in red letters on the bill-head.

'No. 10' had had Christian baptism and a name of her own. To Violet and me, she remained a numerical cypher that sucked pins. Always she was bent double at our feet, measuring our skirts, slithering round on her poor, old knees, and stabbing a pin into each hem from the apparently inexhaustible supply she kept in her mouth.

Woollands, by that time, had socially soared from its beginnings as a servant's bazaar and had become one of the most fashionable shops in London, particularly noted for its beautiful tea-gowns.

The fashion, the *passion* for cascades of lace, for clouds of *tulle illusion*, for intricate embroideries and finely pleated linens, for blouses and tea-gowns and boudoir wraps, had created a new kind of specialist shop, devoted to the intimacies of lingerie, blouses, lace and linen. And it was in Bond Street that the most reverent shrines to femininity were set up. In 1899, George Givan of Belfast established himself in New Bond Street as a leading specialist in Irish linen goods. By 1902, he had opened a ladies' salon for the sale of underwear, and had established workrooms in which were executed 'the finest hand embroideries in

London'. In 1906 the White House, directed by Jean Valentin from Paris, opened at 51 New Bond Street, offering the most exquisite and expensive lingerie, blouses and children's wear. Later it came under the direction of Monsieur Jean Dellière, whose son Robert Dellière is now at the helm. Next Louvet Frères of the *Grande Maison de Blanc*, set themselves up at 62 New Bond Street. The Irish Linen Company, originally established at 4 Bloomsbury Square in 1800, moved to 112 New Bond Street—it was here that the intensely modish Miss Heather Firbank bought her blouses, a dozen at a time, for an average price of £2 9s 6d. Another specialist house, this one dealing exclusively in blouses, was Leighton and Joseph of 105 and 106, New Bond Street.

The blouse reached its peak of elaborate perfection in the Edwardian period with its high boned collar and exquisitely turned cuffs, its delicately, deliciously worked front which hung pouched over the waistband of the skirt. The Edwardian blouse always did up at the back, usually with a myriad tiny hooks and eyes—it was essential to have a lady's maid and/or husband, and the ironing of the blouses defeated all but the most skilled and patient. In 1906, the White House began a laundry service for customers, staffed with trained laundresses versed in the mysteries of 'getting up' blouses and fine lingerie.

This concentration of femininity in Bond Street was something quite new, since for most of the nineteenth century it was regarded as a man's street. Even in the 'nineties, when women were beginning to assert their right to be seen anywhere, Mrs Peel reported: 'Young ladies in Society seldom walked alone except in retired situations, and never in Bond Street, Piccadilly or St James's Street'. This, of course, was because these streets were on the prostitute beat; but all the more does that emphasise that they were masculine streets. The shops were mainly occupied by tradesmen specializing in expensive goods and services for men about town; but since the 'nineties, tradesmen with attractions for the lady of fashion had set their snares in Bond Street.

The Post Office Directory of 1911 shows that there were 101 establishments in Bond Street directly concerned with women's fashions, the majority of them being court dressmakers, but many of them milliners. Twenty-five were ladies' hairdressers and beauticians, these being called 'Complexion Specialists'. There were three electrolysis specialists, and three manicurists. There was Augustus Bide, the famous glover, and Alan McAffee the fashionable shoemaker. It was at McAffee's that Miss Heather Firbank had her shoes made, ordering eight pairs at a time.

It was still not possible to buy anything ready-made in Bond Street, other than underclothes and blouses; and nearly all the shops catering for the fashions and foibles of the feminine half of Society were in New Bond Street: Old Bond Street still held aloof. This is how it was according to Frederick Willis who was a gentleman's hatter in Edwardian days. He writes in *A Book of London Yesterdays*:

Yes, Regent Street was the superb shopping centre, but Old Bond Street was the really aristocratic shopping street. It was unique. But let me make it quite clear that between Old and New Bond Streets was an impregnable social barrier that nobody ever attempted to cross. Up to 1914, Old Bond Street was the quintessence of aristocratic shopping. New Bond Street was a parvenu, a hanger-on at the gates of the *imperium in imperio*. Shopkeepers in Old Bond Street were not tradesmen but critics, connoisseurs, and authorities on the goods they dealt in. No buses were allowed in the street . . . a bus might befoul the carriages. There they stood, rows of them, gleaming and embellished with crests, sleek horses and coachmen as dignified as dukes ought to be, waiting their lords' pleasure.

After the first war, the LCC became active in tidying up the names of London Streets. It was then proposed to combine Old and New Bond Streets and call the result Bond Street. New Bond Street residents were quite agreeable to the change, but the howls of execration that came from Old Bond Street shook even the LCC into an understanding of the enormous gaffe they had made.

89. CLOTH STAND—*'for Tailors, Drapers, Warehousemen, and Others'*. Harris & Sheldon, 1888.

CHAPTER XXII

FROU-FROU LADIES AND
SPLENDID SPORTSWOMEN

The Swan Silhouette. Trousseaux and frou-frou Underskirts.
Coloured silk stockings. Haberdashery, Dress shields. Farthing
change pin-sheets. Golf and Motoring clothes.

THE blouses that bloomed in the shop windows of New Bond Street were worn over that other projector of Edwardian womanhood, the straight-fronted corset. This garment was the fundamental factor in creating the famous 'S' Curve, or swan silhouette, which reached its supreme expression in the magnificent figure of Camille Clifford as the Gibson Girl in '*The Belle of Mayfair*', 1906.

Lucile's majestic mannequins swanned around languidly with S-curving figures; but Lucile was not the creator of the straight-fronted corset. No-one without expertise in corsetry could have achieved, or even conceived this miracle of cutting and shaping. Norah Waugh in *Corsets and Crinolines* says:

> Never before or since has the corset been quite so complicated. It was constructed from numerous curved pieces—as many as ten to fifteen each side, plus gussets—all expertly joined and traversed by a quantity of whalebone and steel of varying thickness and weight.

Miss Waugh attributes the design of this astounding structure to Madame Gaches-Sarraute of Paris, a corsetière who had studied medicine and considered that women's anatomy was being dangerously distorted by heavy corsets shaped to minimize the waist. Madame Gaches-Sarraute's design of 1900 had a straight-fronted busk, which started very low on the bust-line and continued down over the stomach without going in at the waist. Suspenders, now attached to the corset itself, kept the line taut and unbroken to the knees. The theory was

XV   Delivery vans lined up outside the Summer Sale windows of Kendal Milne, Manchester, in the 1890's.

Three-wheeled, motorized delivery van of Trewin Bros., Watford, first used in 1912.

Harrods: photographed from Montpelier Street in 1906.

Nicholsons of
St. Paul's Churchyard
traditional heart of
the drapery world.
Photograph taken the
day before demolition
for the City Barbican
began in November
1963. Nicholsons
opened new premises
at Bromley in
May 1963.

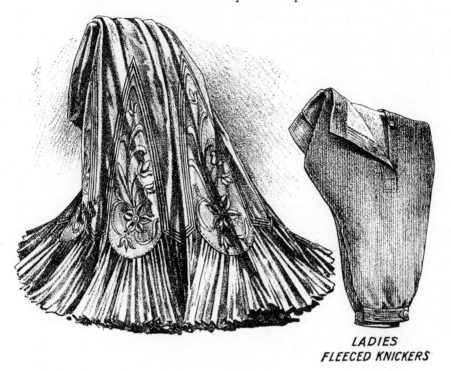

LADIES
FLEECED KNICKERS

90. Ready-made underskirt in embroidered Moreen or Moirette. Grey
fleeced knickers, also available in tweed, striped tweed, Bedford cord, or
serge. I. & R. Morley, 1909.

that this design supported the abdomen and left the thorax free. But
fashionable women were not interested in freedom. They preferred a
small waist. So they laced in the corset, and this resulted in the bust
billowing over its low front, while the abdominal flesh, pressed flat
by the heavy front busk, swelled out at the sides and back.

Over, and also under, this compelling corset went the Edwardian
underclothes. And although Lucile had induced ladies of Society and
the stage to wear delicate chiffon and crêpe de chine lingerie, the
underwear departments of the stores still kept their stock *sans peur et
sans reproche*, even in the eyes of their most conservative customers.
Under-garments were elaborately trimmed with ribbons, lace and
embroidery, but the materials they were made of were uncompro-
misingly opaque.

The relative standing of the stores in fashion at this time can be
gauged by the prices of their trousseaux. As an example, Harrods

quoted trousseaux for brides from £7 7s 8d to £33 18s 0d—their customers were evidently interested in shillings and pence as well as pounds; whereas Debenham & Freebody's trousseaux were from £25 to £100, and most of the items were 'convent made'. This is their £100 trousseau of 1912:

	£	s	d
6 chemises, cambric or batiste, trimmed lace or hand embroidery, at 10/6	3	3	0
6 linen chemises, hand embroidered and ribbon, at 18/9	5	12	6
3 evening chemises, fine lawn, trimmed lace and ribbon, at 18/9	2	16	3
6 nightdresses, cambric or nainsook, trimmed embroidery, at 15/9	4	14	6
6 nightdresses, trimmed lace, at 21/9	6	10	6
6 pairs knickers, trimmed hand embroidery or lace, at 15/9	4	14	6
6 linen knickers, trimmed hand embroidery and ribbon, at 18/9	5	12	6
3 knickers, trimmed lace and ribbon, at 21/9	3	5	3
1 crêpe de chine evening petticoat trimmed lace, etc.	3	5	0
1 coloured satin petticoat	1	1	9
3 white petticoats, embroidered flounces, at 12/9	1	18	3
2 white petticoats, trimmed hand embroidery at 18/9	1	17	6
2 white petticoats, trimmed lace and ribbon, at 25/6	2	11	0
6 camisoles hand embroidered or lace, at 8/11	2	13	6
3 linen camisoles, trimmed hand embroidery and ribbon, at 14/9	2	4	3
3 camisoles, trimmed lace and ribbon, at 16/9	2	10	3
3 dozen diaper towels, at 18/9	2	16	3
4 crêpe de santé petticoats, trimmed lace, at 14/9	2	19	0
4 cream Japanese silk petticoats, at 14/9	2	19	0
1 pair Milanese silk knickers		18	9
4 Indian gauze combinations, at 14/9	2	19	0
3 fancy gauze combinations, at 18/9	2	16	3
1 pair Milanese combinations, for evening wear	1	15	3
1 silk dressing gown	2	9	6
1 muslin dressing gown, trimmed lace	1	9	6
1 tea-gown	4	4	0
1 flannel gown	2	9	6
1 silk dressing jacket	1	9	6
1 muslin dressing jacket		18	9
2 boudoir caps, at 18/9	1	17	6
1 nightdress sachet	1	1	9
1 dozen fancy bordered handkerchiefs		12	6
1 dozen fancy cambric handkerchiefs		15	0
1 pair spun woven knickers	1	7	6

Debenham's £40 trousseau seems to have been selected with a different type of bride in mind, for it includes a bathing costume and two pairs of sports woollen knickers. But the sports girl had her languorous moments, for there was also a rest gown and two boudoir caps.

Although the term lingerie was now used for underclothes of the more delicate kind, anything thick, warm, or woven was still underwear. Debenhams sold sets of chemise, knickers, nightdress, and camisole, under two different headings: 'underclothes sets' and 'lingerie sets', the latter being more exquisite than the former. Decidedly not in the lingerie class was a range of Viyella nightdresses (outsize always in stock) and ladies' sleeping suits, in striped silk.

Drawers were now called knickers, and were made in cambric, longcloth, nainsook, linen. Satin, crêpe de santé, and Japanese silk knickers were 'suitable for evening wear'. For combinations, there was a choice of (1) longcloth, embroidered and tucked, (2) nainsook or cambric, hand-embroidered with ribbons and lace, (3) finest nainsook trimmed torchon lace, tucks, etc., (4) linen, elaborately trimmed with hand-embroidery, real lace and ribbon. Combinations, it seems, although doomed to flower unseen, were almost as beautiful as blouses.

Even in the woven underwear department, combinations were not of much sterner stuff, except the 'extra heavy-weight merino'. Otherwise, they were of Milanese silk, China silk, or spun silk embroidered with low neck and edged lace. Spencers were in merino, silk and wool, Anglo-Indian gauze or spun silk, Directoire closed knickers, black, white, or coloured, were in mercerised cotton, wool, Milanese silk, spun silk, pure silk. Cashmere knickers were supplied also in open shape. Cycle shape knickers buttoned across the back.

Petticoats and underskirts were insistently seductive. Kilted or pleated frills, ruching, and lace gave them 'intriguingness', for they were intended to be seen when a lady picked up her skirt in walking. Hidden persuasions, petticoats spoke louder than skirts, which were often less costly. Daytime clothes were now of wool and heavy tailoring fabrics, silk being used only for linings and underskirts. The skirt of a costume or dress would be lined with silk, and worn over a taffeta underskirt; and the rustling frou-frou of silk on silk sounded more costly than if the dress itself were of silk. It was the pyschology of the mink-lined raincoat.

Lingerie and underwear counters were always discreetly upstairs, sited where there was no possible danger of a man walking through the department. Hosiery, however, was always on the ground floor; and this was not without its subtle suggestiveness. The elaborate frill of an underskirt was not the only thing that gentlemen could hope to observe occasionally—there was also the glimpse of an ankle. Moreover, the Edwardian days were the great days of the hammock, which gave opportunities for more intriguing glimpses. In the Heather Firbank collection there are yellow silk stockings, white silk stockings with lace fronts, and violet stockings with clox. Even Miss Firbank's woollen stockings were purple with black embroidery. Her garters were black with clusters of fruit. She must have been a hammock girl.

The variety of stockings at this time can be seen in Harrod's catalogue of 1900:

White cotton, white lisle
Unbleached cotton with silk clox
Black cotton, clean and fast
Black cotton with white feet *(some black dyes stained when feet got hot)*.
Black lisle with silk clox
Black lisle with embroidered fronts
Plain lisle, coloured lisle, lace lisle
Black ribbed cotton, clean and fast
White gauze hose, in cotton or merino
Black cashmere ribbed hose
White merino
Black cashmere, embroidered fronts
Black spun silk, coloured spun silk
Black spun silk with white feet
Black lace
Pure white silk, embroidered fronts
Coloured silk, all shades

The haberdashery counter of a store was always sited somewhere near the main entrance. Compared with other departments, the cash turn-over was small, and the ratio of shop assistants' time to sales was disproportionately high . . . a customer might spend quarter of an hour choosing exactly the right shade and width of a few yards of binding, the colour of a reel of cotton, the size of a linen button . . . and the resulting sale would add up to perhaps less than a shilling. But haberdashery was an expected service, and ladies purchasing a card of mending cotton might move on to other counters. And it was the recognized training ground for apprentice assistants: all sales girls started their career in 'Haby'. They must have found it bewildering at first to work out $2\frac{1}{2}$ yds. at $6\frac{3}{4}$d a yard, and to find what was required in the innumerable little drawers and shelves. Contemporary catalogues give an idea of the variety of stock:

Stay laces	Pins and needles, needle cases
Hat pins	Combs and hairslides
Garter elastic	Muff chains
Shoe buckles	Veils and fichus
Buttons and fasteners	Feather trimmings, Passementerie
Hooks and eyes	edgings

Silk cord, petersham, ribbons
Belts and fans
Jet garniture
Mantle fasteners, plackets
Whalebone
Jet and sequin collars
Jewelled collar bands
'Vanities'—egg-shaped, on a chain, fitted with mirror in lid
Paste bandeaux
Linen fronts, collars, cuffs
Hair bands

Japanese antimony pin boxes
'Housewifes'
Circular leather work bags
Eye-glass chains
Bodice fronts
Shaped braid and fringe garniture for skirts
Tassels, pendants, mantle fasteners
Jet garniture for bodice fronts
Velvet-grip stocking suspenders
Transfer designs
Dress preservers

Much more detailed lists of haberdashery are in I. & R. Morley's catalogues for the trade. That of Autumn 1899 includes:

Cotton balls
Fingering and worsted balls
Beltings
Berlin wools
Bindings
Blouse protectors
Bodice bones and steel
Bodice busts
Bodkins
Bone casing
Bonnet cotton
Book muslins
Bootakins
Boot laces
Mantle borderings
Braids
Buckram
Bullion fringe
Busk protectors
Button hole gimp and twist
Coffin dometts
Collar protectors, frames and stiffeners
Cork soles
Corset busks and shields
Crochet cotton
Embroidery cotton
Machine cotton
Marking cotton, Ferret cotton
Mending cotton and wool
Cotton wool, Crape cords

Dress weights
Dressing gown girdles
Eye-glass cords and guards
Fascinators
Felt soles
Filletings, Filoselle
Name tapes
Frillings, Galloons
Garters
Glacé webbing
Hair curlers and wavers
Hair falls
Mourning hat bands
Hat guards
Knitting pins
Linen buttons
Measuring tapes
Madapollams
Motor scarves
Mourning handkerchiefs
Night caps
Nursery pins and toilet pins
Night socks and hose
Penny articles
Puggarees
Satin wire
Chamois skins
Skirt edging, Skirt steel, Skirt web
Sleeve lifts, Suspenders
Thimbles
Waddings

That list gives an indication of the variety of haberdashery a good drapery shop would be expected to carry; but under each heading are sub-headings. There are, for instance, ten different types of elastic, sixteen of mendings, twenty-one of pins, twenty-six of braid, with all the variations of colour and width within the type. And this particular catalogue gives no fewer than forty-six kinds of dress-shields, including perfumed dress-shields.

The dress-shield, or dress-preserver, was essential when few dresses were washable, and when there were no chemical perspiration checks. They were most particularly important for evening dresses. Hot ballrooms, the excitement and exercise of the dance, made these tightly corseted and abundantly-fleshed ladies perspire freely. Dress-shields saved the dress from getting stained under the arms; but even the perfumed ones were not deodorant. However, the scent of sweat was not always considered unattractive—in fact it seems to have been numbered amongst the abundant charms of Edwardian womanhood. An old lady, a beauty in her day, was surprised to learn about the modern use of deodorants and anti-perspirants: 'Dear me, when I went to balls, the gentlemen used to *like* what we called a 'bouquet de corsage'.

Although haberdashery counters always stocked pins, ladies were ordinarily well supplied owing to the custom in drapery departments of giving papers of pins in lieu of a farthing change. The farthing was used to make goods seem cheaper than they were: 1/11¾d sounded so much less than 2/–. And instead of the farthing change, the customer was given a paper of pins. Occasionally a customer, perhaps feeling that she had enough pins to last her a lifetime, insisted upon her farthing, but most accepted the pins meekly. They probably imagined they were getting pins at a bargain price. But a study of Morley's trade catalogues reveals the interesting fact that the customer paid more for her pins than if she bought them in penny sheets—and the shopkeeper made a profit on his 'change pin sheets'. In 1883, the price at which drapers bought their change pin sheets by the gross allowed them a profit of 2d a gross—that is to say, he was 2d better off than giving the customer her farthing change. And the customer, who got fifty-two pins on the farthing sheet, could have bought two hundred and fifty pins on a sheet for one penny. By 1908, the draper was making 6d a gross on the change paper pins. Some, in lieu of the pins which were in lieu of the farthing change, substituted 'Farthing Novelettes'. Morley's evidently ran rather more instructive or informative publications, since theirs were called 'Wonderful Books', and 'Citizen Books'. These cost the draper exactly the same, 2/6 a gross, as did the change pin sheets.

91. RINKING OUTFIT and an all-in-one undergarment named THE
BODYSKIRT. Both ready-made from wholesalers Cook's of St Paul's,
selling at drapers' shops all over the country. 1910.

Frederick Willis in *A Book of London Yesterdays*, describes the Farthing
Novelette: 'A Farthing Novelette consisted of four smudgily printed
pages of letterpress and a picture showing a scene in high society.
They all dealt with life in aristocratic circles. The people were gluttons
for information about the upper ten and, presumably, the authors of
these Farthing Novelettes were well equipped to supply it.'

Farthing Novelettes would not have been used in West End shops
whose proprietors liked to think their customers were drawn exclusively
from aristocratic circles—'the nobility and gentry' that they addressed
in their advertisements. They would have been used by small town
drapers and 'fancy goods' shops, like the Camberwell one which
Frederick Willis describes:

It was run by the Misses Crabb, two maiden ladies of questionable age but
unquestionable respectability, whose small shop was crammed in the neatest

way with all the tiniest requirements of a housewife's needlework life: pins, needles, bodkins, buttons, tapes, thimbles, cottons, hooks and eyes, elastic— everything was always in stock, and one or the other of the good ladies would instantly find what was wanted in a great nest of tiny drawers which completely covered the wall at the back of the counter.

This hiding away of all stock in little drawers at the back of the counter was a system the very opposite to self-service.

¥　　　¥　　　¥

It hardly seems possible that those Edwardian ladies with all their frou-frou femininity could also have been sportswomen. Yet many of them most certainly were . . . yachtswomen, huntswomen, cyclists, roller skaters (or 'rinkers'), tennis and hockey players, balloonistes, automobilistes; there were also the lady golfers.

The Ladies' Golf Union was formed in 1893; and although the early ladies' clubs were nearly all in Scotland (the first in 1867 at St Andrews), by the beginning of the new century there was almost equal enthusiasm in the south. Bicycles and golf went together, since the bicycles made the ladies sufficiently mobile to get to the golf courses.

Ladies' golf courses consisted of some short putting holes, some longer holes admitting of a drive of seventy or eighty yards, and a few mild hazards. The drive was confined to this length because, according to Lord Moncrieff in The Badmington Library, 'The postures and gestures requisite for a full swing are not particularly graceful when the player is clad in female dress.' It was this humiliating state of affairs which Thomas Burberry determined to alter, now that he was established in the Haymarket and was making ladies' clothes as well as gentlemen's. He designed a Ladies' Free-Stroke Coat, with patent Pivot Sleeve and Adaptable Skirt:

No other sleeve is fit to golf in, or will ever be used again after this. The coat is fitted with special shaped pockets which keep out wet and carry contents well forward. The skirt loops up by a simple contrivance and shortens its length some six or eight inches.

There was also the Burberry coat and skirt, which 'unites the freedom in the upper part of a Norfolk jacket with expanding pleats, and the smartness below the waist of a skirted coat'. The illustration of this outfit, which was recommended for walking and shooting as well as for golf, shows an ankle length skirt, just short enough to reveal white spats. The hems of golf skirts were very often bound with leather so that the mud could be washed off them. Harrod's sold 'highly starched

BURBERRY
CYCLING GOWN

BURBERRY NORFOLK.
No. 1

92. Leather lapels, pocket flaps and buttons. Skirt has deep inverted pleat to hang in graceful folds each side of the saddle.

93. Adjustable skirt with cords to draw the skirt up (as in picture) or let down to full-length walking skirt.

linen golf collars and golf cuffs—it is surely one of the ironies of fashion that ladies adopted from men golfers these instruments of torture which men themselves would have done well to have discarded. Miss Mabel Stringer gave a tortured account in her golfing memoirs of playing in a starched collar which made sores on her neck.

Burberrys designed only outer garments. But what went on underneath can be seen in Harrod's catalogues, which illustrate cycling and golf knickers, with band beneath the knee and a back opening—in black and navy serge, black and grey alpaca, or black and coloured satin. Linings for these knickers could be chosen in pink flannelette, calico, nainsook, or nun's-veiling. *Very special* were black serge knickers with chamois leather seat for cycling. The 'Rideasy Skirt', for cycling and walking divided at the back to go over each side of the saddle . . .

but it avoided looking like trousers, since there were fan pleats on the inside.

Golf was a middle-class sport. The fashionable sport *par excellence* was automobilism. And automobilism called for an altogether new mode of dress. From 1900, according to Julius Price in *Dame Fashion* (1912) 'firms supplying all that was requisite for the equipment of an up-to-date lady motorist sprung into existence. They sold hats, caps, motor veils, dust-coats, capes, costumes, gauntlet gloves, and goggles'. One of these was 'Allweathers', motor clothing specialists, of 13 New Burlington Street and 43 Brompton Road, whose Illustrated Book included ladies' tailor-made leather motoring knickers, fitted with detachable flannel lining. The 'Montague' was a three-quarter lined leather coat with skirt to match, the coat fitted with storm fronts and windguards to sleeves. Made to measure or from pattern bodice in ten days'. Advertisements of these days refer to driving on a motor-car, not in it. You were completely exposed to the elements.

Ladies were not just passengers . . . many of them took the wheel. And the names of these early automobilistes were as resounding as their vehicles: The Baroness Campbell de Laurentz, first British lady owner-driver, who drove her steam dog-cart with a groom in the tiger's seat; the Duchess of Sutherland, President of the Ladies' Automobile Club which was founded in 1903, *grande dame* of automobilism in England, frequently seen at the helm of her Mercedes; Miss Vera Butler, racing-motorist daughter of the celebrated racing balloonist, herself a ballooniste; Mrs George Thrupp, whose infant son had the first motoring christening; Mrs Bazalgette driving in the one thousand miles trial in 1900 . . . the names of these pioneers were as challenging as the names of their cars.

Formidable as they sound, their photographs in the illustrated magazines show them adorable. Even Mrs Coote, *en automobile* with the Rev Coote, is quite a poppet in her sporting tweed cap fashioned like a man's; and another very county style of motoring millinery was Liberty's motor bonnet of 1900, designed not to crush the hair—a designing triumph, considering those carefully created coiffures. Harrods had a motoring toque, which sounds more crushing. Miss Dorothy Levitt, who set up a women's world record of 91 m.p.h. in 1906, advised about clothes in her book, *The Woman in the Car*:

Gaiters specially made almost to the knee, a plain tailor-made with shirt-blouse; under no circumstances must you wear lace or fluffy adjuncts to your toilette—if you do, you will regret them before you have driven half a dozen miles. Tweed, frieze, or homespun lined with 'Jaeger' or fur. For summer, the ideal coat is of cream serge, which does not crease like silk,

94.　　　　　　95.

96.

94. Full coat with cape-like sleeves and deep roll front to swing right across and fasten with catch at hip. In Vicuna, Game-feather Tweeds, or Homespuns.

95. For automobilising or winter travel, in tweeds lined with Camel Fleece, Vicuna, or Irish Frieze. Also lined Squirrel, Marmot, Mink, with fittings of Astrachan or Nutria.

96. Tussore silk dust-proof head veil—*'serves as a capital guard to the hat, though the Burberry hats do not need anything of the kind to keep them on'.*

alpaca, or linen. A cloth cap to match the tweed should be pinned securely, and over it put a crêpe-de-chine veil, of length a-plenty. Alternately, a close-fitting turban of fur. A long scarf or muffler, good soft kid, fur-lined gloves, made with just a thumb. Don't wear rings or bracelets. Indispensable to the motoriste is the over-all, butcher blue or brown linen, fastening at the back.

Miss Levitt advised having a vanity mirror to hold up to see vehicles approaching from the rear. There were no driving mirrors then, and no windscreens; hoods were optional extras. The hazards of the lonely road had to be guarded against:

If you are to drive alone, it is advisable to carry a small revolver. I have an automatic Colt and find it easy to handle as there is practically no recoil—a great consideration for a woman.

For other kinds of encounters Miss Levitt had other weapons in her armoury:

In a little drawer in the motor-car is the secret of the dainty motoriste. In its recesses put clean gloves, veil and handkerchief, powder-puff, pins, hair pins, and a hand-mirror. Some chocolates are soothing sometimes.

This dainty motoriste was no fair-weather amateur. She was the first Englishwoman to enter for an official non-stop run. Leaving Glasgow at 3.30 a.m. in her 4-cylinder Gladiator, and arriving at Leeds in the evening, she started at 5 o'clock the next morning and drove non-stop to London. Her pleasure motoring was equally determined. For instance, there was a trip from London to Warwick for Sunday luncheon and back—182 miles, with an official speed limit of 12 m.p.h. Before she had been driving eight months, Miss Levitt was twice convicted and fined for exceeding the 'legal twelve'; and she advised all motorists to join the Automobile Association, since the AA scouts, placed on the roads to warn motorists of police-traps would, within a few months, save three or four times the two guinea annual subscription.

Thomas Burberry must surely have had Miss Levitt in mind when he prepared the motoring section of his catalogue:

The rapid growth of Automobilism with its new conditions of exposure and, until now, unheard of rates of speed, has created a demand for a class of garment to meet the requirements of this branch of sport, in which the essentials wind, cold, dust, rainproofness are required to be developed in a greater degree than ever before. For this Burberry's combination plan is absolutely unapproachable. Garments can be built of 2, 3, 4, or any number of layers of their various materials, calculated, in the sportsman's opinion, to supply the necessary protection: Winter gabardine, Frieze, Melton, Beaver, Vicuna, Box Cloth.

For hot weather there were Silk Gabardines, Burberry-proofed, which made 'Slip-ons of zephyr lightness'. Unproofed balloon silk was also beautifully light and very smart for ladies' wear as dust cloaks. The Automo Slip-on and Laprobe was made in five qualities to suit the requirements of different seasons:

1. Airy light—Gabardine or Urber silk.
2. Summer—Gabardine and camel fleece.
3. Winter—Gabardine, elk skin interlining, camel fleece inside.
4. Arctic—Shetland frieze with camel fleece lining.
5. Blizzard—Shetland frieze with elk skin interlining, and camel fleece inside.

Blizzard conditions were also met by Burberry's skirt-sacs, made to match the Automo Slip-on. These were ingenious affairs which enveloped the skirt in a rug formed like a sack, with camel fleece lining and rubber footboard. They prevented the wind from getting underneath ladies' skirts. The slip-on went over the skirt-sac, so that the rain ran down outside. Burberrys suggested 'These articles should be regarded as part of the furniture of the car, to be cared for by the engineer'.

In the matter of headgear, Burberrys were equally thorough . . . proofed motor-caps worn with tie-on hood; forage-caps, mica hoods, which were cages with oblong windows from which lace curtains hung. Alternately, there was an adjustable veil, which could be worn open or closed. When closed, it completely covered the face and tied round the neck. All this protection was against the dust which motorcars raised in summer as they scorched along the unmacadamised country lanes at the legal twelve, or exceeding it. Burberry's dustwrappers were designed by an expert automobilist—long, loose overalls, sufficiently large to go easily over any thickness of underwear. The car-coat, worn under the slip-on, was so designed that at the end of the journey, when the fair motoriste dismounted from her motor car, she could shed her slip-on (leaving it in the care of the engineer) and present 'a smart and well-groomed appearance'.

Burberry's not only applied tremendous thought and ingenuity to equipping society for the new combustion age . . . they also had very definite ideas about what was good taste, and what was conspicuous opulence:

Automobilism and the demand amongst its votaries for cold-excluding, warmth-holding, rain-resisting and dust-proof clothing is bound to lead eventually, and in extreme cases, to the use of fur. But English gentlemen do not take kindly to the *Continental monstrosities* in the shape of horse-skin, sheepskin, wolfskin, and other variations of coats which have the hair, wool, and fur outside. The more distinguished form is to use the fur simply as a lining, the outside presenting the appearance of ordinary travelling ulsters.

In fact, the fur-lined Burberry anticipated by about half a century the mink-lined raincoat that in the 1950s was the ultimate of chic.

The ordinary Burberry raincoat had become a thing that every gentleman possessed as a sign of good breeding. As a Burberry publication of the nineteen-twenties (*Open Spaces* edited by 'Coracias Garrulus') pointed out:

The most casual reader of popular novels must have noticed that the handsome heroes and beautiful heroines always galvanise their attractions by wearing 'Burberrys' when rushing with open arms and Pivot sleeves to their several fates. On the other hand, villains, doubtful females and unsuccessful detectives invariably cower round corners in hideous macintoshes or 'Slickers'.

THE CHELTENHAM

97. Solid leather travelling trunk—a necessity for the Victorian lady, in addition to hat boxes and dressing case, even on a short visit.
I. & R. Morley, 1883.

270

CHAPTER XXIII

THE STORES REACH THEIR ZENITH

Majestic Edwardian women; hot-house femininity. Debenham's new building. Harrod's Diamond Jubilee. Selfridge conquers Oxford Street. Bourne & Hollingsworth's island site. Harrods acquire Dickins & Jones. Shopping in the country and in Manchester. Customer loyalty to shops and stores.

A s the reign of King Edward soared to its zenith, extravagance was the prevailing mood of Society, with mature and triumphant womanhood the focus of all glory, laud, and bonheur. With a middle-aged but still pleasure-loving king, and a middle-aged but still beautiful queen, the age of conquest was raised and the horizons of flirtation extended. 'Oh, those Edwardian women!' recalls Frederick Willis. 'To see them in their glory one had to be in Old Bond Street between the hours of four and six in the afternoon. The street was full of their carriages, and there was an air of reverence in the shops as they entered. On the stage they were represented in every musical comedy. No matter where the setting of the play might be, Hong Kong, Arcadia, or Floradora, there they were among the palms and mimosa, and described on the programme as "English visitors". All they had to do was to wear the most expensive gowns, look delightfully bored and majestically useless. We fawned upon them; they ruled the world with a gentle wave of a delicately gloved hand; they were omnipotent. They achieved their prestige simply by putting the accent on femininity. We were charmed or terrified by their mystery and aloofness'.

This hot-house, conservatory atmosphere was exactly right for the growth, burgeoning, and blossoming of fashion shops. And in Wigmore Street, Debenham & Freebody, like the divinities they served, reached a splendid maturity of prosperity and prestige. In 1907 they completed

271

their handsome new building, which was in far better taste than the routine 'French Renaissance style' which had been the accepted and expected architectural expression of the grand emporiums of the late Victorians. In the following year, a Franco-British Exhibition was held in London, and Debenhams issued a souvenir booklet for visitors to their store:

> You may visit the various departments, then, if you wish, have lunch or tea at very moderate charges in the quiet, elegant Restaurant, to which a Smoking-room and Gentlemen's Cloakroom are attached. The Ladies' Club Room, which adjoins a luxuriously appointed suite of Dressing and Retiring Rooms, is open to lady visitors, who may there read the papers and magazines, telephone, write letters, or meet their friends. Parcels and letters may be addressed to the Cloak Room.

The appointments of the whole store were of a restrained but rich solidity, and although reticence kept the details out of this souvenir booklet, there never was a more comfortably contrived Ladies' Room, with its range of separate retiring rooms, each one containing a dressing-table and mirror, a marble wash basin, tessellated walls. Mahogany seating completed the sanitary fitments which bore the name of 'The Cavendish'. Was this a happy coincidence or by special arrangement to tie up with the original Cavendish House? This Ritz of retiring rooms remained exactly as then until the alterations of 1964.

Debenham & Freebody never attempted to be a department store in the manner of Harrods and Whiteleys. It was first and foremost and always a drapery and fashion shop with extensive workrooms and a very large country trade by post. Soft furnishings, linen, a little stationery and jewellery, and a gallery for modern and antique furniture, old brocades, embroideries, and tapestries, were the only other departments. At the time of their re-building in 1907, their wholesale business was 'one of the largest and most flourishing in the world, and affords an interesting study for those who are interested in the creation, growth and expansion of a big firm. The centre of the wholesale business is in Wimpole Street, behind the retail premises, and another important branch is in St Paul's Churchyard. By degrees the business has pushed its way, not only to the continent of Europe, but also to New York, Canada, South Africa, and Australia, where allied Debenham companies are established, as well as buying agencies all over the world'.

Meanwhile Harrods had grown from small beginnings as a grocery and provision shop into an immense emporium faced with Doulton's terra-cotta, having eighty departments with a thirty-six acre shopping area, in which the variety of merchandise justified the telegraphic address of EVERYTHING, LONDON. At the time of its Diamond Jubilee in 1909, Harrods claimed, not only to be the shrine of fashion, but also 'a recognized social rendezvous; in fact, one of the few smart rendezvous acknowledged and patronized by Society'. It was perfectly proper to meet a gentleman in the ground-floor banking hall—there could be no danger, as the Paddington magistrates had implied over Whiteley's Refreshment Room, that it would become a notorious 'place of assignation'.

On Harrods' Brompton Road frontage, there were still a few small shops, three public houses, and a Board school which had yet to be eliminated; and it was not until 1911 that the complete island site of four and a half acres belonged to Harrods, not until 1939 that the final touches were put to the old familiar façade that we know today. But it had become decidedly the most remarkable store in London, with the highest possible prestige. In their Jubilee Book, Harrods claimed to have been pioneers of shopping by telephone and of an all-night telephone service, of special shopping trains from the country and of free delivery to customers in the country. It does not say at what date this service was inaugurated. Whiteleys had a free delivery service to Brighton in 1886. Harrods' list of special amenities enjoyed by their customers is impressive:

Elegant and restful waiting and retiring-rooms for both sexes, writing rooms with dainty stationery, club room, fitting rooms, smoking rooms, etc., free of charge or question.

Public telephones provided in all departments.

Post Office, Theatre, Steamer Tickets, and Tourist Office. Appointment bureau where notes can be left for friends. Circulating Library and a music room.

Ladies Hairdressing Courts: No less than 33 private hairdressing, manicure, and chiropody courts in this wonderful saloon, as well as comfortable lounges, etc. Adjoining is a handsome sales-room where are sold Wigs, Transformations, Fringes, Combs, Manicure Sets, Hair Preparations, Pin Curls, Frames, Curling Pins, Hair nets, etc., and round the corner is the *LADIES' CLUB*, furnished in Adam style in figured satinwood, the chairs upholstered in green corded silk, tastefully decorated with appliqué embroidery. The Retiring Room is nicely fitted out, the effect in marble being admirable. The windows are of stained cathedral glass, while the walls are covered throughout with panelled Brecchi Sanguine, Pavannazi, Levantine marble, and onyx panels, the whole rendering an unique effect.

THE GENTLEMEN'S CLUB is furnished in the style of the Georgian period carried out in richly carved and moulded mahogany.

THE GRAND RESTAURANT has prices of a strictly moderate tendency. Afternoon Tea is served to the strains of Harrod's Royal Red Orchestra.

Harrods' customers, if not quite so fashionably exclusive as those of Debenham & Freebody, were 'carriage trade'. They belonged to the dog-owning upper-classes—'Dogs of all breeds may be seen chained at the entrance at all hours of the day, awaiting the return of their owners from within'. William Whiteley some time earlier had taken the brave step of forbidding man's best friend to enter his premises. Other tradesmen had prophesied an immediate decline in trade following this unsporting, not to say un-British, veto; but they were disappointed to find that Whiteley's stores suffered no noticeable withdrawal of two-legged customers.

The year that Harrods reached their diamond jubilee, was the year when Gordon Selfridge opened his great emporium in Oxford Street. And Harrods chose the actual week of Selfridge's highly dramatized inauguration to put on a series of jubilee concerts. These concerts were decorous, dignified affairs, with Landon Ronald conducting the London Symphony Orchestra. Selfridge must surely have been speaking sarcastically when he said Harrods had 'put up a magnificent counterblast to our opening'. His own blast was given by an army trumpeter blowing a fanfare from the first-floor parapet above the main entrance as the Selfridge flag was unfurled. Harrods did, however, have some more popular publicity than the symphony concerts in that the musical comedy *Our Miss Gibbs* at the Gaity Theatre had some scenes set at 'Garrods'. The managing director evidently felt this warranted an afternoon off, and afterwards noted in his diary: 'To matinée, which I much enjoyed. Representations of Harrod's Royal Exchange and Millinery Departments very good indeed.'

꙳   ꙳   ꙳

Gordon Selfridge had held an important position with Marshall Field's great store in Chicago; but in English trade circles he was looked upon as a bit of a buccaneer. There was underground rumour, a certain amount of open hostility, and prophesies of early disaster. There were difficulties over raising capital at some stages, and frustrations over what Selfridge considered the antiquated laws of property protecting the Oxford Street premises that he needed to acquire in order to clear the way for his grandiose neo-classical building.

This was far and away the biggest building in England to be constructed as a store from its first foundation. It had been preceded by the Bon Marché at Brixton in 1877, Lewis's Manchester store in 1880, Lewis's Birmingham store in 1885, and John Barnes of Hampstead in 1900; but Selfridges was not only bigger than these, but was the first

OUR MAMMOTH STORES.

Shopman. "Excuse me, Madam, but am I not right in presuming you come from the Toy Department?" *Lady.* "Certainly. Why?"
Shopman. "Would you very kindly direct me to it? I'm one of the assistants there and I've lost my way."

98. *Punch,* December 7, 1911.

brand-new store to be built in the West End. And despite the immense scale of the enterprise, and the financial and legal set-backs, Selfridge's determined optimism drove through all obstacles and the store was opened to the public less than a year after the foundation stone was laid. During that year, public curiosity was whetted by stories and speculations in the press; and as the opening day drew near an unprecedented advertising campaign was launched in the national newspapers.

Selfridge summoned over from America Marshall Field's head window-dresser, Goldsman, to prepare dramatic displays of quality goods—dramatically different from the crowded windows of Oxford Street into which the cheapest goods were crammed and ticketed to attract the customers in. Moreover, Selfridge's windows were kept lighted until midnight. The idea of having members of the staff exclusively concerned with window-dressing and interior display was new to England, as was that of co-ordinating the colours of carpeting, wrapping paper and string, delivery vans, and bill-heads. All these were in 'Selfridge Green', like the flag which flew over the main entrance; and later the same colour was incorporated in Gordon Selfridge's racing colours. Mr Selfridge asked the National Telephone Company to install a public exchange in his store. This was refused, but a special number, Gerrard 1, was offered as a consolation and accepted. There were 120 main lines to Gerrard 1, and over 600 extensions.

On the opening day, purse calendars and shopping notebooks were given as souvenirs, everyone was invited to walk round the 130 departments, to use the writing, reading, and rest rooms, the restaurants, and the 'airiel garden', the post office, and the information bureau. Next day the opening was variously reported as 'one of the great show sights of London', to be 'like the inauguration of a national exhibition or museum or art-gallery' and 'to present the appearance of a fair'. Selfridge's own description was significant of his whole outlook upon the function of a department store: a social centre, not a shop. Later his slogan was WHY NOT SPEND THE DAY AT SELFRIDGES?

Not even Selfridge, the social climber from the new world with small knowledge of London society, can have expected that fashionable women would spend a day at Selfridges—not those aloof and intimidating Edwardian creatures described by Frederick Willis. The customers he envisaged were of the great new middle and lower middle classes. These might equally well afford to spend a day at Harrods, and would find the amenites equal to those that Selfridge was offering to them, if not better—but they were shy of strolling into Harrods just to have a look round and use the public services. In contrast, when they walked along Oxford Street they were irresistibly sucked into Selfridges.

An early innovation was the Ice-cream Soda Fountain. In 1912 came the Bargain Basement, the first in London and a success from the start. On the ground floor, Selfridge brought cosmetics out into the open instead of selling them from under the counter; and he had them sited just inside the main entrance so that the scents should entice passing shoppers. But it seems that 'respectable' women were still shy of being seen buying cosmetics and perfumes, for in the first year the department's turnover was only £500, the best selling line being an innocent, unsophisticated lily of the valley scent. The great reputation of Selfridge's stocking department dates from a vast order placed with the Lyons Syndicate for silk stockings in five sizes and no less than three hundred shades. The order took nearly a year to be delivered; but when the stockings were put on sale as 'Crown Silk Hose' at 5/– a pair, preceded by an advertising campaign claiming that any foot could be fitted, any shoe matched, they were eagerly bought—not only by the public, but by dress houses, shoe shops, and other competing businesses in the fashion trade.

Gordon Selfridge's biographer, Reginald Pound, sums up Selfridge's influence on the retail trade of England after his first five years, that is on the eve of the 1914 war: 'He could claim to have been a transforming influence on the world of retail selling, to have accomplished greater changes in the shopping life of the metropolis than any of his rivals. He would rather lose business than give shoppers the impression that the store existed only to sell them goods, which was the old way. 'I want them to enjoy the warmth and light, the colours and styles, the feel of fine fabrics. That is the basis of this business'; and it was a new basis. He had completely revolutionized store organization, layout and display. He had introduced new methods in staff training which had brought round him what was probably the ablest body of workers in the distributive trades and certainly one of the most loyal.'

Nevertheless, one must not discount the influential changes in shopping brought about by English pioneers before him—by William Whiteley in Westbourne Grove and Richard Burbidge at Harrods, by the Army & Navy Stores, and in the north by the Fenwicks in Newcastle and Louis Cohen of Lewis's in Liverpool, Manchester and Birmingham. Cohen made more goods available to more people. Selfridge did the same but with illusions of luxury and without democratizing down quite so far, except in the Bargain Basement.

The other shopkeepers of Oxford Street found that Selfridges did them more good than harm. They benefited because Selfridge attracted people to Oxford Street from far and wide: no visitor to London, either from the provinces or from abroad, could not go to Selfridges, any more than he could not go to Westminster Abbey. Selfridges, never like Harrods 'the shrine of fashion', was a Mecca for all men and women on a shopping spree. Only Selfridges' next door neighbour, the long established drapery business of Thomas Lloyd & Co. was overwhelmed. Lloyd's, which occupied eight shops to the east of Selfridges, benefited temporarily from the crowds on the pavement but were engulfed by their powerful neighbour in 1914, when Selfridge also acquired more property in Orchard Street and Somerset Street. He had very nearly achieved the goal of every ambitious shopkeeper—a complete island site.

The complications of acquiring an island site in Oxford Street can be comprehended by this list which Mr Hollingsworth once made of the tenancies that had to be shifted before Bourne & Hollingsworth acquired their island site: It is given exactly as he wrote it:

1 pub	1 brothel
1 dairy	1 private residence
A branch of Finch's	A wholesale lace merchant
A barber	A nest of Polish tailors
A coffee house	A sweet shop
A carpet layer	Doan's Backache Pills
A costume manufacturer	A cigarette factory (Savory's)
A wholesale milliner	A wholesale blouse maker (Frances)
A retail milliner	A wine-merchant's cellar
A music publisher	A soda water manufacturer
A musical instrument shop	A jeweller
(German)	A baby linen manufacturer
A palmist	A wallpaper merchant
A beauty parlour	An estate agent
British headquarters, New Columbia	2 solicitors
Gramophone Co.	1 chapel

＊　　　＊　　　＊

To the trade, as indeed to the public, the Harrods of these pre-1914 years was the Eton of stores, admired above all others. A member of Dickins & Jones's staff made some notes of his experiences in the trade before he retired, and recalled Harrods' first 'take-over':

As regards myself, I think the biggest thrill was when I was told Harrods had obtained the controlling interest of Dickins & Jones, and from then, July 1914, was under their management. This was good news for me and the whole of the staff. I remember Sir Richard Burbidge when he was manager of Whiteley's provision department. I was an apprentice there from 1887–1889 and took the cash in many of the departments he controlled. He was a real live wire and I was proud when he came to Regent Street to know that he remembered me as a boy.

The other thing I recollect about Sir Richard was that a day or two after he became chief of Dickins & Jones he arrived there at 7 a.m. Fortunately the superintendent was an excellent disciplinarian and was on duty with the whole of the staff to the delight of Sir Richard. Sir Richard commenced his working day always at 7 a.m. at Harrods and had his breakfast with the supervisors.

Mr Haynes added, 'Next year, if I live long enough, will be a memorable one for me and Mrs Haynes as it will be the completion of my being on the pay-roll for sixty years. Mrs Haynes was also an apprentice at Dickins & Jones, and we have been married for fifty years.'

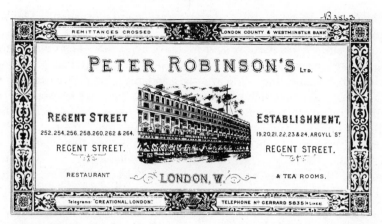

99. Bill-head of December 1910 shows growth of the Regent Street premises
from the original 'Black Peter Robinson' of 256–262 Regent Street and
19–21 Argyll Street. Peter Robinson's Oxford Street shop at this time
had almost achieved its complete island site on the north-east corner of
Oxford Circus. They also had premises for Boys' Clothing at 278 Regent
Street, and Ladies' Outfitting (underwear) at 282 Regent Street.

Such length of service in one store together was not unique. Young
men in the drapery trade more often than not married young women in
the same employment, because the hours were so long that there was
no time for courting after work. One shopkeeper's rules for his staff
included 'Men employees are given one evening each week for courting
purposes, and two if they go to prayer-meeting regularly'. Even when
an 'understanding' had been reached with a young lady in the shop,
there were few opportunities to enjoy leisure pursuits together. As
one old lady at the Linen & Woollen Drapers' Cottage Homes almost
nostalgically put it, 'But we had the summer evenings, and just to take
a walk was a pleasure'. She had been apprenticed to Thomas Burberry
in Basingstoke, and had met her husband when they were both at
Edwin Jones, Southampton. They married when he was earning 34/–
a week and she 11/–.

❧   ❧   ❧

Despite the rapid growth of department stores in the cities, small-scale
retailing was still the most important business form in all trades in 1914.
Drapery and millinery in the smaller towns was entirely in the hands of
individual shop-keepers: the multiple shops, which were by now beginning to multiply rapidly, did not yet deal in clothes, with the exception

of the Scotch Wool Shops and the cheap chain shoe shops. The little country towns and villages were still little changed in their way of shopping since Miss Mitford and Miss Austen's day. The village stores still stocked everything you could possibly need but had always just run out of the one thing you wanted; and the village dressmaker was still an essential member of the community. The big houses still had their sewing woman who came regularly to mend the household linen and make the children's clothes; and in some parts of the country there were still itinerant tailors who worked at the houses they visited for as long as the job lasted. Scotch drapers, or talleymen, still went their rounds of the hamlets and outlying farms. Margaret Penn wrote of an Edwardian talleyman in *Manchester Fourteen Miles*:

> The Talleyman came to Moss Ferry and the surrounding villages regularly every month. He would spread out his huge shiny black American cloth pack by the kitchen door, talking all the time, quick and brightly. . . . He sold frocks and pinafores; stays and drawers, chemises and petticoats; men's working shirts and Sunday shirts and collars; ladies' and children's black woollen stockings; reels of cotton and hanks of mending wool; coarse roller towels; pins and needles; tablecloths and collar studs and combs; rolls of red flannel for weekday, and cream flannel for Sunday, petticoats; sheets and pillowcases, prints and serges and even pearl bead necklaces.

When it came to an important purchase such as the material for winter frocks, Grandma took the train to Manchester and the young man serving at the dress-material counter of Lewis's would take great pains in showing her many rolls of cloth. She would finger them and ask innumerable questions as to their serviceability. If it was for a winter frock she would, in order to satisfy herself that it was 'nowt but wool', request the assistant to snip a bit off and apply a match: if it wouldn't burn then it was wool all right and not 'shoddy'.

Hilda, the narrator in *Manchester Fourteen Miles*, was apprenticed to the village dressmaker, but later Grandma took her to find a better opening 'at one of the grand shops in St Anne's Square—Hankinson & Sankey, or Kirby Nicholson'. Hankinson & Sankey was 'a beautiful big shop. There was a rich-looking carpet all over the floor and covering the staircase as well. Behind the different counters were young ladies, all dressed alike in plain but smart black frocks. "We are Court Dressmakers here", Miss Jackson explained proudly, "and only do the very best work. You would be apprenticed for three years before beginning to earn anything . . . it's the rule everywhere in dressmaking"'. But she agreed to take Hilda on as a workroom errand-girl at 5/– a week for the first year, then 7/6 till she was taken on as an improver. Customers of Hankinson & Sankey expected quality, not speed:

The Stores reach their Zenith

First of all Mrs Honeywell came to the shop downstairs and selected the material. Then she spent days, even weeks, in choosing a pattern. Then she came to be measured. Then the material was given to the cutter; after this it was tacked up. Then she had to be fitted before the dress was actually made up. Several girls worked on different parts of it—one girl did nothing all day long but press, keeping two flat irons going for this purpose. Every seam was pressed flat as soon as it was finished, and just as much trouble was taken with the over-sewing of a lining seam as with the more showy parts of a garment.

Hilda was sent out frequently to match up sewing silks and cottons, for Hankinson & Sankey did not deal in those. Best of all she liked to be sent to Lewis's in Market Street . . . 'It was so big and, no matter what time she went there, always full of people moving up and down the aisles or buying at the many counters. Being in Lewis's was nearly as exciting as being in Market Street itself. There were almost as many people in the shop as in the street.'

The attractions of a big store, whether it was Lewis's in Market Street, or Selfridges in Oxford Street, was irresistible to a generation which had few entertainments. All over England before the First World War, before the cinema, before the radio, before the motor-car was anything but a rich man's possession, the warmth and light, the pervasion of luxury, the ever-changing delights of fashionable merchandize made shopping, whether actually purchasing or just looking round, a stimulating pleasure. More and more women of all classes were beginning to earn money of their own before marriage and, after marriage, to have control over the family purse. The growth of the stores can be seen to run parallel with the social emancipation of women —their emancipation from the restrictions of inhibiting home life, from their dependence upon father or husband for money to spend, and from the tyranny of private dressmakers and their interminable fittings.

Yet the personal, individual element remained strong, even in the departments of the big stores. Daughter inherited from mother her affectionate loyalty to Marshalls, to Debenhams, to D. & J., to Swans, or to Peter Rob., according to family tradition. Osbert Lancaster, in *All Done from Memory* writes of 'Messrs William Whiteley's emporium, an establishment which bulked very large in our family life'. He goes on:

It is difficult nowadays to realise how very personal was then the relationship, even in London, between shop-keeper and customer and the enormous importance, comparable almost to that attained by rival churches, which late Victorian and Edwardian ladies attached to certain stores. All my female relatives had their own favourites, where some of them had been honoured customers for more than half a century and their arrival was greeted by frenzied bowing on the part of the frock-coated shopwalkers, and where certain of the older assistants stood to them almost in the relationship of confessors, receiving endless confidences on the state of their health, the behaviour of their pets and the general iniquity of the Liberal Government. Thus for my Great Aunt Bessie the Army and Navy Stores fulfilled all the functions of her husband's club and her undeviating loyalty was repaid by a respect and consideration which bore little or no relation to the size of her account.

Goodwill, that intangible but invaluable asset, was something which flowed both ways: goodwill from the shopkeeper to the customer surged back as customer goodwill to the shop. There was a *rapport*. A shop is more than a building, fittings, stock and staff, particularly a shop where clothes are bought. So much of the heart, so many high hopes, so many hesitations, go into the purchase of personal adornment that where there is a sympathetic atmosphere, an ambience of interest and understanding, someone who knows your name, that is the shop to which you return again and again. The human element is a factor too elusive to be assessed by accountancy and remote control. Especially is it incalculable when dealing with those two most capricious of customers, women and fashion.

100. For gay displays
—Telescopic Sunshade
Stand.

DATES OF ESTABLISHMENT

Only firms mentioned in the text, whose dates or approximate
dates are known, are included in this list. Where there is conflicting
evidence about a date, the earliest one is given.
It was not possible for all firms with long histories to be included
in the narrative; but those brought in are a representative selection,
indicative of the pattern of shopping in England as a whole during
the period covered.

Before 1800

1707   Fortnum & Mason, Piccadilly.
1760   George Hitchcock & Son, St. Paul's Churchyard.
1770   Hayward's Lace Warehouse, 73 Oxford Street.
1777   William & John Sangster, Umbrella & Parasol Manufacturers, Fleet Street.
1774   Harborow, Woollen Specialists, 15 Cockspur Street.
1778   Flint & Clark (Clark & Debenham 1813), 44 Wigmore Street.
1780   Browns of Chester.
1780   Nicholay, Furriers, Oxford Street.
1784   City Clothing Establishment (E. P. Doudney & Sons), 49 Lombard Street.
1785   Sneiders, Furriers, 92 Oxford Street.
1790   Dickins & Smith, 54 Oxford Street (later Dickins & Jones).
1791   Peal & Co., Bootmakers, Wigmore Street.
1795   I. & R. Morley, Hosiery Manufacturers, Nottingham.
1796   John Watts. Draper, Manchester (1821, The Bazaar, 1836 Kendal Milne).
1796   Harding, Howell & Co., Schomberg House, Pall Mall
1799   The Fore Street Warehouse (Todd & Morrison, later Morrison & Dillon).

1800–1809

1800   Irish Linen Company, 4 Bloomsbury Square (later 112 New Bond Street).
1804   John Townsend, 9 Long Row, Nottingham (later Jessop's).
1806   James S. Carter, Tourist Outfitter, 369 Oxford Street.
1808   William Cook, Linen Draper, Clerkenwell.
1808   Hanningtons of Brighton.
1809   T. Olney, Haberdashery, 139 and 140 Borough (later Olney Amsden & Son, City).

1810–1819

1810   Breeze & James, 32 Kensington High Street (later Moss & Cooke).
1810   John Harris Heal, Rathbone Place (later Tottenham Court Road).
1812   Swan & Edgar, 10 Piccadilly.
1812   (approx.) Stagg & Mantle, Leicester Square.
1812   Carter & Houston, Corset Makers, Blackfriars Road.
1813   Mrs. M. Caley, Castle Street, Windsor.

1813   Clark & Debenham, Cavendish House, 44 Wigmore Street.
1813   Benjamin Harvey, Knightsbridge (later Harvey Nichols).
1814   Mrs. Carter's Parisian Corset Warehouse, Stamford Street.
1814   Shoolbred, Cook & Co., City.
1815   Goodman & Davis, Tailors & Habit Makers, 200 Oxford Street.
1816   Soho Bazaar.
1816   Samuel Courtauld's Silk Factory, Bocking, Essex.
1817   **Shoolbreds, Tottenham Court Road.**
1817   Wheeler & Co., Glovers, 210 Regent Street and 23–4 Poultry.
1817   William Cook, Manchester and Scotch Warehouse, St. Paul's Churchyard.
1817   (approx.) Urling's British & Foreign Lace Warehouse, 224 Regent Street.
1818   Pooley & Smith, Cheltenham (later Cavendish House).
1818   Peck's Drapery Shop, Liverpool (became Lewis's Bon Marché 1877).
1819   **Lord, D. H. 66-70 Burlington Arcade.**

1820–1829

1820   Howell & James, 5–9 Regent Street.
1820   John Morgan, Tailors, West Cowes (London 1883).
1821   The Bazaar, Manchester, later Kendal Milne.
1822   Henry Heath, Hatmaker, 393 Oxford Street.
1824   (approx.) Mrs. Bell's Magasin de Modes, 3 Cleveland Row, St. James's.
1825   (approx.) J. & J. Holmes's Shawl Emporium, 171 Regent Street.
1826   Thos. Wallis & Co., Holborn Circus.
1826   (approx.) Pullars of Perth, dyers (dry-cleaning 1866).
1827   Elton, Dyers & Cleaners, Sloane Street (later 113 Gloucester Road).
1829   Hitchcock & Rogers, Ludgate Hill (became Hitchcock, Williams, 1853).

1830–1839

1830   Jolly & Son, 20 Old Bond Street, Bath (from Margate).
1830   The Pantechnicon, Motcombe Street, Belgravia.
1830   Jas. Smith & Sons, Umbrellas.
1831   William Wink, Laceman, Southsea (later Knight & Lee).
1832   Lilley & Skinner, Paddington Green.
1832   Townsend & Daft, Nottingham (later Jessop's).
1833   Peter Robinson, 103 Oxford Street.
1834   The Pantheon opened as a Bazaar.
1834   Maison Helbronner, embroiderers, Oxford Street.
1835   Dickins, Son & Stevens moved to 232 Regent Street (Hanover House).
1835   Madame le Plastrier, 29 Ludgate Street, Millinery, Dressmaking, Corsets.
1836   Kendal, Milne & Faulkner, Manchester (ex. Watts Bazaar).
1836   S. & J. Watts & Sons, Wholesalers, Manchester.
1837   Marshall & Wilson, 11 Vere Street (Marshall & Snelgrove 1848).
1837   **Daniel Neal, Shoemaker, Edgware Road.**
1837   D. Nicholson & Co., Wholesale Mantle Manufacturer, City.
1838   Bainbridge, Newcastle.
1839   John Sangster, Umbrellas, Regent Street (Fleet Street 1777).
1839   The Scotch House, Aldgate (Gardiner Bros. from Glasgow).
1839   William Reynolds, linen draper, Streatham.

Dates of Establishment

1840–1849

1840   Robert Sayle, Cambridge.
1840   Sykes, Josephine & Co., 280 Regent Street and 56A Old Steyne, Brighton.
1840   (approx.) Marshall & Wilson, Scarborough.
1840   H. J. & D. Nicholl, Regent Street.
1840   Spencer & Hall, Lisson Grove (later Spencer, Turner & Boldero).
1841   Jay's General Mourning Warehouse, Regent Street.
1841   G. Yapp, Shoemaker, 200 Sloane Street.
1842   Lilley & Skinner
1842   Maples, Tottenham Court Road.
1842   Lush & Cook, Dyers and Cleaners.
1843   D. Nicholson & Co., St. Paul's Churchyard.
1845   (approx.) Cole Brothers, Sheffield.
1845   National Linen Co., Fleet Street (later 130 New Bond Street).
1846   W. Bill, Homespun Merchant, Mold, Flintshire (later Tenby).
1847   Jules Duvelleroy, Fan Manufacturer, 167 Regent Street.
1848   B. Benjamin & Sons, Tailors, Ulster House, Conduit Street.
1849   Pugh's Mourning Warehouse, Regent Street.
1849   Henry Charles Harrod, Grocer, Brompton Road.

1850–1859

1850   Farmer & Roger's Great Shawl & Cloak Emporium, Regent Street.
1851   A. Abrahams, Bootmaker, Westbourne Grove.
1851   Bax & Co., 46–8 Regent Street (1852 Emary & Co., then Aquascutum).
1851   Mrs. Washington Moon, Regent Street, lingerie.
1851   G. Pratt, Linen Draper, 5 Bedford Row, Streatham.
1852   Bon Marché, Paris.
1853   (approx.) Argyll General Mourning Warehouse (D. Nicholson & Co.).
1853   George & Henry Lee, Liverpool.
1854   John Heelas, Reading.
1854   Scott Adie's Royal Scotch Warehouse.
1855   Henry Creed, Queen Victoria's tailor, opened Paris branch.
1856   Thomas Burberry, Basingstoke.
1856   Lewis's of Liverpool.
1856   Singer Manufacturing Co. opened first retail shop, Glasgow.
1857   Gayler & Pope, Marylebone High Street.
1857   Sélincourt & Colman, Wholesale Costumiers, 16 Cannon Street.
1858   Frederick Gorringe, Buckingham Palace Road.
1858   S. Bradley & Co., Furriers & Silk Mercers (Westbourne Grove 1871).
1858   Jolly's of Bath opened Bristol branch.
1858   Joseph Smith, Habit Makers, Hastings (later S. Kensington, then Bond Street).
1859   Jones Sewing Machine Co., first retail shop.

1860–1869

1860   (approx.) Wellsteed of Reading.
1860   William Hatch, 23 Gloucester Road.
1860   Jessops of Nottingham.

1861 Morris & Co.
1862 Derry & Toms, Kensington High Street.
1862 S. W. Greves, Glove and Fan Depot, Burlington Arcade.
1863 William Whiteley, Westbourne Grove.
1864 Post Office Supply Association (1866 Civil Service Supply Ass.).
1864 John Lewis, Oxford Street.
1865 Charles Russ, Court Furriers, 70 New Bond Street.
1867 Jones Brothers, Holloway.
1867 Bentalls of Kingston.
1867 Handley's of Southsea.
1867 James Smith, Umbrellas, New Oxford Street.
1869 Stockman Frères, French Busts.
1869 Woollands, Knightsbridge.

1870–1879

1870 John K. Hubbard, Worthing.
1870 John Barker, Kensington High Street.
1870 Seaman, Little & Co., Kensington High Street.
1870 Edwin Hide's Drapery Emporium, Southsea.
1870 Achille Serre, Dry-cleaning.
1870 Matthews, Watford (later Trewin).
1870 The London Glove Co., Cheapside.
1870 (approx.) The Lyons Silk Co., 179 Regent Street.
1870 Bradley's Arctic Fur Store, Chepstow Place.
1871 Peter Jones, Draycott Avenue (later Sloane Square).
1871 Army & Navy Co-operative Society.
1873 Butterick Paper Pattern Company established at 171–5 Regent Street.
1873 William Owen, Hatherley Grove and Westbourne Grove.
1873 John, Sydney and William Ponting, Kensington High Street.
1873 Tom Ponting, Westbourne Grove.
1875 Liberty's, East India House, 218a Regent Street.
1875 Irish Linen Co., 35 Burlington Arcade and 163 New Bond Street.
1877 Lewis's Bon Marché, Liverpool.
1877 Bon Marché, Brixton.
1878 National Fur Company, Brompton Road.
1879 D. H. Evans, Oxford Street.
1879 Junior Army & Navy Stores, Waterloo Place.
1879 Burberry, Basingstoke.

1880–1889

1880 Lewis's, Manchester.
1881 Fleming Reid's first Scotch Wool Shop, Greenock.
1881 Noble Jones, Burlington Arcade (previously French Glove Co. Newington Causeway).
1882 International Fur Store, T. S. Jay, 163–5 Regent Street.
1882 Fenwicks of Newcastle (London 1891).
1883 Jaeger Company, Fore Street, City.
1883 Penberthy, Oxford Street.
1884 Lewis's, Sheffield.
1885 Lewis's, Birmingham.

Dates of Establishment

1885 A. Stephens & Co., oriental fabrics, 326 Regent Street.
1887 Knight & Lee bought William Wink, Southsea.
1887 Bobby's of Margate.
1889 'Lucile' opened in Davies Street. (1891 Maison Lucile, Hanover Square.)

1890–1899

1891 Mr. Fenwick came to New Bond Street.
1892 W. Bill from Tenby to Bond Street.
1894 Robinson & Cleaver, Regent Street (from Belfast).
1894 Bourne & Hollingsworth, Westbourne Grove (Oxford Street 1902).
1897 Calman Links, Furriers.
1898 William Hill, Hove.
1899 Givans came to Bond Street from Belfast.

1900–1915

1900 John Barnes, Hampstead.
1900 Worth opened in Grosvenor Street.
1901 Thomas Burberry came to Haymarket, London, from Basingstoke.
1904 Bobby's, Leamington branch.
1906 Bobby's, Folkestone branch.
1906 Reville & Rossiter, Hanover Square.
1906 The White House, 51 New Bond Street.
1906 Mascotte, 89 Park Street, then Berkeley Square.
1909 Selfridges, Oxford Street.
1910 Bobby's, Eastbourne branch.
1913 Bobby's, Torquay branch.
1914 John Lewis Partnership.
1915 Bobby's, Bournemouth branch.

REFERENCES

HARDY AMIES. *Just So Far*. Collins, 1954.

ANON. *The Habits of Good Society:* A Handbook for Ladies and Gentlemen. James Hogg, *c.* 1860.

Jane Austen's Letters. Edited by R. W. Chapman. Oxford University Press, 1952.

ADA S. BALLIN. *The Science of Dress in Theory and Practice.* Sampson Low, 1885.

T. C. BARKER and MICHAEL ROBBINS. *A History of London Transport.* Allen & Unwin, 1963.

ARNOLD BENNETT. *The Old Wives' Tale.* 1908.

A. R. BENNETT. *London and Londoners in the 1850's and 1860's.* T. Fisher Unwin, 1924.

MARY REED BOBBIT. *The Life and Letters of Lady Jebb.* Faber & Faber, 1960.

MAX VON BOEHM and DR OSKAR FISCHEL. *Modes and Manners of the 19th Century.* Translated by Grace Thompson. Vol. IV. 1879–1914. J. M. Dent, 1927.

CHARLES BOOTH. *Life and Labour of the People of London*, 2nd Series. Industry, Vol. III. Part I, Dress. Macmillan, 1903.

MARY ELIZABETH BRADDON. *The Rose of Life.* Hutchinson, 1905.

ASA BRIGGS. *Friends of the People;* The Centenary History of Lewis's. B. T. Batsford, 1956.

IVOR BROWN. *Balmoral—The History of a Home.* Collins, 1955.

ANNE M. BUCK. *Victorian Costume and Costume Accessories.* Herbert Jenkins, 1961.

LADY COLIN CAMPBELL. *The Etiquette of Good Society.* Cassell, 1912.

IRENE CLEPHANE. *Our Mothers*, 1870–1900. Victor Gollancz.

IRENE CLEPHANE. *Ourselves*, 1900–1930. John Lane the Bodley Head, 1933.

MARY CLIVE. *Caroline Clive.* From the Diary and Family Papers of Mrs Archer Clive, 1801–1873. Bodley Head, 1949.

HAROLD P. CLUNN. *The Face of London.* Phoenix House, 1951.

C. WILLET CUNNINGTON. *Englishwomen's Clothing in the Nineteenth Century.* Faber & Faber, 1937.

C. WILLET CUNNINGTON. *Englishwomen's Clothing in the Present Century.* Faber & Faber, 1952.

C. WILLETT and PHYLLIS CUNNINGTON. *The History of Underclothes.* Michael Joseph, 1951.

LADY DUFF-GORDON ('Lucile'). *Discretions and Indiscretions.* Fred. A. Stokes, New York, 1932.

GEORGE ELIOT. *Middlemarch*, 1871.

JOHN WILLIAM FERRY. *A History of the Department Store.* Macmillan, New York, 1960.

J. P. FRITH. *My Autobiography and Reminiscences.* Richard Bentley, 1889.

ROGER FULFORD. *Votes for Women*, Faber & Faber, 1957.

MADGE GARLAND. *Fashion.* Penguin Books, 1962.

MRS GASKELL. *Cranford*, 1853.

ROSAMUND BRUNEL GOTCH. *Mendelssohn and His Friends in Kensington.* Letters from Fanny and Sophy Horsley, 1833–36. Oxford University Press, 1934.

LADY VIOLET GREVILLE. *The Gentlewoman in Society.* Henry & Co., 1892.

References

GEORGE G. HARPER. *Revolted Woman*, Elgin Matthews 1894.

MRS H. R. HAWEIS. *The Art of Beauty*. Chatto & Windus, 1878.

SIR AMRBOSE HEAL. *London Tradesmen's Cards of the XVII/XVIII Century*. Batsford, 1925.

GEORGIANA HILL. *A History of English Dress*. Richard Bentley, 1893.

M. VIVIAN HUGHES. *A London Home in the 90's*. Oxford University Press, 1936.

SARA HUTCHINSON. *Letters, 1800–1835*. Edited by Kathleen Coburn. Routledge & Kegan Paul, 1954.

JAMES B. JEFFERYS. *Retail Trading in Britain, 1850–1950*. Cambridge University Press, 1954.

SONIA KEPPEL. *Edwardian Daughter*. Hamish Hamilton, 1958.

CHARLES KNIGHT, Editor. *London*. Vol. V. Henry G. Bohn, 1851.

RICHARD LAMBERT. *The Universal Provider*. A Study of William Whiteley and the Rise of the London Department Store. Harrap, 1938.

OSBERT LANCASTER. *All Done from Memory*. John Murray, 1953.

LORD WILLIAM PITT LENNOX. *Fashion Then and Now*. Chapman & Hall, 1878.

J. G. LINKS, *The Book of Fur*. James Barrie, 1956.

JAMES PELLER MALCOLM. *Anecdotes of the Manner and Customs of London during the 18th Century*, with a Review of the State of Society in 1807. Longman, Hurst, Rees & Orme, 1810.

MARGARET MARE and ALICE C. PERCIVAL. *Victorian Best-seller—The World of Charlotte M. Yonge*. George G. Harrap, 1948.

HENRY MAYHEW, Editor. *The Shops and Companies of London*, and The Trades and Manufactories of Great Britain. Vol. I. 1865.

SOMERSET MAUGHAM. *Of Human Bondage*, 1915.

MARY RUSSELL MITFORD. *Our Village*. George G. Harrap, 1947. (Orig. published 1824–32.)

NANCY MITFORD, Editor. *The Ladies of Alderley*. The letters between Maria Josepha, Lady Stanley of Alderley and her daughter-in-law, 1841–1850. Chapman & Hall, 1938.

LAWRENCE E. NEAL. *Retailing and the Public*. George Allen & Unwin, 1932.

H. PASDERMADJIAN. *The Department Store*—Its Origins, Evolution, and Economics. Newman Books, 1954.

HON MRS C. C. PEEL. *Life's Enchanted Cup, 1872–1933*. John Lane, 1933.

MARGARET PENN, *Manchester Fourteen Miles*, Cambridge University Press, 1947.

VALERIE PIRIE. *A Frenchman Sees the English in the 'Fifties*. Adapted from the French of Francis Wey. Sidgwick & Jackson, 1935.

JAMES POPE-HENNESSY. *Queen Mary, 1867–1953*. Allen & Unwin, 1959.

PAUL POIRET. *My First Fifty Years*. Translated by Stephen Haden Guest. Gollancz, 1931.

REGINALD POUND. *Selfridge. A Biography*. Heinemann, *1960*.

JULIUS M. PRICE. *Dame Fashion*, Paris–London, 1786–1912. Sampson Low, 1913.

GWEN RAVERAT. *Period Piece*. Faber & Faber, 1952.

REV J. RICHARDSON. *Recollections of the Last Half Century*. Printed for the Author by Saville & Edwards, 1855.

SOPHIE VON LA ROCHE. *Sophie in London 1786*, trans. from the German by Clare Williams. Jonathan Cape, 1933.

GEORGE AUGUSTUS SALA. *Twice Round the Clock*. 1859.

GEORGE R. SIMS, Editor. *Living London*, 1901–3. Cassell.

SIR OSBERT SITWELL, Editor. *Two Generations*. Macmillan, 1940.

Shops and Shopping

SACHEVERAL SITWELL and DORIS LANGLEY MOORE. *Gallery of Fashion*, 1794–1802. (Plates by Heideloff & Ackermann.)

ROBERT SOUTHEY. *Letters from England by Don Manuel Alvarez Espriella.* Longmans, 1807.

NORAH WAUGH. *Corsets and Crinolines.* B. T. Batsford, 1954.

H. G. WELLS, *Kipps*, 1905.

LLOYD WENDTH and H. KOGAN. *Give the Lady What She Wants.* Rand McNally, New York, 1952.

LOELIA, DUCHESS OF WESTMINSTER. *Grace and Favour.* Weidenfeld & Nicolson, 1961.

FRANCIS WEY. *A Frenchman Sees the English in the 'Fifties.* Adapted from the French by Valerie Pirie. Sidgwick & Jackson, 1935.

H. B. WHEATLEY. *Bond Street Old and New.* 1686–1911. Fine Art Society, 1911.

HENRY B. WHEATLEY. *London Past and Present. Its History, Associations and Traditions.* John Murray, 1891.

H. D. WILLCOCK, Editor. *Browns and Chester: Portrait of a Shop, 1780–1946,* by Mass Observation. Lindsay Drummond, 1947.

A. H. WILLIAMS. *No Name on the Door—a Memoir of Gordon Selfridge.* W. H. Allen, 1956.

FREDERICK WILLIS. *A Book of London Yesterdays.* Phœnix House, 1960.

Parson Woodforde's Diary. Vol. V. 1797–1802.

BARBARA WORSLEY-GOUGH. *Fashions in London.* Allan Wingate, 1952.

J. P. WORTH. *A Century of Fashion.* Little Brown, Boston, 1928.

EMILE ZOLA. *Au Bonheur des Dames.* English Translation: *Ladies' Delight* by April Fitzlyon. John Calder, 1957.

Sponsored Books

KEITH JOPP. *The Hewitson Story,* 1898–1958.

H. L. KARLEY. *An Autobiography of D. H. Evans,* 1879–1956. 1958.

IVOR HALSTEAD. *Bond Street.* Barcliff Advertising and Publishing Co., 1953.

JAMES LAVER. *The Liberty Story,* 1959.

ALICE LYNES. *A History of Coventry Textiles.* Coventry Textile Society, 1952.

D. W. PEEL. *A Garden in the Sky: The Story of John Barker's of Kensington,* 1870–1957. W. H. Allen, 1960.

STANLEY PIGOTT. *Hollins. A Study of an Industry, 1785–1949.* William Hollins & Co., Nottingham.

REGINALD POUND. *The Fenwick Story,* 1972.

ALISON SETTLE. *A Family of Shops.* Marshall & Snelgrove.

Berisfords, The Ribbon People, 1858–1958. William Sessions Ltd., York.

Cash's of Coventry. J. & J. Cash, Ltd., Coventry.

MRS BAILLIE SAUNDERS. *Memories of Marylebone,* 1857–1907. Gayler & Pope, Ltd.

A Story of British Achievement, 1849–1949. (Harrods.)

Wool Through the Ages. Department of Education of the International Wool Secretariat.

Learning about Lace. Federation of Lace & Embroidery Employers' Association.

References

Guide Books and Trade Directories

The Picture of London, 1803 edition. Being a Correct Guide to all the Curiosities, Amusements, Exhibitions, Public Establishments, and Remarkable Objects in and near London. Richard Phillips, 1803.

Johnston's Commercial Guide and Trade Directory, 1817.

Tallis's Street Views. 1837–1838.

Grand Architectural Panorama of London. Regent Street to Westminster Abbey. I. Whitelaw, 1849.

A Visit to Regent Street. c. 1860. Printed by Henry Vizetelly.

Modern London. The World's Metropolis. An Epitome of Results. Published by the Historical Publishing Co., *c.* 1887.

Post Office Directories.

Survey of London, Vols. XXXI and XXXII, Part 2. The Athlone Press, University of London, 1963.

Newspapers and Magazines

Great Stores of the World; a *Guardian* pamphlet. Article by Phyllis Heathcote on the Bon Marché, Paris.

The Fortnightly Review, January 1895. Article by Lady M. Jeune on 'The Ethics of Shopping'.

The World of Fashion.

The What-not, or Lady's Handbook.

Illustrated London News.

Englishwoman's Domestic Magazine.

Sylvia's Home Journal.

Queen.

Lady's World.

Punch.

Weldon's Home Journal.

The Gazette of the John Lewis Partnership.

Chamber's Journal of Popular Literature, Science and Art. Oct. 15, 1864. Article on London Shop Fronts.

Catalogue of First Silk Exhibition, 1890.

British Warehouseman, February 1895. Article on 'The Liberty' Art Movement.

Morning Post, July 7th 1854.

The Times, August 15th 1821, October 4, 1884.

La Belle Assemblée.

The Drapers' Record, from 1887.

The Liberty Lamp, staff magazine of Liberty & Co.

Country Life. 'Europe's First Department Store' by G. Bernard Hughes, May 15, 1958.

INDEX

Figures in italics refer to page numbers of illustrations in the text.

Index

Lewis's, Liverpool, 142, 194, 214, 277; Manchester, 274, 277, 280, 281; Birmingham, 274, 277

Liberty, Arthur Lasenby, 100, 154, 173–4; country house of, 168; interviewed by 'The Warehouseman', 181

Liberty & Co., 100, 173–5, 181; agencies, 183; in Holland, 183; motor bonnet, 266; in Paris, 181–2; at Silk Exhibition, 179; *175, 182*

Life's Enchanted Cup, 197, 245

Lifts, passenger, 217, 234, 239

Lighting, Bude, 96; candles, 95; electric, 181, 234; gas, 7, 95; described by Knight, 96; oil lamp, 7; of shops and streets, 7, 95

Lilley & Skinner, 32

Linen & Woollen Drapers' Cottage Homes, Mill Hill, 126, 151, 237, 279; foundation of, 167

Linen drapers, 6, 97

Lingerie, 37, 253–4, 257–9

Links, Calman, 211

Links, J. G., *quoted*, 211

Linsey Woolsey, 74

Linton & Curtis, 220

Lisson Grove, 95, 152

Liverpool, 78, 141, 170, 191, 194, 238

Lloyd, Thomas, 54, 277

Locke's Scotch Tartan Warehouse, James, 72

Lomas, Thomas, Manchester, 225

London, Knight's, *quoted*, 23, 96, 97

London and Londoners in the 1850's and 1860's, 69

London Fur Company, 212

Lord, D. H., Burlington Arcade, 108

Louvet Frères, 254

Lucile, 244–9, 256

Lush & Cook, 57

Lynden's Hat Manufactory, 52

McAffee, shoemaker, 254

Macdougall's Scotch Warehouse, 75–6

Macintosh, Charles, 81–3

MacLintock, Sandy, 73

Magazin of the Belle Anglaise, 40

Mail order, 233

Malcolm, James P., *quoted*, 2, 6

Manchester, 18, 78, 82, 194, 214, 228, 280–1; Bazaar, 18–21; Guardian, 19

Manchester Fourteen Miles, 280–1

Manchester goods, 42, 201

Mandelberg, Joseph, 83

Mangas, Madame, 219

Mannequin figures, 199, 201–3, 247; milliners', 10

Mannequin parades and mannequins, 247–250

Manners, Lady Margery, 244

Mantle manufactory, 42, 123

Manufactory, definition of, 14

Maples, 14, 142

Margate, 49, 52, 205

Marion, Madame, 107

Markets, open, 15, 31; St James's, 15

Marks & Spencer, 22

Marshall, James, 45, 167

Marshall, James C., 167

Marshall & Snelgrove, 45, 167; limited company, 240; mail order, 233; model costume rooms, 208; Paget elopement, 147–8; Scarborough branch, 45–6; window dressing, 242, 127, 144, 192

Marshall & Wilson, 45

Marshall Field, Chicago, 237, 274

Mary, Queen, 252

Mascotte, 250, *251*

Mason, Mrs, 220

Maternity clothes, 30, 130, 143

Mauds, wrapping, 74, *23*

Maugham, Somerset, 243

May, Princess of Teck, 219

Mayhew, Henry, *quoted*, 6, 65–6, 68; on crinolines, 91, 93–4, 117

Meeking & Co., Charles, 85, 142

Merino, 189, 190–1

Merton Abbey, 174

Mesger, R. H., 90

Metcalfe, Miss, 218

Metropolitan Catalogue, 118

Metz & Co., Amsterdam, 183

Meurice, Madame Valentine, 220

Meysey-Wigley, Caroline, 63; Clive, 91

Middlemarch, 62

Millais, 174, 177

Millard's East India Warehouse, 59

Milliners and millinery, 27–8, 34, 40, 106–8, 211; country, 41

Mills, Mr and Mrs, 29

Mills, Cecil, 195

Mills, William, servants' bazaar, 195

Mitford, Miss, 3

Model girls, *see* Mannequins

Modern London, 103, 118, 156, 157, 158, 166–7, 233

Mohair, 82

Moliere & Co., 31

Monro of Edinburgh, 193